CROSS-BORDER SECURITY AND INSOLVENCY

CROSS-BORDER SECURITY AND INSOLVENCY

edited by

MICHAEL BRIDGE

Professor of Law,
University College London;
Director of Research,
Norton Rose, London

and

ROBERT STEVENS

Barrister, Fellow, and Tutor
in Law: Lady Margaret
Hall, Oxford University

OXFORD
UNIVERSITY PRESS

OXFORD
UNIVERSITY PRESS

Great Clarendon Street, Oxford OX2 6DP

Oxford University Press is a department of the University of Oxford.
It furthers the University's objective of excellence in research, scholarship,
and education by publishing worldwide in

Oxford New York

Athens Auckland Bangkok Bogotá Buenos Aires Calcutta
Cape Town Chennai Dar es Salaam Delhi Florence Hong Kong Istanbul
Karachi Kuala Lumpur Madrid Melbourne Mexico City Mumbai
Nairobi Paris São Paulo Shanghai Singapore Taipei Tokyo Toronto Warsaw
with associated companies in Berlin Ibadan

Oxford is a registered trade mark of Oxford University Press
in the UK and certain other countries

Published in the United States
by Oxford University Press Inc., New York

British Library Cataloguing in Publication Data
Data available

Library of Congress Cataloging in Publication Data
Data available
ISBN 0–19–829921–4

1 3 5 7 9 10 8 6 4 2

Typeset by J&L Composition Ltd, Filey, North Yorkshire

Printed in Great Britain
on acid-free paper by
Biddles Ltd
Guildford and King's Lynn

Foreword

Prudent creditors seek to protect themselves against the risk of their debtor's insolvency by taking security. With the growth of the multinational corporation and the increasing globalization of the market-place, cross-border insolvency has become a major commercial risk. Much academic, judicial, and legislative consideration has been given to this problem, and international conventions and major legal textbooks have been devoted to the subject. Less consideration, however, has been given to the connected and equally important, but possibly more intractable, issue of cross-border security. This book should prove a major contribution to understanding the nature of the problems involved, without which even tentative solutions are unlikely to be found.

It owes its origin to an important colloquium held at St John's College, Oxford in April 2000. The distinguished speakers came from different jurisdictions, England, the United States, Germany, and France, and included bankers and practitioners as well as academics. They contributed valuable papers on their own domestic security laws and their domestic choice of law rules. These expose the many problems which remain unsolved even in domestic laws and for which conflicting solutions have been proposed.

The problem are exacerbated by two features which are inherent in the subject. The first is that, because of its relationship with insolvency, security law is heavily influenced by policy considerations, and these tend to differ from country to country. The second is that, with diverse investment portfolios increasingly held in electronic form by intermediaries and the arrival of instantaneous electronic commmerce, the development of new intangible and non-territorial assets and securities is proceeding apace. New forms of property require new conditions of ownership. The old analogy with tangible movables had already broken down; it is entirely out of place in today's global market-place.

Perhaps we shall live to see a new form of international security, a genuine floating charge but one floating in cyberspace and owing all allegiance to no single legal system but recognized by all. Some such concept will be needed to meet the challenges of the new age when we bring to reality the additional Chapter of the Report of the Cork Committee on Insolvency, written in jest by the secretariat 20 years ago and never published, entitled 'Extra-Terrestrial Insolvency'.

The Rt. Hon. The Lord Millett
January 2001

Contents — Summary

Contents

List of Contributors

HAMISH ANDERSON, Partner, Norton Rose, London

PROFESSOR MICHAEL BRIDGE, Professor of Law, University College London; Director of Research, Norton Rose, London

RICHARD F BROUDE, New York City

RICHARD CALNAN, Partner, Norton Rose, London

PROFESSOR ULRICH DROBNIG, Max Planck Institute for Foreign and Private International Law, Hamburg

PROFESSOR IAN F FLETCHER, Herbert Smith Professor of International Commercial Law, University College London

MARTIN GDANSKI, Norton Rose, Paris

PROFESSOR SIR ROY GOODE, St John's College, Oxford

MARK HOMAN, PricewaterhouseCoopers

DR BURKHARD JÄKEL, Partner, Gleiss Lutz Hootz Hirsch, Frankfurt am Main

PROFESSOR CATHERINE KESSEDJIAN, Professor at the University of Paris II Parthéon-Assas

PROFESSOR CHARLES W MOONEY JUN, Associate Dean for Academic Affairs and Professor of Law, University of Pennsylvania Law School

ROBERT STEVENS, Barrister, Fellow, and Tutor in Law: Lady Margaret Hall, Oxford University

LINDSAY J TOWN, Head of Asset Finance, Halifax Group Treasury and Wholesale Banking

Table of Cases

ECJ/CFI

GERMANY

Tables of Legislation

International

List of Abbreviations

AG	Aktiengesellschaft (stock corporation)
AktG	Aktiengesetz (Stock Corporation Act of 6 September 1965)
ALI	American Law Institute
BGB	German Civil Code
BGBL	Bundesgesetzblatt
BGH	Bundesgerichtshof (Federal Supreme Court, Germany)
BGHZ	Official Collection of Decisions of the Federal Court of Justice in Civil Matters
Brussels Convention	Brussels Convention on Insolvency Proceedings
C & N	P North and JJ Fawcett (eds), *Cheshire and North's Private International Law* (13th edn, 1999)
CAC	French Code of Civil Aviation
CC Proc	Code of Civil Procedure (Germany)
D&M	L Collins (ed), *Dicey and Morris on the Conflict of Laws* (13th edn, 2000)
DGAC	*Direction Générale de L'Aviation Civile* (French Civil Aviation Authority)
EBRD	European Bank for Reconstruction and Development
EGBGB	Einführungsgesetz zum Bürgerlichen Gesetzbuche (Introductory Law to the German Civil Code 1896)
EU Convention	European Union Convention on Insolvency Proceedings
FOSFA	The Federation of Oil Seeds and Fats Associations
Gaz Pol	Gazette du Palais
GBO	Grundbuchordnung (Land Registry Act of 24 March 1897)
GmbH	Gesellschaft mit beschränkter Haftung (private limited company)
GmbHG	Limited Liability Companies Act (Germany)
HGB	German Commercial Code
IATA	International Air Transport Association
ICAO	International Civil Aviation Organization

InsO	Insolvency Code (Germany)
IPrax	Praxis des Internationales Privat und Verfahrensrechts
IPRspr	Die Deutsche Rechtsprechung auf den Gebiete des Internationalen Privatrechts
JD	Juris Doctor
MCC	Maxwell Communications Corporation
NCCUSL	National Conference of Commissioners on Uniform State Laws (USA)
NJW	Neue Juristische Wochenschrift
OLG	Oberlandesgericht (Higher Appellate Court, Germany)
PIL Act	Swiss Private International Law Act
PMSI	Purchase money security interest
PRIMA	The place of the relevant intermediary
Rome Convention	European Convention on the Law Applicable to Contractual Obligations
UCC	Uniform Commercial Code
UCITS	Collective investment undertakings
UNCITRAL	United Nations Committee on International Trade Law
UNIDROIT	International Institute for the Unification of Private Law
ZIP	Zeitschrift für Wirtschaftsrecht und Insolvenz Praxis (Journal of Business Law and Insolvency Practice)
ZPO	German Civil Code of Procedure
ZVG	Act Governing Public Auctions and Administrative Receivership of 24 March 1897 (Germany)

1

Introduction

ROBERT STEVENS

(Fellow and Tutor in Law, Lady Margaret Hall, Oxford)

It is easy for even the most incompetent lawyer to give an account of an area of law which makes it seem difficult and abstruse. The trick is to explain the law so that it seems simple and may be readily understood. Where the subject is cross-border security and insolvency this is a particularly hard trick to pull off.

This collection originated at a colloquium held at St John's College Oxford in April 2000. A case study, set out in Appendix 1, was used as the basis of discussion and as a direction pointer for the various papers, which are set out in this collection in a revised form. This book is divided into five parts, as was the colloquium itself. The first part takes the form of a plea for help from a banker. The second part is an attempt to provide an overview of the ways in which security may be taken in England, the United States, France, and Germany. The third section considers the choice of law rules in relation to security in those countries. In the fourth, Professor Goode discusses the attempts through international conventions to solve the problems raised by the inadequacies of and the conflicts between current choice of law rules. Finally, the international impact of insolvency upon cross-border security is considered.

The purpose of this introduction is to give both a brief overview of the subjects discussed and to give some of the flavour of the discussion of both the contributors and those who attended. In particular the contributions of Lord Millett and Professor Burrows who chaired the sessions should be mentioned.

Lindsay Town considers the fears of a banker taking security outside a wholly domestic context. Legal confusion deters business. Even if a bank chooses to embark upon lending on a cross-border basis uncertainty creates risk and risk creates expense. Unlike the position where contractual rights alone are in issue, a particular choice of jurisdiction and governing law will not necessarily protect a bank.

Set alongside the legal problems, the language barrier would appear easy for a banker to overcome. However, the unwary can be easily misled. Even where lawyers think that they are speaking the same language, words may have different or indeed no meaning for someone from another system. 'Lien', 'Collateral', 'Conditional Sale', 'Floating Charge', 'Trustee in Bankruptcy', 'Receiver', and even 'Bankruptcy' do not have the same meanings or connotations for lawyers from England and the United States. At least when we converse with lawyers from different legal traditions we tend to be wary.

The comparative overview of security interests demonstrated that there was a great deal of common ground in the creation of security rights over immovable property and possessory security over tangible movables. The most important differences are in relation to the ability to create effective non-possessory security rights over tangible and intangible movables. Richard Calnan and Richard Broude demonstrate that, perhaps unsurprisingly, English and American law are very similar in their approach to non-possessory security. Both systems permit the granting of non-possessory security over all forms of property. Both systems permit the creation of security over both the present and future assets of a debtor. Both have in place a method of registration for such rights. However, in its detail English law is very much the poor relation. In particular, the complexity of the English rules concerning priority have long been recognized to be defective. Despite repeated calls to reform English law[1] no steps have yet been taken. Revised Article 9 of the Uniform Commercial Code (UCC) provides a more intellectually coherent model for harmonizing the law of secured transactions, therefore.

Anglo-American law differs sharply from that found in many civilian jurisdictions, however. Burkhard Jakel's analysis demonstrates that there are many aspects of German law which are surprising to the common lawyer. Non-possessory security rights are capable of being created but are potentially more problematic. For an English lawyer, the peculiarity of the floating charge is that the debtor has a general authority to dispose of the charged assets free of the charge, without the necessity for the specific consent of the creditor at the time of disposal. By contrast, for a German lawyer the peculiarity of the floating charge is that it allows a general security to be taken over the entirety of a company's undertaking without particularizing which individual assets are subject to the charge. A general charge of this form is unknown in German law.

The absence of a regime for registration in German law, except in relation to land and aircraft, contrasts sharply with Anglo-American law. Any system which does not require registration of non-possessory security is almost certain to be hostile to the widespread recognition of such rights.

The recent changes in German insolvency law will be striking to anyone familiar with the recommendations of the report of the English Insolvency Law Review Committee under Sir Kenneth Cork.[2] The German

---

[1] *Crowther Committee Report on Consumer Credit* (Cmnd 4596, 1971); A Diamond, *A Review of Security Interests in Property* (DTI, 1989).

[2] *Insolvency Law and Practice* (Cmnd 8558, 1982).

Insolvency Code's virtual abolition of preferred debts reflects what was recommended by Cork. English insolvency law, unlike German law, generally allows a security holder to enforce his security rights outside the insolvency proceeding. The German deduction of the costs of determining and realizing the assets subject to security from the amount paid to the security holder resembles the recommendation by Cork that a 10 per cent fund should be set aside for unsecured creditors from the assets caught by a floating charge. Again, Cork's recommendations did not find their way into the English Insolvency Act 1986.

Perhaps the most surprising rule of German law to an English lawyer is that concerning 'over-securitization'. That a bank may lose its security if it takes 'too much' security is startling. How this rule can be extracted from the principle of good faith under section 138 of the German Civil Code (BGB) is difficult for a common lawyer to grasp.

Suppliers of goods under retention of title clauses are to an extent afforded greater protection under German law than they would be under English law. Under German law 'retention' of title clauses which cover the proceeds of assets supplied will be effective. In England, whilst it is perfectly possible to retain title to the original assets supplied, attempts to extend retention of title to cover proceeds will usually fail as this will be interpreted as creating a charge over book debts and will be potentially void if not registered.[3]

As Martin Gdanski explains, in French law, like German law, the forms and rules governing security vary according to the type of asset over which security is to be taken. Whilst French law does recognize the creation of security over a company's undertaking (*fonds de commerce*) this is much less significant than Article 9 of the UCC or the English floating charge because of the assets excluded from the *fond de commerce* (for example, land, goods, book debts). French law's hostility towards the creation of non-possessory security over stock in trade and the absence of a centralized system for the registration of security rights contrasts sharply with Anglo-American law. Further, under French insolvency law the security right holder cannot stand outside the proceedings and cannot enforce security in the manner available pre-insolvency.

Whether the (relative) generosity of English law towards security holders when compared to the (relatively) niggardly approach of French law is better or worse is outside of the scope of this book. Since the rules are so obviously different, however, it becomes important to know which ones a court ought to apply. In the choice of law context, the strongest division is not between Anglo-American law on the one hand and civilian law on the other but between American law and the law of European

---

[3] *Pfeiffer (E) Weinkellerei-Weineinkauf GmbH & Co v Arbuthnot Factors Ltd* [1989] 1 WLR 150.

countries. In part this is a result of the ongoing harmonization of European private international law. The conflicts of law rules for contractual obligations have been harmonized by the Rome Convention whilst the Regulation on Insolvency Proceedings has recently been adopted. Further, as Ulrich Drobnig, Catherine Kessedjian, and Robert Stevens discuss, many of the rules found in Germany, France, and England resemble each other. According to orthodoxy, under each system the *lex situs* at the time of the creation of the security right determines the validity of the creation of security in tangible movables. The *lex situs* rule appears attractive in a simple case involving a single asset the *situs* of which remains constant. Where successive global charges are created over different forms of property located in several different jurisdictions, the *situs* of which may change over time, serious difficulties occur in applying the *lex situs* rule.

Michael Bridge argues that wherever possible the courts should look to the law governing the contract which created the proprietary interest to solve the problems which arise. A recent example of the courts adopting this approach may be found in the judgment of Neuberger J in *Re Harvard Securities (in liq)*.[4] It must be confessed, however, that this cannot provide a solution in all situations. Where successive security interests are created over a single asset it may be that different laws govern each contract. Since the different contracts may be governed by different systems of law which may provide for different results, a contractual approach cannot resolve the priority between the security holders.

During discussion some support was expressed in favour of applying the *lex loci actus* to determine security rights.[5] As Catherine Kessedjian states, the usual argument given in favour of applying the *lex situs* rather than, say, the *lex loci actus* or the law governing the contract under which a proprietary right is created, is the protection of third parties. If a charge is created over an asset in Ruritania by a contract governed by English law and executed in London, why should a creditor who seeks to execute against the asset have his ability to do so determined by English law of which he knows nothing? However, unless the creditor who seeks execution knows the history of the asset, the *lex situs* rule will not necessarily protect him either. Whilst the asset may now be in Ruritania, the security right may have been created whilst the asset was in England.

In Germany, France, and England the law governing the proprietary effect of the assignment of intangibles either absolutely or by way of security is controversial. Robert Stevens argues that Article 12(2) of the

---

[4] [1997] 2 BCLC 369.
[5] *Macmillan Inc v Bishopsgate Investment Trust (No 3)* [1995] 1 WLR 978 (Millett J). Cf [1996] 1 WLR 387 (Court of Appeal).

Rome Convention provides the solution. This is inconsistent, however, with the assumptions of the Working Group for the UNCITRAL Draft Convention on Assignment in Receivables Financing which is discussed by Roy Goode. Article 29 of the Draft Convention is substantively identical to Article 12(2) of the Rome Convention but clearly does not govern priorities as this is separately dealt with in Article 30 of the Draft. Further, as Catherine Kessedjian comments, an earlier draft of Article 12 of the Rome Convention did cover the issue of priorities in competing assignments but this was removed.

As the simple case of the law applicable to the proprietary effect of the transfer of a single intangible is controversial, it is hardly surprising that there was little agreement as to the correct approach to be taken in more difficult cases, where securities are held through intermediaries, for example.

The approach adopted in the United States may offer a way forward. Charles Mooney served as a Reporter for the Drafting Committee to Revise Uniform Commercial Code Article 9. The primary rule is that the location of the debtor governs the perfection and priority of a security interest.[6] Such a rule makes considerable sense. Forum shopping would be deterred. The location of the debtor is a single system of law which will not change over time and could determine priority in all of a debtor's assets regardless of type. A security holder would know whether and where to register his security. Currently, if a security holder takes a global security over assets situated in a number of jurisdictions he may not be confident that his security is perfected in relation to each asset unless he registers not only at the place of the debtor but also at the *situs* of each asset. Further, as Robert Stevens demonstrates, an English court will give extraterritorial effect to its registration rules.

Where, however, is the location of the debtor? Under the new European Union Insolvency Regulation a court will have jurisdiction if a debtor's main interest is situated within the jurisdiction. In the case of a corporate debtor this is rebuttably presumed to be the place of its registered office. If the approach of Article 9 were to be adopted, it would make sense to define the location of the debtor in the same way, thereby ensuring that the law governing priorities would be that of the state which would have principal jurisdiction if a debtor enters an insolvency proceeding.

More controversial, however, are the rules for determining the location of the debtor under Article 9. If the law of the place of the debtor does not 'generally require information concerning the existence of a non-possessory security interest to be made generally available in a filing, recording or registration system' the debtor will be deemed to be located in the District of Columbia. As we have seen, many European

---

[6] Article 9–301(1).

legal systems do not require or provide for the registration of non-possessory security rights. A German bank which takes security over the German assets of a German customer runs the risk, therefore, that a court which has adopted Revised Article 9 may refuse to apply German law to determine the validity of the security, owing to the absence of German registration requirements. Charles Mooney argues that such an approach is justifiable as it would provide an incentive for lawmakers in Germany to enact provisions equivalent to Article 9. However, it seems harsh that the perceived failings of the German State should be visited upon a particular creditor. The fact that other modern legal systems have not introduced general requirements for the registration of security may indicate that the policy in favour of introducing them is not so overwhelming as to require severe results being inflicted upon particular creditors. It may be that the approach of Revised Article 9 is more easily justifiable where the conflict is between the systems of law of a federal state such as the United States.

Revised Article 9 is not as dramatically different from the current approach of European states as might appear. Article 9–301(3) has retained the *lex situs* rule for certain forms of tangible property and documentary intangibles. Roy Goode provides us with an overview of attempts to harmonize and improve upon the rules individual states have in relation to cross-border security, which in some respects are more radical. The Draft Convention on International Interests in Mobile Equipment is particularly interesting as it proposes the abandonment of the *lex situs* rule in relation to forms of movable property which frequently cause difficulties by changing where they are situated. For English law the most striking change would be the creation of an international registration system for interests in the assets covered. For systems which are more reluctant to recognize non-possessory security rights, the greatest change will be the creation and recognition of an international security interest unknown in the state's domestic law.

Mark Homan explores the difficulties faced by an insolvency practitioner where a single debtor company has entered into formal insolvency proceedings in more than one country. In addition to the legal problems, an insolvency practitioner faces the considerable difficulty of actually running a company. Harmonizing domestic insolvency law regimes is clearly not an immediate practical solution. The only alternative is to attempt, by international conventions, to harmonize the rules concerning where an insolvency proceeding may be opened and the law which will be applied. Following the Colloquium the Council Regulation on Insolvency Proceedings was adopted. The Regulation is almost identical to the ill-fated European Union Convention on Insolvency Proceedings. Further, clause 13 of an Insolvency Bill currently before Parliament will empower the making of regulations to give effect with or without modifications to the UNCITRAL model law on cross-border insolvency.

It is fair to say that Mark Homan is sceptical as to whether either the Regulation or the UNCITRAL Model Law provide the legal certainty which is necessary to remove the legal obstacles that he and fellow insolvency practitioners will face. Certainly there has yet to be substantial consideration of how the Regulation and the Model Law are to fit together if incorporated together into a single system of law.

Ian Fletcher and Hamish Anderson are more optimistic. They consider the effect of the opening of insolvency proceedings upon security rights. The EU Regulation is an ambitious attempt to provide rules of jurisdiction for the opening of proceedings, the applicable law once opened, and the recognition to be afforded by other member states. That the Regulation is subject to interpretation by the European Court of Justice is unlikely, in the short term, to be of any practical help in removing uncertainty. The current gross delays in obtaining a decision from that court make the Regulation unlikely to be of use in resolving many of the pressing questions faced by an insolvency practitioner.

Ian Fletcher has produced the fullest consideration of both the Regulation and the Model Law available in English.[7] There are, however, many questions which have either not been raised or are as yet incapable of being answered. For example, Article 5 of the Regulation stipulates that the opening of insolvency proceedings shall not affect the rights *in rem* of creditors or third parties in respect of tangible or intangible, movable or immovable assets belonging to the debtor which are situated within the territory of another member state at the time of the opening of the proceeding. Future assets are not covered by this protection nor are assets situated outside a member state. On one view, therefore, it may be for the domestic law of place where the insolvency proceeding is opened to determine the priority of proprietary rights in future assets and those outside a member state.

---

[7] Fletcher, *Insolvency in Private International Law* (Clarendon Press, Oxford, 1997).

PART 1

The Problem of Cross-Border Security and Insolvency

2
A Banker's Perspective

LINDSAY J TOWN

(Head of Asset Finance, Halifax Group Treasury and Wholesale Banking)

At the time of writing, I have been involved in the asset finance business for twenty-five years and, of all the issues faced, the cross-border finance arena has often thrown up the most complex of challenges—and the most complex responses. It is for the foregoing reasons that I was delighted to be invited to present a short overview of the concerns that the secured lender faced when dealing on a cross-border basis. Although my own background is primarily in the leasing market, my views may well be considered to be equally appropriate for any form of cross-border transaction where the value of the asset being financed is a material part of the risk and reward calculation.

The first challenge of a brief introductory essay is to find a suitable example on which to base the subsequent points. In cross-border financing it is usual to consider single high value items such as ships and aircraft. These two asset types generally represent the areas where most people consider that the rules are fairly well understood—but I would emphasize the word 'fairly'. It is, however, also worth adding another example to the study. Consider a hypothetical high value item of equipment that may be moved from country to country, albeit that there is not any real intention to do so. We could therefore further extend the example to include the financing of power stations and other high value assets that are often financed on a cross-border basis.

When one considers the nature of the transactions from a practical financier's perspective certain initial fears surface. We can start with the so-called language barrier. It is said that the United Kingdom and the United States are two nations separated by a common language—if only it was that easy in cross-border transactions! We only need to consider some very basic words and expressions to highlight the potential problems:

Lease
Insolvency Proceedings
First Priority Charge
Movable or Fixture

In our domestic activities, these words and phrases have very specific connotations and most financiers have a good view as to their position in relation to each. However, as one moves the concepts to different jurisdictions the familiar implications rapidly evaporate. The category of movables and fixtures raises sufficient problems in the United Kingdom but is a potential nightmare for the cross-border financier, especially if what was thought to be movable turns out to be a fixture when recovery proceedings are commenced. The issue of terminology and the implications of the differing local interpretations of words is one of those classic circumstances where a little knowledge can generate a disproportionately large amount of trouble.

If we overcome the terminology issues we then reach the next basic level of concerns for the financier:

What happens if the deal goes wrong?
What is the attitude of the courts?
What are the prospects for enforcement, even if we win?
What if the equipment has been moved to another country?

And the final question for the financier new to the cross-border market tends to be: Do we really want to do this business at all?

The financier has lost the 'comfort zone' of the home territory and in reality faces little consistency between countries, and the long established precedents of the home market rapidly evaporate. A far worse circumstance then ensues if the asset actually moves from country to country. As each jurisdiction is passed through the asset may pick up liabilities of various types all of which become rapidly manifested if a work out of the financing is required.

The questions set out above produce a dilemma for the financier. The choice of law, who can overturn or interfere with the process, who really controls the underlying asset and what extraneous liabilities has the asset acquired in its travels are some of the most basic building blocks of a secured transaction.

The simple conclusions that one comes to are, to an extent, self-evident:

- The more jurisdictions that an asset moves through, the higher the chance of a successful challenge to the security and the higher the risk of additional parties claiming an interest.
- The implications of an asset being deemed to be fixed to land or part of the land can destroy the most carefully crafted structure—if one thought that the asset was movable to start with.

- If the asset has moved then other parties may have acquired an interest in that asset that was not contemplated in the original structure—and certainly may interfere with the recovery and realization process.

In any work-out situation the financier needs certain conditions to apply to ensure the best possibility of a recovery. The whole thrust of these conditions is to ensure a clarity of contractual relationship, rights, remedies, and recovery of security. Given those conditions, where does the brief analysis of the initial concerns leave us? Regrettably, we are left with the possible view that none of the conditions are satisfactorily met. We have little consistency or common ground and come away with the distinct feeling that practical outcomes rarely meet the theoretical prognosis and that the foreign lender will always be at a serious disadvantage. Stories often recounted tend to start, 'Just when we thought that it was all going to be fine . . . '.

For a successful transaction the financier needs to have certainty of recovery of the asset together with a total confidence in the processes involved. In order to provide the finance requirement, the initial viability of the transaction requires an assessment of the level of confidence in the processes involved. Where there are unknowns, or there is a lack of confidence, the financier has a range of possible reactions:

- Decline the transaction. This is the 'easy' route, but the most negative and potentially damaging to wider relationships.
- Increase the price to nearer to the price of an unsecured loan. This is a pragmatic response to a fear that security may be severely impaired or the recovery process may be ineffective.
- Limit dealings to the highest quality borrowers only. This limits the financier's potential market and also denies a large section of business access to cross-border financing structures.
- Limit dealings to the most understood countries. Again, this may damage relationships where one is dealing with truly multinational companies and also means that the financier is severely limiting the market potential.
- Engage in contractual 'overkill' to cover as many possibilities as can be conceived. This is not an uncommon response but this approach makes documentation unwieldy and possibly opens up more opportunity for confusion in foreign courts.

This range of reactions is not an unnatural response for the financier who relies on the security of an asset as an integral part of the viability of a transaction. It should also be borne in mind that the 'asset' in question may be an intangible as well as the more obvious ships, planes, or trains that spring easily to mind. If one considers the problems set out above in relation to a limited recourse financing of a power station with security over the asset plus off-take agreements (from a third jurisdiction) then one may see the extent of the issues involved.

We face increasingly global markets where the movement of trade and capital must happen rapidly and with minimum interference. The financier always wishes to see new markets open up as the profit motive must never be underestimated and, more seriously, there is a need to be able to support banking relationships at a global level, not just in one or two locations. The clear difficulties for the cross-border financier who looks to assets in particular do not sit at all well with global market concepts. As we are today, the multiplication of risks and relative uncertainty in dealing with such cross-border transactions are material threats to the development of the business for both financier and customer alike.

The move to have a consistent, clearly understood and applied process for cross-border transactions involving security is an important goal in assisting the development of the efficient financing of business.

The views expressed in this chapter are the personal observations and opinions of the writer and do not necessarily reflect the views of Halifax plc.

PART 2

Security under Domestic Law

3

Taking Security in England

RICHARD CALNAN

(Partner, Norton Rose, London)

The purpose of this chapter is to provide a brief outline of the ways in which security is taken in England. It assumes that the person providing the security (the 'debtor') is a company and that the person receiving the benefit of the security (the 'creditor') has lent money to the debtor or provided some other form of credit to it. After an initial discussion of the principal types of security interest which can be created under English law, there will be an analysis of the main priority issues which arise, the way in which the security is enforced, and the effect of insolvency proceedings in relation to the debtor. The chapter will then examine how those principles impact on the taking of security over three specific types of commercial asset (goods, receivables, and shares), before considering how security can be taken generally over all present and future assets of the debtor. Finally, there will be a brief discussion of other ways in which a transaction can be structured so as to avoid the creation of security but to give the creditor substantially the same rights as it would have had if it had taken security.

I. THE CREATION OF SECURITY INTERESTS

There are three principal types of security interest which can be created by agreement between the debtor and the creditor: a pledge, a mortgage, and a charge.[1] Certain types of security interest (most notably common law and equitable liens) arise by operation of law, without the necessity for any agreement between the parties, but they will not be covered in this chapter. Nor will it deal with what is sometimes referred to as 'personal' (as opposed to 'real') security, such as guarantees. It is limited to security created by the debtor over its assets.

At the outset, it should be mentioned that any type of liability for the payment of money can be secured under English law. The liability can be present, future, or contingent; and it can relate to a primary obligation of

---

[1] In *Re Cosslett (Contractors)* [1998] Ch 495 at 508, Millett LJ referred to a fourth type, contractual liens. They will not be covered in this chapter because they have many of the same characteristics as a pledge and are not used by lenders in practice.

the debtor or to a secondary obligation (for instance, a guarantee). It will frequently relate to the repayment of a loan, but can include a liability to pay damages for breach of a non-monetary obligation. Nor does the liability have to be owed by the person granting the security: 'third party' security can be given to secure the obligations of another person.

Pledge

The pledge is the oldest form of security available in England. It is a common law concept and its essential characteristic is that it requires the creditor to have possession of an asset of the debtor until the secured liability has been paid.

It accordingly has two main limitations. The first is that the asset concerned must be capable of being possessed by the creditor. It is therefore only available in respect of chattels, and not land or, generally, intangibles. The second is that it is generally only effective to the extent that the creditor actually obtains possession of the chattel and retains that possession until the secured liability has been paid. Security is constituted by the possession of the chattel by the creditor. It is possible to document the basis on which the security has been granted (and it is common for a 'letter of pledge' to contain its terms). But the document does not create the pledge, it only evidences it.[2] If the creditor loses possession of the chattel before the secured liability has been paid, the letter of pledge is worthless.[3]

In most commercial transactions, therefore, a pledge is not an appropriate form of security. The debtor will normally require the use of its assets for the purpose of its business. There are, however, three aspects of a pledge which enable it to be of some value in commercial transactions.

The first is that the assets which can be the subject of a pledge do not only extend to physical chattels, such as goods. They also include documents of title to goods (such as bills of lading) and documents of title to intangibles (such as bearer securities).[4] This is because such documents of title are capable of being transferred by delivery (and, if necessary, endorsement); and the effect of such a delivery is, if the parties intend it to do so, to transfer not only the document itself, but also the underlying asset.[5] So, for instance, the endorsement and delivery of a bill of lading to

---

[2] *Ex p Hubbard, re Hardwick* (1886) 17 QBD 690 (CA).

[3] Certain types of transfer of possession to a third party (for instance under a sub-pledge) do not terminate the pledge: *Donald v Suckling* (1866) LR 1 QB 585.

[4] *Carter v Wake* (1877) 4 Ch D 605.

[5] Whether the transfer of possession of the bill of lading transfers title to the goods or just constructive possession of them depends on the intention of the parties: *Sewell v Burdick* (1884) 10 App Cas 74 (HL).

a transferee will transfer not only the bill of lading, but also the goods which are the subject of the bill. Similarly, the transfer of a bearer security will transfer not just the physical piece of paper itself, but also the underlying rights against the maker of the security. Since the transfer of the document also transfers the underlying asset, it follows that the possession by a creditor of (say) a bill of lading will give the bank constructive possession of the underlying goods; and much international trade is financed by banks taking pledges over bills of lading.

It must, however, be stressed that the document over which a creditor takes a pledge must be a document of title. Although it is clear that a bill of lading is a document of title, many other forms of document relating to goods (such as most warehouse receipts) are not, and cannot, therefore, be pledged.[6] Similarly, although a bearer share certificate can be pledged, a certificate relating to registered shares cannot.[7] A transfer of a share certificate relating to registered shares cannot transfer the title to the shares.

The second aspect of a pledge which can extend its usefulness in commercial transactions is the use of the concept of 'constructive possession' where the goods are held by a third party. The possession which a creditor has over goods which are the subject of a bill of lading held by the creditor can be regarded as a form of constructive possession, but the expression is often used in a different sense. If chattels of the debtor are in the hands of a third party, the third party can 'attorn' in favour of the creditor and thereby give the creditor constructive possession of the chattels.[8] An attornment is simply a confirmation by the third party, at the request of the debtor but to the creditor, that it holds the chattels on behalf of the creditor. If, for instance, the debtor is an art dealer who has deposited works of art with an auction house, the auction house can, by attorning in favour of the creditor (ie by confirming, at the request of the debtor, that it holds the works of art on behalf of the creditor), transfer constructive possession in the works of art to the creditor.

The third aspect of a pledge which can increase its usefulness is that the powers of the creditor can be extended by the use of a 'trust receipt'. If, for instance, the creditor has possession of a bill of lading and delivers it to the debtor for a limited purpose (for instance to recover the goods from the shipper), the use of a trust receipt (which confirms that the debtor only obtains physical possession of the goods for a limited purpose) may enable the bank to continue in constructive possession and thereby to

---

[6] *Official Assignee of Madras v Mercantile Bank of India* [1935] AC 53, 59 (PC).
[7] *Harrold v Plenty* [1901] 2 Ch 314.
[8] *Official Assignee of Madras v Mercantile Bank of India* [1935] AC 53, 58–59 (PC).

retain its pledge even though the physical possession of the assets has reverted to the debtor.[9]

As was mentioned earlier, although a pledge is established by the possession of the chattel by the creditor, the terms of the pledge are normally set out in a letter of pledge, which will evidence such matters as the extent of the liabilities secured by the pledge and the scope of the powers of the creditor. Although the creditor only has possession of the chattels (rather than title to them), it has an interest in the chattels which is sometimes referred to as a 'special property', as a result of which it can sell the chattels on default by the debtor.[10] In practice, however, the letter of pledge will itself give the creditor wide powers, including the power to sell the chattels.

The disadvantages of a pledge are manifest, but it is still used in practice, particularly in relation to the financing of international trade. The reason is that it has one important advantage over most other forms of security interest: a pledge is not registrable against the debtor.[11] This is because registration is intended to provide third parties with notice of the creation of a security interest. It is not necessary in the case of a pledge because the requirement that the creditor must be in possession of the asset concerned is thought to provide sufficient notice of the existence of the security interest.[12]

Mortgage

The second form of security interest available under English law is the mortgage. The characteristic feature of a mortgage is that title to an asset is transferred from the debtor to the creditor. If it is legal title to the asset which is transferred, the mortgage is a legal mortgage. If only beneficial title is transferred, it is an equitable mortgage.

What distinguishes a mortgage from an outright transfer of title is that the mortgage secures a liability and, therefore, the debtor has residual rights in the asset. In the case of a legal mortgage, the debtor has the right, on payment of the secured liability, to have the asset retransferred into its name. This is not merely a personal right against the creditor; it is a proprietary right, frequently referred to as an 'equity of redemption'. Whilst the mortgage subsists, there are therefore two proprietary interests in the

---

[9] *Re David Allester* [1922] 2 Ch 211 (Ch D); *Official Assignee of Madras v Mercantile Bank of India* [1935] AC 53, 63 (PC). [10] *Donald v Suckling* (1866) LR 1 QB 585.
[11] A pledge is not a 'bill of sale' within the Companies Act 1985, s 396(1)(c): *Ex p Hubbard, re Hardwick* (1886) 17 QBD 690 (CA).
[12] This is the case where the creditor has physical possession of the chattels. It is more difficult to justify where the chattels have been redelivered to the debtor under a trust receipt, although the debtor will usually have them only for a limited time before selling them on.

asset, the creditor having a legal interest in the asset to secure the debt and the debtor having a residual equitable interest. In the case of an equitable mortgage, the creditor has the beneficial interest in the asset and the debtor retains bare legal title and the residual equitable interest. Possession of the asset almost invariably remains with the debtor.

A mortgage may be taken over any type of asset, the title to which is capable of being transferred. At common law, it is possible to transfer land and chattels but not, generally, choses in action. Bearer securities are, however, capable of transfer by delivery, and can therefore be mortgaged at common law, and registered shares can also be the subject of a legal mortgage.

In equity, most types of asset can be transferred, including choses in action, although certain types of chose in action cannot be assigned, such as those of a 'personal' nature and other limited categories of chose in action, the assignment of which would be contrary to public policy.[13] More importantly in practice, because the creditor can obtain no better right to the chose in action than the debtor, the benefit of a contract cannot be assigned in breach of a prohibition on assignment, even if the creditor was not aware of the prohibition.[14] Those choses in action which can be assigned in equity are also capable of being assigned by statute.[15]

Accordingly, most types of chose in action (including rights under contracts and receivables) are capable of being assigned in equity or by statute, but cannot be transferred at common law.

In relation to certain types of asset, specific statutory provisions have affected the way in which mortgages are taken. For instance, since the 1925 property legislation, legal mortgages over land are no longer created by the transfer of title to the creditor. There is now a statutory procedure, known as a 'charge by way of legal mortgage', as a result of which the creditor is given a statutory interest in the land which is effectively equivalent to a legal mortgage.[16] Particular statutory provisions also apply to mortgages over ships, aircraft, and certain types of intellectual property (such as patents).[17]

In practice, therefore, legal mortgages can generally only be taken over chattels and shares (and, in a modified form, over land), whereas equitable mortgages can be taken over most types of asset. Two differences

---

[13] *Nokes v Doncaster Amalgamated Collieries* [1940] AC 1014 (HL).

[14] *Linden Garden Trust v Lenesta Sludge Disposals* [1994] 1 AC 85 (HL). A purported assignment might, however, confer proprietary rights on the creditor if the interests of the person who owes the chose in action are not affected: *Don King Productions v Warren (No. 1)* [2000] Ch 291 (CA). [15] Law of Property Act 1925, s 136.

[16] Law of Property Act 1925, ss 85–87.

[17] This is because there are asset registers for such assets. For ships, see the Merchant Shipping Act 1995; for aircraft, the Mortgaging of Aircraft Order 1972; for patents, the Patents Act 1977, s 30.

between legal and equitable mortgages are particularly important in practice. One is that they have different priority rules, a legal mortgage generally offering greater protection against third parties than an equitable mortgage. These are discussed in part II of this chapter.

The other main distinction between legal and equitable mortgages is particularly important in practice. A legal mortgage is only available in relation to property in existence and owned by the debtor at the time the mortgage is created.[18] In equity, however, it is possible for the debtor to create security not only over its existing assets, but also over assets which it subsequently acquires. Although the mortgage does not attach to the asset until it becomes owned by the debtor, as soon as this happens the equitable mortgage automatically attaches to the asset without the requirement for the execution of any further document.[19] In practice, this is a very important advantage, because it enables after-acquired property to fall within the scope of an equitable mortgage without the requirement for any further action on the part of the debtor or the creditor.

In order to obtain a legal mortgage, the formalities of the transfer of legal title have to be complied with. There are few such requirements in relation to chattels, the title to which can be transferred either by delivery or by execution of a document. In practice, a legal mortgage over chattels is created by the execution of a mortgage document, rather than by transfer of possession (which will normally remain with the debtor). In the case of registered shares, a legal mortgage is effected by the creditor becoming the registered holder of the shares on the share register of the company concerned. A mortgage document will also be executed, evidencing such matters as the scope of the secured liabilities and the powers of the creditor.

The transfer of beneficial title under an equitable mortgage does not require many formalities to be complied with. It can generally be effected by the execution of a mortgage document by the debtor, beneficial title passing simply as a result of the execution of the document. The creation of an equitable mortgage is therefore rather more straightforward than a legal mortgage. Both types of mortgage confer enforcement powers on the creditor, including a power of sale, although these powers are invariably supplemented in the mortgage document.

Where the debtor is a company, most types of mortgage (whether legal or equitable) require to be registered against the debtor under the Companies Act 1985.[20] The requirement extends to companies incorporated in England and, where the asset concerned is situated in England, to foreign

---

[18] *Lunn v Thornton* (1845) 1 CB 379.

[19] *Holroyd v Marshall* (1862) 10 HL Cas 191 (HL); *Tailby v Official Receiver* (1888) 13 App Cas 523 (HL).   [20] Companies Act 1985, ss 395 and 396.

companies which have an established place of business in England.[21] Failure to submit the mortgage and the required details for registration within twenty-one days after the creation of the mortgage will have the effect that the mortgage is void against a liquidator, administrator, or creditor of the debtor. A mortgage is only registrable if it is created over an asset which falls within one of the categories listed in section 396(1) of the Companies Act. The categories of registrable charges have been extended piecemeal by amendments to the companies legislation over the last century, with the effect that mortgages over most types of asset must now be registered. One of the principal exceptions is that mortgages over shares do not require to be registered, although in practice they frequently are.

Charge

The third type of security interest available under English law, the charge, is only available in equity. Its main features are, accordingly, the ease of creation and the corresponding limitations against certain third parties which are characteristic of all types of equitable proprietary interest.

It is easier to describe what a charge is not, than what it is. It does not involve the transfer of possession of an asset. Nor does it require title (even beneficial title) to be transferred to the creditor.[22] A charge is created if an asset of the debtor is appropriated in discharge of a liability to the creditor. It is normally created by the execution of a document by the debtor, under which the debtor is expressed to charge the asset concerned to the creditor as security for the discharge of a liability. The creditor obtains an equitable proprietary interest in the asset, even though it does not obtain possession of it, or title to it. Once the secured liability has been paid, the creditor's rights under the charge are automatically released.

Like an equitable mortgage, a charge can be created over any asset other than the very limited category of choses in action which are incapable of being assigned. A charge can also be created over assets not yet owned by the debtor, although the charge only attaches to the assets concerned once they become owned by the debtor. The importance of a charge is that it provides a creditor with a very flexible form of security over both present and future assets of the debtor. It can be created very simply by the execution of a charge document by the debtor, although a charge requires to be registered against the debtor in the same way as a mortgage. Because a chargee does not obtain title to the asset, it cannot

---

[21] Companies Act 1985, s 409; *NV Slavenburg's Bank v Intercontinental Natural Resources* [1980] 1 All ER 955.
[22] *Carreras Rothmans Ltd v Freeman Mathews Treasure Ltd* [1985] Ch 207.

sell it unless a power to do so is contained in the charge. Since, however, the charge invariably confers broad powers on the chargee, in practice there is no material difference between the rights of the creditor under a charge or under an equitable mortgage.

The flexibility of the charge was extended further during the latter half of the nineteenth century by the creation of the floating charge. If a creditor has a normal (ie a fixed) charge over the assets of the debtor, the debtor cannot dispose of the asset free of the charge without obtaining the consent of the chargee. Since it is impracticable to obtain such a consent in relation to assets, such as stock-in-trade, which are regularly disposed of, it is not possible to obtain a fixed charge over such assets. The courts of equity accordingly developed the concept of the floating charge. The floating charge was created for the purpose of enabling security to be taken over assets which would not be susceptible to a normal (ie fixed) charge because of the frequency of their disposal. The way in which the courts dealt with the problem of frequent disposals of assets was to recognize that a charge could contain a prospective general authority for the chargor to dispose of the assets which were the subject of the charge. The essential characteristic of a floating charge is therefore that it gives the debtor a general authority to dispose of the charged assets free of the charge, without the necessity for the specific consent of the creditor at the time of the disposal. A floating charge accordingly enables a creditor to obtain security over all of the chargor's present and future assets, including stock in trade, by containing an authority for the chargor to dispose of the floating charge assets in the ordinary course of its business. This authority will continue until the floating charge crystallizes on those assets which are owned by the chargor at the time of crystallization. Normally, a floating charge will crystallize by the appointment of a receiver.

Although there are some statements in the authorities which suggest that a floating charge does not affect particular assets of the debtor until crystallization,[23] the effect of the cases is that a floating charge does create security over the debtor's assets from time to time, rather than just over those assets which the debtor owns at the time of crystallization.[24] In practice, therefore, the main difference between a fixed charge and a floating charge is that, in relation to a floating charge, the debtor is given a general authority to dispose of the assets which are the subject of the

[23] See, for instance, the judgment of Lord Macnaghten in *Illingsworth v Houldsworth* [1904] AC 355, 358. There is much academic discussion of the nature of a floating charge, but it has little impact on the practical effect of such a charge. For a discussion of some of the arguments, see Calnan, 'Priorities between Execution Creditors and Floating Chargees' (1982) 10 NZULR 111.

[24] For instance, the priority rules (which are discussed in part II) are based on the assumption that the floating chargee does have a proprietary interest in the charged assets before crystallization.

floating charge whereas, in relation to a fixed charge, it requires the specific consent of the creditor to do so.

The availability of fixed and floating charges means that security can be taken over all of the present and future assets of the debtor by the execution of a single document, commonly described as a 'debenture'. Such a document, if executed by the debtor and duly registered, will create fixed charges over all present and future assets of the debtor which are susceptible to the creation of fixed charges (ie those which are not disposed of in the ordinary course of business) and a floating charge over all of the debtor's other present and future assets (such as stock-in-trade which, by its nature, will be disposed of in the ordinary course of business).

The distinction between fixed and floating charges, and the desire of creditors to extend the scope of fixed charges at the expense of floating charges, is a subject which has been at the forefront of discussions of security interests for the last thirty years. The reason that creditors would prefer to have a fixed charge rather than a floating charge is that the legislature has imposed certain limitations on floating charges which do not apply to fixed charges. For instance, those creditors (known as 'preferential creditors') whose claims rank ahead of ordinary unsecured creditors of the debtor on a winding-up (and which include certain taxation and employee liabilities) also rank ahead of floating charges, but not ahead of fixed charges.[25] Similarly, on liquidation or administration of the debtor, the rights of floating chargees are a little more vulnerable than those of fixed chargees.[26]

This statutory intervention has required the courts to draw a distinction between fixed and floating charges, but there is still a great degree of uncertainty in practice. Indeed, the distinction between fixed and floating charges is much easier to state in general terms than it is to apply in practice. A charge over land which is registered at the Land Registry is clearly a fixed charge; the debtor cannot dispose of the land without the consent of the creditor. Equally, a charge over all of the debtor's stock-in-trade from time to time, by which the debtor is entitled to dispose of the charged assets at any time, is clearly a floating charge. Between those two extremes, a line has to be drawn between fixed and floating charges, but it is by no means clear in practice where the line should be drawn. Ultimately, the test is whether the chargor has sufficient general authority to dispose of the asset free of the charge such that it can be said to have the ability to deal with that asset in the ordinary course of its business. Case law can indicate which particular types of transaction fall which side of the line, but the ultimate test will necessarily remain imprecise.

[25] Insolvency Act 1986, ss 40 and 175(2)(b); Companies Act 1985, s 196.
[26] Insolvency Act 1986, ss 15(1) and (3) and 245.

There is no doubt, however, that the ability of a creditor to obtain, in one document, fixed and floating charges over all of the debtor's present and future assets is a very material advantage. The main limitation of such an approach is in relation to priorities. Before considering security over particular types of asset, it is therefore necessary to discuss priority issues in outline.

II. PRIORITIES

When a creditor wishes to obtain security over a debtor's assets, there are two main concerns. The first is to ensure that the security is effective against the debtor and its insolvency officers (such as liquidators or administrators). The security will be effective against them if the appropriate procedures described in part I of this chapter have been complied with. Thus, for instance, in the case of a pledge, the creditor must have possession of the chattel concerned. In the case of a legal mortgage, the creditor must obtain legal title to the asset concerned and the document setting out terms of the mortgage must have been registered at Companies House within the twenty-one-day time period. In the case of an equitable mortgage or charge, the debtor must have executed the appropriate document, which must have been duly registered at Companies House.

Because compliance with these rules gives the creditor a proprietary interest in the asset concerned, the creditor's interest is, in principle, effective not only against the debtor, but also against its insolvency officer. This is because the assets available to an insolvency officer do not include those owned by a third party, or in which the third party has a proprietary interest.[27]

The creditor's second main concern is to ensure that its security is effective against third parties who also obtain a proprietary interest in the asset concerned. Whether or not it is effective against them depends on the priority rules, which must now briefly be considered.

Time of creation of the interest

The basic priority rule of English law is the obvious one that priorities between two competing security interests in an asset (or between a security

---

[27] This has been the case since at least the early 18th century: *Godfrey v Furzo* (1733) 3 P Wms 185. In the past, it was subject to the 'reputed ownership' rule in bankruptcy, as a result of which assets of which the bankrupt was the 'reputed owner' could be made available to his unsecured creditors. This rule never applied to companies and has now been abolished for individuals.

interest and any other proprietary interest in the asset) depend on the time of creation of each interest. The first in time prevails.

There are, however, a number of exceptions to this basic principle, the five most important of which in practice are:

- the bona fide purchaser rule;
- the rule in *Dearle v Hall*;
- registration;
- cases where 'the equities are unequal'; and
- the 'purchase money security interest'.

After considering these exceptions, the chapter will then examine the priority rules relating to floating charges, which are completely different.

The bona fide purchaser rule

The general principle that priorities depend on the time of creation of the interest concerned will apply as between two competing legal interests (for example two legal mortgages) or as between two competing equitable interests (for example two equitable charges). Where, however, an equitable interest is followed by a legal interest, the subsequent legal interest will take priority if the holder acquired it in good faith and for value, without notice of the equitable interest. This is simply a reflection of the underlying principle of equity that an equitable interest only affects the conscience of a legal owner if he is aware (or ought to have been aware) of its existence. This principle developed in relation to mortgages of land, although it applies equally to security interests over chattels. Indeed, since priorities relating to registered land (which now constitutes the bulk of land in England) are now governed by the date of registration of the interests concerned at the Land Registry, the main application of the rule is now in relation to chattels and shares.

Two points should be stressed in relation to the rule. The first is that it only benefits a purchaser for value of the legal title. The expression 'purchaser' includes a mortgagee, but volunteers (such as execution creditors) cannot take advantage of the rule. Secondly, the rule will only apply if, at the time he took his interest, the purchaser did not have either actual or constructive notice of the existence of the prior equitable interest. He will have constructive notice of a matter if it would have come to his knowledge if he had made such enquiries as he ought reasonably to have made. It will be appreciated that there is scope for considerable uncertainty in the application of this principle.

The rule in *Dearle v Hall*

The second exception to the basic priority principle is the rule in *Dearle v Hall*.[28] For these purposes, its importance stems from the fact that it governs the priorities of all dealings in most types of chose in action, including receivables (although it does not apply in relation to security over shares). Priorities of dealings in such assets are governed by the time that notice is given to the person who owes the chose in action (in this chapter, referred to as the 'counterparty'). The first to give notice will take priority. The rule has been criticized,[29] but is now firmly ensconced in English law. The reason for the rule seems to have been that the giving of notice to the counterparty was seen to be analogous to the taking of possession of a physical asset. The rule applies to all types of proprietary interest in the chose in action, including security interests and outright assignments

There are, however, two main exceptions to the rule. The first exception is that a person who, at the time of creation of his interest, has actual or constructive notice of the existence of an earlier interest in the asset concerned is not entitled to gain priority simply by giving notice to the debtor first.[30] It would be wrong for him to take priority in such circumstances. Where, however, he only became aware of the existence of the earlier interest after his own interest had been created, he is not prevented from giving notice first, and thereby obtaining priority.[31] The other main exception to the general rule is that it does not apply to volunteers, such as execution creditors.

Registration

The third exception to the basic priority principle is the fact that certain types of security interest are registrable. This can have three effects on priorities.

In the first place, the priority of security interests over certain types of asset depends on the time they are registered in a particular asset register. Thus, for instance, priorities of security interests over ships and aircraft are governed by their respective dates of registration in the appropriate register, whether or not the secured creditor had notice of an earlier unregistered charge.[32] Similar rules apply in relation to security

---

[28] (1828) 3 Russ 1.   [29] *Ward v Duncombe* [1893] AC 369.
[30] *Warburton v Hill* (1854) Kay 470.
[31] *Mutual Life Assurance Society v Langley* (1886) 32 Ch D 460 (CA).
[32] Ships: Merchant Shipping Act 1995, Sch 1, para 8. Aircraft: Mortgaging of Aircraft Order 1972, Art 14.

over registered land[33] and certain intellectual property rights, such as patents.[34] The determining feature of such assets is that they are of a type which is sufficiently valuable that they are the subject of specific asset registers.

The second way in which registration can affect priorities is indirect. As has been mentioned above, most types of mortgage or charge created by a company are void against a liquidator, administrator, or creditor of the company concerned unless they are registered against the debtor at Companies House within the prescribed period. If they are not registered within that period, such security interests are, for most practical purposes, ineffective, so that priority issues do not generally arise. If registered within the prescribed period, however, priorities are governed by the normal rules and not by the date of registration.

The third way in which registration can affect priorities is the effect it can have on the concept of notice. It has been seen that neither the bona fide purchaser rule, nor the rule in *Dearle v Hall*, is available to a subsequent mortgagee or chargee if he had notice of the existence of a prior mortgage or charge at the time he took his interest. Does registration of the prior security interest constitute notice of it?

The registration of a security interest in an asset registry is often deemed to constitute actual notice of it from the date of registration.[35] There is no corresponding provision in the companies legislation. It provides that the penalty for non-registration is that the security interest is, for most practical purposes, void. It does not specifically provide that registration constitutes notice of it. There is, however, some authority for the proposition that, at least in certain circumstances, registration of a security interest at Companies House can constitute notice of the existence of it.[36] What is the extent of the notice?

Where the security interest has been registered and the third party searches the register, it will obtain actual notice of it. But if it does not search, will it be deemed to have notice, simply because the security interest has been registered? The law is by no means clear, but it is considered that a person will only have constructive notice of the contents of the register if he ought reasonably to have conducted a search.[37] A bank taking security from the debtor is therefore more likely to have constructive notice than a person buying assets from the debtor in the ordinary course of business. This principle does add further uncertainty to the

[33] Land Registration Act 1925, s 29   [34] Patents Act 1977, s 33 (in a modified form).
[35] For instance, in relation to aircraft: Mortgaging of Aircraft Order 1972, Art 13.
[36] *Wilson v Kelland* [1910] 2 Ch 306.
[37] The introduction of Part IV of the Companies Act 1989 would have clarified the position, but it is unlikely, now, to be brought into effect.

rules concerning the circumstances in which a subsequent encumbrancer
has notice of an earlier interest.

Unequal equities

A further exception to the basic priority principle is that it only applies
'where the equities are equal'. The courts may decide that the basic priority rules should be overridden because, in the particular circumstances
of the case, it is inequitable to apply the first in time rule. An example of
this could be where the fraud or misrepresentation of a first chargee had
caused a subsequent chargee to be misled into thinking that the asset concerned was unencumbered. In certain circumstances, the negligence of
one of the parties may also postpone him to the other. There is a great
deal of case law on these points, and not all of it is easy to reconcile.

The 'purchase money security interest'

The courts have also recognized that, where a creditor has specifically
financed the acquisition by a debtor of a particular asset on the basis that
the asset will be charged to that creditor, its charge (often described as a
'purchase money security interest') will take priority over an earlier general charge over the present and future assets of the company.[38] Most of
the cases involve land, but the reasoning can equally be applied to the
financing of other assets. The reasoning in the cases is that, when money
is lent to a debtor on a secured basis to finance the acquisition of an asset:

- the lending of the money and the acquiring of the asset are, in substance, one transaction;
- the debtor, therefore, only ever obtains its rights in the asset subject to
  the rights of the lender;
- the debtor's existing secured creditor can get no better right than the
  debtor; and
- the lender's security accordingly takes priority over the existing
  secured creditor.

There is no particular logic to this rule. The courts could equally well
have decided (and the earlier cases, which have now been overruled, did
so) that the asset was acquired immediately before the lender's security
interest attached, in which event the existing secured creditor would
have an earlier interest and could then, depending on the nature of the
asset concerned, take priority. In essence, the courts have taken a policy
decision that a lender who has obtained a purchase money security inter-

---

[38] *Abbey National Building Society v Cann* [1991] 1 AC 56 (HL).

est should take priority over a general chargee of the present and future assets of the company concerned, because the acquisition of the asset has been financed by the lender and the general chargee would otherwise obtain a windfall benefit.

Tacking further advances

There is one major qualification which must be made to the rules discussed above. Assume that creditor A has lent money to the debtor and secured it by a charge over an asset of the debtor. If creditor B then takes a second charge over the same asset, he will generally rank behind creditor A to the extent of the existing loans. But if creditor A lends more money to the debtor after he has received notice of the later security interest, the later loans will rank behind creditor B's security unless creditor A had an obligation to lend the money.[39] This can be a particular problem where creditor A is lending on an overdraft because of the way in which payments are appropriated.[40] In practice, once creditor A receives notice of the later mortgage, it should not (unless it is obliged to do so) lend further money to the debtor until it has entered into a priority agreement with creditor B.

Floating charges

The rules relating to the priority of floating charges are completely different from those governing the priority of fixed charges. As has been seen, the essence of a floating charge is that, although it creates a proprietary interest in the assets of a debtor on creation, the creditor gives the debtor a general authority to deal with its assets before crystallization of the charge and therefore to dispose of its assets, and to create proprietary interests over them, in priority to the rights of the creditor. In principle, therefore, later disponees, mortgagees, and fixed chargees of the company's assets before crystallization of a floating charge will generally rank ahead of the floating charge.[41]

The position is different in relation to subsequent floating charges. In the absence of any express permission in the floating charge for the creation of prior floating charges, a later floating charge created over substantially the same assets will rank behind the first floating charge.[42]

[39] Law of Property Act 1925, s 94; *Hopkinson v Rolt* (1861) 9 HL Cas 514 (HL).
[40] As a result of the rule in *Clayton's Case* (1816) Mer 572.
[41] *Wheatley v Silkstone and Haigh Moor Coal Co* (1885) 29 Ch D 715.
[42] *Re Benjamin Cope & Sons* [1914] 1 Ch 800. But a subsequent floating charge over only some of the same assets will rank ahead of the earlier floating charge: *Re Automatic Bottle Makers* [1926] Ch 412.

Most floating charges will, however, contain a negative pledge which prohibits the creation by the debtor of other mortgages or charges over the assets concerned. Such a clause is unlikely to prohibit outright dispositions of the assets, because the company will require to dispose of floating charge assets in order to carry on its business. A floating chargee would not, however, expect the company to create security interests over its assets. Hence the negative pledge.

A negative pledge does not, itself, create any proprietary interests in the assets concerned and therefore a subsequent mortgagee or fixed chargee who takes his charge without notice of a negative pledge will rank in priority to the floating chargee, even if he knows of the existence of the earlier floating charge. If, on the other hand, the subsequent mortgagee or fixed chargee has actual notice of the negative pledge, he will rank behind the floating chargee.[43] This is because the proprietary interest of the floating chargee in the assets of the company is created at the time that the floating charge is created, and not merely on crystallization. In the absence of knowledge of a negative pledge the fixed chargee can assume that the company has authority to deal with its assets free of the charge but, where the subsequent chargee has notice of a negative pledge, he will be aware that the company has no such authority, and the charges will therefore rank in order of creation.

Floating charges are registrable at Companies House.[44] In practice, in addition to registering the floating charge, the chargee will also register the negative pledge. Since, however, the negative pledge is not a matter which requires to be registered, a person dealing with the company will not have constructive notice of the negative pledge even if he ought to have searched the register. In practice, however, he is likely to search the register and therefore discover the existence of the negative pledge. If he then takes his fixed charge, he will have actual notice of the negative pledge and therefore rank behind the floating chargee.

Priorities with owners

There is one final principle which ought to be mentioned in relation to priorities. It is a fundamental principle of English law that a person claiming a security interest in an asset of the debtor will obtain no better right to the asset than the debtor had. For instance, if the debtor does not own the asset concerned (for example, because it is a chattel which is held subject to a reservation of title clause or which the debtor only holds

---

[43] *English and Scottish Mercantile Investment Co v Brunton* [1892] 2 QB 700 (CA).
[44] Companies Act 1985, s 396(1)(f).

under a lease), the chargee will take subject to the rights of the owner, because he can obtain no better rights to the asset than the debtor.

Priority agreements

The priority rules are a potential minefield for secured creditors. The rules vary depending on the nature of the assets concerned, floating charges are governed by a different set of rules altogether, and there is yet another set of rules for money lent after the creditor has received notice of a subsequent charge. Even if the creditor knows which set of rules to apply, many of them depend on matters of fact, such as the extent to which the creditor has actual or constructive notice, which makes it very difficult to be confident of the outcome of any dispute. For all these reasons, it is common practice for secured creditors to enter into a priority agreement with any other secured creditor of which they become aware.

III. ENFORCEMENT AND INSOLVENCY

The security document (whether it is a letter of pledge, a mortgage or a charge) will provide when and how the creditor may enforce the security.[45] It will generally provide that the security is enforceable once the underlying secured indebtedness is repayable (for instance, once the creditor has demanded repayment following an event of default). It will also give the creditor very wide powers to enforce the security, including by selling the asset concerned. Provided the security document contains appropriate powers, it is not generally necessary for the creditor to apply to the court before enforcing the security. The time at which the security is enforceable and the powers of the secured creditor are a matter for the security document itself.

The only material restriction on the power of a secured creditor to enforce the security is relatively recent. The Insolvency Act 1986 introduced the concept of administration as an alternative to the liquidation of companies. If a debtor goes into administration, a secured creditor cannot take any steps to enforce security over the debtor's assets without the consent of the administrator or the leave of the court.[46] No such restriction applies in a liquidation of the debtor.

---

[45] Pledgees (*Donald v Suckling* (1866) LR 1QB 585) and mortgagees (Law of Property Act 1925, s 103) have certain implied powers of sale. Chargees do not: their remedy is to apply to court. In practice, however, these distinctions do not matter because all security documents confer extensive powers on the creditor.

[46] Insolvency Act 1986, s 11(3)(c). The Insolvency Act 2000 will, when it comes into force, give 'small' companies the power to prevent secured creditors from enforcing their security for a limited period if the company is proposing to enter into a voluntary arrangement with its creditors.

In the case of a straightforward security interest, such as a charge over a deposit held by the creditor itself, or security over money payable under a particular contract, the creditor would most likely enforce the security itself. In the case of security over its own deposit, it would apply the deposit in discharge *pro tanto* of the secured indebtedness. Where it had obtained security over moneys payable under a particular contract, it would require the other contracting party to pay those moneys directly to itself.

In most cases, however, the creditor will want to enforce the security by appointing a receiver over the secured assets. The receiver will generally be an insolvency accountant, who will be able to deal with all aspects of the enforcement of the security on behalf of the creditor. In order to be able to appoint a receiver without the intervention of the court, the security document will need to confer the power on the creditor to do so, but such a provision is almost invariably contained in security documents. Where the creditor has security over all or substantially all of the assets of a debtor, the receiver is described as an 'administrative receiver' and, in addition to his contractual powers and duties under the security document, has certain additional statutory powers and duties. An administrative receiver has wide powers to run the business of the debtor, with a view to selling the successful parts of the business as a going concern.[47]

As has been mentioned above, except in the case of an administration, insolvency proceedings in relation to the debtor do not deprive the secured creditor of his ability to enforce his security. Indeed, it is precisely because of the risk of the debtor's insolvency that the security is taken in the first place. There are, however, certain statutory provisions which are available to a liquidator or administrator which enable him to apply to the court to set aside certain types of security interest. In this context, there are two main provisions. The first is that security granted within six months before the liquidation or administration is capable of being set aside if it was a preference (ie if the debtor was influenced, when giving the security, by a desire to put the creditor in a better position than he would otherwise have been in).[48] In addition, floating charges created within one year before the liquidation or administration will be set aside, except to the extent of new credit granted to the debtor after the date on which the floating charge was created.[49] Both provisions generally only operate if, at the time the security was given, the debtor was insolvent; and the time limit is extended to two years where the creditor is a connected person.

---

[47] Insolvency Act 1986, ss 29(2) and 42–49.   [48] Insolvency Act 1986, s 239.
[49] Insolvency Act 1986, s 245.

IV. SECURITY OVER PARTICULAR ASSETS

Having considered the creation, priority, and enforcement of security interests under English law in general terms, the purpose of this part of the chapter is to focus on security interests over three particular types of asset: goods, receivables, and shares; as well as considering how security is taken generally over all of the debtor's present and future assets.

Goods

Stock in trade can, in practice, only be the subject of a floating charge, the use of which is considered at the end of this part. But how should a creditor take security over valuable goods of a debtor which will not be disposed of in the ordinary course of its business? A pledge is impracticable in most cases, because the debtor will require possession of the goods concerned. The choice is therefore between a mortgage and a charge.

The creditor could obtain a legal mortgage, by the transfer to it of legal title to the goods. Alternatively, it could obtain an equitable mortgage by the transfer of beneficial title. Either way, this can be done by the debtor executing a mortgage document in favour of the creditor. Transfer of possession is not required and, unlike the transfer of outright title under a bill of sale, no stamp duty is payable on a mortgage document. The essential difference between a legal mortgage and an equitable mortgage relates to priorities: if duly registered, they are both perfectly effective against the debtor and its insolvency officers.

Alternatively, it is possible for the debtor to create an equitable charge over goods, by executing a charge document. Provided that the charge gives the creditor appropriate powers to enforce the security, there is no practical distinction between the rights of the creditor under an equitable mortgage or an equitable charge; and, in practice, a creditor will generally take a charge rather than an equitable mortgage.

The real choice for a creditor is therefore between a legal mortgage and an equitable charge. Both require to be registered at Companies House within twenty-one days after their creation, failing which they will be rendered void for most practical purposes.[50]

The benefit of an equitable charge is that it can extend to future goods, and not just to those goods which are owned by the debtor at the time the charge is created. Provided the assets concerned are of a kind which the debtor does not require to dispose of regularly, there is no reason why the charge created over future goods should not be a fixed charge. The

---

[50] A charge over goods falls within the Companies Act 1985, s 396(1)(c).

advantage of an equitable charge over a legal mortgage therefore relates to its ability to extend to future assets.

The disadvantage of an equitable charge is that it is less effective against third parties than a legal mortgage. As has been discussed earlier in this chapter, the basic principle that security interests over goods rank in order of their times of creation is subject to the exception that a bona fide purchaser for value of the legal title to goods will take free of a prior equitable interest if he obtains his legal title without actual or constructive notice of that interest. A mortgagee is a purchaser for these purposes. Accordingly, a creditor who obtains only an equitable charge over a chattel is vulnerable to a person who subsequently obtains a legal mortgage over the goods in good faith, for value, and without notice of the earlier equitable charge.

The main issue is the extent to which the subsequent legal mortgagee will be likely to have actual or constructive notice of the earlier equitable charge. As has been seen, a charge created by a company over its chattels requires to be registered at Companies House. Although it is unlikely that this constitutes constructive notice to the world of the existence of the charge, it is nevertheless likely in practice that a creditor obtaining a legal mortgage over a valuable chattel will conduct a company search and obtain actual notice of the earlier equitable charge. It is also likely that a court would decide that a creditor has constructive notice of the existence of the charge if the creditor ought to have searched the register before completing the transaction. In deciding whether it ought to have done so, the court will take account of the practice that banks do, in most cases, conduct a search before taking security over a material asset. This would not be the case, however, in relation to a purchaser of the asset in the ordinary course of business; and the equitable chargee could therefore be in a better position with respect to a subsequent legal mortgagee than it would be in relation to a subsequent purchaser.

There is no doubt that the registration of the equitable charge at Companies House will provide material protection to an equitable chargee of goods, but the possibility of a third party obtaining priority cannot be ruled out. This disadvantage does, however, have to be weighed against the advantage that an equitable charge can extend to after-acquired property. In practice, the creditor may want, at the outset, to take an equitable charge over all present and future goods of a defined class, whilst reserving the power to take a legal mortgage over those future goods which are particularly valuable as and when they become owned by the debtor.

As has been mentioned above, there are particular priority rules for those goods which have their own asset registers, in which dispositions and security interests are noted. For instance, in the case of ships and aircraft, priority of security interests is governed by the time that they are registered at the appropriate registry.

Enforcement of security over the goods will be governed by the document creating the mortgage or charge. In practice, it will be enforced by the appointment of a receiver, who will sell the goods and account for the net proceeds to the creditor. It is only if the debtor is in administration that the court needs to be involved in the enforcement exercise.

Receivables

As in the case of goods, if the debtor is given the ability to deal with its receivables (the proceeds of debts) in the ordinary course of its business, the creditor will be limited to taking a floating charge over them.[51] It is beyond the scope of this chapter to join the debate concerning the extent to which a creditor can take a fixed charge over the debtor's present and future receivables whilst still giving the debtor some control over the proceeds. A brief outline of the distinction between fixed and floating charges is contained in part I of this chapter. In this part, it is assumed that the debtor is not given any control over the receivables concerned or their proceeds and that the creditor is taking security over particular receivables.

It is not possible to take a pledge over receivables because the asset is incapable of being rendered into possession. A mortgage is, however, possible, and would be effected by an assignment of the receivables concerned to the creditor. Assignments of such choses in action are not recognized at common law, but it is possible to assign the benefit of receivables in equity. Since the nineteenth century, it has also been possible to effect a statutory assignment of receivables, under what is now section 136 of the Law of Property Act 1925. Both a statutory assignment and an equitable assignment are capable of being given by way of security.

An equitable assignment of receivables is normally effected by the debtor executing a document assigning the benefit of the relevant receivables to the creditor. An equitable assignment is effective without the necessity to give notice of the assignment to the person which owes the receivables (the 'counterparty'). It is, however, good practice to give notice of the assignment to the counterparty for various reasons. In the first place, as discussed above, the priority rules are generally dependent on the time at which notice is given to the counterparty. In addition, until such notice is given, the counterparty can obtain a good discharge by paying the debtor,[52] and rights of set-off can continue to accrue between

---

[51] *Re Brightlife* [1987] Ch 200.   [52] *Brice v Bannister* (1878) 3 QBD 569 (CA).

the counterparty and the debtor.[53] For these reasons, notice should always be given to the counterparty if it is practicable to do so.

If the creditor wishes to take advantage of a statutory assignment, it must give written notice to the counterparty, because that is one of the conditions of an effective statutory assignment. In order to comply with the statutory provisions, the assignment must also be of an existing receivable and must be in writing and signed by the debtor; and it must be an assignment of the whole debt, rather than just a part of it. The assignment must also be an 'absolute' assignment, a requirement which is generally complied with by stating that the assignment is an absolute assignment of the relevant receivables, subject to reassignment on discharge of the secured indebtedness.[54]

It is also possible for the debtor to create an equitable charge over the receivables. The requirements are effectively the same as for an equitable assignment, except that the document is expressed to create a charge rather than an assignment. Provided that the security document gives the creditor appropriate powers, there are no material differences between an equitable assignment or a charge, as far as the creditor is concerned.

It follows, therefore, that the real choice for the creditor is between a statutory assignment and an equitable charge. As will be seen, if notice is given to the counterparty, there is no difference in the priority rules between a statutory assignment and an equitable charge; and they both require to be registered against the debtor at Companies House within twenty-one days after their creation.[55] The only advantage of a statutory assignment is that it enables the creditor to sue the counterparty in its own name, without joining the debtor. Since, however, it is relatively straightforward to join the debtor as a party to proceedings, a statutory assignment has no material advantages over an equitable charge; and the fact that an equitable charge can be taken over future receivables as well as existing ones[56] (which a statutory assignment cannot) means that the practical advantages of an equitable charge far outweigh the benefits of a statutory assignment unless the creditor is intending to take security over the benefit of valuable existing contracts. It is, however, common to take a statutory assignment where the receivables arise under major existing contracts.

As was mentioned above, the priority rules relating to statutory assignments are the same as those relating to equitable charges or

---

[53] *Roxburghe v Cox* (1881) 17 Ch D 520 (CA).

[54] *Durham Bros v Robertson* [1898] 1QB 765 (CA).

[55] Companies Act 1985, s 396(1)(e). Most receivables are 'book debts', ie debts which arise in the ordinary course of the debtor's business and ought, in accordance with normal accounting principles, to be entered in the books of the debtor's business: *Shipley v Marshall* (1863) CB (NS) 566.   [56] *Tailby v Official Receiver* (1888) 13 App Cas 523 (HL).

assignments.[57] Neither the 'first in time' rule nor the bona fide purchaser rule apply to assignments of receivables. Accordingly, the rules discussed in relation to chattels have no bearing in relation to competing charges or assignments over receivables. The basic principle is the rule in *Dearle v Hall*. The first to give notice to the counterparty will take priority. This is the case whether the interests created in the receivables are statutory or equitable and whether they arise by way of assignment or charge. As has been discussed in part II, however, if the person giving notice to the counterparty had actual or constructive notice of an earlier encumbrance over the debt at the time its interest was created, that person will take its interest subject to the existing encumbrance.

If the first interest to be created was a security interest, it will generally require to be registered against the debtor at Companies House. For the reasons discussed in part II above, registration of the security interest does not constitute constructive notice to the whole world of the existence of that interest, but a subsequent creditor is likely to search the register and to discover the existence of the earlier security interest. Even if it does not search the register, it will have constructive notice of the earlier interest if, in the circumstances, it ought to have searched.

Where, however, the earlier interest is not registrable, there will be no possibility of the subsequent assignee or chargee obtaining actual or constructive notice by registration. Where, for instance, a factor has taken an outright assignment of the receivables, the transaction does not require to be registered because the assignment is not given by way of security. A factor will often give notice to counterparties but, where the arrangement is entered into on an 'undisclosed' basis, it will not do so and the factor will be vulnerable to a subsequent assignee or chargee giving notice first.

In practice, therefore, the choice for a creditor taking security over receivables is between a statutory assignment and an equitable charge. Whichever form of security the creditor takes, however, it must be registered at Companies House and, if practicable, should be perfected by giving notice to the counterparty.

When the creditor comes to enforce the security, it can generally do so without the intervention of the courts, either by appointing a receiver in accordance with powers contained in the security document or simply by requiring the counterparty to pay the creditor direct. The receiver will generally be authorized to collect the receivables or sell them to a third party. The main exception to the principle that the court is not involved in the enforcement is where the debtor is in administration, in which event the creditor will require the consent of the administrator or the leave of the court to enforce of its security.

---

[57] *Marchant v Morton, Down & Co* [1901] 2 KB 829 (KBD).

Shares

Unless the shares are bearer shares (which are extremely unusual in England), it will not be possible to take an effective pledge over the shares, because they are incapable of being rendered into possession.

In practice (as in the case of goods) the choice lies between a legal mortgage and an equitable charge. A legal mortgage can only be obtained over existing shares, whereas an equitable charge can extend to after-acquired shares. In order to obtain a legal mortgage, the creditor needs to become the registered holder of the shares in the books of the company concerned. An equitable charge can be created simply by the execution of the appropriate charge document. Mortgages and charges over shares do not require to be registered at Companies House, although in practice they frequently are.

As in the case of goods, the principal advantage of a legal mortgage over an equitable charge is in relation to priority issues. Although a share is a chose in action, the priority rules relating to shares are the same as those for goods. The rule in *Dearle v Hall* does not apply to shares.[58] This is because companies must generally deal only with the registered holders of their shares, and not with others claiming an interest in them.[59] Instead, the priority of interests in shares is governed by the 'first in time' rule, as varied by the bona fide purchaser rule. The principal difference from the rules relating to goods is, however, that a security interest over shares does not require to be registered at Companies House. The effect is that an equitable chargee of shares is more vulnerable than an equitable chargee of chattels. In the absence of a registration requirement, it is less likely that a subsequent legal mortgagee will have notice of the earlier equitable charge. Although security interests over shares are frequently registered, and a subsequent mortgagee might therefore discover the existence of the charge by searching the register, the absence of any requirement to register means that the subsequent mortgagee is unlikely to be bound by constructive notice. It is very unlikely that a court would decide that a person had constructive notice of a matter on the register which did not require to be there. If a legal mortgagee (or purchaser) becomes the registered holder of the shares without notice of the prior equitable charge, it will obtain priority over the equitable chargee.

It is nevertheless the case that most security over shares in England is taken by way of equitable charge, rather than legal mortgage. Creditors do sometimes go on the register of members, but very rarely do so. In practice, they obtain an equitable charge, together with the share certifi-

---

[58] *Société Générale de Paris v Walker* (1885) 11 App Cas 20, 30 (HL).
[59] Companies Act 1985, s 360.

cate and a signed blank stock transfer form, which the charge document gives them the authority to complete, so that they (or a purchaser from them) can subsequently go on the register.

The creditor will be able to enforce the security at the time, and in accordance with the powers, set out in the charge document. Frequently, this will be by the appointment of a receiver who will sell the shares and account to the creditor for the net proceeds. It is only if the debtor is in administration that the court needs to be involved in the exercise. Where the shares concerned are in a public company and are listed on a stock exchange, the mechanics of transfer of the shares are likely to be straightforward; and the shares should have an ascertainable value. But the prevalence of an absolute discretion for the directors to refuse to register transfers of shares in private companies means that enforcing security over shares in private companies is not straightforward; and the value of such shares is, of course, frequently a matter of considerable uncertainty.

Fixed and floating charge debentures

The previous discussion of security over chattels, receivables, and shares has assumed that specific security is being taken over assets (whether present or future) which are of a kind which are not regularly disposed of by the debtor. Where a creditor wishes to take security over all of the debtor's present and future assets, it will do so by the debtor executing a debenture which creates fixed charges over all present and future assets which are capable of forming the subject matter of fixed charges and a floating charge over all other present and future assets of the debtor. Those assets which are expressed to be the subject of fixed charges will generally include present and future land, fixed assets, shares, goodwill, intellectual property, and receivables. The categories of assets over which it is possible to create fixed charges are still unclear and there has been a continuing debate as to whether it is possible to create an effective fixed charge over receivables in circumstances where the debtor is entitled to use the proceeds in its business. That debate continues and is yet to be resolved by the English courts. In the meantime, creditors continue to purport to take fixed charges over such receivables, being aware of the uncertainties, on the basis that if they do not have a fixed charge they will at least have a floating charge.

The debenture is registrable against the debtor at Companies House. The priority of a debenture depends on the nature of the security interest created by it and the assets over which it is created. The priority of fixed charges contained in the debenture will depend on the nature of the assets over which they are created (and the priority principles relating to chattels, receivables, and shares have been described above). The principles in relation to floating charges are described in part II above.

Enforcement of a debenture is invariably by means of the appointment by the creditor of an administrative receiver over the company. The administrative receiver will have the power to run the business of the company for the purpose of disposing of the valuable parts of its business as a going concern. The net proceeds of the fixed charge assets are paid to the secured creditor. The net proceeds of the floating charge assets are first paid to the preferential creditors, with any balance going to the secured creditor. Again, there is no requirement for court involvement unless the debtor is in administration. Indeed, so ingrained is the concept of receivership in English law that a secured creditor with a debenture over all or substantially all of the assets of the debtor is entitled to prevent the appointment by the court of an administrator over the debtor simply by appointing an administrative receiver before the court hearing.[60]

V. QUASI-SECURITY

As well as recognizing the types of security interest described in this chapter, English law enables parties to structure transactions which have the same commercial effect as the creation of security interests, without the necessity for security to be created. For instance, if the debtor wants to obtain a new piece of equipment, but does not have the cash to pay for it, it could borrow the money from a bank to pay for the equipment and then charge the equipment to the bank as security for the loan. Alternatively, the bank could buy the equipment and lease it to the debtor. The lease can have the same commercial effect, but avoids the creation of security and the requirement for registration.

The position is the same even if the debtor already owns the equipment and then sells it to the creditor for the purpose of enabling it to be leased back to the debtor. The English courts will generally only look behind the terms of a document if it does not reflect the intention of the parties.[61] If the parties intend to enter into a sale and leaseback transaction, and the documents have that effect, the transaction will not be reclassified as a secured loan simply because it has the same commercial effect.[62]

Similarly, one of the debtor's major assets will be its present and future receivables. It could charge them to a bank to secure a loan. Alternatively, it could factor (ie sell) the receivables to the bank for a discounted price. The arrangement will normally provide for the customer to repurchase the receivables if they are not paid when due. If properly structured, such

---

[60] Insolvency Act 1986, s 9(3).   [61] *Re Watson* (1890) 25 QBD 27, 35 (CA).
[62] *Welsh Development Agency v Export Finance Co* [1992] BCLC 148 (CA).

an arrangement does not involve the creation of a security interest and thereby avoids the necessity for registration.[63]

Again, rather than sell goods to a purchaser on deferred payment terms and take a charge over them to secure the purchase price, a supplier of goods on credit can retain title to the goods until payment. Although this arrangement has the commercial effect of the creation of security, no security is created because the supplier is simply retaining title to its own goods, rather than obtaining security over them from the debtor. There is, therefore, no requirement to register the arrangement.[64]

One of the advantages of such forms of 'quasi-security' is the avoidance of the need to register a charge. The principal factor determining the type of transaction used is, however, usually the tax treatment of the arrangement.

Finally, a creditor (particularly a bank) will often rely on rights of set-off in addition to (or instead of) taking security. Under English law, a creditor can obtain contractual rights of set-off against the debtor which are effective unless and until the debtor goes into liquidation. On liquidation, those rights of set-off cease to be effective, but are replaced by a very broad automatic set-off of all monetary cross-claims between the debtor and the creditor under the Insolvency Rules 1986.[65] Although there are circumstances where a charge is preferable to a right of set-off, rights of set-off do have certain advantages over charges. For instance, a contractual right of set-off is effective in an administration of the debtor, whereas a charge cannot be enforced without the consent of the administrator or the leave of the court. A creditor will, therefore, normally take an express right of set-off in addition to taking security over its own credit balances.

VI. CONCLUSION

Where a creditor is intending to take security over the assets of a debtor, there will be circumstances (particularly in relation to the financing of international trade) where it will take a pledge over chattels or documents of title, particularly because pledges do not require to be registered. In most cases, however, the creditor will make a choice between a legal mortgage and an equitable charge. Both generally require to be registered at Companies House. The advantage of the former is that it often

---

[63] *Lloyds and Scottish Finance v Cyril Lord Carpet Sales* [1992] BCLC 609 (HL, 1979).
[64] Sale of Goods Act 1979, s 17. *Clough Mill v Martin* [1984] 3 All ER 982 (CA).
[65] Insolvency Rules 1986, r 4.90. *Stein v Blake* [1996] AC 243 (HL).

affords greater protection against third parties; the advantage of the latter is that it is easier to create and can extend to after-acquired property.

It is also very common for a creditor to obtain security over all present and future assets of the debtor, the debenture concerned containing fixed charges over those present and future assets which are susceptible to a fixed charge and containing a floating charge over all other present and future assets of the company. Such security is relatively easy to create, and can often be created by one document, although it does require to be registered at Companies House.

Priority issues are much more complex. Ultimately, the priority of a security interest depends on the nature of the asset secured. There are different rules for different assets. Floating charges have their own set of rules. The complexity of the rules, and the fact that many of them depend on difficult factual issues concerning notice, mean that the creditor should always try to obtain a priority agreement with any other secured creditor of which it is aware.

The enforcement of security interests is relatively straightforward. It does not generally require the involvement of the court; and the ability to appoint a receiver enables businesses to be sold as a going concern, with consequent increased returns for the creditor.

Finally, English law recognizes that transactions which have the commercial effect of secured lending can be structured in such a way that security is not taken, the creditor being (in the case of a reservation of title clause or a lease) or becoming (in the case of a factoring agreement or a sale and leaseback) the outright owner of the asset. Such arrangements do not require registration at Companies House.

4

Secured Transactions in Personal Property in the United States

RICHARD F BROUDE

(*New York City*)

I. INTRODUCTION: THE ROLES OF THE STATE AND FEDERAL GOVERNMENTS

The federal system of government under which the United States operates has meant that, while the Federal Government is responsible for bankruptcy laws, laws governing secured transactions in real and personal property are the province of the various states. The Constitution grants Congress the power to enact 'uniform Laws on the subject of Bankruptcies throughout the United States'.[1] Although it is not necessary that there be a federal bankruptcy statute,[2] a bankruptcy law has been continuously in effect since 1898.[3] When there is a federal bankruptcy statute, contradictory state laws are superseded.[4]

A good deal of the history of commercial law in the United States grows out of the tension between federal and state legislation in this area. For example, a transaction pursuant to which a debtor creates a security interest[5] in favour of a creditor may be perfectly valid and enforceable

---

[1] US Const, Art I § 8.

[2] Indeed, during much of the 19th century, the United States struggled along without one. For the most part, bankruptcy laws were enacted to deal with specific financial crises, expiring when the crisis did. CJ Tabb, 'The History of the Bankruptcy Laws in the United States' (1995) 3 ALI Law Rev 5, 12–21.

[3] The current Bankruptcy Code became effective on 1 October 1979.

[4] US Const Art VI, cl 2 (the so-called 'Supremacy Clause') states in part that: 'This Constitution, and the Laws of the United States which shall be made in Pursuance thereof . . . shall be the supreme Law of the Land; and the Judges in every State shall be bound thereby, any Thing in the Constitution or Laws of any State to the Contrary notwithstanding.'

[5] A note about terminology. Practitioners and academics in the United States (including the author) tend to use the words 'lien', 'encumbrance', and 'security interest' somewhat interchangeably. In point of fact, each has its own specific use and I shall try to conform my usage accordingly. Article 9 of the Uniform Commercial Code, which is the governing statute in dealing with the creation of encumbrances against personal property, uses the phrase 'security interest' to describe the nature of the creditor's interest in the property of the debtor. The phrase is almost never used in the realm of real property encumbrances, in which the title of the security document—mortgage or deed of trust—frequently performs the function of the descriptive term. Thus, a debtor and creditor may create a mortgage on Blackacre, but they create a security interest in the machinery located thereon. The word 'debtor' also performs two functions. The 'debtor' is the entity whose property is subject to the creditor's security interest, UCC § 9–105(1)(d); it is also the subject of a bankruptcy case, 11 USC § 101(13).

under state law but voidable under one or more of the avoiding powers of the bankruptcy statute in effect at the time. Another example is this: a secured party has certain enumerated rights following default[6] which are automatically stayed if the debtor becomes the subject of a bankruptcy case.[7] And, most importantly, the rights of secured creditors may be dramatically changed by a chapter 11 plan, even if the secured creditor dissents.

II. A SHORT HISTORY OF SECURED TRANSACTIONS LAWS IN THE UNITED STATES

During the nineteenth and first half of the twentieth centuries, secured transactions laws (when indeed there were any) varied dramatically from state to state. To add to the problem it took a long time and a good deal of debate before states began to accept the possibility that certain types of collateral, such as accounts receivable and inventory, which were ever-changing, could even be the subject of security interests. Populist political theory, which argued that some types of property should be available for payment to general unsecured creditors, had a role to play as well. As the nineteenth century drew to a close, however, and the previously agrarian nature of the economy of the United States began to change, the need for operating capital in the form of secured financing became apparent, as did the need for some uniformity among the states. The task of bringing such uniformity about was undertaken by two institutions well suited to the job.

The American Law Institute (ALI) and the National Conference of Commissioners on Uniform State Laws (NCCUSL) are both non-profit institutions committed to the improvement of the law. The NCCUSL, which was created in 1892, is comprised of more than 300 lawyers, judges, and law professors appointed by the states, as well as by the District of Columbia, Puerto Rico, and the US Virgin Islands, to draft proposals for uniform and model laws and work toward their enactment in legislatures. The ALI is a non-profit organization comprised of practitioners, judges, and academics, established in 1923 'to promote the clarification and simplification of the law and its better adaptation to social needs, to secure the better administration of justice, and to encourage and carry on scholarly and scientific legal work'. A number of uniform laws in the secured transactions arena, including the Uniform Conditional Sales Act and the Uniform Trust

---

[6] See text at n 38 *et seq*, below.   [7] Bankruptcy Code § 362(a)(4).

Receipts Act,[8] were proposed. These statutes were enacted in some, but by no means all, of the states. As the economy developed, and more particularly at the end of World War II, the hotchpotch of state laws dealing with secured transactions in personal property became extremely unsatisfactory to the lending and borrowing communities. The cost of complying with the various state laws was excessive, and, if the borrower did file a bankruptcy case, bankruptcy judges (then called referees) were perceived as far too ready to find non-compliance with those laws on extremely technical grounds and free the assets of the debtor for the benefit of unsecured creditors.

The Uniform Commercial Code

ALI and NCCUSL together were responsible for the drafting and ultimate enactment in all states of the Uniform Commercial Code (UCC) in the 1940s and 1950s. First enacted in Pennsylvania in 1953, the UCC deals with almost all aspects of commercial law, including negotiable instruments, warehouse receipts, investment securities, and, most importantly for our purposes, secured transactions. The latter is the province of Article 9 of the UCC, entitled, appropriately enough, 'Secured Transactions'. Article 9 replaced most if not all laws dealing with secured transactions in personal property. Although non-uniform amendments were made by some of the enacting states, Article 9 did perform the paramount function of rationalizing and unifying the previously undisciplined series of laws, uniform or not, and judicial decisions dealing with personal property secured transactions.

After almost forty years of experience under Article 9, which underwent a number of revisions to deal with problems not foreseen when it was first promulgated, and thousands of judicial decisions dealing with some of the statutory language and attempting to fill in some of the interstices, ALI and NCCUSL created a drafting committee to modernize Article 9, and, if necessary, rewrite it entirely. In the late 1990s, the job of the drafting committee ended, and the sponsoring organizations adopted Revised Article 9[9] and recommended it for enactment in the fifty states.

[8] There never was a uniform law dealing with security interests in inventory or accounts receivable. Where no state statute was in effect as to the former type of collateral, field warehousing was developed as an alternative. The taking of a security interest in receivables was always problematic.

[9] In this chapter, when Revised Article 9 is mentioned, it shall be cited as 'R § ___'. At this time, Revised Article 9 has been adopted in more than 30 states and introduced in the legislatures of many others. To ease the very complicated problem of transition from old to Revised Article 9, the common effective date of 1 July 2001 is provided for all states that will have, as of that date, enacted the revised article: R § 9–701.

Revised Article 9 is not uncontroversial. Its proponents argue that it improves upon its predecessor by resolving many ambiguities and providing answers to many unanswered questions. And, as one might expect from a statute written at a time of rapid technological change, Revised Article 9 is medium-neutral; it contemplates that agreements may be entered into and notices given electronically or on paper. But Revised Article 9 does much more than this. Taking account of developments in financing over the past decades, during which intangible property has become increasingly important for asset-based lending, Revised Article 9 provides a more complete treatment of complex transactions in intellectual-property rights, rights to payment of various kinds, and other intangible assets than does its predecessor. Its provisions also reflect the substantial increase in the number of cross-border secured transactions and the increasing sophistication and complexity of routine, domestic transactions.[10]

There are sceptics:

The revision is in the words of the late Barry Zaretsky, 'a love feast for secured creditors,' . . . Since the time of *Twyne's Case* (1602), the whole idea of security interests in personal property has been controversial. Today the supporters of secured credit see it as the linchpin of prosperity. But at the same time vigorous attacks question the efficiency and fairness of the whole system. This new 'fast-lane' Article 9, which so unreservedly embraces secured credit, may well intensify the debate. Will Revised Article 9 allow creditors adhesively to extract electronic consents to security interests and financing statements from . . . small businesses? Will the more-comprehensive floating liens permitted by Revised Article 9 give secured creditors a veto over corporate reorganizations by eliminating any 'free assets' to support reorganization attempts? Will Revised Article 9 encourage preemptive filings against all assets of a firm even though no financing is contemplated in the foreseeable future? Will Revised Article 9 undermine the long-standing policy of public notice by expanding the list of interests which are automatically perfected or may be perfected by control? These are the concerns which the future will dispel or confirm—assuming, as most predict, that Revised Article 9 is adopted by the states.[11]

This chapter will explore the way in which Article 9 works, pointing out, when relevant, the analogous provision of Revised Article 9. It will deal with, successively, the creation, perfection, and enforcement of security interests in personal property, tangible and intangible, with occasional detours into the provisions dealing with priorities. The chapter would not be complete, of course, without some explication of the manner in

---

[10] SL Harris and CW Mooney, jun, 'Introduction to the Symposium on UCC Revised Article 9' (1999) 74 Chicago-Kent L Rev 857. Messrs Harris and Mooney served as Reporters for the Drafting Committee.

[11] JB McDonnell, *Uniform Commercial Code Analysis of Revised Article 9* (Matthew Bender, 1999) 2–3.

which Article 9, current and revised, impacts upon the rights and powers of a bankruptcy trustee.

III. ARTICLE 9: AN OVERVIEW

Article 9 is divided into five 'Parts': 'Short Title, Applicability and Definitions'; 'Validity of Security Agreement and Rights of Parties Thereto'; 'Rights of Third Parties; Perfected and Unperfected Security Interests; Rules of Priority'; 'Filing'; and 'Default'.[12] In broadest outline, the five parts tell us what transactions and types of property fall within the scope of Article 9; the manner in which one creates a security interest and when it 'attaches' to the collateral; how a security interest is 'perfected' (ie, when the rights of the secured party attain priority over a 'lien creditor' (including a trustee in bankruptcy)); the rules governing priorities between secured creditors, and between secured creditors and third parties such as lien creditors and buyers of collateral; and the rights and obligations of secured parties and debtors upon the debtor's default.

To use a rather simple example, if a lender is prepared to make a loan to a borrower but wants to secure the loan with a piece of machinery used by the borrower in its business, Part 1 tells us that the transaction is covered by Article 9,[13] Part 2 tells us how the security interest is to be created, Parts 3 and 4 how it is perfected, and Part 5 tells us how it is enforced.

The scope of Article 9

While current Article 9 was never intended to be all-encompassing, its scope is nevertheless quite broad. It replaced a number of disparate and sometimes irreconcilable statutory schemes. With exceptions noted below, Article 9 applies to any transaction 'which is intended to create a security interest in personal property or fixtures including goods, documents, instruments, general intangibles, chattel paper [namely, a record evidencing both a monetary obligation and a security interest] or

---

[12] Revised Article 9, by contrast, has 7 parts: 'General Provisions'; 'Effectiveness of Security Agreement; Attachment of Security Interest; Rights of Parties to Security Agreement'; 'Perfection and Priority'; 'Rights of Third Parties'; 'Filing'; 'Default'; and 'Transition'.

[13] Working through Part 1, we find that the collateral in question is, in Code terminology, 'equipment'. Section 9–102(1) states that Article 9 'applies (a) to any transaction (regardless of its form) which is intended to create a security interest in personal property or fixtures including goods . . . .' 'Goods', in turn, 'includes all things which are movable at the time the security interest attaches': § 9–105(1)(h). Goods are '"equipment" if they are used or bought for use primarily in business . . . or if the goods are not included in the definitions of inventory, farm products or consumer goods': § 9–109(12).

accounts; and also . . . to any sale of accounts or chattel paper'.[14] To avoid any doubt, section 9–102(2) provides that Article 9

applies to security interests created by contract including pledge, assignment, chattel mortgage, chattel trust, trust deed, factor's lien, equipment trust, conditional sale, trust receipt, other lien or title retention contract and lease or consignment intended as security.[15]

There are some excluded transactions; these are set out in section 9–104. The most important examples, for our purposes, are security interests subject to any statute of the Federal Government, state-created statutory liens, and the transfer of an interest in a 'deposit account'.[16]

IV. CREATION, ATTACHMENT, AND PERFECTION OF SECURITY INTERESTS

Creation of security interests

A security interest is created by a 'security agreement'[17] which need not in all cases be in writing, but usually is.[18] In the typical case, the parties (the 'secured party' and the 'debtor') will enter into a written security agreement which will provide for the creation of a security interest in the 'collateral', which is defined as 'the property subject to a security interest, and includes accounts and chattel paper which have been sold'.[19] Title to the collateral is immaterial; that is, whether the parties use a title retention device (in US parlance, a 'conditional sale') or actually transfer title to the personal property to the debtor, the provisions of Article 9 apply in the same way.[20] The security agreement may provide that the obligation

---

[14] UCC § 9–102(1).

[15] The scope of Revised Article 9 is even greater. R § 9–109(a) states that R Article 9 applies to '(1) a transaction, regardless of its form, that creates a security interest in personal property or fixtures by contract; (2) an agricultural lien; (3) a sale of accounts, chattel paper, payment intangibles, or promissory notes; [and] (4) a consignment . . . '. The expansion of Article 9's scope is much more encompassing than the foregoing would indicate, however, because (1) some of the definitions, such as that of 'accounts', have been significantly broadened, and (2) some transactions formerly excluded from the scope of Article 9 are now included.

[16] A 'deposit account' is 'a demand, time, savings, passbook or like account maintained with a bank . . . or like organization': § 9–105(e). A few states enacted non-uniform amendments permitting security interests in deposit accounts. Security interests in deposit accounts are within the scope of Revised Article 9.

[17] '"Security agreement" means an agreement which creates or provides for a security interest': § 9–105(1)(l). But for cleaning up the grammar by replacing 'which' with 'that', the definition in Revised Article 9 is identical: R § 9–102(a)(73).

[18] When a security interest is perfected by possession, an oral security agreement will generally suffice: § 9–203(1)(a).   [19] § 9–105(1)(c). See also R § 9–102(a)(12).

[20] § 9–202.

may be secured by after-acquired property and that the collateral may secure future advances.[21] While this provision is commonplace today, it was positively revolutionary when proposed, and dealt with issues that had caused considerable controversy and differences among the various states.

Granting a security interest in collateral automatically gives the secured party a security interest in certain types of proceeds.[22]

Another significant change to the law of many states was made by section 9–205, which provides, in part, that '[a] security interest is not invalid or fraudulent against creditors by reason of liberty in the debtor to use, commingle or dispose of all or part of the collateral . . . '. The reason for this was that, under the pre-Code law of many states, the ability of the debtor to use collateral that was encumbered was considered fraudulent, resulting in the invalidation of the security interest. It was this view that was primarily responsible for the difficulty in financing inventory on a secured basis.

Attachment of security interests

The next step in the process is for the security interest to 'attach' to the collateral. When a security interest has attached, it becomes enforceable against the debtor and third parties. 'Attachment' occurs when '(a) . . . the debtor has signed a security agreement which contains a description[23] of the collateral . . . ; (b) value[24] has been given; and (c) the debtor has rights in the collateral'.[25]

EXAMPLE 1. Secured party 'S' and borrower 'D' enter into a written security agreement. S agrees to lend D up to $10 million, secured by D's accounts, inventory, chattel paper, and equipment. The collateral is appropriately described in the security agreement. When S makes the first advance to D, the security interest will attach to D's then existing accounts, inventory, and equipment. When D acquires new inventory, the security interest will automatically attach, and when S advances an additional $1 million, the new advance will automatically be secured by all of the collateral.

---

[21] § 9–204(1), (3).

[22] §§ 9–203(3), 9–306. The right to proceeds is even greater under Revised Article 9: R §§ 9–203(f), 9–315. The definition of 'proceeds' has also been considerably expanded: R § 9–102(a)(64).

[23] 'For the purposes of this Article any description of personal property . . . is sufficient whether or not it is specific if it reasonably identifies what is described': § 9–110. Numerous cases deal with the issue of reasonable identification and some rules have emerged. It is not sufficient to say 'all assets of the debtor' or 'all personal property of the debtor'. This rule is continued in R § 9–108(c).   [24] 'Value' may consist of antecedent debt.

[25] § 9–203(1), (2). The same general rules are continued by R § 9–204(b), although that section speaks of the debtor having 'rights in the collateral or the power to transfer rights in the collateral to a secured party . . . '.

Perfection of security interests

The ultimate purpose of taking a security interest, of course, is to permit the secured party to realize upon its collateral to the exclusion of the rights of other creditors if the borrower falls upon hard times. This means that the goal of the secured lender is to ensure that, if other creditors obtain judicial liens on its borrower's property, or if the borrower files for bankruptcy, the lender's priority will be recognized. In Code-speak, this sublime state is called 'perfection'.

The manner in which a lender perfects a security interest varies with the type of collateral. With some exceptions, the preferred method of perfection is by filing a document called a financing statement with the appropriate state officer, generally the Secretary of State of the appropriate state, which is ordinarily where the collateral is located or where the debtor has its chief office. The financing statement contains, at a minimum, the names and addresses of the debtor and secured party and a description of the collateral.[26] Sometimes filing is the only method of perfection; at other times, it is a possible method of perfection. Filing is the only method to perfect a security interest in accounts and general intangibles.[27] A security interest in inventory or equipment may be perfected by filing or by the secured party's taking possession of the collateral.[28]

For certain types of collateral, such as money and certificated securities, possession is the only method of perfection.[29]

EXAMPLE 2. Same facts as Example 1. D's chief executive office is located in New York City. D's inventory and equipment are located in plants and warehouses located in New York, California, Michigan, and Texas. To perfect its security interests, S must file financing statements in each of the four states. If, in addition, S's collateral included negotiable instruments or stock in D's subsidiaries, S can perfect only by taking possession of the instruments and stock. If S has accomplished all of this, its security interests have been perfected.

V. PRIORITIES

Part 3 of Article 9 deals with priorities among various entities which may have dealings with the property of the debtor. Before we turn to the pri-

---

[26] § 9–402. Compare R §§ 9–502, 9–521.

[27] The financing statement in this instance must be filed in the state in which the chief executive office of the debtor is located: § 9–103(3).

[28] When inventory or equipment is collateral, the financing statement must be filed in the state in which the property is located: § 9–103(1). One of the most significant changes made by Revised Article 9 is to simplify the rules when perfection is by filing. For corporations, filing will only have to be made in the state of incorporation, irrespective of the type or location of the collateral: R §§ 9–301, 9–307. Under the pre-Code law of many states, a security interest in inventory could be created only by possession. This led to the security device known as 'field warehousing', which is sometimes used today as a policing device.   [29] § 9–304(1).

ority provisions, one significant difference between the floating charge of England and the US security interest should be noted. A floating charge over collateral such as accounts or inventory is junior to certain obligations of the debtor, such as taxes. This is not true of the Article 9 security interest, irrespective of the nature of the collateral. Thus, there is no need in the United States to distinguish between floating charges and fixed charges.

With that out of the way, the following is a simplified exposition of the various priority provisions of Article 9:

- As between conflicting security interests in the same collateral, priority goes to the first to file or perfect.[30]
- As between unperfected security interests, the first to attach has priority.[31]
- An unperfected security interest is subordinate to the rights of a lien creditor.[32] Because the term 'lien creditor' includes a trustee in bankruptcy,[33] this is by far the most important rule of priority.

EXAMPLE 3. Same facts as Example 2, except that S neglected to file a financing statement in California, in which D has a warehouse and manufacturing facility. If D files for bankruptcy (either chapter 7 liquidation or chapter 11 reorganization), S's security interest, while valid as between S and D because the security interest has attached, will be invalid as against a trustee in bankruptcy or a debtor in possession in chapter 11. Why this is so illustrates the interaction between state and federal law discussed above. Under state law (UCC section 9–301) the unperfected security interest is subordinate to the rights of a lien creditor. Under section 544(a)(1) of the Bankruptcy Code (the so-called 'strong-arm clause'), a trustee is given the rights of a hypothetical 'creditor that extends credit to the debtor at the time of the commencement of the case, and that obtains at such time and with respect to such credit, a judicial lien on all property on which a creditor on a simple contract could have obtained such a judicial lien, whether or not such a creditor exists'. In this Example, the interplay between sections 9–301 and 544 means that the equipment and inventory located in California comes into the bankruptcy estate free of S's unperfected security interest.

- Special priority rules apply to purchase-money security interests.[34]
- A buyer in the ordinary course of business takes free of a perfected security interest created by the seller even if the buyer is aware of it.[35] This

---

[30] § 9–312(5)(a).   [31] § 9–312(5)(b).   [32] § 9–301(1)(b).

[33] 'A "lien creditor" means a creditor who has acquired a lien on the property involved by attachment, levy or the like and includes . . . a trustee in bankruptcy from the time of the filing of the petition . . .': § 9–303(3). R § 9–102(a)(52), is nearly identical.

[34] § 9–312(3), (4). The term 'purchase money security interest' is defined in § 9–107.

[35] § 9–307(1).

provision is almost always restricted to the sale of inventory; equipment, for example, is seldom sold in the ordinary course of business.

• In certain instances, the priority rules change based upon the method of perfection. If a security interest in chattel paper is perfected by filing rather than possession, the secured party loses to a purchaser of the chattel paper who, in the ordinary course of business and without knowledge of the security interest, gives new value and takes possession of the chattel paper.[36] If perfection is by possession, the result would be different. The Bankruptcy Code's strong-arm powers do not include the status of a hypothetical purchaser of personal property, so this provision does not impair S's security interest in chattel paper when perfection was by filing rather than possession even if D goes into bankruptcy. The lack of status of a trustee in bankruptcy as a hypothetical purchaser of personal property was used to advantage by the drafters of Revised Article 9, one of whose goals was the enhancement of the priority of an Article 9 secured party *vis-à-vis* a bankruptcy trustee.

The floating lien and the trustee in bankruptcy

For years before and after Article 9, a debate raged as to the effect of the floating lien on accounts and inventory when the debtor goes into bankruptcy.

EXAMPLE 4. In the 90 days before bankruptcy, D acquires $500,000 in inventory which is subject to S's security interest under the after-acquired property clause of their security agreement. If S had not made any advances during this period of time, the newly-acquired inventory secures only antecedent debt. The trustee in bankruptcy would argue that, if the other requirements of a preferential transfer (such as insolvency) are satisfied, the attachment of the security interest constitutes a preference under section 547 of the Bankruptcy Code. After much debate, a special rule was inserted in section 547[37] to deal with the situation. This special test is called the 'two-points' test, is extremely complicated, and is the subject of few reported decisions.

VI. DEFAULT AND ENFORCEMENT

Article 9 leaves to the parties the definition of what constitutes a default. Once an event of default has occurred, however, the rules of Part 5 of Article 9 govern the conduct of both the secured party and the debtor.

---

[36] § 9–308.   [37] Bankruptcy Code § 547(b)(5).

The current version of Part 5 of Article 9 is very short—it consists of only seven sections—for the ground it has to cover.[38] While its simplicity is a virtue, it has proved to be fertile ground for controversy and judicial interpretation. As one commentator has noted:

[T]he enforcement provisions [of Article 9] have been a weak link. Numerous commentators have recognized that enforcement, particularly the flexible concept of 'commercial reasonableness,' has been one of the most litigated areas in the entire UCC. . . . That is wasteful, expensive, inefficient, unfair, and detrimental to secured financing. Secured parties need clear guidance in establishing practices and procedures when enforcing their rights and remedies; debtors need protection from arbitrary and capricious enforcement.[39]

Choice of remedies

The secured party has a choice of remedies, consisting of those provided in Part 5 as well as those provided in the security agreement.[40] The secured party 'may reduce his[41] claim to judgment, foreclose or otherwise enforce his security interest by any available judicial procedure'.[42]

That is the general rule. Certain specific rules apply for specific types of collateral. For example, if the collateral is accounts, the secured party may notify the account debtor to make payment directly to the secured party rather than to the debtor.[43] (Of course, even before default, and if the parties had agreed, the secured party could have been receiving payments on the accounts all along under a so-called 'lock box' or other arrangement.) However, in collecting accounts, the secured party must proceed in a 'commercially reasonable' fashion.[44] (This is the first time that we encounter the phrase 'commercially reasonable'. As shall be demonstrated, this concept, for the most part, governs all action taken by a secured party in realizing upon its collateral.)

The secured party may take possession of the collateral upon default and, in doing so, may proceed 'without judicial process if this can be done without breach of the peace or may proceed by action.'[45] If the

[38] By contrast, its counterpart in Revised Article 9 (Part 6) consists of 28 sections. And while the author has not counted words, the verbiage seems to be much more than four times as long as the current version.
[39] DJ Rapson, 'Default and Enforcement of Security Interests Under Revised Article 9' (1999) 74 Chicago-Kent L Rev 893, 893–894.
[40] § 9–501(1). However, the remedies provided in the security agreement are subject to certain constraints: § 9–501(3).   [41] Revised Article 9, you may be sure, is gender neutral.
[42] § 9–501(1). The same choice of remedies will be available under Revised Article 9. See R § 9–601(a)(1).   [43] § 9–502(1). See R § 9–607(1) for much the same rule.
[44] § 9–502(2).
[45] § 9–503. The corresponding section is R § 9–609. A summary of cases discussing what might constitute a breach of the peace may be found in TR Zinnecker, 'The Default Provisions of Revised Article 9 of the Uniform Commercial Code: Part I' (1999) 54 Bus Law 1113, 1140–1146.

parties have agreed, the secured party may require the debtor to assemble the collateral and make it available to the secured party at a convenient location.[46] (This assumes, of course, that the debtor is co-operative, although the secured party might persuade a court to order the debtor to live up to its agreement.)

Finally, the secured party may dispose of the collateral via foreclosure;[47] this is the remedy most frequently pursued[48] and the one which has given rise to most of the litigation.

Foreclosure

The entire subject of foreclosure is dealt with in section 9–504. Revised Article 9 takes ten sections to cover the same subject matter and, along the way, attempts in its own long-winded fashion to resolve some of the issues which have bedevilled the courts and led to sometimes conflicting decisions.

The key to the obligations of the foreclosing secured party is found in section 9–504(3), which provides, in part:

Disposition of the collateral may be by public or private proceedings and may be made by way of one or more contracts. Sale or other disposition may be as a unit or in parcels and at any time or place and on any terms *but every aspect of the disposition including the method, manner, time, place and terms must be commercially reasonable.*[49]

The secured party may buy in only at a public sale, or at a private sale if the collateral is of a type 'customarily sold in a recognized market or . . . the subject of widely distributed standard price quotations'.[50]

The separate ingredients of a commercially reasonable sale will now be described.

Notice

Currently, and with but few exceptions, notice must be given of any intended public or private disposition of the collateral.[51] It is common to provide in security agreements that ten days' notice is reasonable. Revised Article 9 makes ten days' notice the statutory norm.[52] Both versions provide a list of the parties to whom notice must be sent.[53]

---

[46] § 9–503.   [47] § 9–504.

[48] The secured party may, but seldom does, agree to retain the collateral in satisfaction of the obligation. § 9–505(2). Revised Article 9 would permit retention in partial as well as full satisfaction of the obligation: R § 9–620.   [49] Emphasis supplied.

[50] § 9–504(3). The same rule applies under R § 9–610(c).   [51] § 9–504(3).

[52] R § 9–612(2).   [53] § 9–504(3); R § 9–611(c).

While current Article 9 says little about the content of the notice, the revised article conveniently goes so far as to provide a statutory form.[54]

Commercial reasonableness

As noted above, the requirement of commercial reasonableness has led to a great deal of litigation. Revised Article 9 attempts to resolve some of the more contentious issues that have arisen. For example, an Official Comment to revised section 9–610 discusses the situations in which the secured party may sell the collateral in its then current condition and those in which the secured party must prepare the collateral for sale. Revised Article 9 also differs from its predecessor by providing that certain warranties are given at a foreclosure sale but that they may be disclaimed.[55]

The concept of commercial reasonableness is, in a sense, rounded out by section 9–507(2), which provides, in part, that

[t]he fact that a better price could have been obtained by a sale at a different time or in a different method from that selected by the secured party is not of itself sufficient to establish that the sale was not made in a commercially reasonable manner.[56]

The Code also provides that

[a] disposition which has been approved in any judicial proceeding or by any bona fide creditors' committee or representative of creditors shall conclusively be deemed to be commercially reasonable . . .[57]

Failure to comply with the provisions of Article 9

An enormous amount of judicial time and effort has been spent in cases dealing with allegations that a secured party did not conduct itself in a commercially reasonable manner following default and that, as a consequence, the debtor was harmed. The current statute furnishes no guidance regarding the quantum of damages in the event that non-compliance is proved.

Revised Article 9 adopts the 'rebuttable presumption' rule that had found widespread judicial acceptance. The statute provides that if the secured party 'fails to prove that the collection, enforcement [or] disposition . . . was conducted in accordance with the provisions' of Part 6, the

---

[54] R § 9–613.   [55] R § 9–610(d), (e).   [56] This rule is continued in R § 9–627(a).
[57] § 9–507(2). The same rule appertains under R § 9–627(a). It is for this reason that some secured creditors are quite content for their debtors to file bankruptcy so that the bankruptcy court might approve the method of foreclosure.

deficiency that may be recovered by the secured party is limited to the amount by which the secured obligation plus expenses exceeds the greater of actual proceeds and the amount of proceeds that would have been received had the secured party complied with Part 6.

The aforementioned presumption is that

[t]he amount of proceeds that would have been realized is equal to the sum of the secured obligation, expenses, and attorney's fees unless the secured party proves that the amount is less than that sum.[58]

VII. CONCLUSION

In whichever incarnation, Article 9 provides a broad and inclusive statutory scheme governing the creation and enforcement of security interests in personal property and everything in between. Revised Article 9 would increase the breadth of its reach.

It is hard to remember, at this time, how revolutionary Article 9 was when first promulgated. It is for economists to tell us of its impact on the growth of the US economy over the past fifty or so years. Whether the revisions will have such an impact is doubtful; at best, Revised Article 9 is evolutionary more than anything else. Be that as it may, the general satisfaction with what original Article 9 has wrought is testimony to the genius and far-sightedness of its creators.

[58] R § 9–626(a).

5

Taking Security in France

MARTIN GDANSKI

(*Norton Rose, Paris*)

I. TYPES OF SECURITY IN FRENCH LAW

Introduction: pledge and lack of a comprehensive security structure in France

Other chapters have explained that, in Anglo-American legal systems, it is frequently possible for a creditor to obtain security over all present and future assets of the debtor. In the United Kingdom a debenture may contain fixed charges over those present and future assets which are susceptible to a fixed charge and contain a floating charge over all other present and future assets of the company. Such security is relatively easy to create and can often be created by one document, although it does require to be registered at Companies House.

France does not possess a unified regime for the taking of security over assets. Rather, each category of assets is subject to a different set of statutory provisions which provides the framework pursuant to which security over such assets is created and perfected. As a general rule, security over tangible movable assets is created and perfected only by the physical delivery of the pledged asset either to the pledgee or to a third party (*tiers convenu*) mutually agreed upon by the pledgor and the pledgee. Failure to accomplish this formality will render the pledge of the asset unenforceable as against both the pledgor and third parties. Fortunately, there are several exceptions to this general rule, permitting pledge without dispossession (*gage sans dépossession*) of certain categories of assets in certain circumstances. However, the notion of a 'floating charge' which crystallizes upon enforcement of the charge does not exist under French law.

Remedies of the secured party are limited in many cases to the sale of the pledged asset at public auction pursuant to specified procedures for such auctions and the satisfaction of the secured debt out of the proceeds of such sale, or petition to a court for judicial self-attribution, but in the latter case only after an evaluation of the value of the pledged asset by a court-appointed expert. Contractual clauses in the pledge instrument which permit the pledgee to sell the asset by private sale or to appropriate the asset for the pledgee's own use are null and void, and, where considered by a court to be central to the pledge instrument, may even avoid the pledge altogether.

Charges over land: real estate mortgages (*hypothèques immobilières*)

French real estate mortgages (*hypothèques immobilières*) are governed by the provisions of Articles 2114 ff of the Civil Code. A mortgage is defined as a right over real property granted to a creditor (known as a *créancier hypothécaire*) by a debtor, relating to real property which the debtor owns and has the right to dispose of, in order to secure payment of a debt by the mortgagor to the mortgagee.

The mortgage will automatically cover any personal property which is a fixture (*immeuble par destination*) of the real property, as well as any improvements made to the property during the term of the mortgage. Assignment of a mortgaged debt by the creditor to a third party automatically transfers the benefit of the mortgage, and such transfer is noted on the mortgage register.

The creation of a *hypothèque immobilière* does not involve the transfer of title to the real property and should not be confused with a 'legal mortgage' under English law. The creation of a *hypothèque immobilière* gives the creditor the right to obtain attachment (*saisie*) of the mortgaged property despite subsequent transfer by the mortgagor of title to the property (*droit de suite*) and to be paid out of the proceeds of the sale of the attached property (*droit de préférence*). The granting of mortgages is subject to a statutory monopoly in favour of French notaries (*notaires*); in order to be valid, the mortgage deed must be signed as an *acte authentique*, which in practice means before such a notary.

The granting and registration of mortgages requires a lengthy time period. The first step is for the *notaire* to obtain proof of title from the local land register; as these institutions are frequently slow, even this step may take from one to two months, and actual registration may take as long as six months or more. However, the creditor has an actionable document once execution of the mortgage deed has occurred. Perfection of the mortgage and enforceability as against third parties requires registration of the mortgage (*inscription*) with the local land registry (*conservation des hypothèques*). he priority of mortgages is normally determined by the order of filing. wever, in the event that two mortgages are filed on the same day over ame property, the mortgage granted pursuant to the deed bearing the t date will have priority; if both deeds bear the same date, then they ual priority regardless of the time of day at which the mortgages ally filed.

perly recorded, the mortgage is effective as against any urchaser of the property (subject to the 'purging' rights described below), any subsequently filed (and therefore lesser ranking) mortgage, and all unsecured creditors. The mortgage will secure the amount of principal of the debt secured and three years of interest. The registration is effective until the date specified in the registration, provided that where (as will usually be the case) the mortgage is recorded prior to the due date of the amount secured thereby, the date so specified cannot exceed the second anniversary of the due date (or, where the amount secured is to be paid in instalments, two years from the due date of the final instalment) or thirty-five years in all from the date of registration. In the event that the mortgage is registered on or following the due date (or where the mortgage instrument does not specify a due date), then the total duration of the mortgage cannot exceed ten years from the date of registration. The *inscription* is renewable.

The costs of obtaining a real estate mortgage are relatively high and virtually impossible to be compressed. Taxes and registration fees in and of themselves can account for up to 0.6 per cent of the amount being secured under the guarantee, and notarial fees will generally account for approximately an additional 0.55 per cent of the amount being secured.

In the event of default by the debtor, the mortgagee may cause the mortgaged property to be attached (*saisie immobilière*) and sold at public auction (*vente aux enchères*), with the proceeds of the sale being used to satisfy the amount due. The sale must occur publicly pursuant to the strict rules on *saisie immobilière* provided in the French Code of Civil Procedure. Any clause in the mortgage deed which permits the mortgagee to sell the property itself or to dispose of the property directly is null and void.

In the event that the mortgaged property is transferred by the mortgagor to a third party, the mortgagee continues to benefit from the mortgage (*droit de suite*), so long as certain notices are served on both the mortgagor and the transferee. However, the transferee may choose to 'purge' the mortgage by offering to pay to registered mortgagees the purchase price (or the value of the real estate if acquired without payment of a purchase price). If the creditors accept the offer, they are paid out of the purchase price (even if the total amount of the purchase price is not sufficient to satisfy the full amount of the debt secured by the mortgage). If the creditors do not accept the offer, then they must request that the mortgaged property be put up for auction, and undertake to submit or cause to be submitted at such auction a bid for 10 per cent higher than the purchase price.

The right to a mortgage can be transferred independently from the underlying debt obligation; such a transfer is referred to as '*subrogation à l'hypothèque*' and is noted on both the mortgage deed and the mortgage register. The holders of two different-ranking mortgages can agree to exchange priorities under an agreement known as a *'cession d'antériorité'*. The exchange is noted on the mortgage register. If there is an intermediate ranking mortgage between the two mortgages, the transferee ranks ahead of the intermediary mortgagee only up to the amount of the lesser of the two debts secured.

Charges over share accounts and fractional ownership interests in French companies

Since 1981, shares in French companies have not been materialized by physical share certificates. In companies in which ownership interests are represented by negotiable securities (*valeurs mobilières*), such as the *société anonyme* or the *société par actions simplifiée*, ownership is evidenced solely by entries on a master share movement register (*registre de mouvement de titres*) and on individual share accounts (*comptes d'actionnaires*) opened in the name of each shareholder. Transfers of ownership interests are recorded by changes to the register and debit and credit entries on the share accounts, with new accounts being opened as necessary.

The legal structure of certain forms of closely-held companies, such as the private limited liability company (*société à responsabilité limitée*), is such that ownership interests are not represented by negotiable securities, but rather by fractional ownership interests with limited transferability (*parts sociales*). In these cases, ownership is recorded by statements in the Articles of Association (*statuts*) of the company, with transfers being recorded by amendment to the Articles.

Legislation was adopted in 1983 which created, in the case of companies issuing shares (or other negotiable securities), a streamlined procedure for the pledge of such securities. Pursuant to those provisions as originally adopted in 1983, such a pledge was created by the simple delivery, by the pledgor to the entity acting as the share registrar of the shares (usually the issuer company itself), of a statement of pledge (*déclaration de gage*). The registrar was then obliged to record the pledge on the books of the company by transferring the entry in the register relating to the pledged shares to a special account in the name of the pledgor but which stated the existence of the pledge in favour of the pledgee. The registrar then issued a certification of pledge (*certification de gage*) to the pledgee.

The 1983 law was modified substantially by Law no 96–597 of 2 July 1996 on modernization of financial activities and supplemented by Decree no 97–509 of 21 May 1997. These modifications have the effect of broadening the scope of the streamlined procedure originally applicable only to dematerialized negotiable securities to any account in which there are deposited one or several 'financial instruments' (a term which includes not only shares or other securities which can give rise to share capital or voting rights but also other negotiable instruments, shares in collective investment units, and all other financial instruments payable at term).

As it is henceforth the account, rather than the financial instruments deposited therein, which is pledged, the composition of the portfolio of financial instruments contained in the account may change from time to time, permitting considerable flexibility. The revised version of the law provides that the pledgee must agree with the account holder as to the conditions under which the holder may dispose of the financial instruments and the sums recorded as pledged. The parties have full discretion to agree as they wish; they may decide to grant the pledgor the right to dispose freely of the financial instruments and sums or for greater or lesser supervision and control by the pledgee.

Under the text of the 1983 law, as modified, the pledge is perfected as soon as the pledgor has delivered the declaration of pledge to the account administrator (*teneur de compte*). The delivery by the account administrator to the pledgee of a certification of pledge is now optional at the request of the pledgee.

In the case of a *société à responsabilité limitée* and certain other French companies, the rules are different. Since fractional ownership interests in such companies are not represented by recording on a share movement register or on individual share accounts, pledges of such interests cannot be created by simple declaration or perfected by recording on a register. For this reason, the pledge of such equity interests is accomplished in the same manner as any other pledge of intangible rights under French law,[1] ie either by service of a written pledge instrument on the company by authorized bailiff (*huissier*) or acceptance of such an instrument by the company by notarized deed (*acte authentique*), in both cases following registration (*enregistrement*) of such written instrument with the tax authorities.[2] Whichever alternative is chosen, the pledge instrument should first be registered with the local tax authorities.

Dividend and voting rights relating to the pledged shares

During the term of existence of the pledge, the pledgor retains all voting rights with respect to the pledged shares. The practice prevalent in certain jurisdictions, of providing by contract that, upon the occurrence of an event of default in the underlying financing documentation, the pledgee may exercise voting rights, has traditionally been considered as not being enforceable under French law, since the effect of such provisions would

---

[1] See 'Charge over intangible property and contractual rights' below.
[2] Article 2075 of the Civil Code.

be assimilated to a *pacte commissoire*.[3] The sole rights of a pledgee of share accounts or fractional ownership interests to enforcement of the pledge are, as detailed below, deemed to be to sell the pledged asset at public auction and to be satisfied out of the proceeds of such sale, or to petition to a court for judicial self-attribution, but only after an evaluation of the value of the pledged shares by a court-appointed expert.

However, by way of exception to the foregoing rule, the 1983 law as modified and supplemented in 1996 and pursuant to the 1997 decree, specifies that the pledgee may, with respect to negotiable securities in the pledged account, whether issued by French or foreign entities, which are traded on a regulated market (for example, a stock exchange), as well as any shares in collective investment undertakings (UCITS) and cash in the pledged account, enforce the pledge eight days (or such other period previously agreed between the parties) following formal notice to the debtor (*mise en demeure*), by any of the following means:

- full title transfer to the pledgee for amounts in cash;
- sale on a regulated market; or
- self-attribution up to the value of the debt (with no requirement to obtain a court order permitting such attribution), on the basis of the most recent quotations.

The law as modified and supplemented provides that all 'fruits and proceeds in any currency' are subject to the pledge. When read with other language in the revised version of the provision, the statute now appears to permit the parties to determine whether dividends on negotiable securities deposited in the account will be paid to the pledgor or the pledgee. In practice, however, pledgors generally negotiate the right to retain dividends unless and until the pledge is enforced upon the occurrence of an event of default.

Charges over goods and pledges of inventory

Unless covered by one of the exceptions described in the following sections, charges over goods are difficult propositions under French law, because the relevant provisions of the Civil Code and the Commercial Code provide that, in order to create and perfect an effective charge over tangible personal property, it is necessary for the pledgor to be physically dispossessed of the assets in question and for control over such assets to be exercised either by the beneficiary of the pledge or by a third party (*tiers convenu*) named by mutual agreement of the pledgor and pledgee (a process known as *entièrcement*). Moreover, unlike the situation in several

---

[3] See 'Enforcement—Power of sale of attribution of the secured asset' below.

other jurisdictions, there is no public register at which pledges over tangible personal property (other than those assets which are pledged pursuant to one of the exceptions described in the following sections) are recorded; the physical delivery of the pledged asset is both necessary and sufficient for the perfection of the pledge.

Owing to the exceptions to the foregoing rule existing for pledges of going concerns and certain purchase money security interests,[4] the practical consequences in the context of cross-border secured financial transactions are felt most particularly in the case of pledges of inventory (stock-in-trade). However, there do exist companies specialized in acting as *tiers convenu* and in the construction and supervision of 'on-site' third-party controlled inventory pledge warehouses in such capacity. A portion of the pledgor's plant is closed off by fencing erected by the specialized institution, and all inventory is moved into this closed-off area by the pledgor as completed. Access to the area is supervised by the specialized company, which permits inventory to be moved out of the closed area only either upon instructions signed by both the pledgor and the pledgee or upon satisfying itself that the inventory remaining in the closed area has an aggregate value in excess of the amount secured by the pledge.

The rights of enforcement of a pledgee of tangible goods are limited to sale of the pledged goods at public auction and satisfaction out of the proceeds of such sale, or to petition to a court for judicial self-attribution, but only after an evaluation of the value of the pledged goods by a court-appointed expert; contractual clauses which permit the pledgee to dispose of the asset at private sale or to appropriate the asset for the pledgee's own use are null and void.

Charge over going business

Articles L. 141–5 ff of the Commercial Code provides a statutory framework under French law for the pledge of the 'going business' (*fonds de commerce*) of a French company without the pledgor being required to be physically dispossessed of the pledged assets and in a manner which results in public registration of the pledge.

A *fonds de commerce* is the bundle of assets, other than real estate, which constitute the means by which a company exercises its business to satisfy its clientele. A *fonds de commerce* has a legal existence under French law, and can be sold, leased, and pledged as a unit. A pledge of a *fonds de commerce* may cover all or some of the following elements thereof: the commercial name and any logos, the right to be a lessee under a lease (but not

---

[4] See 'Charge over going business' and 'Purchase money security interest over material and equipment' below.

the leased asset itself), goodwill and client lists, commercial furniture and equipment used in the exploitation of the business, licences, trade marks, patents, industrial designs and other intellectual property, and any rights to occupy land.

Inventory (*marchandises*), although encompassed in the concept of a *fonds de commerce*, cannot be pledged within the framework of a *fonds de commerce*.[5] Other assets which do not form part of a *fonds de commerce* and which are therefore not included in a pledge of a going business include real estate,[6] book debt or accounts receivable,[7] and most contractual rights.[8]

Unlike a pledge of inventory, a pledge of a *fonds de commerce* does not require the pledgor to be physically dispossessed of the pledged assets. Perfection is accomplished by execution of a written pledge agreement, submitted for tax registration and then recorded within fifteen days of execution with the commercial court having jurisdiction over the place in which the business is carried out, and the commercial courts of any branches in which the business is also carried out.[9]

In addition, where intellectual property such as trade marks and trade names is included in the going business, an additional filing must be effected with the French National Institute of Industrial Property no later than fifteen days following the filing with the commercial court. The registration of a pledge of a *fonds de commerce* is valid for ten years and then expires if not renewed prior to the end of such term.

Pledges of a *fonds de commerce* are a matter of public record and lists of all existing pledges over a specific *fonds de commerce* can be ordered from the relevant Registry of Commerce and Companies by mail or can be viewed (and 'hard' copies ordered) via any of a number of computer network databases accessible by way of the French national 'Minitel' network or on the Internet. Rank of pledges is determined by order of filing; two pledges filed the same day will have equal priority.

In the event of default by the debtor, the pledgee of a *fonds de commerce* may cause the going business to be attached and sold at public auction (*vente forcée*), with the proceeds of the sale being used to satisfy the amount due; unlike the case of the pledgee of tangible assets (or of the beneficiary of a purchase money security interest, as described in the fol-

---

[5] It must be pledged as described under 'Charges over goods and pledges of inventory' above.

[6] This can be mortgaged, as described under 'Charges over land: real estate mortgages' above.

[7] These can be assigned or pledged, as described under 'Security assignment or pledge of book debts' below.

[8] These can be pledged, as described under 'Charges over intangible property and contractual rights' below.

[9] If the intention is to cover such branches in the pledge and this is made clear in the pledge agreement.

lowing section), the pledgee may not apply to the court for an order of judicial self-attribution. As usual, any clause in the pledge agreement which permits the pledgee to sell the property itself or to dispose of the property directly is null and void.

Purchase money security interest over material and equipment

Pursuant to Articles L. 525–1 ff of the Commercial Code, a specific security interest can be granted over material and equipment (*outillage et matériel d'équipement*) (including material and equipment which are part of the *fonds de commerce* of a business) to secure the purchase price of such equipment or loans made or guarantees given to secure loans made to finance such purchase price. Such purchase money security interest (hereinafter a 'PMSI') has the advantage of giving the pledgee a preferred ranking if there are two secured creditors having equal rank, including ranking over pledges of the *fonds de commerce* which includes such material and equipment.

The general rules applicable to a PMSI under these provisions of the Commercial Code are very similar to those relating to a pledge of a going business, even referring in several instances to such provisions. However, certain procedures and consequences of a PMSI are different from those relating to a pledge of a *fonds de commerce*. The pledge must be contained in the sale or loan instrument itself rather than in a separate document, and the instrument in question must contain a detailed description of the material or equipment in order to distinguish it from similar assets belonging to the pledgor. The pledge must be concluded no later than two months following the delivery of the material or equipment on the site where it is to be used, and must be registered and date-stamped with the local tax authorities and then registered with the Registry of Commerce and Companies no later than fifteen days following such execution. In addition, the pledgee is entitled to require the pledged assets to bear a plaque stating the date, place, and registration number of the pledge. In the event of sale of the pledged asset, the pledgee will enjoy a *droit de suite* only if such plaque has been affixed to the asset.

A PMSI over material and equipment remains in force in the event that the pledged asset becomes a fixture. In the event of enforcement of the pledge, the PMSI will have priority over all other secured creditors, including a pledgee of the *fonds de commerce* of which the material and equipment is a part and a mortgagee of the real estate in which the pledged asset is located. This is so even if such pledges or mortgages have been concluded prior to the PMSI, provided that in such case the pledgee has notified the existence thereof to the other secured creditors and furnished them with a copy of the instrument pursuant to which the PMSI was created, within two months from the date of such creation. Even if such notice has not been served, the PMSI will have preference over any other security interest normally having equal rank (for example, a pledge of *fonds de commerce* filed the same day), and over most liens created by law. A PMSI is valid for a period of five years from the date of registration, and guarantees principal and two years of interest. The PMSI can be renewed twice.

Unlike the case of the pledge of a going business, in the event of default by the debtor, the pledgee under a PMSI may both cause the going business to be attached and sold at public auction, with the proceeds of the sale being used to satisfy the amount due, or apply to the court for an order of judicial self-attribution.

Charge over intangible property (*meubles incorporels*) and contractual rights (*créances mobilières*)

Under French law, the pledge of intangible property (*meubles incorporels*), including rights under contract (*créances mobilières*), is considered to be akin to the pledge of tangible goods.[10]

As in the case of tangible goods, a pledge over intangible rights theoretically requires that the pledgor be physically 'dispossessed' of the pledged asset. Under Article 2075 of the Civil Code, this is accomplished by registration of the pledge instrument with the local tax authorities at nominal cost, followed either by the official serving of such instrument on the underlying contractual debtor by authorized bailiff (*huissier de justice*) or the acceptance of the pledge by the underlying debtor in a notarized deed (*acte authentique*). Owing to language found in a number of early court decisions, some practitioners also require an original signed copy of the contract containing the rights to be pledged to be physically delivered to the pledgee, but this practice is not universally followed.

The enforcement rights of a pledgee of intangible property are theoretically identical to those of a pledgee of tangible goods. In practice, where the property pledged consists solely of a debt to pay a sum of money, it is generally considered permissible to provide that the pledgee may receive directly the payment of such sum and use such amounts to reduce the amount of the debt owed to it.[11]

Article 2075 provides a simple means for creating and perfecting a pledge over contractual rights. However, the requirement of service of the pledge instrument on the underlying debtor renders the technique

---

[10] It is therefore subject generally to the rules described under 'Charges over goods and pledges of inventory' above, with certain exceptions as described under 'Security assignment or pledge of book debts' below.

[11] Or, if the sum is due and paid prior to the time that the secured debt is due, to retain the proceeds as a *gage espéces* as described under 'Cash collateral charge' below.

inefficient where the pledgor does not for commercial reasons wish the underlying debtor to be aware of the pledge, or where there are a great number of underlying contracts all of which are to be pledged. For this reason, Article 2075 is not well suited to the creation of charges over book debts (accounts receivable). Such charges are generally created pursuant to the specific legislation described in the following section.

Security assignment or pledge of book debts (accounts receivable)

French Law no 81–1 of 2 January 1981, as modified (the '*Loi Dailly*'), provides a statutory framework for either the assignment by way of security or the pledge of book debts in favour of a credit institution in order to secure credit granted by such credit institution to the assignor/pledgor. Under the *Loi Dailly*, perfection of the assignment or the pledge is accomplished by the simple delivery to the credit institution of a list of the debts being assigned or pledged (*bordereau*).

Liquid and current debts may be so assigned or pledged, as may debts resulting from an agreement already executed or to be executed, but the amount and the term of which are not yet determined, provided in all such cases that the debt is owed to the assignor or pledgor by legal entities or by individuals in the exercise of a professional activity.

The *bordereau* itself must, by law, contain, in addition to the name and address of the credit institution and a specific reference to the *Loi Dailly*, an enumeration or individualization of the debts being assigned or pledged or information susceptible of effecting such designation or individualization, for example by indication of the underlying account debtor, the place of payment, the amount of the debt, and its term. In practice, the parties generally execute a 'master agreement' (*convention cadre*) requiring the assignor or pledgor to provide *bordereaux* to the credit institution with an agreed upon frequency (for example, on a monthly basis) so as to cover all future debts which are booked during the life of the credit to be secured thereby. As debts mature and are paid by the underlying debtor, they are replaced with new debts which are booked and recorded on the next *bordereau* delivered.

The *Loi Dailly* is one of the few circumstances under French law where an assignment of rights by way of security (*cession à titre de garantie*) has received statutory recognition. An amendment made to the basic text of the law in 1984 specifies that, even 'when made by way of security', an assignment of book debts made pursuant to the law passes actual title to the debt to the assignee. For this reason, most security granted pursuant to the *Loi Dailly* has taken the form of security assignments rather than pledges. This provides the credit institution with a significant advantage in the event of the insolvency of the assignor, since the debts listed in any *bordereau* executed prior to the date of the insolvency filing will be the property of the credit institution.

Assignments or pledges effected pursuant to the *Loi Dailly* are effective as against third parties (including the underlying account debtor) once the *bordereau* is dated by the recipient credit institution, even if the fact of assignment or pledge is not notified to the underlying debtor.[12] The assignor/pledgor is thereafter estopped from modifying the nature or the scope of the underlying debt without the permission of the credit institution.

However, the credit institution may also, at any time (for example, if and when it begins to feel uncomfortable about its own customer), notify the underlying account debtor that all future payments in respect of the debt must be made directly to the credit institution. Thereafter, any payments made by the account debtor to the bank customer are made at the account debtor's risk. Moreover, the credit institution may obtain from the account debtor a written undertaking to pay only the credit institution. If the underlying debtor executes such an undertaking, it may not oppose to the credit institution any defences to payment which it had against the bank's customer unless the credit institution, in acquiring the book debt, knowingly acts to the detriment of the debtor.

It should be noted that there is some doubt as to whether a *Loi Dailly* assignment or pledge would be valid in favour of a bank other than one which is registered in France as a licensed credit institution or enjoying 'passport rights' under the EU Second Banking Directive. The literal text of the *Loi Dailly* states that such assignments or pledges can be granted in favour of a 'credit institution' (*établissement de crédit*) which has extended credit to the assignor/pledgor. The term 'credit institution' is identical to the term used under the French banking law (Law no 84–46 of 24 January 1984) to refer to a bank or financial institution licensed by the French banking authorities to effect credit operations in France. There is therefore an argument that an assignment under the *Loi Dailly* is effective only when the debts are assigned to a French bank (or the subsidiary or branch of a foreign bank licensed by the French banking authorities to operate in France or an EU bank enjoying 'passport rights' to lend into France) which has granted the credit. There is some doctrinal authority in France to the effect that such an assignment should be valid in favour of any banking institution that is licensed under the laws of its home country, but the question has not yet been formally raised in any court decision, and there is some intimation that the Bank of France does not share this view.

---

[12] The master agreement usually provides that during this time the assignor/pledgor will continue to collect the debts, but as the agent for the credit institution.

Charges over cash and bank accounts

French law recognizes two forms of charges over cash, the cash collateral charge and the charge over account balance.

Cash collateral charge (gage espèces)

In the cash collateral charge (*gage espèces*), a specific sum of cash is remitted by the pledgor to the pledgee, or, more frequently, placed on account with a bank which is either itself the pledgee or acting as the agent of the pledgee, as security for the debt. Such a pledge is assimilated under French law to a pledge of tangible personal property.[13] The physical dispossession of the pledged asset required for perfection of a pledge of tangible goods is deemed accomplished by the remittance of the cash or the payment of the pledged sums into the account maintained by the pledgee or the bank acting as its agent; service of the pledge instrument by *huissier* is not required. In order to maintain such dispossession, the pledgor must have no rights to withdraw sums from the account or otherwise control the flow of funds into or out of the account. Some practitioners extend this to a prohibition on the payment of interest to the pledgor on the pledged sums, but this is not universally accepted.

The French Cour de cassation has ruled that, since by definition there can be no contestation as to the value of cash and since money is perfectly fungible, there is no requirement upon enforcement of a *gage espèces* for the pledgee to sell the pledged asset at auction or seek judicial attribution of the asset. The pledgee is therefore entitled to retain the cash pledged and satisfy the secured debt out of such cash; the prohibition against *pactes commissoires* (ie, the self-appropriation of the pledged asset rather than sale at auction) apparently therefore does not apply to *gages espèces*.

Charge over bank account (nantissement de solde de compte)

In the charge over account balance (*nantissement de solde de compte*), a charge is created over the balance of a bank account rather than over a specific sum of cash deposited in the account and, in the event of enforcement, only such funds as are actually standing to the credit of the account at the time of enforcement are available to satisfy the creditor. Such a pledge is assimilated under French law to a pledge of intangible property.[14] For this reason, a written instrument of pledge is always required and perfection is accomplished by service of such instrument by *huissier* upon

[13] See discussion under 'Charges over goods and pledges of inventory' above.
[14] See 'Charge over intangible property and contractual rights' above.

the underlying debtor (ie, the bank at which the account in question is maintained) or acceptance of the assignment in a notarized deed. However, as in the case of the *gage espèces*, it is considered by certain authors—but this position is by no means unanimous—that, since the subject of the security is a right to obtain cash, there is no requirement upon enforcement for the pledgee to sell the pledged account or seek judicial attribution, the pledgee being entitled to the cash on balance in the account at the time of enforcement.

Registrable mortgages over assets other than real property

As in the case in many other jurisdictions, specific statutes permit the creation of security modelled on the real property mortgage[15] in the case of certain large items of valuable movable equipment.

Aircraft mortgages

The French Code of Civil Aviation (the 'CAC') provides for the creation of an aircraft mortgage which is registered on the centralized nationwide aircraft register of French-registered aircraft maintained by the French Civil Aviation Authority (*Direction Générale de l'Aviation Civile* or 'DGAC'). Mortgages of aircraft must be in writing and, to be binding upon third parties, must be registered in the aircraft register.

So long as they are also owned by the owner of the aircraft, an aircraft mortgage automatically covers the hull, engines, propellers, on-board equipment, and any other equipment intended to be used for service of the aircraft, whether installed or temporarily separated from the body of the aircraft. Provision is made for the granting of a single mortgage over all or part of an entire fleet owned by the same owner, so long as the different portions of the fleet are separately stated in the instrument. Spare parts may also be covered by the mortgage if individually itemized. However, such spare parts must be stored in a place where notice of the mortgage (including a statement of the register in which the mortgage is inscribed) is displayed, and an inventory of such spare parts must be attached to the instrument as registered. Any such spare parts which are used on the aircraft must be replaced by other parts, and the creditor must be notified of such use. Mortgages may be granted over aircraft under construction, but must be declared to the DGAC, such declaration indicating the main characteristics of the aircraft under construction.

As in the case of a real estate mortgage, aircraft mortgagees enjoy a *droit de suite* preserving the mortgage in the event of sale of the aircraft to

---

[15] See 'Charges over land: real estate mortgages' above.

a third party. In the case of forced sale of an aircraft, the purchaser may 'purge' the mortgage by notifying the mortgagee of the purchase and offering to pay the mortgagee out of the proceeds of sale. If the mortgagee does not accept the offer of 'purge', it has five days (or longer depending on the location of the mortgagee) in which to request that the mortgaged aircraft be sold at auction, by undertaking to offer to submit a bid of at least one-tenth higher than the planned purchase price.

France is a signatory to the Geneva Convention on the International Registration of Rights on Aircraft and will therefore recognize and give effect to mortgages and other security granted over aircraft in other jurisdictions which are also parties to the Geneva Convention.

Ship mortgages

As in the case of aircraft, specific rules relying on registration of both title and security interests, set forth in Law no 67–5 of 3 January 1967 (the 'Ship Law') and Decree no 67–967 of 27 October 1967 (the 'Ship Decree'), apply to the creation of charges over ships, with the relevant security being the ship mortgage (*hypothèque maritime*). Unlike the case of aircraft, France does not maintain a nationwide ship register, but relies on local registration of interests in ships effected at the home port (*port d'attache*) of the vessel. Registration of a ship mortgage against a vessel under construction is permitted in certain circumstances.

A French ship mortgage may be made 'to order': in such case, endorsement of the agreement automatically results in transfer of the mortgagee's rights. Registration of a mortgage will be cancelled only upon production of a document setting forth the agreement of the parties to such effect, or a judgment incapable of appeal.

The mortgagee enjoys a *droit de suite* and the mortgagee's rights follow the vessel into the hands of any purchaser thereof. In the event of voluntary sale of the ship, mortgagees are entitled to be paid out of the purchase price of the vessel, according to their rank. In the event that only a portion of a vessel has been mortgaged, the mortgagee's rights extend only to the portion of the vessel so mortgaged; however, if more than one-half of the vessel is mortgaged, the mortgagee may cause the entire vessel to be sold and share the proceeds among the other mortgagees. The purchaser can 'purge' the mortgages by notifying all registered mortgagees, within fifteen days of the purchase of the vessel, of the fact of purchase, the purchase price, and the current registered mortgages, and offering to pay off all such mortgages. Any creditor may, within ten days thereafter, require the vessel to be put up for sale at public auction, upon offering to bid at least 10 per cent over the original purchase price and providing sufficient security for the payment of such increased price.

Quasi-security

As is the case in other jurisdictions, French law enables parties to structure transactions which have the same commercial effect as the creation of security interests, without the necessity for security to be created. Several examples of such 'quasi-security' are discussed below.

Finance leasing

As an alternative to borrowing funds to finance the purchase of equipment and creating security over the equipment,[16] specific legislation (Law no 66–455 of 2 July 1966) provides for the creation of finance lease (*crédit-bail*) agreements under which the financing entity purchases the equipment and leases it to the customer. *Crédit-bail* agreements can be concluded with respect to any item of machinery or equipment (which includes 'big ticket' items such as aircraft) so long as they are purchased by the lessor, the lessor maintains title, and the lessee is accorded a purchase option the exercise price of which depends at least in part on previously paid rental payments. *Crédit-bail* agreements may be registered at the commercial court with territorial jurisdiction over the lessee or, failing that, at the court with territorial jurisdiction over the place where the leased asset will be used. Failure to register the existence of the finance lease will render the lessor's property rights unenforceable as against third parties unless the lessor can show that such third parties had knowledge of such rights.

Délégation

As mentioned above, security assignments of book debts are generally not recommended unless effected pursuant to the *Loi Dailly*, which is subject to certain constraints on the identity of the beneficiary and the nature of the obligations secured.[17] Where a single receivable is to be assigned, another useful technique is that of delegation (*délégation*) under Article 1275 of the Civil Code. Under this procedure, a debtor (the delegator, or *délégant*) owing sums to its own creditor (delegation beneficiary, or *délégataire*) but who is in turn owed other sums by another party (delegated party, or *délégué*), delegates such third party to pay to the creditor the sums which the third party in turn owes the debtor. Thus, for example, a debtor, which has purchased an aircraft funded by a bank loan and then leases such aircraft to an airline, may 'delegate' the airline to pay all

---

[16] See discussion under 'Purchase money security interest over material and equipment' above.   [17] See discussion under 'Security assignment or pledge of book debts' above.

or part of the rental payments directly to the bank, with such payments discharging *pro tanto* the obligations of the lessor to the bank under the loan (as well as discharging the obligations of the lessee under the lease itself). Delegation requires the consent of all three parties, typically embodied in a written delegation agreement. If the delegation beneficiary agrees that acceptance of such payment obligation by the delegated party discharges the obligations of the delegator, this is referred to as a '*délégation parfaite*' and has the same effect as if the original debt had been novated. Typically, however, the delegator remains liable on the underlying debt unless and until the delegated party pays the delegation beneficiary the relevant amounts; the effect is therefore that of making the delegated party the guarantor of the delegator for the debt owed by the delegator to the delegation beneficiary, but only up to the amounts due by the delegated party to the delegator. Such a delegation is known as a *délégation imparfaite*.

II. PRIORITIES

Priority as between competing charges

The issue of priority as between competing charges arises rarely under French law, since, as described above, in most cases each specific category of asset is subject to different security. Where such conflict does arise, priority is determined according to the following rules:

- Where a tangible asset over which security has been taken under specific legislation permitting the granting of security without physical dispossession (for example, pledge of a going business[18] or purchase money security interest over material and equipment[19]) is pledged anew by physical dispossession,[20] the second pledge will have priority unless the pledgee was aware of the existence of the prior pledge.
- Where an asset which forms part of a pledged going business is made subject to a purchase money security interest over material and equipment, the purchase money security interest has priority if notified to the pledgee of the going business within two months of the creation of the security interest.
- A purchase money security interest granted over material and equipment which, upon installation, becomes a fixture (*immeuble par destination*) ranks ahead of any real estate mortgage which is extended to such fixture.

---

[18] See discussion under 'Charge over going business' above.
[19] See discussion under 'Purchase money security interest over material and equipment' above. [20] See discussion under 'Charges over goods and pledges of inventory' above.

- Assets which form part of a group of pledged assets but which are the property of a third party are not subject to the pledge.

Priority as against unsecured creditors

Unsecured creditors are entitled in certain cases to exercise a possessory lien (*droit de retention*) over assets of the debtor or to obtain seizure and forced sale of such assets. The possessory lien is effective as against all other creditors, including those with security over the asset. The right of seizure and forced sale may be exercised notwithstanding the existence of security over the asset, but the secured creditor will be entitled to priority over the proceeds of the sale.

Preferential debt

As in other legal systems, French law provides for a number of categories of preferential debt (*créances priviligées*), some of which have priority over contractually created security interests. Occasionally, the specific legislation pursuant to which the security interest is created itself provides for certain liens which rank ahead of such security regardless of the date of the lien; this is the case, for example, of certain aircraft and ship liens.

More generally, various categories of French legislation, including the Civil Code, the Labour Code, the Tax Code, and the Insolvency Law provide for a number of *privilèges* which rank ahead of contractual security either in the case of specific assets (*privilèges spéciaux*) or on all assets of the same category (*privilèges généraux*). A full description of all of the various categories of preferential debt would be beyond the scope of this work; however, the following kinds of *privilèges* are among the most significant:

- Court costs and expenses (*frais de justice*) disbursed in the interest of all creditors for the conservation or the forced sale of the asset.[21]
- Liens of the tax administration for payment of various taxes, duties (including customs duties), and imposts,[22] and privileges of the social security administration for payment of compulsory employers' and employees' contributions to the comprehensive French health, unemployment, and retirement insurance system.[23]
- Wages and certain comparable payments such as redundancy payments and payments in lieu of holiday period, including a special lien (*superprivilège*) in the case of the opening of insolvency proceedings,

---

[21] Civil Code, Arts 2101 and 2104.   [22] Tax Code, Arts 1920 ff.
[23] Social Security Code, Arts L138 and 139.

ranking ahead of all other preferred debts and all security interests, securing payment of salaries for the last sixty working days (ninety days in the case of certain employees) up to a maximum monthly amount fixed by decree.[24] In practice, these sums are paid by an insurance organization, the *Association pour la gestion du régime d'assurance des créances des salariés*, which advances the funds necessary upon receipt of the claim.

- A special lien created under the provisions of the Commerical Code relating to insolvency, pursuant to which claims arising against the debtor following the opening of insolvency proceedings rank ahead of all debt incurred prior thereto during the 'observation period' and thereafter unless the debtor is placed in judicial liquidation.
- Various 'special' liens relating to amounts due in respect of specific assets, such as the lien of the seller of certain assets for payment of the purchase price, the lien of the lessor of real estate for rental payments, transporters' and commissioners' liens, and innkeepers' liens.[25]
- Various 'general' liens relating to subsistence payments, medical payments, funeral costs, and similar expenses.[26]

Outside insolvency, most contractual security ranks behind the lien for court costs and the liens for tax and social security, equally with 'special liens', and ahead of 'general liens'; complex rules govern the priority of the general liens as among themselves. The purchase money security interest for material and equipment ranks ahead of all liens other than the lien for court costs. In the event of insolvency, however, these rules are modified so that the employees' *'superprivilège'* ranks ahead of all other liens and all security, followed by the 'the special insolvency lien'.

Subordination

Specific pieces of French legislation permit the creation of certain loans and negotiable securities which are subordinated by law to all unsecured creditors. The majority view of the learned commentary is that contractual subordination in the absence of a legislative text is also permitted under French law, and in fact such contractual subordination is frequently employed in France, particularly in the case of management buy-outs and buy-ins making use of 'mezzanine debt'. In the absence of definitive case law (*jurisprudence*) on the subject, however, it is unclear whether such contractual subordination is effective as against an insolvency administrator.

---

[24] Labour Code, Art L 143–10.   [25] Civil Code, Art 2102.
[26] Civil Code, Arts 2101 and 2104.

Enforcement

The absence of a unified regime for the taking of security in France means that the remedies of secured creditors under French law depend to a considerable degree on the kind of asset over which the security is taken and the form of security obtained.[27] This section will describe more generally the nature of remedies available to secured creditors and the limitations and restrictions on such remedies.

Power of retention

In the case of ordinary charges over tangible assets, where the security is perfected by delivery of the pledged asset to the pledgee,[28] the creditor is entitled to retain the pledged asset until the secured debt, including principal, interest, and expenses, has been repaid in full.[29] This right of retention does not entitle the pledgee to employ the asset for its own use or to sell the asset to a third party, but merely to refuse to surrender the asset to the owner until the debt is repaid. Obviously, similar rights do not exist in the case of charges which do not require physical dispossession, such as the charge over a going business,[30] the purchase money security interest over material and equipment,[31] and registrable mortgages.[32] However, the revisions to the law of 1983 relating to the pledge of financial instruments[33] create a right of retention in favour of the pledgee over all financial instruments and cash in the pledged account. Holders of a real estate mortgage[34] have a quasi-right of retention, since they are entitled to obtain the exclusion of the debtor from the mortgaged premises.[35]

Power of sale or attribution of the secured asset

The principal remedy afforded to secured creditors under French law is the right to cause the pledged asset to be sold and to be satisfied out of

[27] The distinction between the different kinds of security available and the remedies available to creditors in the case of each specific kind of security is described in Section I above.
[28] See discussion under 'Charges over goods and pledges of inventory' above.
[29] Civil Code, Art 2082.   [30] See discussion under 'Charge over going business' above.
[31] See discussion under 'Purchase money security interest over material and equipment' above.
[32] See discussion under 'Charges over land: real estate mortgages', 'Aircraft mortgages', and 'Ship mortgages' above. In the case of aircraft and ship mortgages, the relevant statutes do, however, create specific repairers' liens.
[33] See discussion under 'Charges over share accounts and fractional ownership interests in French companies' above.
[34] See discussion under 'Charges over land: real estate mortgages' above.
[35] Civil Code, Art 2204.

the proceeds of the sale or, in certain cases, to obtain attribution of the asset. However, except in extremely limited cases, the secured creditor is not entitled to effect such sale or self-attribution on its own: sale must be effected at public auction and, where permissible, self-attribution must be authorized by court order. The security instrument may not entitle the secured creditor to self-appropriate the pledged assets in the event of default by the pledgor. Any provision of a security agreement which permits the secured party to self-attribute the assets (*pacte commissoire*) or to dispose of them by private sale (*clause de voie parée*) is null and void. The public policy reason behind this rule is that the value of the pledged asset may be greater than the amount of the debt secured, and attribution or private disposal of the asset upon default of the pledgor may result in unjust enrichment of the pledgee. This policy is considered to be a cornerstone of French security law, and some courts have even held that where a clause of such nature was central to the pledge agreement, the entire pledge (and not merely the remedies clause) was null and void.

In the case of pledges of assets, whether tangible or intangible, the relevant provisions of the French Civil and Commercial Codes provide that in the event of a default by the pledgor, the pledgee has only two remedies under French law:

(a) to petition the court to permit self-appropriation of the assets or the sale of such assets at public auction, but only after the court has actually ruled to such effect, which may require an expert's evaluation of the value of the assets;[36] or

(b) (in the case of a commercial pledge only) following eight days' notice to the pledgor, to sell the assets at public auction or (in the case of shares) through an authorized stockbroker.[37]

Similar restrictions exist in the case of a pledge of a going business (except that judicial self-attribution is not available), and for a purchase money security interest of material and equipment, and, as discussed above, also apply in the case of shares deposited in a pledged account and not traded on a regulated market.

Similar rights and restrictions apply in the case of mortgages. The mortgagee of real estate is entitled to exercise the remedy of 'expropriation',[38] to cause the mortgaged real estate to be sold at auction, and to be satisfied on a priority basis out of the proceeds of the sale. Clauses permitting the mortgagee to occupy the premises or to sell the real estate outside the auction procedure are void. Similarly, beneficiaries of aircraft and ship mortgages are entitled to arrest or attach the aircraft or vessel and to

---

[36] Civil Code, Art 2078.   [37] Commercial Code, Art L. 521–3.
[38] See discussion under 'Charges over land: real estate mortgages' above.

cause the forced sale thereof at auction, being satisfied on a priority basis out of the proceeds of the sale.

Lenders to French companies occasionally attempt to elude application of these rules by requiring the French party to grant an assignment by way of security over the asset rather than a pledge. Where the asset is actually located outside France (which is arguably the case in the event that the asset being assigned consists of intangible rights arising under a contract with parties in other jurisdictions), there is some merit to adopting this approach, at least where the security assignment is made contractually subject to a law other than that of France and such choice of law is justified by the international element of the transaction.

However, outside the special case of the assignment of book debt to a credit institution pursuant to the *Loi Dailly*,[39] where the notion of security assignments has received specific statutory recognition, the status of security assignments under French law is very unclear. At least one French court has ruled that where a debtor transferred ownership of certain shares to a creditor accompanied by an agreement that the shares would be returned upon repayment of the debt, this was a disguised attempt at effecting a *pacte commissoire* and therefore unenforceable. Alternatively, parties attempting to create a security assignment over French assets risk the possibility that a French court will misconstrue their intention and rule that an outright assignment of the asset has occurred.

The problem is compounded by the fact that there is no concept under French law equivalent to that of the trust, so that it is not possible under current law to transfer legal title to assets whilst retaining beneficial ownership. For several years, the French parliament has been considering the possibility of enacting proposed legislation to permit the creation of trust-like arrangements, known as *fiducie*, similar to legislation existing in Luxembourg. However, this legislation has been stalled due to fears that the *fiducie* will be used in order to avoid taxation.

Survival of the security interest in the case of sale of the secured asset: droit de suite

In all of the categories described in part I above in which security is taken over tangible assets which are not delivered to the secured party, the security interest survives any sale of the asset to a third party, and the secured party continues to have the rights described in part III with respect to such assets. This right is known as the *droit de suite*. However, in each such case, the transferee can defeat such rights by using a procedure known as 'purging' the security interest, consisting in offering to pay

---

[39] See discussion under 'Security assignment or pledge of book debts' above.

the purchase price of the asset directly to the secured party. If the secured party accepts such payment, the security interest is 'purged' (although the creditor retains its ordinary right to sue the debtor for the difference between the proceeds of sale and the amount of the debt). If the secured party refuses to accept payment of the purchase price (in practice, because the amount is insufficient to discharge the debt), it must request that the secured asset be put up for auction, and undertake to submit or cause to be submitted at such auction a bid for 10 per cent higher than the purchase price.

Arrest and forced sale

Arrest. Unsecured creditors are entitled in certain circumstances to arrest (seize) certain assets of a defaulting debtor, even when they are in the hands of a third party. Under Law no 91–650 of 9 July 1991, precautionary arrest (*saisie conservatoire*) of tangible movable assets or debts (*créances*) or other intangible property may be authorized on an *ex parte* basis by the courts upon petition of the creditor or be effected directly by the creditor possessing an executory title (for example, a judgment on the merits). The debtor is entitled to obtain a release (*mainlevée*) of the arrest order if certain conditions are not met or to substitute any other measure which safeguards the interests of the parties. Similar provisions in the relevant legislation permit the arrest of vessels and aircraft (subject to certain exceptions, for example, aircraft used in public transport). In the case of real estate, an analogous procedure exists permitting a creditor who fears that the debtor will shortly become insolvent to obtain a 'judicial mortgage' (*hypothèque judiciaire*) over real estate owned by the debtor, and similar provisions in the Commercial Code permit a 'judicial pledge' (*nantissement judiciaire*) of a going business.

Forced sale. Unsecured creditors holding an executory title (for example, a judgment debt) are, like secured creditors having obtained the necessary court order, entitled to obtain the forced seizure (*saisie-vente*) and sale (*vente forcée*) of assets belonging to a defaulting debtor. However, creditors holding security over such assets are entitled to priority over the proceeds of such sale. The creditor must serve a notice to pay (*commandement*) on the debtor; in the event that payment is not forthcoming in eight days then the property is seized, and may be sold at auction. Similar procedures permit seizure of amounts owed to the debtor by a third party in order to obtain forced attribution (*saisie-attribution*).

Insolvency

As is the case in other jurisdictions, the French insolvency law, codified as articles L. 620–1 ff of the Commercial Code.

Vitiation of security created at point of insolvency

Pursuant to Article L. 621–50 of the Commercial Code, security cannot be perfected by filing following the opening of insolvency proceedings. In addition, Articles L. 621–107 and L. 621–108 of the Commercial Code, which are the French equivalent of the 'hardening' or 'preference' rules found in the insolvency laws of other countries, provide that certain transactions are either automatically null and void or are voidable at the discretion of the court if such transactions have been entered into by the insolvent debtor during the so-called 'suspect period' (*période suspecte*). The suspect period begins at the time when the insolvent debtor is in default of payments (*cessation des paiements*), ie, is unable to make payments as they become due. Although in theory a debtor which finds itself in a situation of default of payments is required to file for insolvency at the latest fifteen days thereafter, in practice the court is entitled to fix the date of default of payments (and thus the beginning of the suspect period) as early as eighteen months prior to the judgment opening the insolvency proceeding. Thus, in the event that a pledgee files for insolvency at any time in the eighteen-month period following the signature of a security instrument, there is a hypothetical possibility that the security could be set aside if the security falls within one of the transactions described in Articles L. 621–107 and L. 621–108 of the Commercial Code.

Article L. 621–107 contains a specific list of transactions which, if accomplished during the suspect period, *must* be set aside (ie, the court has no discretion to refuse to do so). Several such transactions can apply to the taking of security. Article L. 621–107(1) provides that any instrument by which real or personal property (which would include intangible rights) is conveyed (which has been interpreted by the French courts as including the creation of security thereon) for no consideration (*à titre gratuit*) must be set aside. Article L. 621–107(2) provides that any bilateral contract pursuant to which the obligations of the debtor exceed significantly the obligations of the other party must also be set aside. Finally, Article L. 621–107(6) provides that any mortgage or pledge granted during the suspect period as security for previously contracted debts (ie, not for new money) must be set aside.

Article L. 621–108, unlike Article L. 621–107, provides that the court may in its discretion (but is not required to) set aside any transaction involving payment for consideration (no specific list is given) after the date of *cessation des paiements* if the parties who dealt with the debtor had knowledge at the time of contracting that the debtor was in fact in default of payments.

Effect of insolvency proceedings on security

Administrator's right to continue agreements. Unless an insolvent debtor is placed in immediate liquidation, the commencement of insolvency proceedings opens a period of observation of from six to twenty months during which the enterprise continues to transact business while the court considers whether it is possible to save the enterprise by the conclusion of a payment plan with creditors or to sell all or part of it as a going business and satisfy the creditors out of the proceeds of such sale. Under Article L. 621–28 of the Commercial Code, once insolvency proceedings have been opened, the administrator appointed by the court has the option of requiring further performance of any contract then under way, on condition that the administrator itself furnishes future performance of the insolvent debtor's obligations. If the administrator determines to 'continue' performance of the contract, then the co-contractant is required to provide further performance of its own obligations, even if the insolvent debtor had defaulted in its own performance of payment obligations prior to the opening of the insolvency proceedings. In such case, the pre-insolvency default gives rise solely to a creditor's claim. A contracting party may make a formal request (*mise en demeure*) on the administrator requesting a determination as to whether a contract will be continued. Notwithstanding any contractual clause to the contrary, a contract cannot be terminated solely due to the opening of the insolvency proceedings. If the administrator continues the contract but does not make payment, then the contract is automatically terminated and an application may be made for the termination of the observation period as well.

The practical effect of Article L. 621–28 in the context of international lending is that, once insolvency proceedings are opened with respect to a French debtor, it can become nigh impossible to enforce security during the observation period. On the other hand, if the administrator does decide to continue performance of the agreement following the opening of the insolvency proceedings, then the lender is entitled to priority of repayment of new sums advanced, pursuant to Article L. 621–32 of the Commercial Code.

Under Article L. 621–40 of the Commercial Code, the judgment opening the insolvency proceedings suspends or prohibits any judicial action on the part of any creditor whose debt originates prior to the judgment and which relates either to the payment of a sum of money or the termination of a contract for default in the payment of a sum of money, as well as any measures of execution (for example, arrest or seizure of assets) commenced by creditors with respect to movable or immovable assets. Nevertheless, there is some case authority for the proposition that a pledgee of a tangible asset who actually holds the asset is entitled to exercise the pledgee's remedy of sale of the asset.[40] In addition, Article L. 621–24 of the Commercial Code of the Insolvency Law permits the debtor, on application to the *juge-commissaire*, to pay debts which arose prior to the opening of the insolvency proceedings if such payment is necessary to release a pledge over an asset which is necessary for the continuation of the bankrupt's business.

The fate of security in an insolvency proceeding. During the observation period, security over assets of the insolvent debtor is essentially frozen. The insolvent debtor or the *administrateur* may propose to holders of security the substitution of 'equivalent security', and may, if the holders do not consent, apply to the *juge-commissaire* for an order to this effect. In the event that any assets of the debtor which are subject to security are sold during such period, the proceeds thereof are deposited in a special account maintained at the *Caisse des Dépôts et Consignations* (a special state-owned bank). When the observation period is over (ie, the debtor presents a plan accepted by the creditors or is declared in judicial liquidation), the secured creditors are paid the amounts in order of priority (subject to payment of certain employee liens). The *juge-commissaire* is even given power to order the provisional payment by the debtor of all or part of debt secured on the assets of the debtor, prior to the end of the observation period, provided that the secured creditor posts a bank guarantee.

At the end of the observation period, the administrator either proposes a plan of recovery or the liquidation (ie, 'straight' insolvency) of the insolvent debtor. The recovery plan in turn can consist either of the continuation of the enterprise or the total or partial sale of its business (*cession totale ou partielle de l'entreprise*) to a third party. Even if the enterprise is to be continued, parts of the business can be sold to third parties (*cession partielle de l'entreprise*). The fate of security granted prior to the opening of the insolvency proceedings will be considered in each of these scenarios:

(i) Continuation of the enterprise pursuant to a recovery plan

The administrator will have proposed to all creditors either the postponement or the reduction of their debt, or both, which each creditor, whether secured or not, has the liberty to refuse. However, the court may unilaterally impose on all creditors who have not accepted the administrator's proposition, whether secured or unsecured, a postponement of reimbursement and may propose a reduction in lieu thereof. Although any security over the debt will survive, the debt itself will thus have been weakened.

The court may order, as part of the continuation plan, either the isolated sale of assets or the sale of a line of business. In either case, if

---

[40] As described under 'Power of sale or attribution of the secured asset' above.

such assets are subject to security, then the proceeds are subject to the same procedure as sales of such assets during the observation period: the proceeds thereof are deposited in a special account maintained at the *Caisse des Dépôts et Consignations* and the secured creditors are paid the amounts in order of priority (subject to payment of certain employee liens). Amounts payable to secured creditors as part of the general continuation plan (as postponed or reduced pursuant to the procedure described in the previous paragraph) are reduced by any amount payable as the proceeds of such sales. The court may order that alternative security be given to the creditor in substitution of the security originally granted on the asset sold.

(ii) Total sale of the enterprise

If the total business is sold to a third party, then the judgment adopting the plan of sale renders any debts not yet due immediately due. If the sale includes assets which are subject to security, then the court must allocate a portion of the proceeds of sale to each of such assets before the distribution of the purchase price and the exercise of preferential rights. Except in cases of fraud or certain criminal proceedings, this is the sole right of the creditors; they do not recover their individual rights against the debtor at the close of the proceedings. However, any security granted by the debtor to secure the financing of the acquisition of assets on which the security is granted survives the sale of the secured asset to the third party, who is thereafter obligated to reimburse the financing according to its terms unless extended payment terms are granted by the court or the parties agree otherwise.

(iii) Judicial liquidation

If the administrator is unable to propose either an acceptable recovery plan or a sale of the business, or if a recovery plan proves unworkable, then the debtor enterprise is placed in judicial liquidation, and the assets are sold and the proceeds used to satisfy creditors. Where the judicial reorganization proceedings are converted into liquidation proceedings, the creditors' representative is usually named liquidator for such purposes.

Real estate is normally sold at auction, with the reserve price (*mise à prix*) being determined by the *juge-commissaire*. However, the *juge-commissaire* may also decide to sell the real estate privately if circumstances so permit. The proceeds of the sale are distributed in the same manner as described above. Units of production consisting in whole or in part of movable or immovable property may be sold pursuant to a special procedure of public solicitation of offers, and the proceeds allocated to creditors. All other assets are sold at auction or privately by the *juge-commissaire*.

However, certain special rules apply to assets subject to security. If the liquidator so wishes, he may, by payment of the debt secured thereby, liberate from a pledge any tangible assets which have been made subject to pledge. If the liquidator does not do so, he must, within six months of the judgment declaring the debtor in liquidation, request from the *juge-commissaire* authorization to sell the asset. The creditor is notified of the impending sale at least two weeks prior to the sale and may petition the court for the judicial attribution to him of the asset.

The judgment which opens judicial liquidation proceedings (or converts reorganization proceedings into liquidation proceedings) renders immediately due all debts which are not yet due. Creditors with mortgages over real estate or recordable security over personal property (for example, pledgees of a *fond de commerce*) may, if such assets have not been sold by the liquidator within three months from the judgment opening the liquidation proceedings, recover their individual rights and may enforce their security[41] (minus any payments they may have received in the course of the recovery plan). However, the *juge-commissaire* may order the provisional payment of all or part of a debt, and may condition such payment on the submission of a bank guarantee. In the event that debts owing to secured creditors are not fully satisfied out of the proceeds of the sale of the secured assets, such creditors rank equally with unsecured creditors for the remainder of the debts owed to them.

IV. ENFORCEMENT OF FOREIGN SECURITY

Basis of recognition

As explained earlier, the domestic French rules governing security are complex and generally follow the type of asset over which the security is to be taken rather than a unified regime. It follows that the rules governing recognition in France of security governed by foreign law and/or executed outside France will be somewhat complex as well. These rules tend to distinguish between the creation of such security and the effects thereof.

---

[41] As described under 'Enforcement' above.

With respect to the creation of the security, the French *doctrine* (learned commentary) and *jurisprudence* (weight of court decisions) appear to give preference to the law applicable to the source of the security (law governing the contract, the court decision, or the provision of law pursuant to which the security is created); the French courts will recognize such security only if the source is valid and binding in the relevant country and gives rise to an effective obligation to create such security. However, the French courts will also require that the security purported to be created actually corresponds to a type of security recognized by the jurisdiction in which the asset over which the security purported to be created is located, the *lex rei sitae*. Thus, for example, it is theoretically possible to create security over an asset located in France pursuant to an agreement governed by the laws of England, provided that the agreement in question is the valid and binding source of such security under English law, *and* that the type of security so created exists under French law.

With respect to the effects of security, the *lex rei sitae* is given virtually exclusive effect. The law of the location of the asset will therefore govern issues such as the rights of the secured party to preferential payment of the proceeds of sale of the asset, *droits de suite*, and the causes of termination of the security. Delicate issues may arise where the asset is in one jurisdiction at the time of creation but is located in another jurisdiction at the time that the security is sought to be enforced. In such case, the tendency of the French courts is to apply the new *lex rei sitae* to the effects of the security.

The remainder of this subsection will deal with issues relating to specific categories of security.

Real estate mortgages (hypothèques)

Article 2128 of the Civil Code provides specifically that, in the absence of international treaty, an agreement entered into outside France is invalid to create a mortgage over real estate situate in France. Hence, it is inadvisable to execute a mortgage over French real estate otherwise than in accordance with the procedures described above (execution before a French notary), except in the rare cases where international treaty permits the execution of such mortgages before a French consular officer or before local authorities.

Pledge of tangible assets

It is a constant principle of French jurisprudence that a pledge of tangible assets must comply with the *lex rei sitae*. For this reason, the French courts have strictly applied the requirement of physical dispossession[42] to any purported pledge of goods located in France, even if the agreement is executed in a country which recognizes the creation of such pledges without dispossession. Where French law recognizes the creation of pledges without dispossession (for example, in the cases described in part I above), a foreign agreement will be recognized, but only if the procedures required under French law for the creation and perfection of such security are effected. For the same reason, it is strongly recommended to avoid execution of agreements purporting to create a security assignment of tangible assets located in France, as such agreements run a strong risk of being declared invalid in France as a *pacte commissoire*.

Aircraft mortgage

France is a party to the Geneva Convention on the International Recognition of Rights in Aircraft, under which the contracting states agree to recognize mortgages and similar rights in aircraft provided that such rights have been constituted in accordance with the law of the contracting state in which the aircraft was registered as to nationality at the time of their constitution and are regularly recorded in a public record of the contracting state in which the aircraft is registered as to nationality.

Where the aircraft is registered in a country which is not a member state of the convention, the tendency of the courts has also been to apply the law of the state in which the aircraft is registered to mortgages and other security created over the aircraft. Hence, it is possible that the French courts would recognize the validity of a foreign mortgage created over an aircraft registered in the country of such mortgage, even if the aircraft is temporarily in France at the time of the creation of the mortgage.

Competing receiverships

The French courts subscribe to the principle of 'territoriality of insolvency proceedings' (*térritorialité de la faillite*), under which different insolvency proceedings can be brought in respect of the same insolvent debtor in as many places as the debtor does business or owns assets, rather than that of 'universality of insolvency' (*unité ou universalité de la faillite*), under which proceedings may be brought only before a single court, usually that of the domicile or principal place of business of the insolvent debtor. Consequently, in several highly publicized instances, the French courts have granted petitions for the opening of insolvency proceedings (or instituted such proceedings *sua sponte*) in respect of foreign companies

---

[42] As described under 'Charges over goods and pledges of inventory' above.

having branches in France, or even (as in the case of the insolvency of BCCI) simply on the grounds that the foreign company had a 'genuine commercial presence' in France. The fact that insolvency proceedings have already been brought in respect of the same debtor in another jurisdiction (including that of the principal office of the debtor) is not a bar to the opening of proceedings against the debtor in France unless the judgment opening the foreign proceedings has been the subject of execution (*exequatur*) proceedings in France or there is a treaty to the contrary. Such insolvency proceedings will be conducted pursuant to the French insolvency law.

For this reason, it is possible for creditors, whether French or foreign, to file a creditor's claim in a French insolvency opened in respect of a French or foreign debtor, even where another proceeding regarding the same debtor has already been opened outside France. Secured creditors may therefore find themselves in a position where their rights will be accorded different levels of priority in two different insolvency proceedings. The position of the French courts is generally that the law governing the security instrument will be applied to determine if such security will be validly created and the effects thereof, but French law will govern the priority to be accorded to such security in a French insolvency proceeding, even where both the creditor and the debtor are not French.

The effect which foreign insolvency proceedings, whether brought against a French or foreign debtor, will have in France will depend on whether the judgment opening such proceedings has been the subject of an execution order (*exequatur*) in France. In the absence of such an order, the French courts will take judicial notice of the foreign insolvency, but will not enforce any order made by the foreign insolvency court.

In the event that a foreign insolvency judgment receives *exequatur* in France, it is entitled to full *res judicata* effect (*force de la chose jugée*), impeding the opening of similar proceedings in France and subjecting to the law of the forum of the insolvency proceedings the question of priority of security.

On a practical level, more than one respected author has stated that the French courts have generally applied a pragmatic approach to the issue of 'competing' bankruptcies. Where the interests of French creditors require that a foreign insolvency judgment be granted *exequatur*, the French courts will do so. Where such interests will be better protected by the opening of insolvency proceedings in France, the courts will order the opening of such proceedings, even if similar proceedings have already been opened outside France.

6

Outlines of Security Interests under German Law

DR BURKHARD JÄKEL

(Partner, Gleiss Lutz Hootz Hirsch, Frankfurt am Main)

I. INTRODUCTION

Function of security

Access to capital is indispensable for the functioning and prosperity of a modern market economy. Capital is the basis for investment by a company, which ideally will deploy the capital to create jobs and growth to the benefit of the economy as a whole.

Third parties, however, will only provide capital over time if they are assured of adequate interest and of the repayment of capital. As it is not possible to foretell whether the borrower will be able to repay the loan, every lender has an interest in being able to have recourse to the borrower's assets exclusively in its favour to recover sums owed in the event of insolvency. Only if this latter condition is satisfied will a lender be prepared to lend money at a reasonable interest rate, a rate which does not contain a high-risk mark-up.

Any legal system which recognizes these goals must have a choice of suitable and flexible security forms at its disposal, which, if they are to fulfil their function, can be enforced on bankruptcy by the secured creditor in preference over all other creditors.

The German Civil Code (BGB),[1] which lays down the main legal framework for the law on securities, offers lenders an assortment of security types, namely the guarantee *(Bürgschaft)*,[2] the charges on property *(Grundpfandrechte)*,[3] and the pledge over goods and rights *(Pfandrecht an Sachen und Rechten)*.[4] Other forms of security can be found in other specially enacted statutes.[5]

In addition, mercantile custom has developed, on the basis of the principles anchored in the BGB, further security instruments such as the 'transfer of title for security purposes' *(Sicherungsübereignung)* and the 'security assignment of receivables' *(Sicherungsabtretung)*, which forms have been endorsed by the courts. A security which is a hybrid of statutory law and business practice is the so-called 'reservation of title'

---

[1] (1896) (in force 1900).   [2] Articles 765 ff BGB.   [3] Articles 1113 ff BGB.
[4] Articles 1204 ff BGB.   [5] eg, the Law governing Rights over Aircraft of 26 February 1959.

(*Eigentumsvorbehalt*). The premise for this form of security can be derived from Article 455 BGB which is a rule relating to the contract of sale. The rules governing such security have been developed and refined by the courts.

Abstract and accessory security

Two forms of security have to be distinguished: 'abstract' and 'accessory' security.

With respect to accessory security, the debt and the security are by operation of law closely linked with each other with the result that the security can only exist if the debt exists. Furthermore, the security cannot be assigned without the underlying debt being assigned with it.[6] Conversely, if the debt is assigned, the security will also pass automatically by operation of law to the assignee.[7] If the debt ceases to exist, so will the security.

Examples of such accessory security are the guarantee (*Bürgschaft*), mortgage (*Hypothek*) and pledge (*Pfandrecht*) over goods and rights.

This close association between debt and security is not, however, present with regard to abstract securities. Here, the security is independent of the underlying debt. Thus, if the secured debt ceases to exist, the security will nevertheless continue in force. An abstract security can also be assigned without the underlying debt and vice versa. Thus, if a debt is assigned to a third party, the security securing the debt must additionally be assigned, if the security is to pass to the assignee.

The link between the debt to be secured and the abstract security is established by a so-called security agreement.[8] The obligations and rights contained in this agreement are of a contractual nature only. German law distinguishes between rights under contractual law and rights *in rem*. Rights *in rem* provide the holder of such rights with certain rights over the thing, for example disposal, transfer of title, possession, and use. Thus, if the security provider possesses certain rights *in rem* over the asset being secured, then it can still deal with the security and these powers cannot be excluded by contractual agreement.[9]

Examples of such abstract security are the land charge (*Grundschuld*), transfer of title for security purposes (*Sicherungsübereignung*), and the security assignment (*Sicherungsabtretung*).

---

[6] Articles 1153(2), 1250(1) BGB.   [7] Articles 401, 1153(2), 1250(1) BGB.
[8] Discussed below.   [9] Article 137 BGB.

Parties

When security is to be taken, the parties to the security arrangement are the security provider and security holder.

The debtor/borrower and security provider need not be the same person. A third party can provide security to secure a debt owed by the borrower. In relation to a guarantee, however, it is mandatory that the guarantor and debtor be different persons.

The security holder and lender/creditor are nearly always the same person. One possible exception to this rule is where a third party holds the security on trust for the lender. It should, however, be noted that a third party can only hold an accessory security on trust for a lender if the underlying debt is also assigned to the third party.

The secured debt

Any validly existing debt can be secured. In addition, future and contingent debt can be secured. This is expressly provided for in the BGB in relation to all accessory security and the land charge (*Grundschuld*),[10] but is accepted too for the transfer of title for security purposes and the security assignment.

It should be noted that German law recognizes so-called incomplete debts (*unvollkommene Verbindlichkeiten*) which are regarded as non-existent, but which nevertheless can be fulfilled. These include obligations arising out of a wager or a game of chance.[11] Such incomplete debts cannot be secured.[12]

The assets over which security can be taken

Any asset, tangible or intangible, movable or immovable, which can be disposed of and which has a value can serve as security. The first limb is a legal requirement: if the asset cannot be disposed of a security interest cannot be granted, because granting a security interest is a disposal of the asset. The second limb is a matter of fact: it does not make sense to take a security interest in an asset which has no value.

Registration requirements

Entering the security in the Commercial Register (*Handelsregister*) is neither required nor possible.

---

[10] Articles 765(2), 1113(2), 1192(2), 1204(2) BGB.   [11] Article 762(1) BGB.
[12] Compare Article 762(2) BGB for wagers and games of chance.

Apart from charges on land which have to be registered in the land register, none of the security based on the BGB (namely the pledge over
goods and rights, the transfer of title for security purposes, the security
assignment, and the reservation of title) requires registration against
the asset. Registration in the pledge register is required if an aircraft is
pledged pursuant to the Law governing Rights over Aircraft.[13]

Usage of terms

In this chapter, German legal terms are translated into their English counterpart. It should be noted that as a general rule the translation is only the
economic equivalent of the meaning of the German term and that the use
of the English term does not mean that the English term is fully identical
to the meaning of the German term. It should, therefore, not be concluded
that the German security which is being described by the use of that
English term corresponds to the security which the English term denotes
under English law. Instead, the description of the security in this chapter
will provide the reader with the meaning to be attributed to the English
term used.

II. INDIVIDUAL TYPES OF SECURITY

Charges on land

In practice, the most important charges on land (*Grundpfandrechte*) are the
'land charge' (*Grundschuld*, pl *Grundschulden*) and the 'mortgage'
(*Hypothek*, pl *Hypotheken*). The BGB deals with the rules governing
Hypotheken first;[14] the rules governing *Grundschulden* following immediately thereafter.[15] The latter rules, however, deal only with the differences
between the *Hypothek* and *Grundschuld*; otherwise the rules applying to
Hypotheken are stated to apply.[16] The systematic order in which these two
forms of security appear in the BGB does not, however, reflect the order
of their significance in practice. As the *Grundschuld*, being abstract, is
materially more flexible than the *Hypothek*, it is far more commonly used
in practice than the *Hypothek*.

Both the *Hypothek* and *Grundschuld* grant the security holder 'a right to
payment of a particular amount against the land'.[17] This does not create a
duty on the owner of the land/security provider to repay the amount of

---

[13] But no registration is required if the aircraft is pledged pursuant to the rules laid down
in Articles 1204 ff of the BGB.   [14] Articles 1113–1190 BGB.
[15] Articles 1191–1198 BGB.   [16] Article 1192(1) BGB.   [17] Articles 1113, 1191 BGB.

the debt as stated in the deeds forming the security or in the land register. Nor may the security holder derive a right to repayment of the debt from this right *in rem*. The owner of the land is only under a duty to tolerate the compulsory enforcement of the sum of money against his property.[18] Thus, the only right the security holder has against the owner of the estate is a right to sell the land by public auction and/or to put it into administrative receivership.[19] It is not permissible for the parties to agree on another form of realization.[20] The owner of the land can, of course, always pay the debt owed in order to avoid enforcement action against the property itself.[21]

The proceeds from a public auction are distributed to the security holder and to any other persons whose debts are secured by the land in the order of priority of their respective interests.[22] Administrative receivership means that an administrative receiver is appointed over the land whose function is to protect and utilize the land.[23] Any proceeds from utilizing the land are thus distributed amongst the secured creditors in their respective order of priority.[24] The procedural rules governing compulsory enforcement are laid down in the Act governing Public Auctions and Administrative Receivership of 24 March 1897 (ZVG).

In order to create a charge on land two prerequisites must be fulfilled: the security provider and security holder must agree that such a right should be created and the charge must be registered in the land register.[25]

If the charged property has been leased, then the charge embraces the lease rentals.[26] The charge also embraces appurtenances of the estate unless the appurtenances are not owned by the owner of the land.[27] If the assets embraced by the charge are insured, then the charge in addition extends to any claim against the insurer.[28]

Although their function is identical in principle, the land charge and mortgage can be distinguished in that the mortgage is accessory and the land charge abstract. Thus, a mortgage can only be created if it is to secure an existing debt owed to the security holder.[29] The owner of the land can therefore raise all defences against the compulsory enforcement of the *Hypothek* which the debtor can raise against the enforcement of the debt pursuant to the loan agreement.[30] This does not apply to a *Grundschuld*

---

[18] Article 1147 BGB.   [19] Compare Article 866(1) ZPO.   [20] Article 1149 BGB.
[21] Article 1142 BGB.   [22] Articles 10(1) no 4, 11(1) ZVG.   [23] Article 152 ZVG.
[24] Article 155(2) ZVG.   [25] Article 873(1) BGB.   [26] Article 1123 BGB.
[27] Article 1120 BGB.   [28] Articles 1127, 1128 BGB.
[29] In fact, if the secured debt has not come into existence, the *Hypothek* will not be acquired by the security holder but the owner of the land, and will then be converted into a *Grundschuld*, Articles 1163(1), 1177(1) BGB. The reason for this technique is to block the priority ranking in the land register. Otherwise, charges ranking behind the charge to be created would climb up the ranking if the charge did not come into existence at all.
[30] Article 1137 BGB.

which is abstract and which can be created irrespective of whether there is an existing debt.

In order to enforce a charge on land, an 'enforcement title' (*Vollstreck-ungstitel*) is required.[31] Such an enforcement title is usually a court judgment which has been obtained after the security provider has been successfully sued, but it can also be, for example, a notarial deed where the debtor has agreed that the charge taken should be subject to immediate enforcement action by the creditor without the prior need for court proceedings by the creditor.[32] Because the security holder does not wish to encounter a delay by having to sue the security provider/owner of the land first, it is common practice that the security provider submits himself in a notarial deed to immediate enforcement action.

A public auction or administrative receivership can only take place after the security holder has made an application to the local court in whose jurisdiction the charged land lies.[33] The public auction is carried out by the local court.[34] Administrative receivership is subject to the supervision of the local court.[35]

Pledge over goods and rights

Pledge over goods

Goods can be charged to secure a debt by conferring a right on the security holder to sell the goods.

A pledge is created by the owner depositing the goods with the security holder and both parties agreeing that the security holder is entitled to the pledge.[36] If a third party is in possession of the goods to be pledged, so that the pledgor has constructive possession of the goods, then the goods can also be pledged by transferring the constructive possession to the pledgee.[37] Instead of delivering the goods or transferring the constructive possession to the pledgee, the pledge can also be created by transferring co-possession or co-constructive possession to the pledgee so that the pledgor only has access to the pledged goods jointly with the pledgee.[38] If the pledgor is not the owner of the goods but deposits them with the security holder, a bona fide security holder will obtain a pledge over the goods; the same rules as to the acquisition of title in goods by good faith[39] apply accordingly.[40]

The pledge like the mortgage is accessory. The existence of the pledge is therefore dependent on the existence of the underlying debt.[41] The

[31] Article 1147 BGB.   [32] Articles 704, 794(1) no 5 ZPO.   [33] Articles 15, 146(1) ZVG.
[34] Article 35 ZVG.   [35] Article 153 ZVG.   [36] Article 1205(1) BGB.
[37] Article 1205(2).   [38] Article 1206.   [39] Articles 932 ff BGB.
[40] Article 1207 BGB.   [41] Articles 1210(1), 1253 BGB.

pledgor is thus able to raise the same defences against enforcement over the goods as the debtor can raise against enforcement of the debt.[42]

A pledge is enforced by public auction.[43] The pledgee is only entitled to sell the pledged goods when the debt has become due, whether in whole or part.[44] The pledged goods may only be sold by way of private sale if the pledged goods have a market or stock exchange price.[45] The parties may not agree on another form of realization in place of the statutorily prescribed public auction until the secured debt has fallen due entitling the security holder to enforce the pledge.[46] In particular, any agreement between the parties, whereby title in the pledged goods is to pass to the security holder upon the pledge becoming enforceable, is void.[47] The pledgee must notify the pledgor in advance of its intention to enforce the pledge. The notice must state the amount of money due. The sale may only be effected one month after service of this notice of enforcement.[48] This time period can be reduced by agreements between the parties.[49] If the creditor and debtor are merchants within the meaning of the German Commercial Code, then the time period is only one week instead of one month.[50]

Pledge of intangible rights

Not only goods but also intangible rights can be pledged.[51] The provisions of the BGB applying to pledges of goods apply also to pledges of rights.[52]

The law governing the creation of the pledge of intangible rights is the law which would apply to the assignment of such rights.[53] Thus, an agreement as to the creation of a pledge of rights is required to be in the same form as an agreement to transfer the rights. Therefore, for example, shares in a *Gesellschaft mit beschränkter Haftung*, where no share certificates are issued, have to be pledged in an agreement before a German notary public, since, pursuant to German law, such shares can only be transferred before a notary public.[54]

If a pledge is to be created of a right, for example, a receivable, then the owner of the debt and the security holder must agree that a pledge is to be created.[55] No form is required because the assignment of a receivable requires no form.[56] In addition, however, the owner of the receivable must notify the account debtor of the receivable of the pledge.[57]

---

[42] Article 1211(1) BGB.   [43] Articles 1228(1), 1235(1) BGB.   [44] Article 1228(2) BGB.
[45] Articles 1235(2), 1221 BGB.   [46] Article 1245(2) BGB.   [47] Article 1229 BGB.
[48] Article 1234 BGB.   [49] Article 1245 BGB.   [50] Article 368(1) HGB.
[51] Article 1273(1) BGB.   [52] Article 1273(2) BGB.   [53] Article 1274(1) BGB.
[54] Article 1274(1) BGB, Article 15(3) GmbHG.   [55] Articles 1274(1), 398 BGB.
[56] Compare Article 398 BGB.   [57] Article 1280 BGB.

If the secured debt has become due in whole or in part, then the pledgee is entitled to collect the pledged receivable, and the account debtor of the receivable must make payment to the pledgee.[58]

Practical significance

A pledge over both goods and intangible rights is rare in practice. The reason is that the preconditions for setting them up are not workable in practice. A prerequisite for a pledge of goods is that the pledgee obtain possession of the goods pledged. However, in practice the pledgor requires the goods, for example, machines or a vehicle fleet, in order to continue his business operations or to sell as part of his business. A pledge of receivables is also not popular, because this requires notification of the security to the account debtor. The security provider, however, usually wants to avoid others attaining knowledge of this fact.

Other types of security have, therefore, been developed by mercantile practice. Thus, the transfer of legal title for security purposes has been created in place of the pledge of goods and the security assignment in place of the pledge of rights/receivables.

The pledge is, however, still of importance where:

- the pledged assets are not required by the pledgor for continuing his business operations so that the transfer of possession does not affect the pledgor. This applies, for example, in relation to the pledge of the share certificates in an *Aktiengesellschaft* (joint stock corporation);
- someone (temporarily) has goods in his possession because he is carrying out works on those goods or is transporting them. In these cases, pledge rights can ensue by operation of law. Examples of such pledge rights ensuing by operation of law are a works contractor for his remuneration,[59] a commission agent in relation to his rights, in particular his commission,[60] a shipper,[61] a forwarding agent,[62] and a warehouse keeper[63] for their claims to be remunerated;
- transfer of possession of the goods to the pledgee is not a condition of its creation. This applies, for example, to the landlord's lien which is created by operation of law over goods brought on to the leased premises by the lessee[64] and the pledge over aircraft pursuant to the Act governing Rights in Aircraft of 26 June 1959. In the latter case, possession of the aircraft by the pledgee is replaced by registration of the pledge in the pledge register managed by the *Amtsgericht Braunschweig* (Brunswick Local Court).

---

[58] Article 1282(1) BGB.   [59] Article 647 BGB.   [60] Article 397 HGB.
[61] Article 441 HGB.   [62] Article 464 HGB.   [63] Article 475b HGB.   [64] Article 559 BGB.

Transfer of title for security purposes

As mentioned above, the transfer of title for security purposes (*Sicherungsübereignung*) is not statute law based but is a product created by mercantile practice along the lines of the law *in rem* regulated in the BGB.

The transfer of title for security purposes is a creation of an interest in the goods in favour of the security holder by the security provider by the transfer of title to the security holder; it is, however, agreed that the security holder can only exercise the rights conferred on it in accordance with the 'security purpose'. The security provider retains possession of the secured goods.

The basic rule in German law is that title in goods passes when (i) the owner of the goods and the prospective transferee agree that title to the property is to pass to the transferee, and (ii) the goods are handed over to the transferee.[65] Statute law, however, allows exceptions to the rule that the goods have to be handed over (see below).

Agreement passing title

In order for the agreement passing title to be valid, the goods must be ascertained (*bestimmt*). This means that the goods have to be described in such a manner in the agreement that any person who obtains knowledge of the agreement will be able to distinguish without difficulty the goods which are the subject matter of the transfer from those which are not. Ascertainability of the goods is not sufficient; it is not permissible to fall back on outside circumstances in order to make the goods certain.

Goods are ascertained if they have a serial number or another type of identification number and this number has been stipulated in the agreement. Ascertainment also exists if the parties agree that title in all goods stored or to be stored in a particular warehouse, which must be exactly described, is to pass. However, the requirement of ascertainment is not satisfied if the parties have agreed that only title in those goods in the warehouse to which the transferor already has title is to pass. The reason for this is because it cannot be ascertained from this description which goods in the warehouse belong to the transferor. Further enquiries would be necessary. In particular, it would have to be determined which goods were still subject to a reservation of title.

The principle of ascertainment never causes problems where goods are to be handed over to the transferee because, at the latest, the goods will be ascertained at the time of handing over. The principle of ascertainment,

---

[65] Article 929 sentence 1 BGB.

therefore, only plays a role where the handing over of the goods is substituted by one of the means laid down in the BGB, for example, the transfer of constructive possession.[66]

Handing over

In addition to agreeing that title is to pass, the goods have to be handed
over. In substitution for handing over the goods, the security holder and
security provider may agree that possession shall be retained by the security provider and only constructive possession be granted to the security
holder.[67] The security holder has constructive possession if another person possesses the goods in question as lessee or custodian or on the basis
of a similar legal relationship.[68]

If the asset which is to be provided as security is to remain in the possession of the security provider, which is generally the rule, the handing
over of the goods is substituted by the security holder and security
provider agreeing that the security provider shall possess the asset for the
security holder as custodian free of charge. The custody agreement must
be based on a concrete asset. Therefore, in order to satisfy the principle of
ascertainment the asset must be defined as precisely as it has to be for the
agreement to pass title. The custody agreement can also encompass assets
which come into the security provider's possession at a future date.

If the asset to be charged is not in the possession of the security
provider but in the possession of a third party, then the handing over of
the asset to the security holder can be replaced by the security provider
assigning to the security holder his right against the third party to repossession of the asset.[69]

Security assignment

A security assignment (*Sicherungsabtretung*) is an unconditional assignment to the security holder of trade receivables owed to the security
provider. The security holder receives security from the assignment by
being able to collect the receivables payable to the security provider. The
security holder is bound, however, to exercise the rights which he has
acquired as a result of becoming the owner of the receivables within the
scope of the security purpose.

A receivable can be assigned merely by the security holder and
provider entering into an agreement of assignment, which requires no
particular form.[70] The assignment does not need to be notified to the

---

[66] Discussed below.   [67] Article 930 BGB.   [68] Article 868 BGB.
[69] Article 931 BGB.   [70] Article 398 BGB.

account debtor. So long, however, as the debtor has no knowledge of the assignment, he can continue to make payments to the assignor to discharge his obligations. Moreover, any legal transaction effected between the debtor and the assignor with respect to the receivable has effect for and against the assignee.[71]

The receivables to be assigned must be assignable. Therefore, it has to be verified that an assignment of the receivables has not been prohibited pursuant to the underlying agreement reached between account debtor and assignor.[72] A receivable of money arising from a commercial transaction between merchants can always be assigned, even if a clause to the contrary has been agreed between the two merchants. However, in this case, the debtor can still discharge his obligations by making payment to the assignor even if he has received notice of the assignment.[73]

The receivables to be assigned must be at least ascertainable (*bestimmbar*), in order for the assignment to be valid. This applies in particular to an assignment of future receivables, namely, those receivables which come into existence at a future date. A receivable is ascertainable if, at the time it comes into existence, it can be determined whether it forms part of the assignment arrangement. This will be the case if, at the relevant time, the creditor, debtor, and the amount of the receivable assigned can be determined. The assignment is still valid even if a substantial amount of work and time is required to make the determination. The following are all ascertainable: an assignment of all receivables owed to the security provider from certain units of his business operations, an assignment of receivables from particular legal transactions, and also an assignment of all future receivables.

The most important types of security assignment are the 'global assignment' (*Globalzession*) and the assignment of receivables within the framework of an 'extended reservation of title' (*verlängerter Eigentumsvorbehalt*). On the basis of a global assignment, all present and future receivables arising out of the security provider's business activities are assigned to the security holder, typically a bank. As far as extended reservations of title are concerned, see the comments under the heading reservation of title (below).

Security assignment agreements normally provide that the security holder may not disclose the assignment to the debtor of the receivables, and that the security provider is authorized to collect the assigned receivables, as long as the security provider is still complying with his contractual obligations. Only when the security provider is in default may the security holder notify the account debtor of the assignment. The security

---

[71] Article 407 BGB.   [72] Article 399 BGB.   [73] Article 354a HGB.

provider must be informed in advance that the assignment will be disclosed to the debtor.

The account debtor is only under a duty to make payments to the security holder after he has received a deed containing the assignment or he has been notified in writing by the security provider of the assignment.[74]

Reservation of title

Creation

The reservation of title (*Eigentumsvorbehalt*) is a security taken by a seller providing goods on credit. The reservation of title is created by the parties agreeing that the agreement necessary to pass title in the goods pursuant to Article 929 BGB[75] shall be subject to the condition precedent that the purchase price for the goods is paid in full.

Simple reservation of title

A simple reservation of title ceases to exist when the purchase price has been paid for the goods subject to the reservation of title or a third party has obtained title to such goods. The latter usually occurs when the security provider on-sells and transfers title in the goods to a third party.

Enhanced reservation of title

An enhanced reservation of title (*erweiterter Eigentumsvorbehalt*) is any agreement between the parties whereby the prerequisites for passing title are greater than for a simple reservation of title. An enhanced reservation of title is where the transfer of title in the goods is not only made subject to the full payment of the purchase price, but also the repayment of all receivables arising out of the business relationship (current account reservation of title) or even repayment of all receivables owed by the purchaser to the security holder's group companies.

Extended reservation of title

An extended reservation of title (*verlängerter Eigentumsvorbehalt*) permits the purchaser of the goods to on-sell the goods, but the proceeds of sale owed to such purchaser from the on-sale are assigned to the original seller. Thus, title in the goods sold under reservation of title is replaced with title in the receivables deriving from the on-sale of the goods. As this

---

[74] Article 410 BGB.   [75] See transfer of title for security purposes, above.

assignment of proceeds is a security assignment, the prerequisites for making a valid assignment must be observed, in particular the assigned receivables must be ascertainable. It is common practice that the assignment is not disclosed and the purchaser is authorized to collect the assigned receivables as long as he is still complying with his contractual obligations.

Contingent right

A purchaser who purchased goods subject to a reservation of title has a secure legal position which the seller cannot impair, provided the purchaser continues to fulfil his contractual obligations. This is the case even though the seller retains title to the goods and, therefore, as legal owner, has all rights *in rem* over the goods. However, once the purchase price for the goods has been fully paid, then any rights which the seller did exercise in connection with the goods and which would impair the acquisition of title by the purchaser become invalid.[76] This legal position of the purchaser is known as a contingent right (*Anwartschaftsrecht*), which is the precursor to ownership of the goods in the future by the purchaser. This contingent right grants the purchaser the right to possess the goods.

The aforementioned contingent right can be assigned pursuant to the provisions of the BGB which apply to the transfer in title to goods.[77] If the contingent right has been assigned and the condition precedent of full payment of the purchase price has been fulfilled, then the assignee acquires full title to the goods. A contingent right can also be pledged in accordance with Articles 1204 ff BGB, ie by the parties agreeing on the creation of the pledge and delivery of the goods into the pledgee's possession.[78]

The contingent right exists only as long as the condition precedent can still be fulfilled. If the seller rescinds the sale agreement by reason of the purchaser's default, which he is entitled to do pursuant to Article 455 BGB, then the contingent right ends.[79] As a consequence, the seller is entitled to demand repossession of the goods from the purchaser.[80]

Charge over business as a whole

German law does not recognize a charge which can be created over the whole business of the debtor such as the floating charge under English law. In order to obtain a charge over all assets of the security provider, it is necessary to follow the rules applying to the creation of a security in the

---

[76] Article 161(1) BGB. [77] Wolf, *Sachenrecht* (15th edn, 1999) 288.
[78] Wolf, *Sachenrecht*, 288. [79] Wolf, *Sachenrecht*, 289. [80] Article 985 BGB.

individual assets: land has to be charged pursuant to the rules of charges on land, title in goods can be transferred for security purposes, and receivables can be made the subject of a security assignment.

However, it should be noted that the creation of (various) charges over all the assets of the security provider exposes the creditor to the risk of over-collateralization with the effect that all created individual charges will be null and void.[81]

Leasing

The leasing of goods contains a financing element if the fixed term of the lease, in comparison with the useful life of the leased asset, is long and the lessee amortizes fully or in part the acquisition costs of the assets through the lease instalments he pays.

Leasing is not a type of security in its true sense. The lessor retains unconditional title to the leased goods. If the lessee does not comply with his contractual obligations, the lessor is entitled to terminate the lease agreement and repossess the leased object.[82] He can then choose at his discretion whether to re-lease the asset or realize it.

Factoring

Factoring is the sale of receivables to a company ('factor') which collects the sold receivables owed by the account debtors. If the transaction is a 'true' factoring, then the factor assumes the debtor's credit risk. If the transaction is a so-called 'untrue' factoring, then the credit risk remains with the seller of the receivables so that in the event that the account debtor of the receivables becomes insolvent, the factor can demand reimbursement of the shortfall from the seller or, as often agreed, the factor can require the seller to repurchase the receivables sold to him in return for repayment of the purchase price.

True factoring is treated as an unconditional sale of receivables. The factor thus becomes the unrestricted owner of the assigned receivables over which he can exercise all rights *in rem*. By contrast, 'untrue' factoring is regarded as a loan. The payment of the purchase price is regarded as payment of the loan, the assignment of the 'sold' receivable as a security assignment for the purpose of securing repayment of the loan. This distinction becomes important if the seller of the receivables goes bankrupt.

---

[81] Discussed below.   [82] Articles 554, 556, 985 BGB.

III. THE SECURITY AGREEMENT

By law, there is a close link between accessory security and the debt to be secured. Thus, when creating an accessory security, one only has to determine which particular debt has to be secured. Statute law lays down in detail the prerequisites that need to be satisfied before the security can be enforced. On account of the close link between the security and the secured debt, it is not possible to realize more security than is necessary to recover the secured debt.[83]

The position is different in relation to abstract security. Here, the security provider has a legal position which is totally independent of the existence of the secured debt. This difference can be seen by the following example, which makes a comparison of an accessory mortgage (*Hypothek*) and abstract land charge (*Grundschuld*). Both charges are entered in the land register for a certain amount of money. Whereas the amount entered in the land register for the purpose of being secured by a *Hypothek* is not the amount which can be enforced against the property, if the amount secured is, in fact, lower than the amount stated in the land register, a holder of a *Grundschuld*, on the other hand, can enforce the full amount stated in the land register against the property, even if the secured debt has long ceased.

The security agreement (*Sicherungsvertrag*) creates the link between the abstract security and the secured debt. It determines what debt is being secured by the security, the conditions on which the security holder may realize the security, and when the security has to be retransferred to the security provider. Although there are contractual limits on the enforcement of the abstract security as between security provider and security holder, these do not necessarily bind third party transferees of the right which has been provided as security, who therefore might be able to enforce it in full.

It is inherent in every security agreement that the security holder may only realize the security if this is within the scope of the so-called 'security purpose', that is, only when the secured debt is not fulfilled in due time.[84] Before realization, the security holder must serve an enforcement notice on the security provider.[85] If the security purpose no longer exists, because all the debt secured by the security has been repaid, then the security has to be retransferred to the security provider.[86]

---

[83] See Articles 768, 771, 1137, 1141, 1142, 1211, 1233 *et seq* BGB.   [84] Wolf, *Sachenrecht*, 322.
[85] Wolf, *Sachenrecht*, 323, compare Article 1234 BGB.
[86] BGHZ 137, 212, 219 (Official Collection of Decisions of the Federal Court of Justice in Civil Matters, with volume and page).

The security can only be realized to the extent it is required for settling the secured debt. The security holder has to realize the security at best price. If the proceeds from realization of the security exceed the secured debt, any excess amount has to be refunded to the security provider.

Once the value of the security exceeds the amount of secured debt by more than 150 per cent, the security holder is required to retransfer that part of the security which is in excess of this threshold in order to avoid over-securitization.[87] 'Value of the security' means with regard to assigned receivables their nominal value and with regard to goods their fair market value.[88] This is also inherent in every security agreement and does not need to be expressly agreed. The Federal Court of Justice no longer pursues its former policy, pursuant to which it held that a security agreement entered into on standard terms and conditions which did not contain an express provision providing for the release of security in the event of over-collateralization was void.[89]

It is thus to be concluded that the main purpose of the security agreement is to limit the powers that the security holder can exercise over the security by reason of the fact that he has become owner of the security. This restriction, however, is of a contractual nature only. Such an agreement, therefore, cannot prevent the security holder from effectively dealing with the security *vis-à-vis* third parties, even if this results in a breach of the security agreement.[90] The security provider, however, will have a claim in damages if the security holder does exercise rights *in rem* over the security in breach of contract.

IV. ORDER OF PRIORITY OF SECURITY INTERESTS IN AN ASSET

Charges on land

Several charges can exist over land. The order of priority of each charge depends on the order in which they were registered in the land register.[91] The order in which the charges are registered in the land register depends, in turn, on the time when the application to the land register was made: thus, the application received first in time is the first to be registered in the land register.[92] For this reason, the registrar is under a duty to note the exact time (date and time) when an application to register a charge on land was received.[93] The respective order of priority can be changed by agreement amongst the security holders, which agreement,

---

[87] BGHZ 137, 212, 224.   [88] BGHZ 137, 212, 233, 234.   [89] BGHZ 137, 212, 220.
[90] See Article 137 BGB.   [91] Article 879(1) sentence 1 BGB.   [92] Articles 17, 45 GBO.
[93] Article 13(2) sentence 1 GBO.

however, requires the consent of the owner of the land over which the charge has been created.[94] Any agreed order of priority has to be entered in the land register.[95]

Pledge

The order of priority of various pledges over an asset depends on the order in which the pledges were created; the pledge created earliest in time ranks before all pledges created later in time.[96]

Transfer of title for security purposes

If the security holder has obtained title in an asset, the security provider cannot exercise a right *in rem* over the same asset a second time and create a further security interest, because he is no longer the owner. However, German law recognizes the principle of a bona fide acquisition of title to goods from a person who has no title[97] and the security holder is not protected by any rights that the security provider exercises over the secured asset as a result of his continued possession of the asset.

   In order for a third party transferee to acquire an asset bona fide, it must not only acquire the asset in good faith but as a general rule must also acquire possession of the asset.[98] A security provider who thus retains possession of the charged asset can, therefore, transfer title to a third party acting in good faith pursuant to Article 932(1) BGB, even though the security provider does not have legal title to the charged asset. However, if the third party only acquires constructive possession pursuant to Article 930 BGB, that is, the security provider remains in possession of the asset, then the third party does not obtain title in good faith, because such third party has not acquired direct possession, as is required pursuant to Article 932(1) BGB. If, on the other hand, the security provider subsequently hands over the asset to the third party, then such third party will acquire title, provided he was acting in good faith.

Security assignment

If the same receivables are assigned for security purposes more than once, then the assignment effected first in time will have priority over all subsequent assignments. This principle cannot be circumvented by a

---

[94] Article 880 BGB.   [95] Article 879(3) BGB.   [96] Compare Article 1209 BGB.
[97] Articles 932 ff BGB.   [98] Article 932 para 1 BGB.

transfer of the receivables in good faith, because a receivable cannot be acquired in good faith pursuant to German law.[99]

An exception does, however, apply as far as the relationship between a global assignment and an assignment of the proceeds of sale pursuant to an extended reservation of title is concerned. Although the principle of first in time also applies here, according to case law, the assignee of receivables pursuant to a global assignment must give priority to an assignment of the same receivables pursuant to an extended reservation of title, even if the latter assignment took place subsequent in time, otherwise the global assignment will be held to be invalid.[100] To give effect to this rule, the terms of the global assignment agreement must exclude receivables which are subject to an extended reservation of title from the assignment. It is not sufficient for the global assignment agreement to provide that the assignee will retransfer the receivables upon request to the security provider.[101] The courts, therefore, give a seller who sells goods to a purchaser subject to extended reservation of title priority over a lender of money.

A further exception exists in relation to the assignment of receivables in a true factoring transaction. Such an assignment would be valid, even if the receivables assigned to the factor had already previously been assigned as part of an extended reservation of title or global assignment to the seller of the goods or a bank. The courts are of the view that the authority granted to the purchaser/debtor to collect the assigned receivables, also encompasses the right to assign the receivables as part of a true factoring transaction. The reason is that the seller/bank will be in no worse position after the factor has made payment of the purchase price than if the underlying debtors had settled the receivables themselves.[102]

V. ENFORCEABILITY OF SECURITY IN THE EVENT OF INSOLVENCY OF THE SECURITY PROVIDER

The purpose of insolvency proceedings and the function of the administrator

The purpose of insolvency proceedings is to satisfy all the creditors of the debtor by realizing the debtor's assets and distributing the proceeds among the creditors or, instead of realizing the assets, to agree on an

---

[99] It should be noted, however, that rights which are incorporated in a deed, so that a transfer of title in the paper itself also transfers title in the incorporated right, can be subject to bona fide acquisition of such right pursuant to the rules of the bona fide acquisition of title to goods.   [100] BGHZ 55, 34, 35, 36; 72, 308, 310; 100, 353, 359.
[101] BGHZ 72, 308, 311.   [102] BGHZ 72, 20 ff; 82, 283 ff.

insolvency plan to maintain the business as a whole.[103] If insolvency proceedings are initiated, then the insolvency court will appoint an administrator (*Insolvenzverwalter*) to whom all rights of the debtor to administer and exercise rights over the assets will pass.[104] The administrator must comply with the provisions of the Insolvency Code and must ensure that all creditors are satisfied equally. Thus, it is not the function of the administrator to satisfy certain or individual groups of creditors, for example secured creditors, in precedence over others. Unlike other legal systems, German law does not recognize a receiver who can be appointed by a creditor to enforce his individual rights over the assets of the debtor.

An administrator appointed over the assets of the security provider will usually be confronted with the problem that all the debtor's assets are charged with security: the debtor's land will be encumbered with charges on property, his movable assets (for example, vehicle fleet or machines) as well as current assets (for example, goods in a warehouse) will have been transferred to the security holders, outstanding trade receivables will have been assigned as part of a global assignment or extended reservation of title. If this position remained as it is, the administrator could call it a day, because the debtor would have no assets at all. Administrators, however, are intent on increasing the assets of the liquidation fund of the insolvent security provider. This the administrator may be able to do by not only exercising rights of challenge granted to him pursuant to the German insolvency laws, but also by calling into question whether the security has been validly created.

Reasons for unenforceability

Invalidity

The administrator could, for instance, challenge a transfer of title for security purposes, because the assets which were transferred were not certain. He could challenge a security assignment by arguing that the receivables assigned are not determinable even after he has made considerable efforts to identify them from the debtor's books.

Over-collateralization

The taking of security is void pursuant to Article 138 BGB, if the taking of such security infringes the principle of good faith. This will be the case if the security agreement constricts the security provider to such an extent that he is no longer able to operate the whole or parts of his business

---

[103] Article 1 InsO.   [104] Article 80(1) InsO.

(*Knebelung*)[105] or if a security holder takes security with reckless disregard of the security interests of other creditors of the security provider. An example of the latter is, in particular, if the security holder takes security over all the assets of the security provider with the intention of deceiving or harming other creditors.[106] The fact that a security holder has taken security over all the assets of the security provider, with the result that other creditors have little chance of securing their debts, is insufficient *per se* for the transaction to be deemed to be a transaction against the principle of good faith.[107] However, a security contract will be against the principle of good faith and thus void pursuant to Article 138 BGB if from the onset there was over-collateralization.[108]

Capital-replacing shareholder loans

Pursuant to Article 32a(1) Limited Liability Companies Act (GmbHG), capital-replacing shareholder loans are subordinated to the rights of other creditors when a *Gesellschaft mit beschränkter Haftung* (GmbH, similar to a private limited company) becomes insolvent. Any security taken in connection with a capital-replacing shareholder loan can only be enforced to the same extent that the loan can be enforced.

Pursuant to the GmbHG, a capital-replacing loan is a loan which a shareholder grants to the company at a time when the shareholders as ordinary businessmen should have injected share capital into the company.[109] The courts have interpreted this provision by holding that a shareholder loan has a capital-replacing character if, at the time that the shareholder granted the loan, the company would not have been able to obtain credit from a third party at normal market conditions to cover the capital the company required in order for it to be able to continue its business activities.[110] It is not necessary in order for Article 32a GmbHG to apply that the shareholder granting the loan was aware that the loan would be characterized as a capital-replacing loan.

A loan, even if it could not have been regarded as a capital-replacing loan at the time it was granted, can become a capital-replacing loan if the shareholders do not demand repayment of the loan upon the company falling into financial difficulties.[111]

The rules governing equity-replacing loans do not apply to shareholders who hold 10 per cent or less of the capital of the company and at the same time are not directors of the company.[112] The rules are also not

---

[105] BGHZ 19, 12, 18; 138, 291, 303.   [106] BGHZ 138, 291, 299, 300.
[107] BGHZ 138, 291, 300.   [108] BGHZ 137, 212, 233; BGH in ZIP 1998, 684, 685.
[109] Article 32(1) GmbHG.   [110] BGHZ 76, 326, 330; 81, 252, 255.
[111] BGHZ 76, 326, 329; 105, 168, 185.   [112] Article 32a(3) sentence 2 GmbHG.

applicable if a lender acquires shares in a crisis-stricken company of more than 10 per cent for the purposes of rescuing the company; neither loans granted prior to an acquisition of shares by a third party lender nor thereafter will be subject to the rules on capital-replacing shareholder loans.[113]

Article 32a GmbHG only applies to a GmbH. The courts have, however, extended these rules with modifications to shareholders of an *Aktiengesellschaft* (AG, stock corporation), provided the shareholder granting the loan has a financing responsibility to the AG. This will only be the case if the shareholder holds more than 25 per cent (blocking minority) in the capital of the AG.[114]

Upstream security

Doubt has been expressed whether a company which has a stated share capital (*Kapitalgesellschaft*) can grant security for loans which its shareholders have borrowed against its assets (upstream security). This doubt is based on the capital preservation rules pursuant to which assets required to preserve the nominal capital of the company may not be paid out to the shareholders, and any shareholder who receives payment in breach of these provisions must repay the amount.[115]

The Federal Court of Justice settled this dispute in its judgment of 19 March 1998,[116] but only where the lender is neither a shareholder nor a director of the company granting the security. In this case, the Federal Court of Justice held that the capital preservation rules did not hinder the granting or realization of upstream security in these instances, because the capital preservation rules only applied to the directors and the shareholders of the company granting the security, and not to third parties.[117] The security will only be regarded as void pursuant to the general rules contained in Article 138(1) BGB, if the creditor wilfully colluded with the shareholders to the detriment of other creditors.[118] In relation to group financing, where typically the loan proceeds are distributed amongst the group companies, the bank will wish, as far as possible, for all the group companies to be liable for the loans granted.[119] Only when the lending bank can no longer ignore the fact that the group is near economic collapse, particularly if a planned rescue is unlikely to be successful, can a bank become liable to other creditors of the group companies pursuant to Article 826 BGB.[120] However, in this regard, the bank's legal position

---

[113] Article 32a(3) sentence 3 GmbHG.   [114] BGHZ 90, 381, 390, 391.

[115] Articles 30(1), 31 GmbHG with regard to the GmbH and Articles 57, 62 AktG with regard to the AG.   [116] BGHZ 138, 291.

[117] BGHZ 138, 291, 298.   [118] BGHZ 138, 291, 298, 299.   [119] BGHZ 138, 291, 301.

[120] BGHZ 138, 291, 301, 302.

is no different than its legal position would be with regard to non-group companies.[121]

Administrator's right of challenge

The administrator's right of challenge (Articles 129 ff Insolvency Code— InsO) is an instrument which the Insolvency Code has granted the administrator in order for the administrator to rescind legal transactions which are disadvantageous to the creditors.

If the challenge is successful, any asset which has been removed from the debtor's property must be returned to the liquidation fund.[122] If the recipient of the asset returns the asset to the liquidation fund, then his claim against the debtor is revived.[123] Any consideration that was paid by the recipient for the asset must be returned to the recipient, provided that such consideration is still identifiable or the liquidation fund has increased in value as a result.[124]

A legal transaction can be challenged if a creditor was granted security or repayment of his debt in the three months prior to the petition for the initiation of insolvency proceedings, the debtor at the time of the transaction was insolvent, and the creditor knew this.[125] Constructive notice where the creditor could have gained knowledge of the insolvency from the circumstances is treated as actual knowledge.[126] If a creditor received security or repayment of his debt at a time when such creditor had no right to such security or repayment, then this transaction can be challenged *per se*, if it was effected in the month preceding the petition for initiation of insolvency proceedings or effected thereafter.[127] If the transaction was effected in the second or third month prior to the petition for the initiation of insolvency proceedings, then the transaction can be challenged if the debtor was insolvent at the time the transaction was made.[128] Knowledge of the creditor of the insolvency is irrelevant in this case. A legal transaction can also be challenged if it was effected within the second or third month prior to the petition for initiation of insolvency proceedings, the debtor was not insolvent, but the creditor knew at the time of the transaction that the transaction would be disadvantageous to other creditors.[129]

If a person benefiting from a legal transaction is a connected person, then there is a presumption that such person had the requisite knowl-

---

[121] BGHZ 138, 291, 302. Article 826 BGB reads: 'Any person who wilfully causes damage to another in a manner which is against good morals, is obliged to compensate the other for such damage.'   [122] Article 143 InsO.
[123] Article 144(1) InsO.   [124] Article 144(2) InsO.   [125] Article 130(1) no 1 InsO.
[126] Article 130(2) InsO.   [127] Article 131(1) no 1 InsO.   [128] Article 131(1) no 2 InsO.
[129] Article 131(1) no 3 InsO.

edge for the purpose of the administrator's right of challenge.[130] If the debtor is a natural person, then connected persons are, *inter alia*, his/her spouse, close relatives of the debtor, as well as persons who cohabit with the debtor or cohabited with the debtor in the year prior to the transaction which is the subject matter of the administrator's challenge.[131] If the debtor is a legal entity, then connected persons are, *inter alia*, members of the debtor's board of directors and supervisory bodies, personally liable shareholders, and shareholders with more than a 25 per cent shareholding.[132]

Legal transactions entered into in the last ten years prior to the insolvency petition with the intent of disadvantaging the creditors can be challenged if the other party knew at the time of the transaction of the debtor's intent. This knowledge will be presumed if the other party knew that the debtor was threatened with insolvency and that the transaction would be disadvantageous to creditors.[133] Any contracts entered into with connected persons for consideration in the last two years prior to the insolvency petition can be challenged if the creditors are directly disadvantaged.[134]

Contracts entered into in the last four years prior to the insolvency petition for no consideration can also be challenged, provided that the subject matter of these contracts did not consist of *ad hoc* gifts of little value.[135]

Security granted in connection with a capital-replacing loan in the last ten years prior to the application for insolvency proceedings can also be challenged.[136] Payment of such a loan can also be challenged within the last year prior to the insolvency petition.[137]

Preferred debts

Essentially the only preferred debts which are recognized by the Insolvency Code are the costs of the insolvency procedure (which consist of the court costs as well as the remuneration payable to the administrator), any liabilities which have arisen as a result of transactions undertaken by the administrator, and liabilities arising out of contracts where the administrator elected performance.[138] All other preferred debts were abolished upon the Insolvency Code coming into force on 1 January 1999. In particular, liabilities owed to the tax authorities, social security contributions, and remuneration owed to employees are no longer preferred debts. Although liabilities that are preferred debts have to be satisfied first, this preferred right does not extend to validly created security.

---

[130] Articles 130(3), 131 para 2 InsO.   [131] Article 138(1) InsO.   [132] Article 138(2) InsO.
[133] Article 133(1) InsO.   [134] Article 133(2) InsO.   [135] Article 134 InsO.
[136] Article 135 no 1 InsO.   [137] Article 135 no 2 InsO.   [138] Articles 53, 54, 55 InsO.

Segregation and preferential treatment

The Insolvency Code distinguishes between two types of rights against an asset: rights which entitle the creditor to segregation (*Aussonderung*) and rights which entitle the creditor to preferential treatment (*Absonderung*).

Segregation means that the asset which is in the possession of the debtor/administrator does not belong to the insolvency fund. In this regard, the creditor is not to be regarded as the creditor of the insolvent debtor. Whether a creditor has a right to segregation of an asset is determined pursuant to acts which apply outside the insolvency proceedings.[139]

Preferential treatment means that the asset in which the security holder has a security interest will be realized and the proceeds of such realization will primarily be distributed to that security holder to settle the secured claim. Any excess amount is to be distributed to the liquidation fund. Creditors who only have the right to preferential treatment against an asset are creditors of the insolvency debtor and, therefore, are subject to the Insolvency Code.[140]

Effect of insolvency on individual security

Charges on land

Holders of charges on land (*Grundpfandrechte*) are entitled pursuant to the Act on Compulsory Public Auctions and Administrative Receivership to preferential treatment.[141] Notwithstanding these rights, the administrator is entitled to file an application for a public auction or administrative receivership with the competent court.[142]

Transfer of title for security purposes

Even though the holder of this type of security is the unconditional owner of the secured asset, he is only able to exercise his rights *in rem* within the scope of the security purpose. He, therefore, only has a right to repayment from the asset and, therefore, has no right of segregation, but a right to preferential treatment.[143]

If the administrator is in possession of the charged asset, then he is entitled to realize the asset by private sale.[144] Prior to the sale, however, he must inform the security holder of the condition of the asset and give the security holder the opportunity to determine whether there is a more

---

[139] Article 47 InsO.   [140] Articles 49 ff, 165 ff InsO.   [141] Article 49 InsO.
[142] Article 165 InsO.   [143] Article 51 no 1 InsO.   [144] Article 166(1) InsO.

favourable method for realizing the asset.[145] The security holder can also purchase the asset if this is more favourable.[146]

After the asset has been realized, the costs of determining and realizing the asset must be deducted from the realization proceeds prior to being paid to the security holder to offset his outstanding claims.[147] The cost of determining who has rights over the asset is fixed at 4 per cent of the realization proceeds and the cost of realizing the asset at 5 per cent of the realization proceeds, unless the realization costs were substantially less or more.[148]

If the administrator allows the security holder to realize the security, then the security holder must nevertheless pay the costs of determining the rights over the assets in the amount of 4 per cent of the realization proceeds to the insolvency fund.[149]

The administrator may also continue to use any charged asset in his possession for the business of the debtor. He must, however, compensate the security holder for the loss in value caused to the charged asset through such continued use by way of continuing payments, provided that the loss in value caused by the continued use impairs the security holder's security.[150] The right to use the security includes the right of the administrator to continue processing the asset, provided that the security holder's security is not impaired thereby.[151]

If the administrator is not entitled to realize the security (because such security is not in his possession), then the security must be realized by the security holder. The court can, however, order upon application by the administrator that the security holder realize the security within a certain period of time. After the expiry of such period, the administrator is entitled to realize the security.[152]

Security assignment

The security assignment also results in the security holder only having a preference right, notwithstanding the fact that the security holder has unrestricted ownership of the receivable. The security holder, therefore, has no right to segregation of the receivables.[153]

The administrator is entitled to collect the assigned receivables.[154] After the receivables have been collected, the costs of determining the rights over them and the costs of realization in the amount of 4 per cent and 5 per cent, respectively, have to be paid to the insolvency fund, before the realization proceeds are paid over to the security holder.[155]

[145] Articles 167(1), 168(2) InsO.   [146] Article 168(3) InsO.   [147] Article 170(1) InsO.
[148] Article 171 InsO.   [149] Article 170(2) InsO.   [150] Article 172(1) InsO.
[151] Article 172(2) InsO.   [152] Article 173(2) InsO.   [153] Article 51 no 1 InsO.
[154] Article 166(2) InsO.   [155] Articles 170(1), 171 InsO.

Reservation of title

A purchase agreement pursuant to which goods were sold subject to a reservation of title is a pending contract as long as the condition precedent of payment of the purchase price has not been fulfilled. The contract is pending, because the debtor/purchaser has not fully paid the purchase price and the seller has not transferred title in the asset to the purchaser.

The administrator, therefore, has a right to demand performance of the purchase agreement.[156] If he does so, the seller's outstanding claim for the purchase price has priority over insolvency claims.[157] The seller can require the administrator to decide whether he wishes to demand performance. As a general rule, the administrator must inform the seller of his decision without delay after receipt of the seller's request. If the administrator does not make a decision without delay, he is no longer entitled to demand performance of the contract.[158] In relation to goods subject to a reservation of title, however, the administrator only has to inform the seller of his decision after the Reporting Meeting (*Berichtstermin*)[159] where he reports as to the financial condition of the debtor and the prospects of continuing the debtor's business operation, and at which the creditors subsequently decide whether to wind up or to continue the debtor's business operations. The purpose of this rule is to ensure that, if the administrator who is endeavouring to maintain the undertaking as a viable concern elects to perform the purchase agreement, the creditors at the reporting meeting may decide instead to liquidate the company.[160] In such a case, performance of the purchase agreement would be economically pointless.

If the administrator decides not to perform the purchase agreement, then the debtor's contingency right expires. The seller can demand repossession of the goods. To this extent, he has a right of segregation. This right of segregation does not, however, extend to proceeds of sale owed by a third party to the debtor from the on-sale of the seller's assets pursuant to an extended reservation of title. The assignment of the proceeds of sale only entitles the security holder to preferential treatment.[161]

Leasing

The lessor is the unrestricted owner of the leased object. He is, therefore, entitled to a right of segregation should the lessee become insolvent.

---

[156] Article 103(1) InsO.   [157] Article 55(1) no 2 InsO.   [158] Article 103(2) sentence 2 InsO.
[159] Article 107(2) InsO.
[160] Balthasar in Nerlich/Römermann, *Insolvenzordnung*, Article 107, annotation 4.
[161] Andres in Nerlich/Römermann, *Insolvenzordnung*, Article 47, annotation 23. Different view Sinz, *Factoring in der Insolvenz*, 111: the factor has a right of segregation.

The lessor, however, only acquires such a right if he acts in accordance with generally applicable law.[162] This means that the lessor can only demand repossession of the leased object from the administrator if he has terminated the lease agreement and has thus revoked the debtor's right of possession to the leased asset. Pursuant to the provisions of the BGB, the lessor is entitled to terminate the lease agreement with immediate effect, if the lessee is in default with two consecutive lease instalment payments.[163] It should, however, be noted in this context that a lease agreement can no longer be terminated for default in payment after a petition for the initiation of insolvency proceedings has been initiated over the assets of the lessee, if the default occurred prior to the petition.[164] This does not apply if, after the application for the initiation of insolvency proceedings has been made, the lessee again defaults in payment of due lease instalments in an amount which would entitle the lessor to terminate the lease agreement for good cause.

Likewise, a lease agreement, after the insolvency application has been made, cannot be terminated on the ground that the lessee's financial standing has deteriorated.[165]

If the lessor is not able to terminate the lease agreement by reason of the above termination rules, then the leased object must remain in the possession of the debtor/administrator. The administrator has a choice as to whether to continue to perform the lease agreement or terminate it.[166] Again, the lessor has the right to demand that the administrator makes a choice without delay.[167] The rule that applies to reservations of title, namely that the administrator need not make his election until after the reporting meeting, does not apply to leased objects, unless the agreement is a hire purchase agreement, whereby the lessee acquires title in the leased object through payment of the hire purchase instalments.

Factoring

In relation to true factoring, the factor has become the unconditional owner of the receivable.[168] Thus, the receivables do not belong to the insolvency fund of the insolvent seller of the receivables. The administrator is not entitled on the factor's behalf to collect the receivables sold to the factor.

In relation to untrue factoring, on the other hand, which is treated as a loan, the sold receivables are treated as if they are security. The factor,

---

[162] Article 47 InsO.   [163] Article 554(1) BGB.   [164] Article 112 no 1 InsO.
[165] Article 112 no 2 InsO.   [166] Article 103(1) InsO.   [167] Article 103(2) sentence 2 InsO.
[168] See above discussion.

therefore, only has a preference right in relation to them.[169] The administrator is, therefore, entitled to collect the receivables sold to the factor pursuant to the rules which apply to the security assignment.

VI. COMPULSORY ENFORCEMENT BY THE SECURITY HOLDER OF ITS SECURITY

The above outline has so far only dealt with the rights that a security holder is entitled to against the security provider or the administrator against the assets of the security provider. A different question is how these rights can be enforced if the participation of the security provider is required.

In principle, for many security interests the question of a participation of the security provider does not arise. If the security is a charge on land, the security holder simply files an application for enforcement of the security in the competent local court. If goods are pledged, the pledgee is already in possession of the goods and can sell them by public auction. If the security holder has obtained a security assignment then the security holder simply discloses the assignment of receivables to the account debtors and demands payment from them. Therefore, the question of participation of the security provider only arises if the security provider refuses to hand over the charged assets in his possession or if he does not allow the security holder access to the property in order to pick up the goods.

The basic rule is that nobody is entitled to enforce his rights through force. Only the State has the power to exercise such rights through its enforcement agencies. However, the State enforcement agencies can only act if the creditor has obtained an 'enforcement title'.[170] Such an enforcement title is usually a court judgment.[171] It can also be, for example, a notarial deed where the debtor has agreed that the security taken should be subject to immediate enforcement action.[172] The security holder must, therefore, often take legal proceedings if the security provider has to be compelled to participate in the enforcement.

Obtaining a court judgment, for example, as to whether a lessee has to redeliver a leased object to the lessor, takes several months. The debtor can also protract proceedings by alleging false facts. The German Civil Code of Procedure (Articles 916 ff ZPO) does provide for expedited proceedings, where an order can be obtained in a number of hours. However,

---

[169] Andres in Nerlich/Römermann, *Insolvenzordnung*, Article 47, annotation 30.
[170] Articles 704, 794 ZPO.   [171] Article 704 ZPO.   [172] Articles 704, 794(1) no 5 ZPO.

such proceedings are only permissible if there is a special reason for them. The fact that the security provider is obviously defaulting in his obligations is not sufficient. Instead, the security holder has to show that there is particular urgency, for example, that there is good cause to believe that the security provider will remove the assets outside the jurisdiction of the court or that the security will drastically deteriorate in value, if proceedings are not expedited.

PART 3

Security in Private International Law

7

English Conflicts Rules for Transfers of Movables: A Contract-based Approach?

PROFESSOR MICHAEL BRIDGE

(Professor of Law, University College London; Director of Research, Norton Rose, London)

I. INTRODUCTION

It is now established beyond recall in developed legal systems that contracting parties are free to choose the law applicable to their contract. The importance of this development cannot be underestimated. It permits the project financier and its advisers to plan a complex transaction and to assess legal risk by reference to a chosen and transaction-friendly legal system. This principle of party autonomy is a long-standing feature of English law, though formerly subject to a limitation of uncertain scope that the choice be *'bona fide* and legal'.[1] In an apparent response to this limitation, a prominent feature of certain standard form commodities contracts providing for the application of English law is a clause deeming that the contract has been concluded in England and has been performed in England.[2] This second element especially is palpably fictitious in the case of the great majority of modern contracts entered into on the basis of those standard forms.

The above limitation, laid down by the Privy Council in a case concerning the application of the Hague Rules on carriers' liability, is not repeated in those same terms in the Rome Convention on the Law Applicable to Contractual Obligations.[3] The Convention, nevertheless, provides for deference to the mandatory terms of the forum state and of closely connected foreign legal systems notwithstanding the choice of another country's law to govern the contract.[4]

Autonomy, however, is not present in the case of property matters where the *lex situs* plays a dominant but not altogether unchallenged role. The absence of autonomy in property matters inhibits transactions in that it limits the prospects of avoiding legal risk. There is also a degree of uncertainty surrounding the applicable choice of law rule in respect of

---

[1] *Vita Foods Products Inc v Unus Shipping Co Ltd* [1939] AC 277.
[2] Form 100 of the Grain and Feed Trade Association (cl 31: the 'domicile' clause).
[3] Article 3(1).
[4] Articles 7 and 3(3). The UK entered a reservation to Art 7(1) pursuant to Art 22(1)(a): see the Contracts (Applicable Law) Act 1990, s 2(2).

some types of property which affects the quantification of legal risk. Furthermore, and especially in the case of intangible property like book debts, uncertainty is compounded by the difficulty of drawing the line between contract and property issues. It is hard enough to do in English domestic law without being complicated further by issues of characterization in private international law. In this chapter I shall argue, taking advantage of the paucity of case law, that the dividing line in matters of movable property between contract and property should be drawn as far as reasonably possible in favour of contract. The justification for this approach is that it encourages the conclusion of contracts and the taking of risk and is therefore conducive to productive exchange.

How then does the lawyer respond to the above uncertainties? First of all, assuming that the *lex situs* applies, in the case of certain types of asset such as ships and aircraft, where the *situs* may be[5] the place of registration, the cause of autonomy is served by registering the ship or aircraft in a transaction-friendly jurisdiction. Secondly, rights in certain assets can be transformed into derivative rights. Instead of dealing with a book debt, parties may deal instead with a bill of exchange that can be negotiated in a jurisdiction of choice. Assets can be transferred to a bankruptcy-remote vehicle located in a preferred jurisdiction and issuing bonds or other commercial paper. In the case of shares, share certificates or global notes can be issued and lodged with a depositary with derivative rights being held at successive intervals by those dealing with the depositary, and those dealing with them in turn.

Not all assets, however, can be possibly or practicably 'relocated' in this way. This explains the attraction of uniform law as sponsored by the Rome Institute for the Unification of Private Law and the United Nations Commission on Uniform Trade Law, which bypasses the private international legal process so far as it relates to choice of law.[6] In a large federal state like the United States, where the great bulk of private international law issues are internal, the evidence of uniform legal activity testifies eloquently to the superior attractions of uniform law. Nevertheless, uniform law is one thing in a unitary state; it is an altogether less predictable creature when taking in divergent legal systems with different legal traditions. It is also a particularly distant prospect, especially when it takes place outside a federal state. Lawyers and financiers cannot suspend dealings until uniform law arrives. They have to work within the present

---

[5] L Collins (ed), *Dicey and Morris on the Conflict of Laws* (London: Sweet & Maxwell, 13th edn, 2000) cites as exceptions to the rule that movables are situate where they are at a given time (Rule 112) ships and aircraft which are situate in the port of registry (ships) and country of registration (aircraft) but, somewhat disconcertingly, only 'at some times'.

[6] It does not of course bypass rules dealing with jurisdiction and recognition and enforcement of judgments.

system, which means that they have to come to terms with a particularly underdeveloped branch of private international law, namely, the choice of law rules for tangible and intangible movables.

II. *SITUS* OF PROPERTY

The *lex situs* exercises a powerful attraction in matters relating to land. Since land does not migrate, it remains firmly within the physical control of the legal system of the country in which it is located. The effectiveness of the local law is matched by the impotence of any foreign law seeking independently of that local law to regulate its use and disposal. That is why English courts will not take jurisdiction in matters concerning title to or the right to possession of foreign land,[7] though for *in personam* matters they will take jurisdiction in actions concerning foreign land,[8] and why the rule is that property issues concerning land fall to be disposed of according to the *lex situs*, including its conflicts rules. Again, this explains why the applicable law for a contract dealing with rights in immovable property is presumptively the *lex situs*, in the absence of any express choice by the parties.[9] It is probably too the reason why English law, in matters of private international law, does not distinguish, as it does domestically, between real and personal property, but between immovables and movables.[10] Any insistence that a leasehold interest in land is personalty and therefore, possibly, subject to a law other than the *lex situs* would necessarily fail in the face of an adamantine law belonging to the majority of legal systems organized around the division between immovables and movables.

Other types of property, namely tangible and intangible movables, do migrate, so the hold of the *lex situs* is less effective. The *situs* of tangible movables is simply the place where they happen to be from time to time, with the possible exception of registered ships and aircraft.[11] In the case of pure, as opposed to documentary, intangibles, it is peculiarly difficult even to identify the *situs* of the property. According to Dicey and Morris, the *situs* of a chose in action[12] is the country where it is properly recoverable or enforceable.[13] This is of course a fiction in that it attributes 'to airy

---

[7] Section 30(1) of the Civil Jurisdiction and Judgments Act 1982. For the position at common law, see *Hesperides Hotels Ltd v Aegean Turkish Holdings Ltd* [1978] QB 215, on appeal *sub nom Hesperides Hotels Ltd v Muftizade* [1979] AC 508.

[8] *Penn v Lord Baltimore* (1750) 1 Ves Sen 444.

[9] Rome Convention on the Law Applicable to Contractual Obligations, Art 4(3).

[10] *Re Berchtold* [1923] 1 Ch 192.   [11] See above.

[12] An expression the authors prefer, despite its domestic connotations, to intangible movables.   [13] Rule 112(1).

nothing a local habitation'. The location of a chose in action will therefore depend upon its particular type. Debts, for example, are considered to exist in the place where the debtor resides.[14] This rule has the benefit of providing constancy, which would not be accorded by a rule, matching English domestic law, that a debt is repayable at the creditor's residence or wherever directed by the contract giving rise to the debt[15] and is therefore located in that place. The rule also suits asset financiers who have freedom, depending upon other considerations arising out of the deal such as tax liability, to organize the incorporation of the debtor, if a special purpose vehicle is desired, in a jurisdiction of choice.

The location of the *situs* is not the only difficulty arising from the private international law treatment of intangible property. The very nature of this type of property renders the drawing of a line between matters of contract and of property acutely difficult. Given this difficulty and the artificiality of ascribing a *situs* to intangible property, there is no case for blindly following the treatment of immovable property and applying the *lex situs*. The principle of effectiveness, in any case, as imposing as it may be in the case of immovables, is not advanced by an application of the *lex situs* to tangible and intangible movables. Any justification for applying the *lex situs* to such items of property has to be found elsewhere. Yet the application of the *lex situs* to immovables seems to raise a presumption of its applicability to other forms of property that is difficult to rebut in the absence of a clear-cut alternative which may be hard to find.

III. CHOICE OF LAW AND TANGIBLE MOVABLES

The authorities on the *lex situs*

The rule that the transfer of property rights in tangible movables is determined by the *lex situs* is authoritatively established in English law. In *Cammell v Sewell*,[16] a Prussian ship carrying a cargo of deals from the Russian port of Onega to Hull struck certain rocks off the Norwegian coast. The consignees of the deals gave notice of abandonment to their underwriters, the plaintiffs, who paid as for a total loss, the effect of which was to invest the underwriters with title to the deals. Despite the protests of the underwriters, the deals were sold at auction in Norway by the ship's master pursuant to Norwegian judicial proceedings. The pur-

---

[14] *New York Life Insurance Co v Public Trustee* [1924] 2 Ch 101. For the case of corporations with more than one place of residence, see *Jabbour v Custodian of Israeli Absentee Property* [1954] 1 WLR 139.

[15] See *Joachimson v Swiss Bank Corpn* [1921] 3 KB 110. Debts, after all, may be assigned.

[16] (1858) 3 H & N 617, affd (1860) 5 H & N 728 (Cam Sc).

chaser, who happened to be the British Vice-Consul, then forwarded the deals to the defendants in London, who had made advances upon them and who were 'defending the present action upon [the purchaser's] right and title'. By Norwegian law, the sale by the master passed a good title to the purchaser. By English law, there was no necessity justifying the sale with the result that title remained in the underwriters.

The decision of the Exchequer Chamber supports the following propositions. First, it was a matter for Norwegian law, the law of the country in which the goods were at the time of the sale, to determine whether title passed to the purchaser. In reaching this conclusion, the court in effect rejected the maxim that personal property has no location and that its disposal, as is the case with testamentary succession, should be determined by the owner's personal law. The court also rejected the view that the issue of title should be referred to the personal law of the consignee. Taking the case of a general ship with consignees in different countries, purchasers in the country where the sale takes place could be assured of no secure title if, on the sale of the entire cargo, different laws had to be consulted to determine the proprietary effect of the transfer as it related to different parts of that cargo. The law of the ship's flag was also rejected.[17] Furthermore, it made no difference that the presence of the goods in Norway was accidental and not consented to by the owner. Although much of the discussion of Norwegian law centred on the question whether the master had authority to sell the deals despite the absence of necessity, it is plain that the majority concluded that title passed under Norwegian law to the purchaser on the judicial sale.[18]

The second proposition flowing from the decision was that a property interest vesting in the purchaser under Norwegian law was not divested by the subsequent bringing of the deals into England. This is but a corollary to the first proposition but it testifies to the court's sense of comity. There was a keen awareness that the transfer of title to property arising out of a domestic sale in England, whether because that sale took place in market overt or was conducted by a landlord pursuant to a distress, could have an expropriating effect on the true owner just as much as the Norwegian sale in the present case. Subject to one reservation, *Camell v Sewell* is strong authority for the proposition that title can pass under the *lex situs* of movables so as to defeat the title of the true owner, even though the presence of the movables in the *situs* country is accidental, and that this title will be recognized in England. The case makes no claims for the private international rules of other states. The reservation

---

[17] (1860) 5 H & N 728, 747 (Cockburn CJ).
[18] (1860) 5 H & N 728, 746 (Crompton J and Cockburn CJ). Of the six members of the court, Byles J dissented.

expressed in the case concerns the bona fides of the purchaser who, it was assumed, did not know that the sale was carried out by the master without the owner's authority.[19]

The decision in *Cammell v Sewell* was followed in *Winkworth v Christie Manson & Woods Ltd*,[20] where certain Japanese works of art, stolen in England, found themselves the subject of a sale in Italy to the second defendant before being brought back to England. There is little in the facts to distinguish the case from *Cammell v Sewell* but the application of the earlier authority to the case of a stolen painting returned to England shows the strength of the court's commitment to the *lex situs* rule as well as its reluctance to introduce a public policy exception of uncertain scope. No special tenderness was to be shown to British subjects and the court would not rule on the supposed superiority of English rules over Italian rules. The plaintiff sought a declaration that the works of art had at all times been his property, which depended upon whether he could demonstrate a right to their immediate possession. This in turn prompted a preliminary issue to be tried, namely, whether English domestic law or Italian domestic law applied to the sale in Italy. By English law, the second defendant would most probably not have acquired title to the works of art. For the purpose of the present proceedings, the court was prepared to assume that under Italian law he would have done so.

The plaintiff's attempt to distinguish the rule in *Cammell v Sewell* centred on the argument that it should not be applied to goods removed from country A and returned to A after a divesting transaction in country B,[21] on the ground the principle of security of titles demanded an exception to the rule of the *lex situs* so that country A could protect title recognized under its own laws.[22] The court regarded this as the plaintiff's strongest point but nevertheless concluded that security of title was just as important to the innocent purchaser in country B and stated in strong terms that commercial convenience demanded the application of the *lex situs* rule to proprietary rights in movables. Commercial certainty would be sacrificed if qualifying factors of the type mentioned by the plaintiff were

---

[19] (1860) 5 H & N 728, 743 (Crompton J).

[20] [1980] Ch 496. The same approach was also taken in the Scots case of *Todd v Armour* (1882) 9 R (Ct of Session) 901 (title to goods, stolen in Ireland and acquired by a purchaser in Ireland, could not have been acquired under similar circumstances under Scots law). In *City of Gotha v Sotheby's* (High Court, 9 September 1998), it was agreed between the parties that the transfer of title to a painting was governed by the *lex situs* at the time of the transfer (subject to five exceptions, listed below, none of which was relevant on the facts).

[21] The case as phrased avoids any reference to England, no doubt to avoid the taint of nationalism.

[22] Logically, there is little reason to distinguish this case from the following: goods are removed from country A, taken to country B, where the purchaser acquires an overriding title, and then brought to country C, neither A nor C in their domestic laws recognizing an overriding title in these circumstances.

to be added to the *lex situs* rule. There is also the argument that additional factors, such as the previous presence of the movables in country A, might be unknown and unknowable to the purchaser in country B. The plaintiff's further point that the principle of effectiveness would not be sacrificed if the goods were back in country A at the time of adjudication foundered when set against the above considerations. In this regard, it is noteworthy that the doctrine of renvoi, understandably absent from *Cammell v Sewell*, receives no mention in the *Winkworth* case and was indeed excluded under the terms of the preliminary issue. Furthermore, the lack of emphasis attaching to the effectiveness principle may turn out to have significance in cases going beyond *Winkworth* itself. Finally, the absence of a voluntary act on the part of the owner to connect the goods to country B, even the 'surreptitious' removal by someone else of the goods to country B, was no reason to depart from the rule in *Cammell v Sewell*.

The last point to consider arising out of the *Winkworth* case was the court's assertion that the rule in *Cammell v Sewell* was 'not likely to be applied' in any of five exceptional cases mentioned in the course of the proceedings. These five cases appear by implication to be a comprehensive list. In the order they appear, they are as follows. First, the goods are in transit and their *situs* is either 'casual' or 'not known'.[23] Now, 'casual' cannot mean 'accidental' or else it absorbs the case of *Cammell v Sewell* itself. It might mean that the goods are just passing through a jurisdiction without ever coming to rest. Conceivably, it might embrace a transaction between parties who are not in the country of the *lex situs* at the time of the transaction and who do not order their affairs by reference to or in reliance upon the *lex situs*. Secondly, the purchaser has not acted bona fide. If the purchaser acquires good title under the laws of country B, it is difficult to see any reason for permitting an exception along these lines, if the case falls short of the limited scope given to English public policy,[24] which is the third exception. The fourth exception concerned statutory provisions of the forum state that are expressed to apply in terms that depart from the forum's own choice of law rules, a necessary qualification to any authoritative statement of choice of law rules. Fifthly, there were special rules dealing with general assignments of movables arising on bankruptcy[25] or succession. In such cases, there are factors at stake other than the inconvenience of having multiple *leges situum*, which in

[23] Applying an exception put forward in the 9th edition of *Dicey and Morris on the Conflict of Laws*, n 5 above.

[24] Something in the order of a 'monstrous' *lex situs* would be called for, in the light of the court's reference to Crompton J's judgment in *Cammell v Sewell*: [1980] Ch 496, 504.

[25] For convenience, bankruptcy refers herein both to individual and corporate insolvency unless the two are being distinguished.

itself may be a reason for departing from the *lex situs* in the case of complex, voluntary, and *inter vivos* transfers of movables.

The claims of the *lex loci actus*?

A case has been made for the application of the *lex loci actus* to title dealings involving shares,[26] though it does not command general support. Instead, the settled position is that title matters are dealt with by the law of the place of incorporation.[27] Of these two laws, the *lex loci actus* alone is capable of being applied to the transfer of title to movables, but it has attracted no appreciable support in modern times. Its superiority over the *lex situs* as the governing law is not easy to see. Just as the *lex loci contractus* has latterly lost all support as the law applicable to the contract—it may be accidental and have no material connection with the performance of the contract—there seems no good reason for advocating a role for the *lex loci actus* in matters of title transfer to movables.

There is also a further objection. If the *lex loci actus* were to rule, this would encourage dealings in movables in countries giving little protection to a vested title and would impose few practical constraints on transactions being artificially situated in such countries. At this point, the domestic concerns of English law in respect of title transfer cannot be clearly detached from its selection of a choice of law rule. In view of its physical attachment to the goods, the *lex situs* rule holds out some hope for an owner seeking to track down stolen goods. Moreover, to move towards the *lex loci actus*, which would facilitate the laundering of title, at a time when title protection has been strengthened in domestic English law with the abolition of the market overt exception to the rule of *nemo dat quod non habet*,[28] would run counter to the flow of legislative policy.

Transfer of title and passing of property distinguished

The above discussion deals only with the classic dispute of a third party purchaser and an owner brought into conflict by an intermediate rogue or innocent wrongdoer. In domestic English law, this is the province of the rule of *nemo dat quod non habet* together with its various exceptions. Consequently, case law supporting the *lex situs* to title transfer does not respond to the problems facing asset financiers since the case law says nothing about the effect of bankruptcy on the ownership of tangible movables and, whilst capable of being applied to the case of a secured creditor standing in for the third party purchaser, was not formulated with

---

[26] *MacMillan Inc v Bishopsgate Investment Trust Plc (No 3)* [1995] 1 WLR 978, 994ff (Millett J).
[27] [1996] 1 WLR 387.   [28] By the Sale of Goods (Amendment) Act 1994.

secured credit in mind. The private international law of property transfer suffers from a lack of critical mass. There are insufficient authorities to goad it into a sophisticated analysis of what constitutes a property issue and whether it is appropriate that the *lex situs* dispose of all of these issues. In particular, before bankruptcy and security are considered, it should first be asked whether a distinction should be drawn between two-party cases and three-party cases. By a two-party case, I mean that the only involved parties are the grantor and grantee of the property interest, whether it be ownership or possession. There will almost always be a contract in existence between them. By a three-party case, I mean that a title dispute has erupted between the third party and one of the two original parties to a transaction involving the transfer of a property interest.

This distinction between two-party and three-party cases is not made in Dicey and Morris, the discussion in which is heavily concentrated on three-party, title transfer problems. This is because title transfer is the area where the authorities, largely Canadian and dealing with cars taken from one province to another, are overwhelmingly to be found.[29] Rule 116 subjects the validity of a 'transfer' of tangible things to the *lex situs* of the thing at the time of transfer. The word transfer is not defined, but it is not phrased only in terms of three-party cases and indeed is capable of extending to two-party cases. For example, Dicey and Morris asserts that, as between seller and buyer, the *lex situs* determines whether the property can pass with or without delivery.[30] Again, support for Rule 116 is proffered in the form of *Inglis v Usherwood*,[31] where a right of stoppage in transit, effective under the local (Russian) law where the goods happened to be when the notice was issued, was recognized in England, where the goods were later discharged, even though the right of stoppage would not have existed on the facts under English law.[32] Nothing in the case, however, identified the law applicable to the contract. This could well have been Russian law since delivery of the goods took place when they were loaded on board ship in the Russian port of Onega. Lord Kenyon refers to this being 'a transaction in a foreign country' and Grose J says that 'delivery here was made in Russia'. Although Russian law was applied, there is nothing in the various judgments to signify that it was applied as the *lex situs*.

A less easy case to distinguish is *Hardwick Game Farm v Suffolk Agricultural Poultry Producers Association*,[33] where the court had to consider if a particular

---

[29] The distinction is, however, to be found in the Hague Convention sur la loi applicable au transfert de la propriété en cas de vente à caractère international d'objets mobiliers corporels (15 April 1958), discussed below.   [30] Note 5 above at p 965.
[31] (1801) 1 East 515.
[32] Because the goods had been delivered to a ship chartered by the consignee.
[33] [1966] 1 WLR 287.

statute[34] applied to goods imported into the United Kingdom under CIF contracts. In considering this issue, Diplock LJ, drawing upon earlier Court of Appeal authority,[35] stated that all sales of goods take place where the goods are located at the time when the property in them passes from seller to buyer.[36] In the course of rejecting the view that the sale took place at the point where documents were taken up by the buyer, he gave his opinion that the property in specific goods could not pass at the contract date in accordance with the English rule if the goods were situate in Germany and German law required delivery for the property to pass. In the words of Diplock LJ: 'This can only be because the property passes at the place where the goods themselves are.'[37] Now, these observations on the passing of property do not form part of the ratio of the case. In any case, to say that a sale takes place *where* the goods are located at the time of sale does not, in and of itself, say anything about the law that determines *whether* and *when* a sale has occurred.

If it is logically possible for English law, as the law applicable to the contract, to determine that a sale of goods occurs at a time when the goods are situate in a foreign jurisdiction, it is useful to develop the distinction between two-party and three-party title cases in the context. The United Kingdom Sale of Goods Act lays down a series of rules concerning the passing of the property (the general property or ownership) in goods from seller to buyer.[38] Pursuant to a contract of sale, the seller has a duty to transfer the general property to the buyer.[39] The performance of this duty takes place in accordance with the dominant rule that the intention of the parties settles the time when the property passes, subject to the overriding rule that, in the case of goods sold as unascertained goods, the property cannot in law pass before they become ascertained. Where no intention is expressed, a series of presumptive rules lays down the time when property passes for different cases. No separate formality or act is prescribed to mark the point when the contract to sell becomes a sale (or conveyance). So stated, the passing of property is so closely connected to performance of the contract that it would seem entirely artificial to subject it to some law, other than the governing law of the contract, such as the *lex situs* of the goods.

---

[34] The Fertilisers and Feeding Stuffs Act 1926.
[35] *CEB Draper & Son Ltd v Edward Turner & Son Ltd* [1965] 1 QB 424.
[36] [1966] 1 WLR 287, 328.   [37] [1966] 1 WLR 287, 330.
[38] Sections 16–19, 20A–B. See MG Bridge, *The Sale of Goods* (Oxford: Clarendon Press, 1997), ch 3.
[39] The Act does not say this in so many words but a seller who insists on reserving the right of disposal despite having been paid and having no legitimate reason not to pass the general property to the buyer would be acting in breach of contract. This duty of the seller is distinct from the undertaking the seller gives (under s 12(1) of the Act) that he has a right to sell the goods for that provision relates, principally, to the strength of the seller's title.

The consequence of this, it is submitted, is that, as between buyer and seller, the effect of a reservation of title clause should as a matter of principle depend upon the applicable law of the contract.[40] If that law, for example, permits simple reservation of title clauses without registration, the clause should be effective even if the goods are situate in a jurisdiction whose law demands registration if the clause is not to be void. This solution avoids complications arising out of any movement of the goods between the contract date and the delivery date, for, if the *lex situs* were to govern, it would have to be determined whether it was the *lex situs* at the contract date or the *lex situs* at the date of delivery. And if the *lex situs* were to be consulted, another difficult question would turn upon the character of the rule laid down by that law. For example, a rule to the effect that a reservation of title clause is ineffectual unless it is registered would seem to encroach upon the domain of the law applicable to the contract; a rule stating that property passes upon delivery unless it is reserved by the seller in a particular way that demands registration has a more proprietary flavour.

If the law applicable to the contract properly governs the effect of a reservation of title clause, the next question concerns the consequences of the buyer's insolvency. Suppose that there are only two relevant laws to consider: first, the law applicable to the contract, and secondly, the law of the insolvent's residence where the goods are also located. Furthermore, the latter law is English law. According to the Insolvency Act 1986, the estate of a bankrupt vests automatically in his trustee in bankruptcy at the date the latter's appointment takes effect.[41] The bankrupt's estate is defined as 'all property belonging to or vested in the bankrupt' at the date the bankruptcy commences[42] and property 'includes . . . every description of property wherever situated'.[43] In the case of company liquidations, the property of the company does not vest in the liquidator but a liquidator in a compulsory winding-up may apply for a vesting order,[44] though such liquidators rarely do so. A liquidator's statutory powers to deal with property[45] are normally adequate for his purposes. According to English domestic law, the trustee or liquidator stands in for the insolvent party and is the means by which his assets are distributed to his creditors. His conscience is burdened in the same way as the insolvent's in respect of

---

[40] Some concession in favour of the law applicable to the contract, away from Scots law as the *lex situs*, is to be found in the Scots case of *Zahnrad Passau Fabrik GmbH v Terex Ltd* 1986 SLT 84. Under the Vienna Convention on the International Sale of Goods 1980, which in its treatment of sales contracts excludes 'the effect which the contract may have on the property in the goods sold' (Art 4(b)), it may be possible to run the same argument that two- and three-party issues are distinguishable since the seller is required under the Convention to transfer the property in the goods 'as required by the contract *and this Convention*' (Art 30) (emphasis added).   [41] Section 306.

[42] Sections 283(1), 385.   [43] Section 436.   [44] Insolvency Act 1986, s 145.

[45] Schedule 4 to the Insolvency Act 1986.

the latter's prior dealings.[46] If a vesting does occur, it should not be regarded in the same way as a disposition by the insolvent to an innocent third party purchaser: the trustee and liquidator are not purchasers.

Now, if English law were to apply a rule that the effect of a simple reservation of title clause depends upon the law applicable to the contract, none of the above should compromise the validity and effect of that clause. Suppose, however, that the goods are located at the time the insolvency regime comes into play in a jurisdiction that provides that the insolvent's assets vest in the trustee or liquidator, as the case may be, and that the property in goods the subject of a contract of sale vests in the buyer on delivery unless the seller registers a reservation of title clause. It is submitted here that the result should be the same if English law refers the issue of reservation to the law applicable to the contract. In this area of law it can be very difficult indeed to define the respective provinces of domestic law and foreign law selected through the choice of law process. An English court, guided by its approach in domestic cases, is likely to decline to treat foreign liquidators and trustees as purchasers.

Hague Convention sur la loi applicable au transfert de la propriété en cas de vente à caractère international d'objets mobiliers corporels (15 April 1958)

The contractual approach to title acquisition and reservation gains support from a 1958 Hague Convention dealing with the transfer of proprietary rights in tangible movables by way of sale. This Convention, which has received singularly little support,[47] distinguishes between the two-party transfer of property rights *inter partes* and the acquisition by third parties of rights in the subject matter of the sale transaction.[48] It also deals with the time when the seller's rights to the 'products and fruits of the things sold' are determined.[49] On the basis of the scheme of the Convention, this expression appears to be synonymous with the passing of the seller's property rights to the buyer.

Elsewhere in the Convention, however, the position of the third party is set out. According to Article 3, as against all persons other than parties to the contract, the transfer of property rights to the buyer is governed by the 'internal law' of the country where the movables are situate at the time of the claim to them being made by the third party.[50] To this rule

---

[46] *McEntire v Crossley Bros* [1895] AC 457, 461; *Madell v Thomas* [1891] 2 QB 230, 238.

[47] With the signature of only Greece and Italy, and the accession of only the latter, the Convention is not in force and is never likely to come into force.   [48] Articles 2–3.

[49] Article 2(1).

[50] Article 3(1): 'la loi interne du pays où sont situés les objets vendus au moment où se produit une reclamation les concernant'.

there is an exception within Article 3 itself: a buyer will retain property rights recognized by the internal law of any country where the movables were previously situate.[51] This is not a conventional application of the *lex situs*: it does not look to the law of the place where the movables were situate at the time of the propietary transaction under review.

Article 3, which supports the law of the place where the movables were situate at the time of the third party's claim, is itself subject to Articles 4–5. According to Article 4, the rights of an unpaid seller, either arising out of an action to avoid the contract[52] or a reservation of title clause, are determined by the internal law of the country where the movables are situate at the time of the first claim or execution against them.[53] Unlike Article 3, Article 4 contains no internal exception dealing with the seller's rights being recognized by the law of any country where the movables were previously situate. Article 5 provides that a conflict between the rights of a buyer and of a third party claiming the property or a real right in the movables sold is determined by the law of the place where the movables are situate at the time of the third party's claim. This rule, however, is without prejudice to rights recognized in the buyer by the law of the place where they were situate at the time the buyer took possession of them.

Apart from its sheer complexity and its failure to define key expressions like third party,[54] the most notable features of the 1958 Convention are its separation of two- and three-party title issues, and its invocation of a sort of roving *lex situs*, which varies from the place where the buyer first took possession of the goods to the place where the goods were situate at the time when a third party first made a claim to them. As an exercise in ineffectual law-making, the Convention and its subsequent failure speak for themselves. That should not, however, be treated as a rebuttal of the distinction drawn in this paper between two- and three-party title issues.[55]

The understanding of the trade

The argument advanced above that the acquisition of a property right in tangible movables should be determined by the law applicable to the contract may accord with contractual expectations. Support for this view flows from well-known standard form contracts in the dry commodities

---

[51] Article 3(2): 'la loi interne de l'un des pays où le objets vendus ont étés antérieurement situés'. A similar exception applies to documents representing the movables where the buyer's property rights were previously recognized by the internal law of the country where he received the documents. [52] Article 4(1): 'en vertu d'une action en résolution'.

[53] There is an identical rule for documents.

[54] 'Tiers'. Does it include a trustee in bankruptcy?

[55] The Convention also contains a useful rule that movables in transit, whether in a state's territory or outside it, should be considered to be situate in the country where they were dispatched: Art 6, 'considerés comme situés dans le pays de l'expédition'.

trade. Forms promulgated by FOSFA[56] deal contractually with the acquisition by buyers of property rights to portions of bulk cargoes. The FOSFA 53 form, for example, provides:

UNASCERTAINED GOODS. In every instance where a parcel of goods sold by this contract forms an unidentified part of a larger quantity of goods of the same description, whether in packages or in bulk, no separation or distinction shall be necessary and, until separation and identification of the parcel sold hereby from the larger quantity has taken place the unpaid Seller and/or the Buyer who has made payment is/are the pro rata owner(s) of the whole of the larger quantity in common with Seller(s) and Buyer(s) of other parts of the larger quantity.

The same assumption, that the source of property rights in common in bulk cargoes is the law applicable to the contract, underpins the Sale of Goods (Amendment) Act 1995. This was enacted in response to a joint report of the Law Commission and the Scottish Law Commission[57] that responded to the frustration of commercial expectations arising when buyers were unable to acquire property rights when paying cash against ship's delivery orders or even bills of lading representing unascertained parts of a bulk cargo. The usefulness of English law was seen to be compromised if it was unable to give support to such legitimate expectations.

Now, the problem of property rights in bulk cargoes is not confined to dry cargoes though it might arise in connection with them more frequently than it does in the case of oil. In both cases, it will be a very rare case indeed where the cargo is present in England at any time when property rights in bulk might arise pursuant to the 1995 legislation. If English law is so unlikely to be the *lex situs* at the relevant time when property rights in common supposedly arise, it has to be asked why Parliament went to the trouble of enacting the legislation if the acquisition of property rights in bulk was a matter for the *lex situs*. It should, however, be mentioned that Dicey and Morris puts forward an Exception to the *lex situs* in matters of proprietary transfer when the chattel is in transit at the time of the transfer and its *situs* is 'casual' or 'unknown'. The exception, for which the authors cannot provide supporting English authority,[58] favours the 'applicable law'. The word 'casual' seems hardly apt to describe a vessel plying the well-known route across the North Atlantic to the major north European ports in the ARA[59] range. Furthermore, 'unknown' hardly fits the case of a vessel whose whereabouts at the time of the transfer can without real difficulty be verified from its log and which may well be already tied up in Rotterdam or some similar port.

---

[56] The Federation of Oil Seeds and Fats Associations.

[57] *Sale of Goods Forming Part of a Bulk* (1993, LAW COM No 215, SCOT LAW COM No 145).

[58] No criticism is intended of the exception, whose existence testifies to the acute difficulties of authors in this part of private international law having to make bricks without straw.

[59] Amsterdam–Rotterdam–Antwerp.

This suggests that English law, as the law applicable to the contract, which it so often is in these oil and dry commodity cases, will rarely be invoked under the Dicey and Morris exception. There is, however, one feature of the exception that deserves closer consideration. The exception, as written, refers to the applicable law *simpliciter*. This prompts the question, 'Applicable law of what?' The comment to the exception refers to the law applicable to the transfer and an illustration deals with a Scots case[60] concerning the release of shipping documents on trust receipt terms. This appears not to be a case of the law applicable to the contract. The comment goes on to justify the exception on the ground that the *lex situs* is not within the contemplation of the parties. The text may not connect with the problem of acquisition of property rights in bulk cargoes, or with the acquisition of property rights in any two-party case, but there are the makings of an argument that in such two-party cases matters of property should be an aspect of contract and party autonomy. This is despite the reference to the Scots trust receipt decision.

Removal of movables from one jurisdiction to another

Regardless of which law governs the passing of property pursuant to a contract, the next question concerns the recognition of that law's role. One of the commonest issues presented by tangible movables arises when they are removed from one jurisdiction and taken into another. If English law were to deal with passing of property issues according to the law applicable to the contract,[61] then the removal of the movables to England should not reverse that result any more than their removal to England would overturn the application of the *lex situs* to a prior transaction. If, for example, the reservation of beneficial title were treated by the law applicable to the contract as effective, the fact that it would give rise to a charge in English law[62] should not pose a threat of subsequent recharacterization so as to make the seller's 'charge' void for want of registration under section 395 of the Companies Act 1985.

A question that has often arisen in Canadian case law is whether the domestic registration requirements of the second jurisdiction have to be satisfied if the interest of the seller out of possession is to be preserved.[63] As the issue is often presented, it is a question of whether the second

---

[60] *Northwestern Bank v Poynter* [1895] AC 56.

[61] The exclusions from the scope of the Rome Convention in Art 1(2) do not list the passing of property. Furthermore, the passing of property is something that a seller is contractually obliged to do. [62] See *Re Bond Worth Ltd* [1980] Ch 228.

[63] Canadian provinces have long had registration systems for conditional sales, in contrast with England, where conditional sales and hire purchase transactions have never been subject to a system of registration.

province's registration requirements are to be imposed upon the conditional sale agreement entered into out of that province. In interpreting their own provincial legislation, Canadian courts have been sensitive to the application of the *lex situs* so as to deny an implied extraterritorial application to their own legislation. Nevertheless, the second province may impose a reregistration requirement to be satisfied within a stated time of the import of the goods.[64] A provision of this sort does not challenge the law applicable to the reservation of the seller's interest under the conditional sale but, rather, imposes its own requirements for the continued holding in the second province of goods on title retention terms.[65] Furthermore, even if a transaction is duly registered in the first province, the seller's retained title will be overridden by a transaction occurring within the second province when this transaction accords with one of the latter province's exceptions to the rule of *nemo dat quod non habet*.[66]

Where, as happened in some of the above cases, the seller's retained title was overridden by the title acquired by a bona fide purchaser under a transaction concluded in the second province, it would follow that the bona fide purchaser's title ought to be recognized in a third province if the goods were subsequently removed there. This would again be in accordance with the *lex situs* principle. There may, however, be scope in some cases for arguing whether the transaction occurring in the second province is truly a transaction that attracts the *lex situs* principle for the purpose of recognition in the third province. An example of such is legislation in the second province that deems a sale by the buyer in possession to have occurred in the second province in favour of the buyer's trustee in bankruptcy.[67] This departs from the common law rule that the trustee stands in the shoes of the bankrupt.

IV. CHOICE OF LAW AND INTANGIBLE MOVABLES

Introduction

The choice of law rules for the assignment of intangible property are especially difficult to state. First of all, they have given rise to very little

---

[64] See *Trans Canada Credit Corp Ltd v Bachand* (1980) 177 DLR (3d) 653; *Re Adair* (1985) 15 DLR (4th) 596. For a more restricted interpretation of such legislation, confining it in the case of conditional sales occurring outside the second province to sales to residents of the second province, see *Industrial Acceptance Corp Ltd v LaFlamme* [1950] 2 DLR 822.

[65] *McAloney v McInnes* (1956) 2 DLR (2d) 666.

[66] *Century Credit Corp v Richard* (1962) 34 DLR (2d) 291; *Traders Finance Corp Ltd v Dawson Implements Ltd* (1958) 15 DLR (2d) 515; *Re Fuhrmann* (1977) 78 DLR (3d) 284; *Re Delisle* (1988) 52 DLR (4th) 106. See also *Price Mobile Home Centres Inc v National Trailer Convoy of Canada Ltd* (1974) 44 DLR (3d) 443.   [67] *Re Delisle* (1988) 52 DLR (4th) 106.

case law. Secondly, the expression 'intangible property' encompasses a very wide range of individual types of property which, as a matter of domestic law, may be transferred either in a very informal manner or only in compliance with a formal registration system. Thirdly, assignments may be made of individual items of intangible property or of such property *en bloc*. Efficiency considerations demand that global assignments should have one governing law rather than as many governing laws as each assignment is capable of presenting. Fourthly, intangible property frequently has its roots in contract, though it need not necessarily do so. In those cases where it does, the dividing line between contract and property is acutely difficult to draw. Fifthly, a distinction should be drawn between pure intangibles and those documentary intangibles that are transferred by means of endorsement and delivery.[68] In the case of the latter, their similarity to tangible movables calls for them to be treated in the same way.[69]

The connection between immovables and the *lex situs* is a powerful one, that between tangible movables and the *lex situs* less so. By the time we come to intangible movables, it is hard to resist the conclusion that the only argument in favour of the *lex situs* is that it applies to other forms of property and so, for the sake of consistency, should apply to intangibles too. And if this means that an artificial *situs* has to be found for a particular item of intangible property then, one way or another, it will be found. The force of the *lex situs* in such cases is hardly compelling when the *situs* can be determined only by artificial means.[70]

Prior to the incorporation of the Rome Convention in English law by the Contracts (Applicable Law) Act 1990, the rules relating to the assignment of intangible movables were severely undeveloped. Taking first the simple case of the assignment of a debt, there was academic authority for the view that the *lex situs* applied[71] but case law was hostile to the notion and inclined to the view that the *lex loci actus* governed.[72] This view was open to the criticism that, as artificial as the *lex loci contractus* was in the case of contracts, so too was the *lex loci actus* for transactions such as assignments. In the face of the sparse authorities, there was scope to argue the case for a separation of the different issues that can be presented by an assignment.

[68] Bills of exchange and bills of lading.
[69] *Embiricos v Anglo-Austrian Bank* [1905] 1 KB 677, 683, referring to *Alcock v Smith* [1892] 1 Ch 238.
[70] Any extravagant pretensions of the *lex situs* to apply to relations between debtor and assignee were firmly rejected in *Raiffeisen Zentralbank Osterreich AG v Five Star General Trading LLC* (High Court, 26 May 2000).
[71] See N Bentwich (ed), *Westlake's Private International Law* (7th edn, 1925) 207–208 and early editions of *Dicey and Morris on the Conflict of Laws*, n 5 above.
[72] *Republic of Guatemala v Nunez* [1927] 1 KB 669; *Re Anziani* [1930] 1 Ch 407.

It is therefore worth perambulating through a simple contractual debt assignment to list the individual issues that might typically arise: (1) whether the right to be assigned is non-assignable because of its personal character or because of a no-assignment clause in the contract; (2) whether equities and defences available to the debtor against the assignor might equally be asserted against the assignee; (3) whether and when the assignor or assignee can give a good discharge for the debt; (4) whether notice of the assignment has to be given to the debtor and with what effect; (5) whether an assignee may take steps individually to recover the debt or whether the assignor must be joined to the proceedings; (6) whether a first or a subsequent assignee has priority rights in the assigned debt and its proceeds; (7) whether the assignee has a proprietary interest in the proceeds of a debt in the hands of the assignor.

The Rome Convention

It is evident that assignment spans contractual and proprietary issues and, in so far as it deals with contractual matters, relates to more than one contract—the contract giving rise to the debt and the contract underlying the assignment itself. With the complex character of assignment in mind, it is time to turn to the scope and interpretation of Article 12 (Voluntary Assignment) of the Rome Convention on the Law Applicable to Contractual Obligations 1980:

1. The mutual obligations of assignor and assignee under a voluntary assignment of a right against another person ('the debtor') shall be governed by the law which under this Convention applies to the contract between the assignor and assignee.
2. The law governing the right to which the assignment relates shall determine its assignability, the relationship between the assignee and the debtor, the conditions under which the assignment can be invoked against the debtor and any question whether the debtor's obligations have been discharged.

Lest it be thought simply that this provision, housed in a Convention dealing with contractual obligations, applies only to the contractual aspects of an assignment, it must be understood that Article 12 speaks to a number of legal systems not all of which draw as sharp a distinction as the common law does between the contractual and the proprietary aspects of an assignment.[73] Courts interpreting the Rome Convention are bound to respect its international character[74] and therefore may not

---

[73] In the common law, the distinction is plainly there but it does not follow that the *location* of the line separating property and contract is easily found: *Raiffeisen Zentralbank Osterreich AG v Five Star General Trading LLC* (High Court, 26 May 2000).

[74] According to Article 18 (Uniform Interpretation): 'In the interpretation and application of the preceding uniform rules, regard shall be had to their international character and to the desirability of achieving uniformity in their interpretation and application.'

impose their own domestic legal principles and character on the Convention. The Dutch Supreme Court has given an expansive interpretation of Article 12, arguing that this accords with the intentions of the drafters of the Convention to cast the net of Article 12 as widely as possible over assignment issues.[75] Nevertheless, simply because some states in Europe do not readily distinguish between contractual and proprietary issues is not in and of itself a justification for giving an expansive reading to Article 12. The cause of uniformity is equally served by all states taking the same view, narrow or broad. A better argument in favour of a broad reading of Article 12 is that this supports party autonomy and therefore gives parties broader freedom in planning their activities. An opposing argument has been advanced,[76] however, that the policy requirements of property law, relating for example to the publicity of security and the protection of creditors misled by apparent wealth, are best served by moving away from the contractual approach, even where there is in favour of the forum state a mandatory rules exception to the applicable law.[77] One response to this is to say that different legal systems approach such policy issues with different policies and varying intensities of interest,[78] which can best be expressed through the mandatory rules of the forum state overriding contract autonomy than by characterization in favour of property rather than contract.[79]

The seven principal issues outlined above will now be considered in the light of Article 12, with the contractual character of assignment pressed as far as it reasonably can be. The first issue concerning the assignability of contractual rights should be determined by the law applicable to the contract giving rise to the right. If, for example, A and B select English law as the applicable law, and under English law a clause is effective when it states that an assignment requires the debtor's consent which will not be unreasonably refused, then the debtor's contractual expectations will be subverted if the clause is denied effect according to some other law taken to govern relations between the debtor and the assignee. The law applicable to the contract should also apply, though the force of the argument is less strong, to cases of implied non-assignability, as where the contract might be characterized as personal in character.

---

[75] See the discussion in Struycken, 'The Proprietary Aspects of International Assignment of Debts and the Rome Convention, Article 12' [1998] Ll MCLQ 345.

[76] Struycken: ibid.   [77] As is the case with Art 7(2) of the Rome Convention.

[78] For example, in contrast with some legal systems, English personal property law attaches little significance to the appearance of wealth (an example being the abolition of the doctrine of reputed ownership in bankruptcy law by the Insolvency Act 1985).

[79] Neverthless, Struycken, n 75 above, favours a property-based approach that applies the law of residence of the assignor instead of the *lex situs* of the debt. The *lex situs* is hardly suitable for global assignments, which in modern times are very likely to appear in the conflict of laws.

Article 12(2) of the Rome Convention supports the commanding role of the law applicable to the contract giving rise to the right. It is for that law to determine whether a contractual right is capable of amounting to a piece of property.

The same arguments favouring the law applicable to the contract giving rise to the right apply to the second principal issue, the raising of equities and defences. Article 12(2) is clear that this law governs. The third issue, which concerns discharge by payment, should also attract the law applicable to the contract. In making payment, the debtor is performing the contract and should not have to consult some other law to determine his position. Article 12(2) supports this approach. It states that the law governing the contract between debtor and assignor should also govern relations between debtor and assignee. The fourth issue concerns the need for and purpose of giving notice to the debtor. So far as this relates to the issue of discharge, the law applicable to the contract between debtor and assignor applies for reasons stated above.

The fifth issue concerns joinder of parties. Essentially, this is a matter of litigation management and should therefore be governed, it is submitted, by the *lex fori*. Article 12 has no role to play here. The sixth issue, the matter of competing assignments, again should fall outside Article 12. If the law applicable to the contract giving rise to the right were to govern the matter of priority, it could only be for lack of any other imaginable law,[80] especially since that law is manifestly inapt to deal with global assignments embracing receivables arising under contracts with different applicable laws. The law governing the contractual relations of assignor and assignee is not compelling: the competing assignments could be governed by different laws. A similar objection could be levied against the *lex loci actus*, which furthermore, as a matter of geographical accident, can hardly be more compelling than the *lex loci contractus* is for contract. The law of the assignor's residence has been put forward. This has the great merit of being a single law in those cases where the assignment is a global one, and therefore superior to the law of the *situs* of the debt in question. Apart from the rare case where the assignor's residence changes between the two assignments, this approach favours a single law for the determination of priority, the need for which is axiomatic.

Finally, there is the seventh issue of payments received by the assignor. Article 12(1) subjects the relations of assignor and assignee to the law

[80] This, nevertheless, is the view taken in the leading English texts, namely PM North and JJ Fawcett (eds), *Cheshire and North's Private International Law* (London: Butterworths, 13th edn, 1999) and *Dicey and Morris on the Conflict of Laws*, n 5 above, based on a broad reading of Art 12(2) of the Rome Convention. At first instance in *MacMillan Inc v Bishopsgate Investment Trust Plc (No 3)* [1995] 1 WLR 978, 991, Millett J rejected the law applicable to the contract between the assignor and assignee without favouring any other law in particular.

applicable to their contract. The merits of simplicity and predictability point to that same law determining the proprietary and restitutionary consequences of a payment received by the assignor.

V. CONCLUSION

In the absence of global, uniform law, the interests of business and productive exchange are best advanced by expanding as far as possible the category of contract since, in matters of private international law, the principle of autonomous party choice is so firmly embedded. There is little doubt that, had property matters in private international law attracted a significant body of case law, this would have been a difficult case to make on the basis of existing authority. Far from being an impediment to advancement, however, this paucity of authority creates an opportunity to advance the case of contract at a time when worldwide legal barriers to trade are coming down or are at least being lowered. The optimal solution to problems arising may well be uniform law but the rate of progress towards uniform law is slow. Furthermore, the adoption of a uniform text is only the beginning of the challenge since its continuing character as uniform law has to be preserved even as it is thereafter being viewed through the prism of different domestic legal traditions. An expanded field of contract represents the preferred choice of those who wish to promote international transactions.

8

German Conflict Rules on Security Interests in Movable Assets

PROFESSOR ULRICH DROBNIG

(*Max Planck Institute for Foreign and Private International Law, Hamburg*)

I. DOMESTIC SOURCES

Apart from international conventions on the conflict of laws, the main source of German private international law in general is Articles 3–46 of the Introductory Law to the German Civil Code. Among these provisions, Articles 27–37 deal with the law applicable to contracts, transposing the corresponding rules of the Rome Convention of 1980 on the same topic. Articles 38–41 contain some conflict rules on extra-contractual obligations and Articles 43–46 conflict rules on tangible property. These latter two sets of conflict rules were only recently adopted by a Law of 1999[1] and are of fairly short and general nature.

In addition to these legislative provisions, there is a rich case law and copious legal writing. These supplemental sources are particularly important in the field of property law since up to now no case law has been reported applying the newly codified conflict rules. Older case law will remain relevant also in future because of the rather general nature of the new legislative provisions. German cases on private international law are collected in annual volumes which since 1926 have appeared under the title 'Die deutsche Rechtsprechung auf dem Gebiete des Internationalen Privatrechts 19 . .' (abbreviated IPRspr). For ease of reference, all citations will be to this collection.

II. CREATION OF SECURITY INTERESTS

Contracting parties: capacity and authority

The issues of legal capacity of the contracting parties and of the authority of the officers and/or agents acting for them arise, in present day practice, usually only with respect to legal entities. Discussion will therefore be focused on these.

---

[1] Law of 21 May 1999, BGBL I 1026.

Within the European Communities, the consequences of *ultra vires* acts have essentially been settled by European law. According to Article 9(1)(b) of the First Directive on Company Law of 1968[2] *ultra vires* acts are, as a rule, valid. The member countries may, however, deviate from this principle if the company proves that the other contracting party knew or ought to have known that the act was *ultra vires*; publication of the articles of association as such does not yet suffice to impute such knowledge.

Article 9(1) of the First Directive also covers the authority of company officers, even if their acts are *ultra vires* the company. There are two exceptions to this rule. The first applies if these officers act beyond the powers which they have, or have attributed to them by law. By contrast, limitations upon their authority imposed by the articles of association or by resolutions (of the shareholders) can never be invoked by the contracting party.[3]

The second exception applies with respect to legal provisions which allow a company to deviate from the statutory rule with respect to the minimum number of acting officers. If the articles of association provide for such a deviation from the statutory scheme by conferring authority upon a single person or upon several persons, the relevant national law may provide that such a charter provision may be invoked by the company, provided it has been duly published according to Article 3 of the Directive.[4]

In the European context, conflicts may arise, if and in so far as the member states have made use of the deviations permitted by Article 9 of the First Directive and also outside the scope of that Directive, which applies only to commercial legal entities.[5] The relationship to companies from non-member states is, of course, entirely subject to the conflicts rules on companies and legal entities. In the absence of a legislative provision, the majority of German courts follow the established practice of the Federal Supreme Court: the powers of a company or legal entity as well as the authority of its directors are governed by the law at the seat of its headquarters/central administration.[6]

Law governing the security agreement

Both German substantive law and German conflict of laws insist upon the strict distinction between the contractual agreement of the parties to create a security interest, on the one hand, which gives rise only to

---

[2] [1968] OJ L658.   [3] Article 9(2).   [4] Article 9(3).
[5] Cf the enumeration in Art 1.
[6] Kropholler, *Internationales Privatrecht* (3rd edn, 1997) s 55 I 2, pp 488–489; Kegel, *Internationales Privatrecht* (7th edn, 1995) 414–416 with copious references.

personal obligations between the parties; and the creation of the proprietary right, on the other hand, which deploys effects also *vis-à-vis* third persons.

A security agreement is no more than a contract and is therefore subject to the general rules for the determination of the law governing contracts.[7] The statutory conflicts rules correspond to those of the Rome Convention of 1980 and therefore need not be set out in detail. The only issue is to which result these rules will lead if applied to security agreements. This issue becomes relevant only if the parties have not themselves agreed upon the applicable law. In the absence of such choice of law, the security agreement will usually be subject to the *lex contractus* of the main contract, which may, for example, be a loan, a contract for work, or a sales contract. Equally, if a security agreement is laid down in a separate document, writers suggest that this agreement will be subject to the same law as that governing the credit to be secured, ie the law of the main contract.[8]

Creation of a security interest

General rules

Generally speaking, a contractual security interest requires for its creation at least an agreement of the parties and often, in addition, a physical act such as delivery of the collateral or registration or a notification. Further, any formal requirements must be observed.

With respect to the parties' agreement, German law, both substantive and conflicts law, as mentioned above strictly distinguishes between the contractual security agreement and the creation of the (proprietary) security interest. The latter is subject to the law applicable to proprietary rights, as specified in the succeeding paragraphs.

This distinction can be easily understood if the conclusion of the security agreement clearly precedes its performance, ie the creation of the security interest. Conceptually and practically, however, the same distinction is made if the two legal acts coincide because the security interest is created at the same time as the conclusion of the underlying security agreement.

[7] Clear distinction in Federal Supreme Court (Bundesgerichtshof, BGH) 4 July 1969, IPRspr 1968–9 no 24 *sub* II; Kreuzer in Münchner Kommentar zum Bürgerlichen Gesetzbuch X (3rd edn, 1998) no 29, Nach Art 38 Anh I with references; Kropholler (preceding n) s 54 I 2, p 479.
[8] Martiny in Martiny/Reithmann, *Internationales Vertragsrecht* (5th edn, 1996) no 156; Firsching/von Hoffmann, *Internationales Privatrecht* (5th edn, 1997) 398.

The creation of a contractual security interest presupposes an agreement of the parties to create this proprietary interest. Notionally, this agreement is considered by German property law to be a proprietary agreement (*Einigung*) and as such it is subject not to the *lex contractus*, but to the law governing the property right to be created.[9]

According to German substantive law the most important consequence of this distinction is that the validity of the proprietary agreement for the creation of a security interest does not, in general, depend upon the validity and existence of the underlying contract but is independent of it. Consequently, in the German conflict of laws the question whether the validity of the agreement for the creation of a security interest depends upon the validity of the underlying security agreement is also submitted to the law governing property rights.[10] The separation between the underlying contractual and the proprietary agreement becomes relevant whenever the underlying agreement is affected by a defect of consent possibly giving rise to avoidance, or when the contract is rescinded or otherwise is terminated.

Any additional physical act intending to give publicity to a security interest, such as delivery of the collateral to the creditor or registration of the security interest, or a notification, is also subject to the law governing the security interest.

Any formal requirements established for the creation of a security interest are also subject to the law governing the security interest.[11]

General tangibles

The general conflicts rule for tangibles, except major means of transport,[12] is the centuries-old principle of the *lex rei sitae*. Article 43(1) of the Introductory Law to the Civil Code confirmed this rule by providing simply: 'Rights in a thing are subject to the law of the state in which the thing is located.' The criterion of the basic rule therefore is the *situs* of the tangible property.

This basic rule fits well for immovables. But a supplementary rule indicating a time element is required for movables which are moved from one jurisdiction to another jurisdiction since in this case there are two successive *situs*. This point will be taken up later.

The general rule of the *lex rei sitae* may be qualified by virtue of two other general rules. The first is a statutory escape clause which is worded as follows: 'If there is a significantly narrower connection with the law of a state other than the law that would be applicable according to Articles

---

[9] Kropholler (*supra* n 6) 479.
[10] Broad discussion by Stoll in Staudinger, *Kommentar zum Bürgerlichen Gesetzbuch, EGBGB/IPR, Internationales Sachenrecht* (13th edn, 1996) no 159, 160, 296; Kreuzer (*supra* n 7) nos 27–28.   [11] Article 11(5) Introductory Law to the Civil Code (Introductory Law CC).
[12] Discussed below.

43–45, then that law has to be applied.'[13] According to general opinion, this escape clause may be invoked only in very exceptional cases given that it runs counter to the general idea of the basic rule, ie to protect third parties at the place of location. Consistent with this general idea, situations in which only the rights of the parties are at stake have occasionally been envisaged as allowing a recourse to the *lex contractus* chosen by the parties for the underlying contractual transaction.[14]

Further, German private international law generally allows a renvoi. According to Article 4(1) of the Introductory Law to the Civil Code, all conflicts rules referring to foreign law comprise also that legal system's conflicts rules. However, in the field of property law, the relevance of renvoi in practice is negligible since the conflict rules of most foreign nations are also based upon the *lex rei sitae*.

Major means of transport

The principle of the *lex rei sitae* implies that the law governing property rights changes upon every border crossing. Such change of governing law, especially if it occurs frequently, as it does for aircraft and ships used in international traffic, is bound to give rise to uncertainties for the financers of valuable means of transport who have secured their credits by security rights in these vehicles.

On the international level, these risks were intended to be met by some conventions relating to rights in ships and aircraft. The relevant maritime conventions have not been very successful, and none of them has been ratified by Germany. By contrast, Germany acceded to the Geneva Convention on the Recognition of Rights in Aircraft of 1948,[15] which has been widely adopted by some seventy countries, although not by the United Kingdom.[16]

The German legislator, taking up an academic proposal, has generalized this idea by establishing a special conflicts rule for proprietary rights in (major) means of transport. Article 45(1) of the statute provides:

Rights in aircraft, vessels and railborne vehicles are subject to the law of their home country. That is

1. for aircraft, the state of their home country,
2. for vessels, the state where they are registered, otherwise their home port or home place,
3. for railborne vehicles, the state which has licensed them.

---

[13] Article 46 Introductory Law CC.
[14] cf Kropholler (*supra* n 6) s 54 II, p 480; and especially Stoll (*supra* n 10) nos 262, 282–293.
[15] cf Bundesgesetzblatt 1959 II 130.
[16] A mortgage created in an aircraft registered in Oklahoma was duly recognized in Germany, cf BGH (*supra* n 7) 7 October 1991, IPRspr 1991 no 72.

This is followed by a second paragraph determining the law governing statutory security interests in these means of transport. The creation of such statutory security interests (typically liens for repairs and supplies) is subject to the law governing the claim to be secured. However, priority among several security interests is subject to the general rule of the actual *lex rei sitae*.

A suggestion to extend the main rule to automobiles has been rejected on the ground that their home country could not so easily be identified and the insignia, such as nationality and licence plates, could too easily be removed or altered. This reasoning *a contrario* explains the *raison d'être* of the exception: the high-value vehicles covered by Article 45 (1) have a clear, firm, and easily recognizable home country. This justifies the exceptional benefit of submitting them to a fixed connecting factor, thus insulating them from the adverse effects of a (more or less frequent) change of governing law.

Negotiable instruments and documents, securities

Instruments and documents are located halfway between tangibles and intangibles. They may represent or incorporate a tangible (for example, goods) or an intangible (such as an account receivable or membership in a public company), but they may also be no more than an ancillary paper. This complex field is not covered by the recently enacted conflict rules for tangible property but is almost entirely dominated by case law and legal writing. In the present context, only the basic rules can be presented[17] which in essence are not controversial.

It is generally agreed that one must distinguish between the law governing the claim or right or thing for which an instrument or document has been issued (the law governing the right), and the law governing the instrument or document itself (the law governing the paper). The law governing the right determines whether or not the right can in such a way be incorporated into an instrument or document so that a disposition of the paper disposes also of the right.[18] If such an incorporation has taken place, both the rights in the instrument or document itself as well as those represented by the paper are subject to the basic rule for tangibles, ie the *lex rei sitae*. The Federal Supreme Court has applied this basic rule in determining who was the holder of a cheque issued in Switzerland and therefore subject to Swiss law when the cheque had been transferred to

---

[17] For a broad, but condensed survey, cf especially von Bar, 'Wertpapiere im deutschen Internationalen Privatrecht,' in Pfister/Will (eds), *Festschrift für Werner Lorenz zum siebzigsten Geburtstag* (1991) 273–295.

[18] Stoll (*supra* n 10) nos 412–416; Kreuzer (*supra* n 7) nos 117–120.

various persons partly in Switzerland and partly in Germany.[19] Another Swiss-German case involved the transfer of bearer shares in a Swiss company: since the Swiss law governing the company refers to the *lex rei sitae* of the bearer shares at the time of dispositions and the transfers had taken place in Germany, German law decided the issue who had acquired the shares and therefore become the shareholder.[20]

The preceding rules also apply to the creation of security interests.[21]

Intangibles, especially accounts receivable

Among the various kinds of intangibles, accounts receivable everywhere are of paramount interest as a means of securing credit. The following discussion will therefore concentrate on the creation of security interests in accounts receivable.

Civil law countries allow and regulate in a detailed manner the pledging of accounts receivable which in practice, however, is becoming less popular. Since the creation of a pledge is a disposition of the pledged account receivable, it is subject to the law governing the receivable.[22] The latter law must be determined, if a contractual receivable is involved, according to the rules of the Rome Convention of 1980 and the corresponding provisions of Articles 27–37 of the Introductory Law to the Civil Code.

Much more frequent than the pledging of accounts receivable is nowadays their assignment by way of security. The contractual assignment of accounts is largely, although perhaps not exclusively, governed by Article 33(1) and (2) of the Introductory Law to the Civil Code which correspond to Article 12(1) and (2) of the Rome Convention. Articles 33(1) and 12(1) submit the security agreement between assignor and assignee to the *lex contractus* of that agreement which must be determined according to the general rules on the law applicable to a contract.[23]

By contrast, the relationship between the assignee and the debtor of the assigned receivable and all aspects of the debtor's protection are subject to the law governing the assigned receivable[24] because the debtor's position should not be adversely affected by the change of creditor.

A very controversial question is which law governs the position of other third parties, especially the assignor's creditors and several assignees of

---

[19] BGH (*supra* n 7) 26 September 1989, IPRspr 1989 no 59 *sub* no I 2 a) aa) (distinction expressly applied).

[20] BGH 19 January 1994, IPRspr 1994 no 54 *sub* A 3 and B 1 (distinction impliedly followed).   [21] Stoll (*supra* n 10) no 418 with references.

[22] Martiny (*supra* n 8) no 312.

[23] This is in contrast with the strict separation in German law between the security agreement and the proprietary right, discussed above.

[24] Article 33(2) Introductory Law CC and Art 12(2) Rome Convention of 1980.

an account receivable, if the latter has been assigned, intentionally or unintentionally, to several persons. The Federal Supreme Court and the majority of writers extend Article 33(2) Introductory Law to the Civil Code and Article 12(2) Rome Convention to these cases.[25] Other writers criticize this solution on both theoretical and practical grounds, especially in cases of assignment of future claims, since the law governing them is at the time of the assignment usually not yet known. The same objection applies in cases of global assignments; in addition, their validity possibly would have to be determined according to a multitude of laws if the assigned receivables are governed by different (and at the time of the assignment not foreseeable) laws. Alternative references that are proposed are either the law governing the security agreement[26] or the law of the assignor's place of business or residence.[27]

III. THE TREATMENT OF FOREIGN SECURITY INTERESTS IN GERMANY

All tangible movables other than the aforementioned major means of transport are subject to the general principle of the *lex rei sitae*. Every change of *situs* across the borders of a country therefore as a rule implies a change of the applicable law. The issue of treatment of foreign security interests will only arise if collateral is moved into Germany.

General rule on change of *situs*

The general rule expressing the principle of *lex rei sitae* for tangible movables is supplemented by a second rule setting out the general effect of a change of *situs*. Article 43(2) provides:

If a thing in which rights have been created is moved to another state, these rights cannot be exercised contrary to the law of this state.

---

[25] Especially BGH (*supra* n 7) 8 December 1998, IPRspr 1998 no 39, NJW 1999, 940 (global assignment and double assignment); also BGH 20 June 1990, IPRspr 1990 no 48 (double assignment, *obiter dictum*). Fully convinced, von Hoffmann, 'Die Forderungsübertragung, insbesondere zur Kreditsicherung, im Internationalen Privatrecht,' in Hadding/Schneider (eds), *Die Forderungsabtretung, insbesondere zur Kreditsicherung, in ausländischen Rechtsordnungen* (1999) 3–25 (*passim*); von Bar, *Internationales Privatrecht* II (1991) no 567; Martiny (*supra* n 8) nos 309–311. Some authors share this opinion *de lege lata* only, cf Kropholler (*supra* n 6) 438.

[26] Stadler, 'Der Streit um das Zessionsstatut—eine endlose Geschichte?' [2000] Praxis des Internationalen Privat- und Verfahrensrechts, 104–110.

[27] Stoll (*supra* n 10) nos 347–351; Kieninger, (1998) 62 Rabels Zeitschrift für ausländisches und internationales Privatrecht 678; Kaiser, *Verlängerter Eigentumsvorbehalt und Globalzession im IPR* (1986) 202, 224.

This provision not only confirms the principle of the *lex rei sitae* for the case of a border crossing. In addition, it implies an important second rule, namely the continuity of the proprietary rights created under the law of the former location. The rights as such are preserved; only their exercise must be in conformity with the law of the new location. The terms used by the statute indicate a willingness to recognize foreign property rights; this is in line with, and inspired by, German practice, as we shall see.

The text could even be (mis)understood as meaning that the exercise of the rights is governed by the preceding *lex rei sitae* and that the new *lex rei sitae* merely may object. This interpretation, however, would not be compatible with the legislative intention. The legislator wanted to emphasize that mere entry of collateral into a new country as such does not change the governing law, unless the imported real right is actively exercised or passively affected by some act in the new country.[28] Any other interpretation would also create indissoluble difficulties if, for example, a motor car passes successively through several countries. Would it then be necessary to trace back the governing law to the very first jurisdiction from which it started? How should that be ascertained after three or five years?

How is this general rule applied to collateral which is subject to a security interest validly created under the preceding *lex rei sitae* and then moved into Germany? It is proposed to deal with this issue by distinguishing between different major forms of non-possessory security interest, namely reservations of title, non-possessory pledges, and enterprise mortgages, including floating charges.

Reservations of title

In German practice, foreign reservations of title have invariably affected imported goods.

Simple reservations

In distorting to some degree the general principle of the *lex rei sitae*, the German courts have fashioned a special rule for simple reservations of title in imported goods. In fact, for more than thirty years German courts have submitted reservations of title in imported goods exclusively to German law; and that was, as one can derive from my German colleague's chapter on the extremely liberal substantive law, to the benefit of the foreign exporters! The leading case, a decision of the Federal Supreme Court of 1966,[29] had still paid at least lip-service to the *lex rei sitae* rule since it first looked to the law of the Italian exporter. Under that law the

---

[28] cf Stoll (*supra* n 10) no 356.   [29] BGH (supra n 7) 2 February 1966, IPRspr 1966–7 no 54.

reservation of title clause, because of non-compliance with Italian formal requisites, was valid *inter partes* only. But then the court took the daring step of imputing to the parties the intention of creating a reservation of title that would be fully effective in Germany, especially also against the German buyer's creditors who had attached the imported goods in Germany. The Supreme Court therefore implied an obligation by the buyer, upon entry of the goods into Germany, to retransfer title to the seller! While this artificial reasoning was rebutted as unrealistic by commentators, they fully approved the result.[30] The result means that the legal situation in the export country is flatly disregarded and that reservations of title in imported goods are subjected only to German law; practically, therefore, they are almost always fully effective, not only *inter partes*,[31] but also and in particular *vis-à-vis* third parties, especially other creditors of the buyer. This is the constant practice of the courts.[32]

Under the new statutory conflict rules, this sensible result may be justified by resort to the escape clause of Article 46.[33] If goods are imported into Germany, there is indeed a 'significantly closer' connection with German law than with the law in the exporter's country. This new provision therefore now furnishes a justification for the rather makeshift judicial departure from the strict application of the *lex rei sitae* principle.[34]

Extended reservations

Agreed extensions of a reservation of title into substitute assets (such as new products and accounts receivable arising from a resale) are subject to separate conflict rules. Whether processing of the original goods results in the production of new things, and whether the seller's title can be extended to these new goods, is subject to the law of the place where the processing is effected.[35] If the sold goods are processed in Germany and

---

[30] Kegel, 'Der Griff in die Zukunft [1968], *Juristische Schulung*, 162; Drobnig, 'Eigentumsvorbehalte bei Importlieferungen nach Deutschland' (1968) 32 *Rabels Zeitschrift für ausländisches und internationales Privatrecht* 450, 468–471.

[31] Higher Appellate Court (Oberlandesgericht, OLG) Koblenz 16 January 1992, IPRspr 1992 no 72, IPRax 1994, 46 with critical commentary by Schurig.

[32] OLG Hamm 13 July 1992, IPRspr 1992 no 76 p 164; OLG Koblenz 23 December 1988, IPRspr 1988 no 35 p 74; OLG Hamburg 2 June 1965, IPRspr 1964–5 no 73 pp 234–236; Lower Appellate Court (Landgericht, LG) Köln 24 March 1992, IPRspr 1992 no 73; LG Hamburg 9 January 1991, IPRspr 1991 no 171a pp 366–367; idem 28 June 1978, IPRspr 1978 no 42.

[33] Discussed above.

[34] The draftsman of the new conflict rules in the Federal Ministry of Justice relies on another statutory rule, ie Art 43(3), to justify the earlier court practice, cf Wagner, 'Der Regierungsentwurf eines Gesetzes zum internationalen Privatrecht' . . . in *Praxis des Internationalen Privat- und Verfahrensrechts* (1998) 429, 435. This justification has, however, justly been criticized, cf Stoll (*supra* n 10), at n 335 and Schurig (*supra* n 29), at 28.

[35] Stoll (*supra* n 10) nos 341 and 267; Kreuzer (*supra* n 7) no 93.

if an appropriately drawn extension clause has been agreed upon then the extension is effective under German law.

By contrast, it is a controversial question which conflicts rule should govern an extension of the seller's title into the claim for the purchase price arising when the original buyer resells the purchased goods to a new buyer.[36] However, there is at least agreement with respect to the basic and most frequent situation, namely a resale to a (German) buyer governed by German law. In this case, the assignment of the future claim for the future purchase price is subject to German law and therefore, as a rule, is effective.

Non-possessory security rights in specific assets

For both factual and legal reasons, the treatment of foreign non-possessory security rights other than reservations of title is more complicated and therefore less certain.

In fact, non-possessory security usually is not connected with an import transaction, so that the collateral is not intended to be moved to Germany. The special reasons motivating the German courts, in dealing with foreign reservations of title, to disregard the primary foreign *lex rei sitae* and to apply only German law, are therefore absent here. Furthermore, the incidence of these cases is much rarer so that few decisions have been rendered in this area.

Legally, special difficulties arise in this area since the types of non-possessory security differ widely from country to country. This has been demonstrated by the various national reports on the substantive law.

It is no accident that only two relevant cases have become known and that both concerned security rights in automobiles. In the first case, decided in 1963, a French lorry had been charged in favour of a French bank financing the acquisition of the vehicle and secured by a non-possessory pledge, entered in a French register. While circulating in Germany, the lorry had been attached by a German creditor of the French owner. The French bank objected to the German creditor's attachment and was recognized as having priority over him. The Federal Supreme Court[37] stated that—contrary to earlier governing opinion—Germany no longer can invoke, as a matter of public policy, a principle of possessory pledge (although this is the only type of pledge regulated by the Civil Code). Apart from a few narrow statutory exceptions, the possessory

---

[36] According to prevailing court practice and opinion, the proprietary effect of the assignment is subject to the law governing the assigned claim according to Introductory Law CC Article 33(2), which corresponds to Rome Convention Article 12(2) (cf above part II, text under subheading 'Intangibles, especially accounts receivable').

[37] BGH 20 March 1963, IPRspr 1962–3 no 60.

pledge has in fact been virtually set aside by the development of the non-possessory security transfer of ownership (that has been alluded to in chapter 6). Thus, the French security right was recognized, offering even some publicity, contrary to its German functional equivalent, as the court expressly remarked; though, one may comment, not in Germany. The court did not have to deal with the important second question, which German rules should be applied to the French secured creditor's rights in Germany. Rather, the procedural basis of defence against an attachment was relevant, although not in controversy. It is characteristic that the relevant provision granting preferential satisfaction in an attachment to a possessory pledgee[38] is also applied to a (mere) security owner, whereas a full owner may recover his goods and therefore object to an attachment of his asset.[39]

Almost thirty years later, a comparable case was brought before the Federal Supreme Court. An Italian in Italy had bought a very valuable luxury car, a Ferrari 208 Turbo; the purchase price was financed by an Italian bank which secured its credit by registering a mortgage on the car; that mortgage was also entered in a licence certificate for the car. Its owner brought the car to Germany and offered it, at the entrance of the Frankfurt Automobile Fair, for sale. A wealthy German lady was persuaded to purchase the car; neither she nor her agent took the trouble to enquire about the legal situation. The Italian bank's claim for recovery of the car in order to obtain satisfaction of its claims was successful.[40] The court followed the aforementioned leading case of 1963 in recognizing the Italian chattel mortgage in Germany.

The Italian bank's claim for satisfaction of its mortgage was made subject to the rules for the German non-possessory security transfer of ownership. The bank's claim for recovery of the car was therefore allowed. The German defendant's plea of good faith acquisition was, contrary to the appellate court, rejected on the ground that the purchaser of a foreign car has an increased duty of enquiry, including recourse to experts who can read the documents and ascertain the legal situation.

The conclusion to be derived from this decision is that the German non-possessory security transfer of ownership is the functional equivalent of foreign non-possessory security interests; it is irrelevant whether or not these are subject to registration. This result is generally supported by most writers.[41] It is also in conformity with the new statutory provision's

---

[38] Section 805 Code of Civil Procedure (CCProc).   [39] Section 771 CCProc.

[40] BGH 9 January 1991, IPRspr 1991 no 71, reversing the appellate court.

[41] cf Kreuzer (*supra* n 7) no 98 with copious references in n 479. The only prominent dissenter is Stoll (*supra* n 10) nos 358–361, who would differentiate between rights securing purchase money which should liberally be recognized, and those securing ordinary credits which as a rule should not be recognized (no 361)! This radical differentiation has no basis

general policy of recognizing foreign property rights validly created under the preceding *lex rei sitae*.

Global non-possessory security rights

There has been some discussion by German writers whether global non-possessory security rights, especially those comprising a whole enterprise or parts of it, can be recognized in Germany; in particular, the English floating charge has been analysed and has given rise to conflicting views. This discussion cannot and need not be reflected here in any detail since the issue does not seem to have been litigated in a German court, but a few words are in order.

Recognition in Germany is impeded by the fact that a global security right of this kind does not exist in Germany and is regarded with suspicion because it gives too much power to the secured creditor and, correspondingly, threatens satisfaction of the enterprise's unsecured creditors. On the other hand, German practice allows a creditor to accumulate single asset security rights within limits. Following this approach, some writers suggest that a comprehensive enterprise security may not be repugnant to the German *lex rei sitae* if the individual element of the charged assets which is at issue can be charged in Germany as well;[42] and in practice, there are hardly any limits in this respect.

IV. FOREIGN SECURITY INTERESTS IN A GERMAN INSOLVENCY PROCEEDING

Collateral located in Germany

If insolvency proceedings are opened in Germany and the collateral is located in Germany as well, in general no conflict arises. The law governing the insolvency and the law governing the security right coincide, since German law applies to both issues—provided, of course, that the security right had been validly created under the law of its preceding *situs*.

Such full coincidence does not, of course, exist for those special means of transport (such as ships and aircraft) which are subject to the law of

---

in German conflicts law; it is true, though, that security for purchase money enjoys some preferences, as it does in many countries.

[42] Generally, cf Kreuzer (*supra* n 7) no 99; similar Stoll (*supra* n 10) nos 185 and 195; for detailed analysis cf Wenckstern, 'Die englische Floating Charge im deutschen Internationalen Privatrecht' (1992) 52 Rabels Zeitschrift für ausländisches und internationales Privatrecht, 624.

their home country. In these cases, therefore, it will be necessary to examine whether any security rights validly created according to the law of the home country of the vehicle can be recognized in Germany. The criteria indicated before for non-possessory security rights in specific assets will apply. By analogy, that is also true for reservations of title since what is here involved is not an import transaction.

The same is true for major means of transport that may be subject to a global enterprise security since there is a special conflict rule which has precedence. In practice, of course, the vehicle's home country often will be at the seat of the enterprise, and then no conflict arises.

Collateral located outside Germany

Do German insolvency proceedings also cover all assets owned or possessed by a debtor which are located outside Germany?[43] Of course, whether a security interest has been effectively created in those assets is, according to the general conflict rules, subject to the *lex rei sitae* or, in the case of major means of transport, to the law of their home country.

Usually in these cases, the *lex concursus* and the *lex situs* will differ. The co-ordination of these two different legal systems is so difficult that the German legislator, in an earlier draft provision, tended to exclude from the reach of German proceedings any security rights in collateral located outside Germany.[44] Such self-restriction has certainly the advantage of avoiding a difficult issue of the conflict of laws. However, whether that is a legitimate justification is open to doubt, and I confess to sharing this scepticism.

[43] BGH (*supra* n 7) 13 July 1983, IPRspr 1983 no 205 b.

[44] This rule must be implied from the unwritten principle that foreign insolvency proceedings as a rule should deploy the same international effects as German proceedings (cf Allgemeines *sub* 5 a) of the reasons for the government draft of the Insolvency Order, reprinted in Balz/Landfermann, *Die neuen Insolvenzgesetze*, 1995, 671). In order to protect domestic trading, a foreign insolvency proceedings does not affect collateral located in Germany (ibid 672, 682–683). The same rule is to be found in Articles 5 and 7 of the recent European Insolvency Regulation of 29 May 2000 (OJ EC 2000 L 160 p 1).

9

The Conflict of Laws Principles in French Law with Respect to Security Interests in Movable Assets

PROFESSOR CATHERINE KESSEDJIAN

(Professor at University of Paris II Panthéon-Assas)[1]

I. INTRODUCTION

The purpose of this chapter is to set out the principles of French conflict of laws rules in relation to security interests created over movable goods as well as over intangible assets. Before we deal specifically with the issues, some general remarks on French private international law may be useful.

The sources of French private international law, international conventions and treaties aside, are mainly case law and legal doctrine. The reasons for this development are the lack of codification of French private international law and the very small number of provisions in French legislation, starting with the French Civil Code, which specifically pertain to private international law.

French private international law on property and other real rights, including security interests, is a good illustration of the above-mentioned principle. The main rules have all been deduced by courts and legal authors from one single provision of the French Civil Code, Article 3(2) which reads in translation: 'real estate, even when owned by foreigners, is governed by French law'.[2] Article 3(2), must be read in the context of the whole Article. Therefore, on the face of it, it only applies to real estate located in France. However, as we will see below, the rule has also been used for assets located in a foreign country.

Over time, the Cour de cassation has broadened the scope of this provision in two directions: first, it has held that Article 3(2) of the French Civil Code not only applies to immovables but also to chattels;[3] secondly,

---

[1] The author thanks Ms Alexandra Schluep, temporary legal assistant at the Permanent Bureau of the Hague Conference, for her assistance in writing the present chapter.

[2] My translation. The original text of Art 3(1), (2) of the French Civil Code reads as follows: '(1) Les lois de police et de sûreté obligent tous ceux qui habitent le territoire. (2) Les immeubles, même ceux possédés par des étrangers, sont régis par la loi française.'

[3] This extension is made for the first time in Cass req 19.3.1872: S 1872, 1, p 238; DP 1874, 1, p 465; the principle is confirmed in Cass req 24.5.1933: Revue critique DIP 1934, p 142, note J-P N; JDI 1935, p 381, note J P; S 1935, 1, p 257, note H Batiffol.

the Cour has bilateralized[4] this rule so as to submit property located in another country to the laws of that country.[5] Thus, case law leads to the bilateral conflict of laws rule that both immovable property and movable goods are governed by the *lex situs*. This rule is still the main rule applied by French courts as we will see below.

In theory, property law, contrary to contract, is subject to the application of 'renvoi'. 'Renvoi' works as follows: the conflict of laws rule of the forum points to the whole legal system of a country and not only to its internal law. This means that one has to look first at the conflict of laws rules of the country designated. If those rules designate yet another country, or France, then the law applied is the law of that other country or of France. In other words, French courts will only apply the internal law of the country designated by French conflict of laws rules if that country's rules 'accept' the designation, ie have the same conflict rule.[6] However, in practice, renvoi is not useful in this field since the *lex situs* is supposedly a universally accepted rule.[7]

When compared to other matters of private international law, it is remarkable that there is relatively little case law with respect to French conflict of laws for property and security interests. This is usually taken to be an indication that few problems arise in practice and that the existing system works satisfactorily. However, one could argue the contrary and say that the whole matter is so complex that parties and practitioners do not even try to submit their dispute to courts and accept the loss they have incurred or settle the matter. Existing divergent opinions within legal doctrine with respect to French conflict of laws on property and security interests would be an argument to comfort the latter view.

Three aspects will be covered in this chapter. First, we shall address the question of the law applicable to the creation of security interests. Secondly, we shall examine whether, and if so, under what conditions, security interests created abroad do have effects in France. Thirdly, we shall give an overview of the law applicable to international insolvency proceedings and its implications for security interests.

[4] The text of Art 3(2) of the French Civil Code contains a unilateral rule, since it provides only for the application of French law to property located on French territory. This rule has been bilateralized, which means that it has been held to apply not only to property located in France but also to property located abroad. The consequence is that property located in France is submitted to French law, whereas property located in Germany, for instance, will be governed by German law. The determining factor remains the geographical localization of the property, but the rule can now lead to the application of any foreign law.

[5] See Cass 1ère civ, 19.1.1999, Epx Baciocchic/Banque Cantonale de Genève, Bull Civ I, no 2.

[6] France does not apply the so-called 'foreign court theory' which prevents the application of renvoi when the courts of the foreign country designated by the French conflict of laws rules would not apply renvoi.

[7] However, it may be useful for some other aspects of the rules applied in the field.

II. LAW APPLICABLE TO THE CREATION OF SECURITY INTERESTS

The capacity to create security interests

Both individuals and legal entities can create securities over movable assets they own. In order to be able to do so, they need to have certain legal qualifications, known as 'capacity' for individuals and 'authority' for the persons acting on behalf of legal entities. In a typical cross-border transaction, as illustrated by the case study set out in Appendix 1, where a company incorporated in jurisdiction A[8] creates in jurisdiction B a security interest over an asset located in jurisdiction C, the question whether the directors of that company have authority to create such a security can only be answered after having determined, in accordance with the applicable conflict of laws rules, which substantive law applies to their capacity/authority.

For individuals, the fundamental conflict of laws rule is to be found in Article 3(3) of the French Civil Code, which reads in translation: 'Rules governing the status and capacity of persons apply to French nationals, even when they reside abroad.'[9] Literally, the French Civil Code submits the personal status and capacity of French citizens to French law. However, like Article 3(2) of the French Civil Code, Article 3(3) was bilateralized by French courts.[10] The law governing the status and the capacity of an individual (*loi personnelle*) is thus his or her national law.[11] The place of domicile or residence is irrelevant as far as capacity is concerned since its personal law follows the individual. However, the scope of the personal law is not unlimited. In the famous *Lizardi* case decided in 1861,[12] the Cour de cassation decided that a 22-year-old Mexican citizen, who had attained majority according to French law but was still a minor according to his national law, could not invoke his minority in order to avoid the purchase contract he had concluded with a French jeweller. He was thus

---

[8] As we will see below, 'incorporation' is not a pertinent connecting factor in French private international law.

[9] My translation. The original text of Art 3(3) French Civil Code reads: 'Les lois concernant l'état et la capacité des personnes régissent les Français, même résidant en pays étrangers.'

[10] See n 4. One of the first decisions setting this rule is a decision from the Paris court, 13.6.1814: S 14.2. p 393.

[11] If a person has two or more nationalities, among which the French nationality, French courts will hold that the French nationality prevails on any other nationality. However, if a dual or multinational person does not possess the French nationality, French courts will look at the 'effective' nationality. For a recent decision, see Cass civ 1ère, 3.6.1998, in: Bull civ I, no 189, p 130; DS 1998, IR, p 160; Gaz Pal 1998, 2, panor p 293; JCP 1998, IV, 2675; Revue critique DIP 1999, som. p 831.

[12] Req 16.1.1861, DP 1861 1, p 193, S 1861.1.p 305, note Massé, *Grands Arrêts de la Jurisprudence Française de Droit International Privé* (Paris, 3rd edn, 1998), no 5, p 34.

condemned to pay the amount agreed upon, on the ground that the French party to the contract had neither acted carelessly nor imprudently but rather in good faith. This decision constitutes the starting point of the theory of appearance or forgivable ignorance of foreign law (*théorie de l'apparence ou de l'ignorance excusable de la loi étrangère*), which protects the party acting in good faith. This party is not supposed to enquire whether the other party is capable of entering a contract. This theory has found its way into Article 11 of the European Convention on the Law Applicable to Contractual Obligations signed in Rome on 19 June 1980 (hereafter the Rome Convention),[13] which entered into force for France on 1 April 1991.

Two provisions apply in relation to capacity of legal entities. Article 1837 of the French Civil Code provides: 'Every company which has its seat on French territory is submitted to French law. Third parties may avail themselves of the statutory seat, but the company cannot invoke it against third parties, if it appears that its effective seat is located else-where.'[14] Article 3 of the Law on commercial companies is almost identical to Article 1837 of the French Civil Code, except for some linguistic differences.[15] These provisions have also been bilateralized.[16] A company is thus submitted to the laws of the country where it has its seat. In most cases, the effective seat of the company will coincide with the statutory seat. However, should there be a dichotomy between these two places (for example, the by-laws of the company indicate a seat in The Netherlands where it is registered, but the effective management of the company takes place in France, the board of directors meets in France, the shareholders' meetings are held in France), then only the effective seat in France is relevant to determine the law applicable to the company. This has been confirmed by French courts in various cases, among others in the case *Banque Ottomane*.[17] The *Banque Ottomane* was a long established Turkish bank whose statutory seat was in Constantinople, as Istanbul was then

---

[13] Article 11 of the Rome Convention under the heading 'Incapacity' reads as follows: 'In a contract concluded between persons who are in the same country, a natural person who would have capacity under the law of that country may invoke his incapacity resulting from another law only if the other party to the contract was aware of this incapacity at the time of the conclusion of the contract or was not aware thereof as a result of negligence.'

[14] My translation. The original text of Art 1837 of the Civil Code reads as follows: '(1) Toute société dont le siège est situé sur le territoire français est soumise aux dispositions de la loi française. (2) Les tiers peuvent se prévaloir du siège statutaire, mais celui-ci ne leur est pas opposable par la société si le siège réel est situé dans un autre lieu.'

[15] Article 3 of the Law on commercial companies (Loi no 66–537 du 24 juillet 1966) reads as follows: '(1) Les sociétés dont le siège social est situé en territoire français sont soumises à la loi française. (2) Les tiers peuvent se prévaloir du siège statutaire, mais celui-ci ne leur est pas opposable par la société si son siège réel est situé dans un autre lieu.'

[16] B Audit, *Droit international privé* (Paris, Economica, 2nd edn, 1997) no 1096.

[17] Tribunal de commerce Paris, 19.10.1984, Banque Ottomane: Revue critique DIP 1984, p 93, n Synvet.

known, but whose management took place in London. The French judge applied his own conflict of laws rule to determine that the law applicable to the bank was English law, being the law of the country where the bank had its centre of decision making, and not Turkish law. Then the 'renvoi' theory was applied. The English conflict of laws referring to the law of the state of incorporation of the company, the French court came to examine Turkish law. However, Turkish conflict of laws contained the same rule as French conflict of laws (based on the effective seat of the company) and, as a matter of consequence, referred back to the law of England. The outcome of the conflict of laws question was that the substantive law of England was applicable to the *Banque Ottomane*.

The *lex societatis* has a wide scope: it not only applies to the foundation of the legal entity, but also to its internal structure, to its operating mode, to the authority of its directors, and to its dissolution and liquidation.[18] The Cour de cassation has repeatedly confirmed that the authority of directors to enter contracts on behalf of the company and the limitations thereof are exclusively submitted to the *lex societatis*.[19] The question whether the directors need special authorization from the board of directors or another collective body to create a security interest on the company's assets will therefore also be answered by the *lex societatis*.[20] According to these precedents, third parties concluding agreements with a company which has its seat in another country bear the risk that its directors lack authority and, therefore, that the transactions are void. To offer some protection to third parties, legal doctrine has suggested to apply to such cases the theory of appearance *mutatis mutandis*.[21] Depending on the circumstances of the case (ie the profession and the good faith of the third party), the degree of diligence required from the third party would vary. A banker signing a contract of pledge would be expected to ascertain whether the director representing the company has authority to create security interests over the company's assets. A person not familiar

[18] M Menjucq ad Cass civ 1ère, 8.12.1998, in Revue critique DIP 1999, p 284.
[19] Cass com, 21.12.1987, Soc Viuda de José Tolra: JCP 1988, II, 21113, concl Montanier; Revue des sociétés 1988, p 389, n Synvet: Revue critique DIP 1989, p 344, n Jobard-Bachellier; Cass com, 8.11.1988, Europe 1 Communication: JCP 1989, II, 21230; Revue critique DIP 1989, p 371; Cass com, 19.5.1992, JDI 1992, p 954, n Kahn; and recently, Cass civ 1ère, 8.12.1998, Soc General Accident: Bull civ I, no 345, p 238; Revue des sociétés 1999, p 93, n Y Guyon; Revue critique DIP 1999, p 284, n M. Menjucq.
[20] Under French substantive law, the directors of a company need an authorization from the board of directors to create a security interest. Art 98(3) of the above-mentioned Law on commercial companies provides: 'Les cautions, avals et garanties données par des sociétés autres que celles exploitant des établissements bancaires ou financiers font l'objet d'une autorisation du conseil dans les conditions déterminées par décret.'
[21] B Audit, n 16 above, no 1097; P Mayer, *Droit international privé* (Paris, Montchrestien, 6th edn) no 1041.

with this kind of transaction might try to plead that his or her ignorance of the lack of power of the director under the *lex societatis* was forgivable given the circumstances and that the contract has to be upheld. So far, however, French courts have not followed the legal writers. Article 11 of the Rome Convention, which is also applicable to legal entities, should bring about a change in this practice.

The creation of security interests

The law applicable to the creation or transfer of security interests or 'quasi-security' interests on movable property depends on the type of assets concerned. There are three main categories of assets to be considered: chattels, receivables, and securities (bearer securities and registered securities). Another distinction can be made between the different ways security interests are created: by contract, by law, or by judicial decision. Since security interests created by law or by judicial decision are almost exclusively mortgages on immovable property (*hypothèque légale, hypothèque judiciaire*), they will not be considered here.

Chattels

The creation of a security interest or reservation of title on chattels agreed upon by transaction between the parties presents proprietary as well as contractual characteristics. According to French conflict of laws, the proprietary aspects of this contract, or more precisely the creation of title on the goods, are exclusively governed by the law of the state on which territory the goods are situated at the moment of creation, ie the *lex situs*. This principle is directly based on Article 3(2) of the French Civil Code. The main justification for the application of the *lex situs* in international situations is the protection of third parties by substantive law. This is particularly true in France where, inherited from Roman law, the system of property and other real rights relies on strict rules of publicity. In this respect, the maxim contained in Article 2279(1), of the French Civil Code,[22] is an illustrative example: ownership of a chattel is inferred from the possession thereof.[23] The rationale of this rule is that third parties must be able to appraise a legal situation involving property, ie to determine who the legal owner is on the basis of the outside appearance or facts. The protection of third parties as well as public interests also justifies the wide scope of the *lex situs*. The *lex situs* determines which security

[22] Article 2279(1) French Civil Code reads: 'En fait de meubles, la possession vaut titre.'
[23] This is a rebuttable presumption. This rule explains modern days difficulties with security interests which do not entail dispossession.

interests are available,[24] the conditions of their validity, their content, and the formalities attached to their creation or transfer, including the rules of publicity. So for instance, under French law, the debtor has to relinquish possession of goods over which a pledge has been created to the beneficiary of the pledge or to a third party. The purpose of this formality, as has been said, is to prevent third parties gaining an incorrect impression of the financial situation of the debtor. A pledge created over such goods located in France in accordance with German law, which does not require the dispossession of the debtor, would be deceptive and therefore void.[25] Another example of publicity of a real right under French substantive law is the appending of a sign on tools and other equipment or material subject to a lien.[26] Contrary to dispossession or registration, this form of publicity is not problematic from a private international law perspective, since it follows the goods. Third parties will not be misled by the apparent situation.

Since the *lex situs* is applicable whenever the interests of third parties are at stake, the scope of the law of the contract will necessarily be limited to the relations between the parties. It is generally admitted that the *lex contractus* governs the mere contractual aspects of the transaction by which the parties agree to create or transfer a security interest, such as the existence and the validity of consent and the mutual obligations of the parties.[27] The fact that the agreement to create a security interest is generally part of another contract, for instance a contract of sale or a loan, is not relevant for the distinction between *lex situs* and *lex contractus*.[28] In principle, parties are free to choose the law which will apply to the main contract and to the contract constituting the security interest. Under Article 4(2) of the Rome Convention, in the absence of a choice of law by the parties, the main contract of loan and the agreement to create the security would be governed by two different laws. The form of the contract itself is still, more often than not, governed by the principle *locus regit actum*, that is to say the law of the place where the contract was concluded, even if the new trend is now to choose in favour of the law which validates

[24] French law knows a closed system of real rights (*numerus clausus*). A frequently heard argument in favour of the strict rule of *numerus clausus* is that fixing the types and content of all real rights enhances the ease of use, the certainty and the simplicity of the law of property.

[25] P Mayer, n 21 above, no 651.

[26] Loi no 51–59 du 18 janvier 1951 sur le nantissement de l'outillage et du matériel d'équipement, Art 4.

[27] H Batiffol/P Lagarde, *Droit international privé* (Paris, 7th edn, 1983) Vol II, nos 518 and 524, and from a comparative law perspective, K Kreuzer, *La propriété mobilière en droit international privé* (Académie de La Haye de droit international 1996, Recueil des cours, tome 259) 89–90.

[28] The distinction of the respective domains of the *lex situs* and the *lex contractus* is rendered more difficult in French conflict of laws by the fact that under French substantive law property and other real rights are transferred by mere consent in one contract.

the contract.[29] Again, the importance of these conflict of laws rules is marginal since the form of the creation of the security interest and the publicity attached to it remain subject to the *lex situs*.

The determination of the *lex situs* with respect to tangible goods is generally easy, since it is just a matter of physically locating the goods. However, some categories of chattels are more difficult to locate. It lies in the very nature of aeroplanes and ships that they seldom are in a certain location. Moreover, they are to be found in 'lawless' regions, as for instance the high seas. To circumvent these difficulties, it has been agreed by international convention to submit aeroplanes to the law of the country where they are registered.[30] For ships, the law of the flag is thought to provide a stable determining factor. This factor is used in various international maritime conventions, for example the International Convention for the Unification of Certain Rules Relating to Maritime Liens and Mortgages signed in Brussels on 10 April 1926 and the International Convention Relating to the Arrest of Seagoing Ships signed at Brussels on 10 May 1952.[31] However, this fictitious localization is only effective as long as the ship does not change flag and sail under a flag of convenience.[32]

Other goods which prove difficult to locate are goods in transit. Legal opinion usually draws a distinction between goods in transit which can be located and goods in transit which cannot. In accordance with the general principle, the former are subject to the *lex situs*; the latter are governed by the law of the state of their destination.[33] If goods in transit are transported by aeroplane or ship, they follow the fate of their means of transport and are thus submitted to the law of the state of registration or the law of the flag.[34]

---

[29] Article 9(1) of the Rome Convention provides: 'A contract concluded between persons who are in the same country is formally valid if it satisfies the formal requirements of the law which governs it under this Convention or of the law of the country where it is concluded.'

[30] Geneva Convention dated 19 June 1948 relating to the international recognition of rights on aeroplanes, ratified by France in 1964 (JO 16 April 1964, 3420 and JO 13 May 1964, 4043).

[31] These Conventions were ratified by France, respectively in 1935 and 1958 (JO 14 January 1958, 515).

[32] The countries of convenience are generally not contracting parties to the international conventions and thus offer no protection of the rights of third parties on ships.

[33] V Bonnet, *Juris-Classeur, Droit international*, Fasc 550 (update 1999), nos 183–184.

[34] J Derruppé, *Juris-Classeur, Droit international*, Fasc 555 (update 1999), nos 148–149. Art 6 of the Hague Convention of 15 April 1958 on the Law Applicable to the Transfer of Ownership in International Sale of Moveable Goods provides that goods in transit are to be considered as being located in the state from which they are sent. This Convention was signed by Italy and Greece and has been ratified only by Italy. Thus it is not in force.

Receivables

Receivables are usually governed by the law of the right to which they relate, for example the law of the contract or the law of tort.[35] This is particularly true for the relationship between the debtor and the creditor. However, because receivables are also considered an element of the creditor's patrimony, and utilized as security interests in the forms of voluntary assignment or right of pledge,[36] they are assimilated to real rights. Given their intangible nature, they can be 'located' only fictitiously. In international assignments of receivables, the legal relationships of the three parties involved (the assignor, the assignee, and the debtor) are generally not submitted to the same law. In addition, the transaction comprises contractual aspects as well as 'proprietary aspects'. Contractual relations arise on the one hand between the assignor and the debtor, and on the other hand between the assignor and the assignee. The 'proprietary aspects' include the effect of the assignment against the debtor and the right of the assignee to claim payment from the debtor, as well as the opposability to third parties of the assignment. Because these different aspects are so closely linked, we will treat them together at this point.

French conflict of laws concerning the voluntary assignment of receivables is now to be found in Article 12 of the Rome Convention,[37] which reads as follows:

1. The mutual obligations of assignor and assignee under a voluntary assignment of a right against another person ('the debtor') shall be governed by the law which, under this Convention, applies to the contract between the assignor and assignee.
2. The law governing the right to which the assignment relates shall determine its assignability, the relationship between the assignee and the debtor, the conditions under which the assignment can be invoked against the debtor and any question whether the debtor's obligations have been discharged.

By referring to the system of the Convention, paragraph 1 of this provision leaves room for party autonomy (choice of law). Article 12(2) clearly governs the effect of the assignment against the debtor. A controversy[38] has arisen as to whether the Convention covers or not the opposability to

---

[35] H Batiffol/P Lagarde, n 27 above, no 538.

[36] French legal doctrine draws no distinction between the assignment of receivables and the right of pledge on receivables. Both institutions are submitted to the same regime; see G Khairallah, *Les sûretés mobilières en droit international privé* (Paris, Economica, 1984) no 269 and n 115. In the Swiss Private International Law Act of 1987, a clear distinction is made between these two types of securities (Arts 105 and 145 PIL Act).

[37] The Rome Convention has a universal scope of application (Art 2).

[38] For an overview of the controversy in various European countries, see THD Struycken, 'The proprietary aspects of international assignment of debts and the Rome Convention, Article 12' [1998] Ll MCLQ 345–360.

third parties of the assignment, and if it does, whether this question falls under the scope of paragraph 1 or 2 of Article 12. Some writers, including the Reporters to the Convention, think that it does not address the question.[39] For others, the solution is to be found in the Convention. In a recent decision,[40] the *Hoge Raad* of The Netherlands held that Article 12(1) was applicable to the question whether the assignment was opposable to the trustee in bankruptcy of the assignor. It has also been suggested in France that the law of the assigned receivable be applied to the opposability to third persons of the assignment, in the sense of Article 12(2) of the Convention.[41] The traditional view taken by French case law is that this question is governed by the law of the domicile of the assigned debtor.[42] Finally, the draft Convention on receivables financing prepared by UNCITRAL,[43] which contains a chapter on conflict of laws rules, takes another view and submits the question of opposability of the assignment to third parties to the law of the state in which the assignor is located at the time of the assignment (Article 30). As in the Rome Convention, the law of the assigned receivable determines the conditions of discharge for the debtor. To summarize, the determination of the law applicable to the question of the opposability to third parties of the assignment of a receivable can lead to very divergent results, which the parties to the transaction cannot necessarily foresee. It is not certain that the *Hoge Raad* will be followed by other courts in its interpretation of Article 12 of the Rome Convention.

Securities

A brief word on securities. Traditionally, securities incorporate a receivable in a material certificate.[44] It is therefore possible to locate them and hence submit them to the law applicable to other movable goods, ie the *lex situs*. However, because they are so closely linked to the existence of the legal entity that issues them, their creation is governed by the *lex societatis*.[45]

---

[39] Giuliano and Lagarde Report; the Reporters found their opinion on the fact that one of the draft projects of the Convention contained a provision dealing with this issue which was then cut out (OJ C282/4).

[40] Hoge Raad, 16 May 1997, *Brandsma qq v Hansa Chemie AG*, Rechtspraak van de Week 126.

[41] D Pardoel, *Les conflits de lois en matière de cessions de créances et d'opérations analogues* (Paris, LGDJ, 1997).

[42] B Audit, n 16 above, no 762; A Sinay-Cyterman, 'Les conflits de lois concernant l'opposabilité des transferts de créances', Revue critique DIP 1992, pp 35–60.

[43] The Working Group has finished its preparatory work. It is hoped that a final draft (for the present text see reference A/CN 9/466) will be approved by the General Assembly in July 2001.

[44] For the purpose of explanation, we first discuss securities incorporated in a document. Problems related to 'dematerialized' securities will be addressed briefly below.

[45] B Audit, n 16 above, nos 763 and 765.

With respect to the transfer and the creation of security interests (mainly a right of pledge, *nantissement*), a further distinction has to be made between bearer securities and registered securities. Bearer securities are assimilated to movable goods and therefore, their transfer as well as the creation of securities interests over them are exclusively submitted to the *lex situs*. Registered securities are subjected to the law of the place where they are registered, which is practically the law of the head office of the issuer, thus the *lex societatis*.[46]

In cross-border financial transactions, it is commonplace nowadays to guarantee loans by providing securities as collateral. However, the interests in securities, which are held through multi-tiered intermediaries, are evidenced by book entries with the immediate intermediary and are no longer tangible. Moreover, the securities given as collateral often originate from issuers located in many different jurisdictions. For these reasons, the collateral taker finds it difficult to determine, at the time of the transfer of the security, what law must be complied with in order to be sure to obtain a valid security. In cases of securities from different jurisdiction, the collateral will have to comply with all the various laws of these jurisdictions. It appears quite clear that the traditional connecting factor of the *lex situs* will not do in such cases. In order to respond to the needs of the financial services market for greater legal certainty, it has been suggested that 'the place of the relevant intermediary' (PRIMA) be used as the unique connecting factor in determining the law applicable to the disposition of securities held through intermediaries. For collateral provided to central banks, to the European Central Bank, or in connection with certain payment and settlement systems, the European Union has followed the PRIMA approach in Article 9(2) of the Directive of 19 May 1998 on settlement finality in payment and securities settlement systems.[47] In implementing it, a number of member states have favoured a broad interpretation of the Directive, extending its scope to all participants in a European Union settlement system, or even, to all participants of all payment and securities systems, whether or not they are European Union systems. France is still working on the implementation of the Directive. However, it appears that implementing legislation, which favours a broad interpretation of the Directive, will be passed before the end of the year 2000.

---

[46] Y Loussouarn/P Bourel, *Droit international privé* (Paris, Dalloz, 6th edn, 1999) no 423.

[47] Article 9(2) of the Directive reads: 'Where securities (including rights in securities) are provided as collateral security to participants and/or central banks of the Member States or the future European central bank as described in paragraph 1, and their right (or that of any nominee, agent or third party acting on their behalf) with respect to the securities is legally recorded on a register, account or centralised deposit system located in a Member State, the determination of the rights of such entities as holders of collateral security in relation to those securities shall be governed by the law of the Member State.'

III. THE EFFECTS IN FRANCE OF SECURITY INTERESTS
CREATED ABROAD

In practice, the question of the effects in France of security interests created abroad occurs almost always in the context of an insolvency procedure. Since 'bankruptcy corrupts everything', the principles which can be inferred from the available case law are necessarily biased. We shall, however, try to reason in general terms and leave aside the prevailing law of bankruptcy. After having defined the problem caused by the importation of foreign security interests in France, we shall expose the ways judges and legal writers deal with it, given that, like most countries, France does not have legal provisions on the recognition of foreign security interests.

Defining the problem: the *'conflit mobile'*

Following the principle set forth in Article 3(2) of the French Civil Code, French courts consider that the effects of real rights vested in movable goods are defined by the law of the country where the goods are situated at that moment.[48] The application of the *lex situs* to both the creation of the security interest and its effects offers the advantage of unity of the conflict of laws rule. If the two systems of law conflict, however, it leads to great difficulties in the case where goods are moved from one jurisdiction to another between the moment when the security interest was created and the time its effects are invoked. Which law should be applied to the security interest? The former or the present *lex situs*? Or both laws cumulatively? This is the *'conflit mobile'* or mobility conflict.

There are typical examples of mobility conflict illustrated by case law: a security interest is validly created over an asset situated in Germany or in The Netherlands in accordance with the national substantive laws, which are both quite different from French substantive law. Thereafter, the asset is moved from Germany or from The Netherlands to France. Quite often, the asset is then seized by a third party who claims to have a right in relation to it. From this standard case, it appears clearly that the parties involved have conflicting interests. The beneficiary of the security interest created in Germany will want this security interest to have effect in France and give him a priority right on the asset against any subsequent creditor. Third parties in France will want to know whether security interests have already attached to the goods. The interest of the owner is to obtain the biggest credit possible in the same asset. These individual interests pair with public interests of the state where the asset is located. As was said earlier,[49] by adopting a closed system of real rights

---

[48] H Batiffol/P Lagarde, n 27 above, nos 519–520.   [49] See n 24.

the French legislator intended to facilitate and protect transactions within national territory. This system is also thought to implement the principle of equality between the citizens. The weight given to these various interacting factors will be determinative in the elaboration of a solution to mobility conflicts.

Solutions to the problem

So far, French courts have applied with great consistency the present *lex situs* to determine the effects of the 'imported' security interest in France on the ground that '*la loi française est seule applicable aux droits réels dont sont l'objet les biens mobiliers situés en France*'.[50] The Cour de cassation elaborated this rule for the first time in connection with a security interest in 1933.[51] A Dutch company, Maas, had lent a certain amount of money to a French company, Ravel. The contract of loan signed by the parties in Mainz, Germany, was explicitly subjected to German law and provided that the loan was secured by a fiduciary transfer of title in favour of Maas over five cars owned by Ravel. At the time the Dutch company claimed the cars, invoking its property right, the cars were located in France. The Cour de cassation dismissed the claim for the reason that the clause agreed upon by the parties, even though valid under the law of the contract, that is German law, contained a *pacte commissoire* which was expressly forbidden by French law, which was the only law applicable to security interests vested in movables situated in France.

This decision was confirmed by the Cour de cassation in 1969,[52] when a German credit company, DIAC, opened a credit in favour of a German company, Schluter, to finance the buying of a car. Following the interpretation of the Cour de cassation, the parties had agreed on a reservation of title clause on the vehicle in favour of DIAC. The car was then brought to France where a French garage owner, Oswald, seized it on the ground that he had not been paid by Schluter for some work done on it. DIAC opposed the seizure claiming it had a better right to the car, but its claim was dismissed. As in the preceding case, the Cour de cassation judged that the contract concluded between the two German companies contained a *pacte commissoire*. As mentioned above, such an agreement being forbidden by French law, it cannot have effect. The *pacte commissoire* does

[50] My translation: 'the only law which applies to real rights on movable goods situated on French territory is French law'.

[51] Req 24.5.1933, Soc. Administratie Kantoor de Maas: Revue critique DIP 1934, p 142, note J-PN.

[52] Cass 8.7.1969, Société DIAC: Revue critique DIP 1971, p 75, note Ph Fouchard; JDI 1970, p 916, note J Derruppé; JCP G 1970, II, 16182, note H Gaudemet-Tallon; *Grands Arrêts de la Jurisprudence Française de Droit International Privé*, no 48, p 387.

not fit in the *numerus clausus* of security interests known in French law. In a decision rendered in 1973,[53] the Cour de cassation confirmed the decision of a lower court which characterized a contract of sale by instalments with a reservation of title for the seller concluded between two Dutch parties as being a contract of loan with a pledge without dispossession. The Cour de cassation concluded that such a pledge without dispossession was not opposable to third parties in France. Legal doctrine criticized the characterization of the foreign security interests as a *pacte commissoire* made by the French judges in the two earlier decisions.[54] It seems that, in all three cases, the Cour de cassation mixed up two different types of security interest known in Germany and in The Netherlands and mistook a fiduciary transfer of property for a reservation of title clause. But, as we will see below, a 'correct characterization' would not have had any influence on the outcome of the cases.

It may be inferred from case law that in order to be effective in France, a foreign security interest has to be 'transposed' into a security interest known in France. Transposition presupposes that the foreign security interest has been validly *created* according to the former *lex situs*.[55] French law does not validate mere facts which have occurred in another country by taking them into account for the creation of a security interest on goods which have entered French territory.[56] Transposition is then a two-step procedure. First, the security interest created according to foreign law must be known to French substantive law or at least be compatible with French substantive law. This is a consequence of the *numerus clausus* principle of real rights in France. Secondly, the requirements for the opposability of the security interest according to French substantive law, ie the formalities intended to protect third parties, will have to be met.

For instance, it seems unlikely that a fiduciary transfer of title as known in Germany,[57] by which the property in the movable is transferred to the creditor as a means of security interest until the debt is paid, the debtor remaining in possession, can, even with adaptations, fit into the system of French security interests. The correct characterization of the German or

---

[53] Cass 3.5.1973, Soc Nederlandsche Middenstands Financieringsbank NV: Revue critique DIP 1974, p 100, note E Mezger; JDI 1975, p 74, note Ph Fouchard.

[54] See note Fouchard, Revue critique DIP 1971, p 76ff; note E Mezger, Revue critique DIP 1974, p 100ff; and *Grands Arrêts de la Jurisprudence Française de Droit International Privé*, no 48, p 388.   [55] H Batiffol/P Lagarde, n 27 above, no 511.

[56] German law (Art 43, para 3 EGBGB) and Swiss law (Art 102, para 1 PIL Act) provide for such a validation of facts which occurred in another country, by taking them into account for the creation of a security interests on their territory. For more details on this question, see K Kreuzer, 'La reconnaissance des sûretés mobilières conventionnelles étrangères', Revue critique DIP 1995, p 485 (hereafter Reconnaissance).

[57] In the new Dutch Civil Code (Burgelijk Wetboek) enacted 1 January 1992, the fiduciary transfer of title has been abolished.

Dutch security interests as fiduciary transfers of property by the Cour de cassation in the aforementioned cases would nonetheless have led to the conclusion that these security interests have no effect in France.

To the contrary, a simple reservation of title clause created in Germany should be recognized in France, since it also exists in substantive law.[58] However, the extended and prolonged forms of reservation of title known in Germany cannot be effective in France.[59] A foreign security interest cannot have other or more effects than those permitted by national law. Finally, to comply with the French condition of publicity the reservation of title clause should be incorporated in a written contract, general contractual conditions being sufficient as long as they have been accepted and form part of the contract.

As for rights of pledge without dispossession, they exist in France for specific types of goods, such as professional equipment and tools[60] or cars.[61] One cannot see why foreign rights of pledge falling into one of these categories should be deprived of effects in France, provided the necessary formalities of publicity (for example registration) are fulfilled.

The English floating charge has drawn the attention of French legal doctrine, but has not, so far, been addressed in French case law.[62] This is quite remarkable given the fact that a floating charge encompasses all the assets of the debtor company, actual and future, wherever they are located. Therefore, if the debtor company owns assets located in France, these assets should also be subjected to the floating charge. The question, however, is whether the creditor can enforce the floating charge in France? Can an English administrative receiver seize and sell the assets located in France in order to pay the debt, after the security has 'crystallized'? And how will the right of an English creditor be treated in insolvency proceedings opened in France? The enforcement of an English floating charge in France raises two main issues: the recognition or 'transposition' of the security in French law and the powers of the English administrative receiver on French territory.

According to Paul Lagarde,[63] a floating charge created in England cannot have effect on movables situated in France. Therefore, the creditor will

---

[58] The reservation of title is opposable to third parties, even in insolvency proceedings (Art 121 of the loi no 85–98 du 25 janvier 1985 relative au redressement et à la liquidation judiciaire des entreprises). For a comparative study of Dutch, French, and German conflict of laws with respect to reservation of title clauses, see JW Rutgers, *International reservation of title clauses* (The Hague, TMC Asser Press, 1999).   [59] K Kreuzer, Reconnaissance, p 483.

[60] Loi no 51–59 du 18 janvier 1951 sur le nantissement de l'outillage et du matériel d'équipement.   [61] Décret no 53–968 du 30 septembre 1953.

[62] There is one case submitted to the Paris Cour d'appel, 19.1.1976: Revue critique DIP 1977, p 126, note P Lagarde; Gaz Pal 1976, I, p 371, note Viatte, which has to do with a floating charge, but the Cour d'appel only examined the problem of *exequatur* of an English decision and did not consider the question of the floating charge itself.

[63] Note under the decision of the Cour d'appel cited in n 62.

not be able to enforce his right. He bases his opinion on two arguments. First, the particularities of the floating charge make it impossible to transpose into a type of security interest known by French law. Secondly, even if such a transposition were possible, the floating charge would not be opposable to third parties in France because the publicity occurring in England does not reach French parties. A more recent opinion[64] is less categorical about the impossibility of a floating charge having effect in France. The floating charge could be transposed in a *nantissement de fonds de commerce*, a right of pledge on a business.[65] According to the author, the transposition of the floating charge into this French type of security interest should be made effective, even if the conditions of validity prescribed by French law (dispossession of the goods or their registration) are not fulfilled. The recognition of a foreign security interest in this fashion would mean that substantive law is applied differently to internal situations and to international situations. This would mean a drastic change in the actual conception. In the case where the right of the beneficiary of the floating charge on the assets is in competition with rights claimed by French creditors in the same goods, the priority of the floating charge would be determined by the date of the 'crystallization'. However, this author is of the opinion that, at least, the beneficiary of a floating charge should make all attempts to register his right in France, if he happens to know that property belonging to the security provider is in the form of a *fond de commerce* located in France. This may help to circumscribe the priority issue and have that part of the floating charge recognized as of the date of registration instead of the date of 'crystallization'.[66]

The question of the powers of the receiver to act with respect to assets located on French territory is the second obstacle that the floating charge faces in its pursuit of effectiveness in France. The capacity of the receiver heavily depends upon whether his rights come into competition with those of other creditors or secured persons in the same assets. If a question of priority exists, then capacity of the receiver to act is linked to the recognition of the floating charge itself.[67] In order to determine which law applies, the capacity and powers of the receiver must be characterized by

---

[64] Frédérique Dahan, 'La *Floating Charge*: Reconnaissance en France d'une sûreté anglaise', JDI 1996, p 381.

[65] The *nantissement du fonds de commerce* is governed by the Law of 17 March 1909 'relative à la vente et au nantissement des fonds de commerce'. This security is more restrictive than the floating charge, since it encompasses neither the stock-in-trade nor the future assets of the company. To be valid, the *nantissement* has to be registered within 15 days after its constitution.

[66] The author understands that this may fall short of the philosophy underlining the floating charge in English law but makes the proposal as a matter of practicality.

[67] See discussion above.

the French judge according to the *lex fori*. Because of his particular function and the powers vested in him by English law, the receiver can be seen in three different ways: as an agent of the debtor company, taking control of and managing the charged assets and even selling the company as a going concern; as a representative of the creditor, for whom he must sell the charged assets; and finally, as a liquidator or administrator of the insolvent debtor company. Another complication arises from the fact that, in most cases, the receiver is nominated 'privately' by the creditor and not appointed by a court. At this stage, we shall only consider the first two possibilities; the capacity of the receiver as insolvency trustee or liquidator/administrator in insolvency proceedings will be addressed below in part V. If the receiver is to be considered as the agent of the debtor company, the law applicable to the receiver's capacity will be the law of the debtor company. As we have seen before, following French conflict of laws rules, the law applicable to a legal entity is the law of the country in which this entity has its seat, the effective seat being relevant where there is a discrepancy between statutory seat and effective seat. In most cases, because the floating charge is a typically English type of security, English law will be applicable. However, if the law applicable to the company is French law, the provisions of the French Civil Code (Articles 1984 ff) will have to be observed: the agency authority must be given in writing and must be specific, mentioning the power of the receiver to manage the company and sell its assets, if deemed necessary. The receiver would then be in the same position as a director of the company, acting in its name and on its behalf. If one considers the receiver to be the representative of the creditor, who in most of the cases appointed him, the law applicable to his capacity will be the law of the contract of floating charge.[68] There again, English law is most likely to apply: the floating charge being a typical English security, it seems difficult to imagine that a different substantive law should apply to the contract. As the representative of the creditor, the receiver does not have wider powers than the creditor himself. In fact, French law forbids creditors to seize 'privately' themselves the assets in which they have real rights.[69] Realization procedures are exclusively state regulated and enforced by public authorities or officials. To realize collateral outside this prescribed procedure would constitute a violation of French public policy.

As shown by the above examples, many foreign securities may fail the test of 'transposition' and are, as a matter of consequence, deprived of any effect in France. In order to overcome the problems caused by a

[68] In agreement, Frédérique Dahan, n 64 above, p 390.
[69] See Art 2078 Civil Code and Art 93 Commercial Code.

mobility conflict, legal doctrine has made various suggestions. Among the most interesting and innovative are the views of Pierre Mayer[70] and Georges Khairallah.[71] The former suggests applying the law of origin (*loi de la source*) to the creation as well as to the effects of real rights, the *lex situs* intervening only as law of police (*loi de police*) when the protection of third parties is at stake. The latter advocates the subjection of the security interest, including its proprietary aspects, to party autonomy. By analogy with the *Lizardi* solution,[72] the law chosen by the parties would have to withdraw, if under the circumstances of the case a third party could not be blamed for not knowing the foreign applicable law. Their solutions, these authors claim, would also do away with the painstaking distinction between contractual and proprietary questions. Moreover, they would be acceptable in view of the evolution in French substantive law towards moving away from the strict rule of possession and publicity with respect to security interests. Finally, legal doctrine draws some hope from a decision rendered by the Cour de cassation in 1982.[73] In this case, two German companies had concluded a leasing contract on a machine. The machine was then sub-leased to a French company. The contract had been publicized neither in Germany, where it was not necessary, nor in France, where the leasing was supposed to be registered at the domicile or seat of the lessee. The Cour de cassation did not agree with the opinion of the lower court which had dismissed the property claim made by the German lessor against the French sub-lessee on the grounds that there had been no publicity in France. According to the Cour de cassation, inasmuch as the Cour d'appel had established that the German lessee and the French sub-lessee were not bound by a leasing contract, publicity in France was not compulsory. Therefore, the German leasing contract, by which the lessor retained title in the machine, was effective in France against the sub-lessee. Some authors have seen in this decision an implicit recognition in favour of the *lex contractus*. The Ottawa Convention of 28 May 1988 on international leasing contracts, which has been in force for France since 1 May 1995, contains uniform material rules which may apply in international situations. The scope of application of the Convention is defined in its Article 3(1).[74] Article 7(1)(a)

---

[70] P Mayer, n 21 above, nos 648ff and 654ff.   [71] G Khairallah, n 36 above, nos 244ff.
[72] See discussion above.
[73] Cass com, 11.5.1982, Soc Localease c Singer: Revue critique DIP 1983, p 450, note Georges Khairallah; D 1983, p 271, note C Witz.
[74] Article 3(1) of the Ottawa Convention reads as follows: 'This Convention applies when the lessor and the lessee have their places of business in different States and: (a) those States and the State in which the supplier has its place of business are Contracting States; or (b) both the supply agreement and the leasing agreement are governed by the law of a Contracting State.'

of the Convention governs the opposability to third parties of real rights of the lessor.

The lack of any effects in France of a foreign security interest does not mean that it is automatically extinguished when the relevant movable is brought into France. According to some authors,[75] the effects of the real right are only suspended until the chattel is brought back to the state of exportation or any other state which recognizes its effects. This opinion is based on the argument that the security interest was validly created and that its validity is not questioned by the change of location.

To conclude, it appears that the solution adopted by French courts is very strict since it usually results in the non-recognition and, as a matter of consequence, in non-enforcement of foreign securities in France. This rigid position allows no room for the flexibility which is demanded by the increase of international trade and the evolution of the economy, in which the factors of wealth are more often movable assets than immovable property. The alternative solutions proposed by legal doctrine have not, so far, been followed by court practice.

IV. INSOLVENCY AND SECURITY INTERESTS

The opening of bankruptcy proceedings has drastic and intrusive effects on the law applicable to security interests. The law of insolvency or bankruptcy (the *lex concursus*) has a predominant rank on any other applicable law. Since the *lex concursus* is the *lex fori*, there is no real conflict of laws problem. However, the question of jurisdiction becomes crucial. After looking at jurisdiction, we will examine the effects of the *lex concursus* on security interests with respect to insolvency proceedings opened in France and abroad. The impact of the Brussels Insolvency Convention will be assessed very briefly. Particular attention will be given to some questions raised by the floating charge.

Jurisdiction for insolvency proceedings

In the past, French courts have taken a resolutely extensive view on this matter and have founded their jurisdiction on various grounds, such as the existence in France of assets of the debtor, the conclusion of business transactions by the debtor in France, or the French nationality of the creditor or of the debtor (Articles 14 and 15 of the French Civil Code). These so-called exorbitant *fori* are no longer accepted internationally today.

---

[75] *Grands Arrêts de la Jurisprudence Française de Droit International Privé* no 48, p 387.

Two factors should bring a change to this practice. In 1985, the French legislator adopted a new statute reforming domestic insolvency proceedings and judicial restructuring of companies.[76] This statute was followed in 1985 by an enacting decree, amended in 1994.[77] Article 1(1) of the enacting decree determines the jurisdiction of French courts: the competent court is the court of the district in which the debtor has its head office or, in the absence of such head office in France, the main centre of its interests in France.[78]

The concept of 'head office', is used in almost every legal system with respect to bankruptcy and insolvency proceedings. In accordance with old principles of French private international law, this criterion for internal competence also determines, by extension, international jurisdiction.[79] A French court will therefore have jurisdiction in a cross-border situation to open insolvency proceedings if the debtor has its head office in France. The notion of 'head office' is a broad one, which is not restricted to companies but also refers to the individual businesses of natural persons. When used in relation to a company, it designates its registered office as specified in the company's by-laws, but only on the assumption that the registered office is also the effective seat where the decisions are taken and from where the company is effectively managed.[80] Because the criterion of the 'head office' is broadly recognized internationally and because it offers many practical advantages (for example, the co-operation of the management of the mother company, the centralization of information), it is in principle admitted by legal doctrine that the court which has adjudicated the bankruptcy of a company at its head office is also competent to decide the bankruptcy of the managers of the insolvent company as well as the bankruptcy of the company's subsidiaries abroad.[81] This doctrine of 'extension of bankruptcy' has not, so far, been followed by the Cour de cassation.

---

[76] Loi no 85–98 du 25 janvier 1985 relative au redressement et à la liquidation judiciaire des entreprises.

[77] Décret d'application no 85–1388 du 27 décembre 1985, amended by Décret no 94–910 du 21 octobre 1994.

[78] My translation. Art 1(1) of the enacting decree no 85–1388 of 27 December 1985 reads as follows: 'Le tribunal territorialement compétent pour connaître de la procédure de redressement ou de liquidation judiciaire est celui dans le ressort duquel le débiteur a le siège de son entreprise ou, à défaut, de siège en territoire français, le centre principal de ses intérêts en France.'

[79] Cass 1ère civ, 30.10.1962, Dame Scheffel c Scheffel: Revue critique DIP 1963, p 387, note Francescakis; D, 1963, p 109, note G Holleaux; *Grands Arrêts de la Jurisprudence Française de Droit International Privé*, no 37, p 278; and recently confirmed again by CA Paris, 5.12.1997: Gaz Pal 1998, 2, 710, note I Chatenet; Revue critique DIP 1999, som p 828.

[80] Cass 1ère civ, 21.7.1987, Sté Ets Bernard: Bull Civ, I, no 242; D, 1988, p 169, note J-P Rémery, where the Cour de cassation says that this rule is of public order and that it may be invoked by everyone, even the debtor himself.

[81] J-P Rémery, *La faillite internationale* (Presses Universitaires de France, 1996), 34.

The second criterion set by Article 1(1) of the 1994 decree[82] is the 'main centre of interests of the debtor in France'. This notion must be equated with that used by the European Court of Justice in the context of Article 5(5) of the Brussels Convention on Jurisdiction and Enforcement of Judgments in Civil and Commercial Matters of 1968, even though this Convention does not apply to insolvency. It is thus a centre of business which can be seen as an emanation of the head office, and which disposes of a certain factual autonomy and power of decision, but is not necessarily a legal person.

Since the enactment of the 1994 decree, there should be no room left for jurisdiction founded on other criteria to pronounce the bankruptcy of the debtor.[83] However, Article 1(1) of the decree only addresses the jurisdiction of the courts to pronounce an international bankruptcy (*faillite*), ie a general and universal decision with respect to all the assets and activities of the debtor. It leaves open the possibility of French authorities seizing individualized assets, receivables, or goods belonging to the debtor and located in France by way of attachment, arrest, or injunction, inasmuch as these measures are followed by individual execution (payment of the 'seizing' creditor on the seized assets).[84]

The second factor which should bring some change to the jurisdiction of French courts with respect to bankruptcy is the Brussels Convention on insolvency proceedings, elaborated under the auspices of the Commission of the European Union and signed on 23 November 1995 (the Brussels Convention)[85] which is due to become a Community Act (probably a Regulation) by virtue of Article 65 of the EC Treaty as amended by the Amsterdam Treaty.[86] The system of the Brussels Convention relies on the distinction between principal proceeding and ancillary proceeding. For the principal procedure, the courts of the Contracting State where the debtor has the centre of his main interests have jurisdiction (Article 3(1)). Where the centre of the debtor's main interests is situated in the territory of a Contracting state, the courts of another Contracting State shall have jurisdiction to open an ancillary procedure if the debtor possesses an establishment in the territory of that State. The effects of this ancillary

---

[82] See n 77.   [83] J-P Rémery, n 81 above, 46.

[84] Loi no 91–650 du 9 juillet 1991 portant réforme des procédures civiles d'exécution et décret d'application no 92–755 du 31 juillet 1992.

[85] There is also an Istanbul Convention on Certain Aspects of Bankruptcy established by the Council of Europe which was opened for signature on 5 June 1990, but has never been enforced because of insufficient ratification. This Convention addresses only particular issues of trustees' powers and cross-border publication of the commencement of bankruptcy cases.

[86] For ease in reading the following developments, the reference will still be made to the Brussels Convention.

procedure are restricted to the assets located in the territory of this state (Article 3(2)).

Finally, it must be mentioned that France has ratified a number of bilateral conventions relating specifically to cross-border insolvency.[87] These conventions contain provisions on international jurisdiction which have pre-eminence over national law. Because of their bilateral character, the scope of these conventions remains limited. Furthermore, they are outdated and no longer respond to the needs of modern practice, even though the Cour de cassation still applies them without any adaptation.[88]

The impact of the *lex concursus* on security interests

The law applicable to the insolvency proceedings (the *lex concursus*) will always be the law of the state where the bankruptcy is adjudicated, ie the *lex fori*. A French court competent to initiate insolvency proceedings will always, in doing so, apply its own substantive law.

The *lex concursus* has a wide scope: it not only applies to the organization of the proceedings, but also to the powers of the bankruptcy trustees, to the determination of the extent to which the debtor is deprived of control over his assets, and to the suspension of individual procedures by creditors.[89] The application of the *lex concursus* to the whole bankruptcy proceedings is justified by the fact that it is a collective procedure involving many creditors, disseminated assets, and numerous different legal relationships between persons and goods. The fair and equitable treatment of all the parties involved as well as practicality and simplicity require the application of the same substantive law to all. Because of the requirement that bankruptcy-related issues be consolidated into a single proceeding with a single applicable law (*vis attractiva concursus, le pouvoir attractif de la faillite*), the *lex concursus* expands into the field of real rights and particularly security interests. As a matter of fact, the crucial question whether a valid security can successfully be opposed by its beneficiary to the other creditors of the debtor within insolvency proceedings is submitted to the *lex concursus* (including the preferential or priority rights attached to the security). The Cour de cassation has confirmed in various cases that the opposability of security interests is submitted to the *lex concursus*. In a relatively recent decision on a reservation of title clause, the highest French court has judged that the question as to whether the beneficiary of the clause (in most cases, the seller of the goods to which the

---

[87] French-Belgian Convention of 8 July 1899; French-Italian Convention of 3 June 1930; French-Monaco Convention of 13 September 1950; French-Austrian Convention of 27 February 1979.   [88] J-P Rémery, n 81 above, 10ff.

[89] J-P Rémery, n 81 above, 76f.

title has been reserved) can claim his title in a bankruptcy procedure is exclusively governed by the provisions of the *lex concursus*, whatever law governs the creation and the general effects of the clause.[90] In a case involving the right of set-off, the Cour de cassation came to the conclusion that again the law of the bankruptcy determines whether this right can be exercised or not.[91] In this case, the bankruptcy had been adjudicated in Italy, but, since the debtor also owned assets in France, a French agent had been nominated. This agent invoked a right of set-off in relation to his fees against the price of the assets of the company to be sold in France, which he was bound to make over to the bankruptcy trustee in Italy. The Italian bankruptcy trustee refused the agent's right of set-off on the ground that the Italian law of insolvency, which was applicable to the case since the bankruptcy was adjudicated in Italy, did not allow it. Subsequently, the Italian trustee filed a claim with a French court against the French agent in order to recuperate the price obtained from the sale in France of the company's assets. The Paris Cour d'appel applied Italian law to the case and adjudicated the claim. This decision was confirmed by the Cour de cassation.

The above-mentioned cases show that the *lex concursus* completely overrides any other law normally applicable to security interests. However, the *lex concursus* only claims application with respect to their opposability to the debtor and third parties in insolvency proceedings. The question of the validity of the security itself must be examined under the law applicable to its creation. For instance, in the examples mentioned above, before discussing whether a reservation of title clause can or cannot be opposed to third parties in insolvency proceedings according to the *lex concursus*, the judge examines whether this clause has been correctly created. The same applies to rights of set-off. To summarize: in order to assess whether a security can be opposed by its beneficiary to parties involved in insolvency proceedings, the judge will have to follow a two-step reasoning process. Initially, he will examine whether the security interest itself was created in a valid manner and is therefore effective. If such is the case, the judge will then consider the conditions of opposability set by the *lex concursus*.[92] This reasoning leads to a plurality of conditions to be fulfilled by the security interest in order to be taken into account in the insolvency proceedings. Taking advantage of this system, French courts have until now often restricted themselves to the second step in the reasoning process (the question of opposability according to

---

[90] Cass 1ère civ, 8.1.1991, Soc Heinrich Otto: Bull Civ I, no 9; D 1991, p 276, note J-P Rémery; JDI 1991, p 991, note A Jacquemont; D 1993, som p 286, obs F Pérochon.
[91] Cass 1ère civ, 6.6.1990, Anger: Bull civ I, no 136; D 1991, p 137, note J-P Rémery; Revue critique DIP 1993, p 425, note M-N Jobard-Bachellier.   [92] J-P Rémery, n 81 above, 87f.

the *lex concursus*). This is, however, bound to change with respect to foreign reservation of title clauses, since the French legislator has decreed that they are opposable, under certain conditions, to third parties in a bankruptcy procedure.[93]

It must be noted that the Brussels Convention of 1995, under certain circumstances, limits the scope of the *lex concursus* with respect to real rights and specific security interests.[94] For instance, Article 5(1) of the Convention provides for the principle that 'the opening of insolvency proceedings shall not affect the rights in rem of creditors or third parties in respect to tangible or intangible, movable or immovable assets belonging to the debtor which are situated within the territory of another Contracting State at the time of the opening of the proceedings'. Paragraph 2 of the same Article contains a number of examples of what must be understood by rights *in rem*.[95] Even though this list of examples does not refer directly to the floating charge, the Contracting States agreed that a floating charge created under United Kingdom law qualifies as a right *in rem* for the purpose of the Convention.[96] For instance, Article 5 would be applicable in the case of an insolvency procedure opened in France (where the debtor company has its registered office or the centre of its main interests) where a floating charge has been created over assets belonging to the debtor but located in the United Kingdom.[97] Indeed, if the assets of the debtor are located in France, Article 5 does not apply. The assets will be submitted to the *lex concursus*, thus to French law. The question which then arises in the context of the French winding-up procedure is: what does 'shall not affect' mean in the context of the Convention? Following the opinion of one of the official reporters of the Convention, it means that a creditor holding a floating charge or another security interest qualified as a right *in rem* is not affected in his right by the insolvency proceedings opened in France and he may therefore proceed to realize the collateral in the United Kingdom to satisfy his secured claim.[98] However, where a secondary

---

[93] See n 58.

[94] Article 15, para 1 of the French-Austrian Convention of 1979 contains a similar provision.

[95] Article 5, para 2 reads as follows: 'The rights referred to in paragraph 1 shall in particular mean: (a) the right to dispose of assets or have them disposed of and to obtain satisfaction from the proceeds of or income from those assets, in particular by virtue of a lien or a mortgage; (b) the exclusive right to have a claim met, in particular a right guaranteed by a lien in respect of the claim or by assignment of the claim by way of a guarantee; (c) the right to demand the assets from, and/or to require restitution by, anyone having possession or use of them contrary to the wishes of the party so entitled; (d) a right in rem to the beneficial use of the assets.'

[96] Miguel Virgos, 'The 1995 European Community Convention on Insolvency Proceedings: an Insider's View', in *FORUM Internationale on Commercial Law and Arbitration* (1998), no 25, p 19.   [97] For the localization of assets, see Art 2(g) of the Convention.

[98] Miguel Virgos, n 96 above, p 19.

proceeding is opened in the United Kingdom, the creditor would have to participate in this proceeding under United Kingdom law. According to the same author, only the rights and not the assets themselves are left unaffected by the opening of insolvency proceedings. The law of the state of the opening, which in our example is French law, determines which assets form part of the estate on a universal basis, ie wherever they are situated (Article 4). The main trustee could thus promptly pay the secured debt in order to avoid a separate realization of the security interest which might devalue the asset and therefore bring up less for the creditor as well as leave a lower surplus for the estate after satisfaction of the secured creditor.[99] According to this view, the right *in rem* remains totally outside the insolvency proceeding and seems to put the creditor in a better position. The question of priority among several creditors holding a security interest with relation to the same asset(s) will then not be submitted to the *lex concursus*, but to the law applicable to the security, which will most likely be the *lex situs*. A slightly different view is taken by Frédérique Dahan:[100] applied to our example, Article 5 of the Convention not only guarantees that the English floating charge will not be declared void by French law, but also invites the French insolvency trustee to take it into account in the proceedings, with the effects attached to it by English law. According to the author, a transposition of the floating charge in French law is therefore essential. The consensus reached by the European states in Article 5 still leaves insolvency trustees with many problems to solve: determining the content of the law applicable to the security interest, transposing the security interest in the national system, reconciling the interests of all the creditors of the insolvent debtor.

V. THE EFFECTS IN FRANCE OF INSOLVENCY PROCEEDINGS OPENED IN ANOTHER COUNTRY

Insolvency proceedings opened in another country can only have effect in France in two cases: first, when there has been an *exequatur* of the bankruptcy adjudication, and secondly, when there is a bilateral or multilateral convention providing for the recognition by operation of law of the effects of insolvency proceedings.[101] In all other cases, the insolvency procedure initiated in another country will produce no effect in France at

---

[99] Art 18(1) of the Convention provides that 'the trustee may remove the debtor's assets from the territory of the Contracting State in which they are situated, subject to Articles 5 and 7'. [100] Frédérique Dahan, n 64 above, pp 402–403.
[101] This would be the case under the Brussels Convention (Arts 16ff).

all.[102] The debtor will not lose his power of disposal over his assets located in France and individual proceedings against him will not be suspended. Also, security interests in assets located in France will not be affected by the bankruptcy opened abroad.

Consequently, insolvency proceedings can be opened in France against a debtor who has already been declared insolvent in another state. However, if *exequatur* is granted to a foreign bankruptcy decision, the consequences which the foreign *lex concursus* attaches to this decision will be effective in France.[103] As for the powers of the foreign insolvency trustee, they too are submitted to *exequatur*.[104] An administrative receiver cannot take any measures against the debtor's assets in France submitted to a floating charge without a prior acceptance by a French court of his powers and capacity in an *exequatur* judgment. Such a French *exequatur* judgment presupposes that there is an English court decision to be enforced. In consequence, if the administrative receiver is to be seen as an insolvency trustee, his capacity to act in France will only be considered if he has been appointed in a court decision. An administrative receiver who has been 'privately' nominated by the creditor will not be given powers in France since no *exequatur* can take place.

Under the 1995 Brussels Convention, the powers of the 'liquidator' to act are recognized in all Contracting States (Article 18). With respect to security interests, this would mean taking measures against the debtor's assets located in France in order to enforce the effects of the opening of insolvency proceedings. Annex C to the Convention contains for each Contracting State a list of the persons and bodies which fall under the definition of liquidator in the sense of Article 2(b). However, the administrative receiver is not mentioned in the list of the United Kingdom under 'liquidator'.

VI. CONCLUSION

The overview given in this chapter shows that the matter of conflict of laws with respect to security interests is, to say the least, quite complex. Simplification of the law applicable to international bankruptcy which, as we

---

[102] For a recent decision on the necessity of *exequatur* for a foreign judgment of bankruptcy to produce effects in France, see Cass 1ère civ, 24.3.1998, Darby c Josephs: Bull no 122, 81; DS 1998, IR, 108; Gaz Pal 1998, 2, panor p 231; JCP 1998, II, 10155, note E Kerkhove; Revue critique DIP 1999, som p 834.

[103] See Cass 1ère civ 25.2.1986, Soc Kléber: Revue critique DIP, 1987, p 589, note H Synvet; JCP, G, 1987, II, 20776, note J-P Rémery, where the law applicable to the bankrupcty was Danish law.

[104] See Cass 1ère civ, 29.6.1971: JDI 1973, 383, note Trochu; Revue critique DIP, 1973, p 343, note Loussouarn.

have seen, is of crucial importance to security interests, seems attainable at least among the twelve European countries bound by Article 65 of the EC Treaty.[105]

However, unification or even harmonization of the conflict of laws rules in relation to security interests in general remains a 'dream'. Most attempts made in this direction by various international institutions have failed.[106] The suggestions made with a view to a uniform substantive law of security interests have been no more successful. However, a few positive steps can be reported. The European Bank for Reconstruction and Development has elaborated a Model Law on Secured Transactions of 25 March 1994 to help with the economic restructuring in Eastern European countries. This is, however, only a model law and not a means towards the international harmonization of rules.

Although the Hague Conference decided ten years ago not to work in this area,[107] the Special Commission on General Affairs and Policy which convened in The Hague in May 2000, decided to put as a new topic on the agenda of the Conference the conflicts of laws relating to securities held through intermediaries. This attempt could be the first step towards more in-depth work in the field alongside UNCITRAL if that institution is to continue working on the substantive aspects.

Meanwhile, and in order to facilitate international credit transactions and to enhance the flexibility required by the global economy, French courts should be more open to foreign security interests and oppose them only when they clearly violate French principles of public policy.

[105] Denmark, Ireland, and the UK have a special status. Denmark is not bound at all and cannot opt in. Ireland and the UK have the possibility to opt in.

[106] For a review of the attempts made to unify or harmonize the conflict of laws on security interests, see K Kreuzer, Reconnaissance, 465ff.

[107] The Special Commission expressed the opinion that 'it would be very difficult, if not impossible, for the Conference to be successful in a field where so far work both on a universal and on the regional level, notwithstanding great efforts, had not led to concrete results'. See the Conclusions of the Special Commission of January 1988, in *Hague Conference on Private International Law, Proceedings of the Sixteenth Session,* Tome I, Miscellaneous matters, Preliminary Document No 14, pp 195ff.

10

Extraterritorial Impact of Choice of Law Rules for Non-United States Debtors under Revised Uniform Commercial Code Article 9 and a New Proposal for International Harmonization*

PROFESSOR CHARLES W MOONEY JUN

(Associate Dean for Academic Affairs and Professor of Law, University of Pennsylvania Law School)

I. INTRODUCTION

After almost a decade of study, meetings, deliberations, and drafting, a new version of Uniform Commercial Code (UCC) Article 9 (Secured Transactions)[1] recently was promulgated in the United States. As of May 2000, Revised Article 9 had been enacted in twenty-two states (including California and Texas), was on the governor's desk for signature in three other states, and had been introduced in fifteen other jurisdictions. It is under study as a part of the legislative process in several others. Former Article 9, which is destined to be replaced by Revised Article 9, is generally believed to have been one of the most successful—if not the most successful—uniform law projects ever undertaken in the United States. I expect that Revised Article 9 will earn a similar reputation.

Revised Article 9 substantially rewrites the former Article. Many stylistic changes were necessary in order to have the statute conform to the modern drafting style now in use for uniform laws. The numerous substantive

---

* The author served as a Reporter for the Drafting Committee to Revise Uniform Commercial Code Article 9 (Drafting Committee) along with Steven L Harris, Professor of Law, and Norman & Edna Freehling Scholar, Chicago-Kent College of Law. The views expressed in this chapter are not necessarily those of the Drafting Committee or its sponsors, the American Law Institute (ALI) and the National Conference of Commissioners on Uniform State Laws (NCCUSL). I wish to thank Katherine Scobey (JD 2000, University of Pennsylvania; BA 1984, Yale University) for her excellent research assistance and comments.
[1] American Law Institute and National Conference of Commissioners on Uniform State Laws, *Uniform Commercial Code Official Text and Comments* (1999). For background, see generally SL Harris and CW Mooney Jun, 'Reflections of the Reporters: How Successful Was the Revision of UCC Article 9?' (1999) 74 Chi-Kent LR 1357. That article is one of several that appear in a symposium issue of the Chicago-Kent Law Review; the symposium is devoted exclusively to Revised Article 9. As used in this chapter, 'Revised Article 9' and 'the revised Article' refer to the 1999 official text of Article 9. References to 'Revised section 9– —' and 'R § 9– —' are to sections of Revised Article 9. 'The former Article' and 'Former Article 9' refer to the 1995 official text of Article 9. References to 'Former section 9– —' and 'UCC § 9– —' refer to sections of the former Article.

changes arose for a variety of reasons. Some seek to impose normatively superior social policies, including provisions intended to override judicial interpretations of the former Article that were thought to be undesirable. Others were occasioned by the need to modernize the statute to take account of developments in financing practices, structures, and patterns. Still others were thought useful by virtue of the increasingly international aspects of many secured financing transactions. This last group of revisions includes new choice of law rules for non-United States debtors. This chapter addresses these new choice of law rules, among other things.

The new Article 9 choice of law rules should attract special attention from those with an interest in modernizing and harmonizing the law of secured transactions worldwide. Were several nations to adopt modern secured transactions laws and also to adopt choice of law rules similar to those provided in Revised Article 9, the impact might be felt in many other nations as well. Modern secured transactions laws, as I contemplate them, would condition the effectiveness of a security interest, against creditors or purchasers, on compliance with a public notice ('filing' or 'registration') requirement, as does Article 9. As explained below, that development could provide strong incentives for the other nations to make their own secured transactions laws conform.[2]

The wild card in this discussion is the intersection of laws governing property and enforcement rights and those governing insolvency, bankruptcy, and reorganization. Past years have seen considerable efforts toward harmonization and rationalization in connection with the administration of insolvency proceedings around the world. Recent examples include the European Union Convention on Insolvency Proceedings,[3] the International Bar Association Concordat,[4] the UNCITRAL Model Law on Cross-Border Insolvency,[5] and the Transnational Insolvency Project of

---

[2] For a pessimistic view of the processes of international harmonization, based on a political economy analysis, see PB Stephan, 'The Futility of Unification and Harmonization in International Commercial Law' (1999) 39 Va J of Int'l L 743.

[3] European Union Convention on Insolvency Proceedings (EU Convention), opened for signature, 23 November 1995, (1996) 35 Int Leg Materials 1223. The EU Convention received only 14 of the required 15 signatures by its self-established deadline of 23 May 1996. See generally LA Burton, 'Toward an International Bankruptcy Policy in Europe: Four Decades in Search of a Treaty' (1999) 5 Ann Surv Int'l and Comp L 205.

[4] International Bar Association Section of Business Law's Committee J, Cross-Border Insolvency Concordat, 15 September 1995. See generally A Nielsen et al, 'The Cross-Border Insolvency Concordat: Principles to Facilitate the Resolution of International Insolvencies' (1996) 70 Am Bankr LJ 533.

[5] Report of United Nations Commission on International Trade Law (UNCITRAL) on the Work of its Thirtieth Session, UN GAOR, 52d Sess, Annex I, at 68–78, UN Doc A/52/17 (1997). See generally AJ Berends, 'The UNCITRAL Model Law on Cross-Border Insolvency: A Comprehensive Overview' (1998) 6 Tulane J Int'l and Comp L 309.

the ALI.[6] These efforts are of enormous importance and the UNCITRAL Model Law and the ALI's project certainly have promise. In general, they seek to find the proper balance among 'universalist' (ie, one principal court administers a debtor's insolvency, with the co-operation of courts in other interested countries), 'territorial' (ie, courts in each interested country administer local assets for the benefit of local creditors, without significant regard for foreign proceedings), and hybrid approaches in transnational insolvencies.[7] Understandably, the focus of these projects has been on procedural aspects of insolvency proceedings, to the end that co-operation, maximization of recoveries, and equitable distributions would be promoted.

For the most part these projects and the commentaries that address them do not seek to resolve the issue of priorities, including priorities of security interests.[8] Yet the 'acid test' for a secured transaction, of course, is the extent to which it is respected in an insolvency proceeding *vis-à-vis* competing claimants. For this reason, this chapter focuses almost exclusively on the local (non-bankruptcy) law of property and enforcement.[9] My focus is on harmonization of secured transactions law as a complementary goal of regulating bankruptcy procedure. As this chapter suggests, as progress continues in the procedural realm, perhaps the next wave of effort should focus on harmonization *per se* and confront the difficult issues of priorities head on.[10]

This chapter is organized as follows. It first describes the choice of law rules under former Article 9 and those that have replaced them under Revised Article 9. In particular, it explains the rules (under both versions) that address directly non-United States debtors. The chapter then explores

---

[6] American Law Institute, *Transnational Insolvency Project, Principles of Cooperation in Transnational Bankruptcy Cases Among Members of the North American Free Trade Agreement* (Tentative Draft, 14 April 2000). [7] See, eg, ibid at 10–11.

[8] For an exception, see, eg, JL Westbrook, 'Universal Priorities' (1998) 33 Texas Int'l LJ 27 (analysing alternative systems for universal cross filing (liquidators in one country would file claims in insolvency proceedings in other countries), cross priority (non-discriminatory treatment for foreign secured claims), and choice of law rules for determining priorities).

[9] Of course, priority rules *in* insolvency proceedings also are important. For present purposes I assume that insolvency rules that substantially impair security interests would be reformed by a nation as a part of modernizing and harmonizing its non-bankruptcy law. Otherwise, the project would hardly be worth the effort.

[10] I advance no overarching criticism of—indeed I applaud—continuing efforts to bring procedural regularity to international insolvency law. Harmonization of secured transactions law, however, will require the efforts of a new group of experts with a very different mindset. The latter project must focus not merely on how assets in *actual* insolvencies are administered and distributed, but on the enormously more important and economically significant question of how the legal regime (including insolvency regime) affects actors outside insolvency proceedings—ie, how it should be structured to encourage extensions of credit. See generally SL Harris and CW Mooney Jun, 'Measuring the Social Costs and Benefits and Identifying the Victims of Subordinating Security Interests in Bankruptcy' (1997) 82 Cornell LR 1349.

the impact of the adoption by other non-United States jurisdictions of Revised Article 9-like statutes that contain Revised Article 9-like choice of law rules. It next advocates harmonization through adoption of modern secured transactions laws that include public notice requirements. It then explains how enactment of expansive domestic choice of law rules in some jurisdictions could affect arguably 'purely domestic' transactions in *other* jurisdictions that have *not* adopted similar laws, thereby providing powerful incentives for modernization and the adoption of public notice systems in the other jurisdiction. It also sketches a proposal for an international registry for secured transactions and a companion model law on choice of law for security interests in personal property. Finally, it advocates harmonization and modernization of secured transactions law through the vehicle of international conventions, such as the projects now being undertaken by the International Institute for the Unification of Private Law (UNIDROIT)[11] and UNCITRAL.[12] In that context, it explains that the very concept of a 'purely domestic' transaction itself may be obsolete, unhelpful, and worrisome.

II. CHOICE OF LAW RULES UNDER FORMER AND REVISED ARTICLE 9

Former section 9–103 governed choice of law concerning 'perfection and the effect of perfection or non-perfection of a security interest'.[13] The reference to 'the effect' is generally understood to refer to the priority of a security interest *vis-à-vis* a competing claim to collateral, that is, prior-

---

[11] UNIDROIT is an intergovernmental organization based in Rome. See Report of the Drafting Committee, Unidroit CGE/Int/2–WP/24, ICAO Ref LSC/ME-WP/27 (1 September 1999), Appendix I (Text of the [preliminary] draft [Unidroit] Convention on International Interests in Mobile Equipment, as reviewed by the drafting committee in the light of the Joint Session's second reading thereof (the Base Convention)), Appendix II (Text of the [preliminary] draft protocol to the [preliminary] draft [Unidroit] Convention on International Interests in Mobile Equipment on matters specific to Aircraft Equipment, as reviewed by the drafting committee in the light of the Joint Session's second reading thereof (the Aircraft Protocol)). Subsequent references to the 'UNIDROIT Convention' are intended to encompass both the Base Convention and the Aircraft Protocol, unless otherwise specified. A recent symposium issue of the Uniform Law Review is devoted to the UNIDROIT Convention: 4 Unif LR 1999–2. Although I was a member of the UNIDROIT Study Group on the mobile equipment project and now serve on the United States delegation, the views expressed in this chapter are not necessarily those of the United States.

[12] See Report of the Working Group on International Contract Practices on the Work of its Thirty-First Session, Annex I, Draft Convention on Assignment [in Receivables Financing] [of Receivables in International Trade], A/CN9/466 (2 November 1999) (UNCITRAL Convention). A recent symposium issue of the University of Pennsylvania Journal on International Economic Law addresses both the UNIDROIT Convention and the UNCITRAL Convention. See (Fall 1999) 20 J of Int'l Econ L.

[13] UCC § 9–103(1)(a). 'Perfection' refers to the steps necessary to create a security interest and to cause it to be effective against a later judicial lien creditor. See UCC §§ 9–303; 9–301(1)(b), (3). The principal perfection steps designed to impart public notice of a security interest are filing a financing statement and taking possession of the collateral. See UCC §§ 9–304; 9–305.

ity. Although the former Article contained some specialized rules,[14] the two principal choice of law rules were found in Former section 9–103(1) and (3). Subsection (1) applied to 'documents, instruments, rights to proceeds of written letters of credit, and goods other than those [subject to specialized rules]'. Under subsection (1), the law of the jurisdiction in which the collateral is located governed perfection (for example, where to file a financing statement) and priority.[15] Under subsection (3), the law applicable to perfection and priority for most intangible collateral, including most 'accounts . . . and general intangibles', as well as 'goods which are mobile and which are of a type normally used in more than one jurisdiction', was '[t]he law (including the conflict of laws rules) of the jurisdiction in which the debtor is located.'[16] Subsection (3) also provided guidance on where a debtor is located; a business debtor with multiple places of business, for example, was located in its 'chief executive office'.[17]

Revised Article 9 has made some bold changes in its choice of law provisions.[18] It has abandoned the *situs* (location of collateral) rule for *perfection* of security interests in most collateral covered by Former section 9–103(1); it has replaced that test with a location of debtor test.[19] It has retained the *situs* rule for most such collateral for purposes of the law governing *priority*, however.[20] In another bold step, it provides that a debtor such as a corporation is located not in its 'chief executive office'[21] as under Former Article 9 but in the jurisdiction under whose laws it is organized (for example, a corporation's jurisdiction of incorporation).[22]

[14] See eg UCC § 9–103(2) ('goods covered by a certificate of title'), (4) ('chattel paper'), (5) ('minerals or the like (including oil and gas)'), (6) ('investment property').

[15] Former § 9–103(1) modified the location rule in a curious way, providing a temporal twist: 'the law of the jurisdiction where the collateral is when the last event occurs on which is based the assertion that the security interest is perfected or unperfected'. This so-called 'last-event' test was highly criticized. See eg H Kripke, 'A Draftsman's Wishes That He Could Do Things Over Again—UCC Article 9' (1989) 26 San Diego LR 1.

[16] UCC § 9–103(3)(a), (b).   [17] UCC § 9–103(3)(d).

[18] For the most complete discussion to date of Revised Article 9's choice of law rules in the international setting, see NB Cohen and EE Smith, 'International Secured Transactions and Revised UCC Article 9' (1999) 74 Chi-Kent LR 1191.   [19] R § 9–301(1).

[20] R § 9–301(3). Although there may be clear cases, in many cases distinguishing and analysing the issues of perfection and priority may be very difficult under the law of a non-Article 9 jurisdiction. See eg Cohen and Smith (1999) at 1206. Revised Article 9, as did its predecessor, also contains some specialized provisions. See eg R §§ 9–301(4) (certain collateral related to minerals); 9–302 ('agricultural liens'); 9–303 ('goods covered by a certificate of title'); 9–304 ('deposit accounts'); 9–305 ('investment property'); 9–306 ('letter of credit rights').   [21] See n 17 and accompanying text.

[22] Revised section 9–307(e) provides: 'A registered organization that is organized under the law of a State [ie, a state or territory of the United States] is located in that State.' Revised section 9–102(a)(70) defines 'registered organization' as 'an organization organized solely under the law of a single State or the United States and as to which the State or the United States must maintain a public record showing the organization to have been organized'. Special rules are provided for certain debtors. See eg R § 9–307(f) (registered organizations organized under United States federal law and bank branches and agencies).

Former Article 9 contained some special provisions dealing with non-United States debtors. Under Former section 9–103(3)(c), if a debtor is located in a foreign jurisdiction that does not provide for perfection by filing or recording in the foreign jurisdiction, then the law of United States jurisdiction 'in which the debtor has its major executive office in the United States' was the applicable law for perfection and priority.[23] Under an alternative provision in paragraph (3)(c), if a debtor is not located in the United States or Canada, a security interest in accounts or general intangibles for the payment of money 'may be perfected by notification to the account debtor'.[24]

While well intentioned, subsection (c) was generally regarded as unsuccessful.[25] For example, the first sentence was of little use when the foreign debtor did not have a 'major executive office in the United States'. And the second sentence is not a choice of law rule at all; it simply provides for a special method of perfection ('notification') when it is applicable. More generally, the drafters of Revised Article 9 thought that the general deference to laws outside the borders of the United States was too broad for purposes of perfection of security interests created by foreign debtors, as discussed next.

Revised section 9–307 provides the basic rules for determining the location of a debtor for purposes of the choice of law rules. Subsection (b) sets forth the baseline rules and subsection (c) contains specialized treatment for debtors located outside the United States. Under subsection (b), an organization with more than one place of business, for example, 'is located at its chief executive office'.[26] Under subsection (c), however, subsection (b) does not apply unless the law of the jurisdiction in which the debtor's chief executive office is located 'generally requires information concerning the existence of a nonpossessory security interest to be made generally available in a filing, recording, or registration system as a condition' of perfection with respect to the collateral involved.[27] When subsection (b) is not applicable, 'the debtor is located in the District of Columbia'.[28] Under subsection (c), then, if the foreign debtor's jurisdiction does not have a qualifying public notice system, 'the debtor is located in the District of Columbia'.[29]

---

[23] UCC § 9–103(3)(c).   [24] ibid.   [25] See Cohen and Smith (1999) at 1197–1199.
[26] R § 9–307(b)(3). The rule of Revised section 9–307(e), discussed above, which locates a registered organization in its jurisdiction of organization, does not apply to foreign debtors.
[27] R § 9–307(c).   [28] ibid.
[29] The District of Columbia is a political subdivision created under the federal laws of the United States. Official Comment 3 to Revised § 9–307 states: 'Under the general rules of this section, a non-US debtor normally would be located in a foreign jurisdiction and, as a consequence, foreign law would govern perfection. When foreign law affords no public notice of security interests, the general rule yields unacceptable results'.

The operation of Revised Article 9's foreign debtor choice of law rules is best understood with an example:

Detter Ltd and Customer SA each are organized under the laws of the nation of Secret and also have their chief executive offices in Secret. Customer owes Detter 100 Million Agents (the local currency of Secret) for services rendered by Detter. As security for a loan made by Confidential Bank, Detter assigned to Confidential its rights in the receivable owed by Customer (among other receivables). Confidential Bank is also organized under the laws of Secret and has its chief executive office in Secret. Confidential notified Customer that its debt to Detter had been assigned to Confidential and instructed Customer to remit payment of the 100 Million Secret Agents to Confidential. This notification is adequate under the law of Secret to protect the assignment from attack by creditors of and purchasers from Detter.

Detter has been sued in a court of the Republic of Public by a creditor, Predator Co. Public has adopted a law substantially similar to Revised Article 9 (including its choice of law rules). After obtaining a judgment against Detter in the Public court, Predator caused process to issue against Customer, under which Customer must pay its debt to Detter into court for application to Predator's judgment.[30] Having learned of this development, Confidential has intervened in the court proceeding in Public, asserting that its rights are senior to those of Predator in Detter's receivable from Customer.[31]

What will be the result in the priority contest between Predator and Confidential?[32] The forum court in Public will look to the applicable choice of law rule in Public to resolve the priority contest. If the court consults Public's Revised section 9–301(1), it will learn that, for accounts such as the one owed to Detter by Customer, the law of the jurisdiction in which the debtor (here, Detter) is located governs priority. Because Secret does not have a qualifying public notice system, Revised section 9–307(c), as enacted in Public, provides that Detter is located in *Public*.[33] Under

---

[30] We need not struggle here with details of Public's local procedural laws and rules. In most states in the United States, for example, a judgment creditor such as Predator would reach the debt owed by Customer to Detter by a garnishment proceeding.

[31] This example assumes that both Detter and Customer are subject to personal jurisdiction in the Public Republic. Alternatively, even if Customer alone is subject to personal jurisdiction in Public, Predator could obtain jurisdiction for purposes of having the debt owed by Customer applied to the satisfaction of Predator's claim against Detter. See Restatement (Second) of Conflict of Laws § 68.

[32] The example might have featured a second assignment by Detter to Predator of the Customer receivable. The example as written may be more plausible, however, inasmuch as the second assignment by Detter probably would have been wrongful at best or even fraudulent. While the example is adequate for purposes of the discussion in this chapter, it is but one of a large number of settings in which cross-border choice of law questions may arise concerning perfection and priority. Many of these are canvassed and analysed in Cohen and Smith (1999).

[33] Revised section 9–307(c) actually provides that a debtor such as Detter is located in the District of Columbia. I have plausibly assumed that, having enacted a similar statute as its national law, Public would have designated a filing office in Public as the proper place to file a financing statement.

Public's Revised section 9–317(a)(2), whether Predator's judicial lien has priority over Confidential's security interest depends on whether Confidential's interest is perfected. Under Public's Revised section 9–301(1) the law of Public also governs *perfection*. A security interest in an account may be perfected only by filing a financing statement (with some exceptions not relevant here).[34] Under Revised section 9–501(a)(2), the proper place to file a financing statement is the designated filing office in Public. Because Detter is located in Public, as explained above, and Confidential has failed to file a financing statement in the proper filing office in Public, Confidential's security interest is not perfected. Consequently, Predator's judicial lien on the Customer receivable is senior to the interest of Confidential under Public's Revised Article 9.[35]

Notwithstanding this clear statutory framework, Confidential might not accept this result without an argument. Confidential would argue that one hardly could imagine a more 'purely domestic' transaction than Detter's assignment of the Customer receivable to Confidential—each of these three entities would be located in *Secret*, not *Public*, under almost any imaginable test of location. The nub of Confidential's argument would be that Public's Revised Article 9, including its choice of law rules, simply does not apply to the assignment transaction. Confidential's argument would find some support in the Official Comments to Revised section 9–307, which state that Revised sections 9–301 to 9–307 inclusive apply only when the relevant 'transaction bears an appropriate relation to the forum State' under section 1–105(1).[36]

If the collateral in the Detter-Confidential transaction were goods physically located in Public when Predator's judicial lien attached, few would doubt that the goods would provide an appropriate relation to Public. Should the result be different in the case of an intangible, when the obligor (Customer, here) is sued in Public? Stated otherwise, does the transaction bear an appropriate relation to any forum jurisdiction in which Customer may be found and sued on the debt? Confidential, of course, would argue that this puts an assignee in an impossible position at the inception of a financing transaction, inasmuch as it would be impossible for the prospective assignee to know where Customer might be found and sued in the future. On the other hand, Public's strong public policy favouring public notice may influence the forum court in Public to take an expansive view of whether the Public's Revised Article 9 bears an appropriate relation to the assignment transaction. Even if the Public

---

[34] R § 9–310(a).   [35] See R § 9–317(a)(2).

[36] R § 9–307, Official Comment 3. UCC section 1–105(1) provides that if the parties fail to agree on the applicable law, 'this Act [ie, the UCC] applies to transactions bearing an appropriate relation to this state'. Note that it does refer to the *most* appropriate relation.

forum court took a more restrictive view, were Customer located in Public (as opposed to Secret), the Public court might easily conclude that an appropriate relation exists.

Customer may be one of many obligors, located in many jurisdictions, on receivables assigned by Detter to Confidential. That fact might make an *ex ante* determination by Confidential of the applicable law as difficult, or almost so, as would be the case under an expansive approach toward the appropriate relation test. Moreover, as discussed in the following section, an instrumental argument for a broad interpretation of the appropriate relation test in this context may be based on the very difficulties of which Confidential would complain. The *baseline* choice of law rule for perfection in Revised Article 9 is the location of the debtor (Detter), which is Secret. It is Secret's failure to enact an adequate public notice law that has created the problem (or potential problem) for Confidential. Instead of rewarding entities located in Secret for this failure, an expansive approach by the forum court in Public would provide an incentive for lawmakers in Secret to wake up, smell the coffee, and reach some of the conclusions that lawmakers reached in the United States and Canada many years ago.

Confidential has at least one other worry in arguing that the Revised Article 9 choice of law rules do not apply to the Confidential-Predator priority contest. As one of the Reporters on the Revised Article 9 project, I generally am loath to question the accuracy and quality of the Official Comments. But the forum court sitting in Public may not be so deferential. UCC section 1–105(1), the general choice of law provision in the UCC, establishes the appropriate-relation test for all of the articles, including Revised Article 9. However, UCC section 1–105(2) provides:

(2) Where one of the following provisions of this Act specifies the applicable law, that provision governs and a contrary agreement is effective only to the extent permitted by the law (including the conflict of laws rules) so specified:

. . .

Law governing perfection, the effect of perfection or nonperfection, and the priority of security interests. Sections 9–301 through 9–307.

Predator will argue that the effect of subsection (2), at least by implication, is to override the generally applicable appropriate relation test in favour of the specific choice of law rules specified in Revised sections 9–301 to 9–307.[37] Whether or not Predator prevails in its argument,

---

[37] Official Comment 5 to section 1–105 supports this interpretation: '5. Subsection (2) spells out essential limitations on the parties' right to choose the applicable law. Especially in Article 9 parties taking a security interest or asked to extend credit which may be subject to a security interest must have sure ways to find out whether and where to file and where to look for possible existing filings'. Ironically, the exceptional rule that would locate Detter in Public actually causes *ex ante* uncertainty for Confidential, as explained above.

it is an argument that Confidential must be prepared to address nonetheless.[38]

The central point for purposes of this chapter is not merely the appropriate interpretation of the Revised Article 9 choice of law rules under the law of an adopting jurisdiction in the United States. Instead, I wish to address the potential consequences of widespread enactment throughout the world of expansively interpreted choice of law rules similar to Revised section 9–307(c).

III. HARMONIZATION OF SECURED TRANSACTIONS LAW

Is it a worthwhile goal to harmonize the law of secured transactions? I believe that it is, but this answer requires qualification. No one would support harmonizing domestic laws with substantive doctrine that fails to achieve the intended purposes and that reflects normatively unwise choices. Moreover, 'harmonized' legal regimes need not reflect nearly identical statutory frameworks, definitions, and the like, such as the 'uniform law' model that is standard in the United States.[39] Instead, harmonization should be grounded in the understanding that secured credit can be a vehicle for the facilitation of credit extensions and the creation of wealth.[40] Given the differences among nations in their judicial systems and personal property law regimes (among many other differences), any

---

[38] I am more sympathetic to Predator's argument than the Official Comment to Revised section 9–307 may suggest. I have found no example of commentary or case law under Former Article 9 indicating that before a forum consults the choice of law rules for perfection and priority in the forum's own Former section 9–103, it first must determine, under UCC section 1–105(1), that the transaction has an appropriate relation to the forum. Professor Cohen and Mr Smith take the position, consistent with the Official Comments, that one must first apply the appropriate relation test, at least under Revised Article 9. Cohen and Smith (1999) at 1238–1240. They concede, however, that it may be necessary to clarify UCC section 1–105 in order to ensure that result, inasmuch as 'the Comment is not the law'. Ibid at 1239. The current draft of Revised Article 1 would provide explicitly that the Revised Article 9 choice of law rules would apply only in cases in which the forum would apply a version of the Uniform Commercial Code under the forum's normal, non-Uniform Commercial Code choice of law rules. Rev UCC § 1–301(e), ALI Annual Meeting Discussion Draft 24 (14 April 2000).

[39] NCCUSL promulgates uniform laws, usually following a few years of study, drafting, and public discussion. NCCUSL is a private organization composed of commissioners selected by states and analogous political subdivisions of the United States. The UCC, unlike other uniform laws, is a joint venture between NCCUSL and the ALI.

[40] See Harris and Mooney (1997); SL Harris and CW Mooney Jun, 'A Property-Based Theory of Security Interests: Taking Debtors' Choices Seriously' (1994) 80 Va LR 2021; A Saunders et al, 'The Economic Implications of International Secured Transactions Law Reform: A Case Study' (1999) 20 Univ of Penn J of Int'l Econ L 309; SL Schwarcz, 'The Easy Case for the Priority of Secured Claims in Bankruptcy' (1997) 47 Duke LJ 425.

comprehensive system of personal property security must be 'seasoned to taste' on a nation by nation basis.[41] Moreover, harmonization in the secured transactions field should focus on the *major* principles necessary to facilitate the extension of secured credit. Thorough discussions of those principles and the social benefits of facilitating secured credit are beyond the scope of this chapter. But the appropriate principles must include a requirement for public notice as a condition for the priority of a security interest over a subsequent judicial lien and a form of first in time priority rule among competing security interests, based on the time of filing, registration, or possession.[42]

Revised Article 9 as a model for harmonization

Granting, for present purposes, the desirability of harmonizing and modernizing secured transactions law, Revised Article 9 provides an appropriate pattern for harmonization because it reflects the major principles of a sound secured transactions law. Revised Article 9's forebears—former Article 9 and the various Canadian Personal Property Security Acts (which built on Former Article 9 and generally incorporate its major principles)—have been proved enormously successful as measured by widespread enactment and the ready availability of secured credit. These successes, of course, have played out in societies marked by advanced economic development, abundant natural and human resources, legal and judicial frameworks that are sophisticated and generally free of corruption, and strong capital markets. If anything, this suggests that a secured transactions law adopting the major (Revised and Former) Article 9 principles would be even more appropriate in some countries with relatively less economic development and a relatively less reliable judicial system. Facilitating secured credit in a less developed economy and in the face of less confidence in the local judiciary calls for an *even stronger* legal framework for personal property security in order to provide *even greater* comfort to prospective creditors. On the other hand, those seeking investment in these less developed economies probably would not need (or benefit from) a statutory framework burdened by the

---

[41] The draft UNIDROIT Convention now under consideration is an important step in this direction. See, eg, Base Convention Arts 37 and 38 (making provision for Contracting States to list categories of non-consensual rights and interests that may be registered and to make declarations concerning priority of non-consensual rights and interests); Aircraft Protocol Art XXX (final provision permitting a Contracting State to declare that it will not apply certain provisions relating to choice of law and default remedies, including remedies on insolvency).

[42] The draft UNIDROIT Convention embraces these principles; the draft UNCITRAL Convention falls short.

level of regulatory detail and complexity embraced by Revised (and Former) Article 9.[43]

To what extent should Revised Article 9's baseline choice of law rule for perfection (namely, where to file) be a major principle in the international harmonization of secured transactions law? Abandoning the *situs* of collateral rule for most collateral in favour of a generally applicable location of debtor rule will substantially reduce the burden of filing financing statements in the United States for many transactions in which filings in multiple states has been required under former Article 9. Perhaps relatively fewer benefits would arise from a location of debtor rule in a nation with a single national secured transactions law and a single national filing office. But in many cases a debtor's goods (such as equipment or inventory) may be located outside the nation's borders and in multiple jurisdictions. Widespread adoption of modern secured transactions laws containing location of debtor choice of law rules for purposes of perfection, then, could render substantial benefits along the lines of those anticipated under Revised Article 9.

More controversial, perhaps, is the wisdom of encouraging widespread enactment of a provision similar to Revised section 9–307(c), which locates a non-United States debtor in the District of Columbia if the debtor otherwise would be located in a jurisdiction whose law does not have a 'generally applicable' public notice requirement as a condition of perfection. Recall the earlier example involving the Detter-Confidential assignment transaction with Revised Article 9 being the law in Public but not in Secret. A cautious Confidential might well insist on filing in compliance with Public's Revised Article 9. To be sure, that step would be prudent if one assumes that Customer is located in Public. If Secret and Public have a substantial common border or are located in the same region, the likelihood of a creditor of Detter, such as Predator, suing in Public may add an additional incentive. Indeed, the more likely it is that priority litigation will transpire in Public the greater incentive for Confidential to file.

Adding some realism to this thought experiment, now assume that a handful of jurisdictions in Europe, in Latin America, and in East Asia adopt modern secured transactions laws with choice of law rules for perfection along the lines of those of Revised Article 9. Confidential might be prudentially compelled in every transaction to comply with the public notice requirements in each of these jurisdictions, as each might present a reasonably foreseeable potential forum for a priority dispute. Viewed from one plausible perspective, this state of affairs has introduced substantial

---

[43] For a discussion of examples of substantial complexity in Revised Article 9 and speculation about the reasons underlying this complexity, see Harris and Mooney (1999) at 1388–1398.

additional uncertainty and transaction costs for financing transactions involving a debtor located in Secret. But, by choosing to eschew a generally applicable public notice regime for personal property security, Secret has only itself to blame. Moreover, Secret's regime *already* imposes material uncertainty and costs. To the extent that Secret's regime recognizes that secured transactions are effective without any public notice, these costs are imposed, for example, on those who would extend credit to Secret-located debtors and who have no sure means of determining the existence of the debtor's secured creditors. Or, costs may be imposed, and wealth creation forgone, to the extent that credit extensions are discouraged or made at a higher cost (that is, a higher interest rate). In sum, under the imagined set of facts, the marginal increases in uncertainty and costs, if any, for Secret's debtors (and for its economy, more generally) may be minimal. But the perception of uncertainty in Secret and among its debtors might be much greater.

At some point, lawmakers in Secret and in other jurisdictions without public notice systems might grow to understand that this set of affairs is unsatisfactory, to the end that these jurisdictions would adopt modern secured transactions laws. This longer term instrumental view suggests that in the harmonization of secured transactions laws around the world, a location of debtor choice of law rule, coupled with a supplemental rule for foreign debtors such as Revised section 9–307(c) (expansively interpreted), deserves serious consideration.

Harmonization of secured transactions law through domestic legislation (including the development of model laws)

The most obvious means of promoting the harmonization and modernization of secured transactions law would be the development of model laws for jurisdictions to consider as they seek to reform their local laws. If the political will exists, there is no shortage of plausible sponsors for such a project, either on a regional[44] or worldwide scope.[45] Model laws would fit well with the goal of fitting secured transactions law into a jurisdiction's existing legal regime, including its insolvency laws, as they relate to secured transactions and priorities.

Notwithstanding this potential, I am not optimistic about the prospects for actually achieving widespread enactment of model laws that would

[44] The European Bank for Reconstruction and Development has done just this, primarily for the benefit of Eastern European countries. See European Bank for Reconstruction and Development, Model Law on Secured Transactions (London, 1994).

[45] Model laws on secured transactions would be a natural next step for UNIDROIT and UNCITRAL following completion of the current projects on secured financing. See nn 10 and 11 and accompanying text.

leave the most important principles of modern secured transactions intact. Experts on a given jurisdiction's legal regime as it relates to secured transactions are likely to be legal academics or practising lawyers. Academics and lawyers may have little interest in reforms that would render obsolete their lifelong efforts to master the esoteric. Insolvency lawyers may see a regime for stronger, more effective security interests as a threat to debtors' 'free' asset base to which they expect to look for their fees. Interested players also are likely to include local financial institutions, who may perceive competitive advantages (*vis-à-vis* foreign institutions) to the jurisdiction's archaic, or at least *sui generis*, regime. These institutions may be reluctant to invite competition from offshore institutions, which might be attracted by a modern regime. Those who would benefit most directly from reforms, the entities for whom access to credit and the terms of credit would be improved, and those with whom they would do business, may lack the expertise or access to the political process necessary to make their case (even assuming they understand the case for secured credit). Time may tell whether my pessimism is warranted. In the meantime, academic attention to a 'public choice' analysis of the market for harmonization and modernization of secured transactions law would be welcome.[46]

Recently I have come to see another possible approach toward overcoming barriers to harmonization in this field. Perhaps the most difficult hurdle has been cultural and institutional opposition to the creation of new public notice systems in jurisdictions that have no tradition of such regimes—at least not regimes of the Article 9 notice filing type. My proposal would attempt to overcome, or reduce, this opposition by drawing on the extraterritorial approach taken by the Revised Article 9 choice of law rules for foreign debtors.[47] My suggestion has two components.

First, I suggest the creation of a new 'international registry', to be operated and controlled by an existing and reliable *intergovernmental* international organization.[48] The registry would be a name-based registry in

---

[46] See DA Skeel, jun, 'Public Choice and the Future of Public-Choice-Influenced Legal Scholarship' (1997) 50 Vanderbilt LR 647, reviewing ML Stearns (ed), *Public Choice and Public Law* (1997). Skeel notes that 'public choice' theory 'assumes that all of the relevant players tend to act in their own self-interest, and explores the implications of self-interest for the legislative and other institutional decisionmaking processes'. Ibid at 651. He characterizes public choice analysis as 'any analysis that incorporates or explicitly challenges the self-interestedness premise in addressing' these processes. Ibid. For an analysis of the role of bankruptcy lawyers in bankruptcy legislation in the United States, see DA Skeel, jun,'The Genius of the 1898 Bankruptcy Act' (1999) 15 Bankr Dev J 321, 336–340.

[47] See nn 18–38 and accompanying text.

[48] I do not underestimate the difficulty of identifying a willing and acceptable organization and the implementation of the international registry. But those details are beyond the scope of this brief outline. Suffice to say that once the international registry under the proposed UNIDROIT convention is a reality, my proposal may seem less daunting.

which registrations and searches would be based on a debtor's name inscribed by use of the Roman alphabet. Although it would be necessary to work out the details of a registration system in which, say, Chinese characters would be converted to a Roman equivalent, this system already exists for the Chinese language and should be feasible for all major language groups as well.[49]

The second component would be a model law covering choice of law for the public notice aspects of secured transactions. The law would provide something like the following (note that I use Article 9 terminology and many terms would require definition):

If a debtor is located in a jurisdiction whose law does not generally require information concerning the existence of a non-possessory security interest to be made generally available in a filing, recording, or registration system as a condition or result of the security interest's obtaining priority over the rights of a lien creditor with respect to the collateral, then:

(a) the perfection and priority of the security interest is governed by the law of this [jurisdiction]; and
(b) the office in which to [file] [record] [register] a notice of the security interest is the international registry.

This new approach would provide incentives for modernization and harmonization inasmuch as a jurisdiction lacking a tradition of public notice would not have to start from scratch—it could itself cause its domestic law to provide that the office for registration is the international registry. That would, of course, remove the jurisdiction from the scope of the proposed choice of law rule because that jurisdiction then *would have* a regime providing for public notice. For other jurisdictions, this approach could provide an incentive to modernize domestic laws and to create domestic registration systems in order to avoid application of the choice of law rule. In sum, the international registry could facilitate modernization for jurisdictions that would choose to embrace the international registry and could provide an incentive for other jurisdictions to clean up their own houses.

Finally, I do not underestimate the difficulties in creating something like this new regime. But, it might be an easier and speedier approach than the development and adoption of international conventions, discussed next.

---

[49] See B Xue (ed), *A Chinese-English Dictionary of Law* (Beijing, 1995) 8 (explaining that 'entries . . . are arranged according to the order of the Chinese Phonetic Alphabet').

Harmonization of secured transactions law through an international convention: towards a twenty-first century view of private international law

In many respects the process of harmonization through an international convention is much more cumbersome and unwieldy than the model law paradigm. An international convention normally would be sponsored by an intergovernmental organization, with all the usual formality and delay. The road from an idea, to a study, to successful meetings of governmental experts, and eventually to a diplomatic conference may be long, winding, and rocky. A model law, on the other hand, need not have explicit or unqualified approval of any government or intergovernmental organization, inasmuch as it is itself not a law at all but only a 'model'.

This said, the international convention route nevertheless has some significant advantages over the model law approach. Even assuming the 'model' version of a model law might be a superior product to the product produced by a diplomatic conference, the version eventually introduced to a legislature and the version eventually enacted (if any), may bear little resemblance to the original prototype. The model will be subject to influences such as those mentioned above, with little discipline from outside the jurisdiction. An international convention necessarily is more of a 'take it or leave it' package, although a successful international convention on secured transactions will find it necessary to provide alternatives that will accommodate local, domestic interests that may vary from jurisdiction to jurisdiction.[50] Moreover, an international convention that limits its bite to discrete types of transactions in an international context may face opposition that is considerably more muted than the opposition to a new domestic law that more generally upsets local doctrine. This advantage is, of course, a disadvantage as well. International conventions commonly (and unfortunately, as discussed below) are not seen as general means of reforming local law. Finally, because an international convention that comes into force necessarily binds several nations, it offers greater potential than a model law for multinational recognition and harmonization of choice of law rules.

In closing, I wish to advance briefly a thesis concerning the harmonization and reform of private law in the context of an international convention. Simply put, the historical conception of the proper domain of international conventions is too narrow and should be expanded during the twenty-first century—at least in so far as secured transactions law is concerned. First, the idea that the project is somehow tied to addressing problems that are peculiarly international or cross-border should be dis-

---

[50] See n 41 and accompanying text.

carded. As a corollary, the idea that a convention's legitimacy dictates that a *transaction* have an international 'connection' or a 'test of internationality' must be abandoned.[51] Consider an example. In the context of the UNIDROIT Convention, what *is* 'international' is *not* the attributes of any particular transaction (for example, an item of equipment has moved across borders). It is the common patterns and practices of financing seen around the world that are international. Financing structures and accompanying financial, tax, and accounting goals and concerns increasingly are shared around the world. Also international are the characteristics and location of market participants, the equipment involved, and where it *might* be necessary to enforce an interest in the equipment *as a general matter*—not in respect of a particular transaction. Secondly, and closely related to the first point, the international law reform community should embrace boldly a new and (hopefully) emerging norm that recognizes that the real project is reforming and overriding domestic, internal laws that simply are not up to the tasks of modern commercial and financial transactions. If model laws or other internal law reform efforts have not succeeded, there is no reason to shy away from an international convention as a means of reform.

The draft UNIDROIT Convention portends an important and beneficial step towards recognizing this new norm. The draft that emerged from the second joint session contains a final provision to the effect that (subject to some remaining square brackets, to be discussed further) a Contracting State may make an effective declaration stating that it will not apply the Convention to 'a purely internal transaction' and it would permit the Contracting State to specify in its declaration 'which types of transaction are to be considered purely internal'.[52] The good news, here, is that the Convention recognizes the possibility that no test of internationality may be necessary. The flip side, of course, is the unfortunate implication that it would be thinkable for a Contracting State to attempt, for purposes of the UNIDROIT Convention, to define a type of transaction that is 'purely internal'. Space does not permit an explication of why any definitional detour in search of the 'purely internal' transaction necessarily would fail in this context.[53] Suffice it to say that if the Convention

---

[51] For example, the approach taken in the UNIDROIT Convention on International Financial Leasing would not be appropriate in the secured transactions context. Article 3(1) of that convention provides: '1. This Convention applies when the lessor and the lessee have their places of business in different States and: (a) those States and the State in which the supplier has its place of business are Contracting States; or (b) both the supply agreement and the leasing agreement are governed by the law of a Contracting State.'

[52] UNIDROIT Base Convention, Art V.

[53] I have undertaken a brief explanation and analysis elsewhere. CW Mooney jun, 'Exporting UCC Article 9 to an International Convention: The Local Law Conundrum' (1996) 27 Can Bus LJ 278, 282–284.

is to carry water in the manner intended, parties to a transaction must know *ex ante* whether it will apply or not. Conditioning application of the Convention on looking back to the history of the equipment or forward to its future is not feasible. Moreover, inasmuch as the rights of third parties are concerned, it would not be feasible to inject a test that implicates the location of a creditor.[54]

IV. CONCLUSION

I have advanced two principal theses, among others, in this brief chapter. First, choice of law rules derived from the approach taken to non-United States debtors by Revised Article 9 offer an attractive approach for worldwide secured transactions law reform efforts. Were such provisions to become common, they could create strong incentives for other nations to adopt secured transactions laws containing a public notice feature. Secondly, I have argued for a more expansive view of international conventions in the context of secured transactions. I have called for abandoning tests of internationality on the transactional level. I also urged consideration of the international convention approach as a conscious strategy for reforming domestic, internal laws. Useful as harmonization efforts concerning procedural aspects of insolvency law for multinational debtors may prove, perhaps it is time to step up efforts to modernize and harmonize the substantive law of secured transactions.

[54] Ibid.

11

The English Conflict of Laws Rules

ROBERT STEVENS

(Barrister, Fellow, and Tutor in Law: Lady Margaret Hall, Oxford University)

I. INTRODUCTION

Assuming that the English courts have jurisdiction, which law or laws will be applied to determine the validity and priority of security rights? In order to answer this question it is necessary to distinguish between contractual (or *in personam*) validity and proprietary (or *in rem*) consequences. Where the debtor is insolvent the proprietary effect of the security will, obviously, be of most importance. The contractual issues cannot be ignored, however. If the law governing a contract of loan determines that nothing is owed, the proprietary effect of any security will be irrelevant.

The ancillary issues of the applicable law to determine the availability of set-off and the extraterritorial effect of the English rules of registration and clawback will also need to be considered in order to give a more complete picture.

II. CONTRACTUAL VALIDITY

Contractual issues generally

The law governing most contracts[1] is now determined by the Rome Convention on the Law Applicable to Contractual Obligations as incorporated into English law by the Contracts (Applicable Law) Act 1990. The parties to the contract are free to choose the law governing most[2] contractual issues, which in most cases well-informed parties will have done.

In the absence of choice, which law will govern? Under Article 4(2) it is presumed that the contract is governed by the place of the central administration of the company which has rendered the characteristic performance. The Giuliano–Lagarde Report on the Rome Convention refers to the 'provision of security' as being the characteristic performance in secured lending.[3] This would lead to the application of the place of the debtor's central administration.

---

[1] Not all, see Art 1(2).   [2] Not all, see Art 1(2).   [3] [1980] OJ C 282 20.

By contrast, where goods are supplied under a reservation of title clause, the characteristic performance under a contract for the sale of goods will be that of the seller/creditor as he provides the performance for which the buyer is to pay the price.[4] Similarly, it is thought that in unsecured lending the characteristic performance will be that of the creditor in making the loan.[5] It is unclear what justification there could be for treating secured and unsecured lending differently in this way.

The presumptively applicable law may be disregarded, however, if it appears from the circumstances as a whole that the contract is more closely connected with another country, in which case the law of that country will be applied.[6] For example, if the only security provided is situated in the country of the creditor's place of business it is possible that the law of that country may be applied.[7]

To the extent that the security provided is immovable property, it will be presumed that the contract is most closely connected with the country where the immovable property is situated.[8] This presumption takes priority over the presumption in favour of the place of characteristic performance. If the security covers both movable and immovable property, the wording of this presumption ('to the extent') might indicate that the presumed law might apply to issues concerning the immovable property but not to other severable issues. Giuliano and Lagarde comment, however, that such severance of the governing law is to be resorted to in only the most exceptional cirumstances.[9] The presumption in favour of the *lex situs* of the immovable property may be displaced where it appears from the circumstances as a whole that the contract is more closely connected with another country. Where, however, the assets secured, the place of contracting, and the parties to the contract are in different jurisdictions, there will not be one country of which this is true.

Formal validity

Some contractual issues are not necessarily determined by the generally governing law. A contract concluded between persons who are in the same country is formally valid if it satisfies the formal requirements of the law governing the contract or the law of the country where it is concluded.[10] Further a contract concluded between persons who are in different countries is formally valid if it satisfies the formal requirements of the law governing the contract or the law of one of those countries.[11] If the

---

[4] L Collins (ed), *Dicey and Morris The Conflict of Laws* (Sweet & Maxwell, 13th edn, 2000) (hereafter '*D&M*') 1326.　　　　　　　　　　　　　　　　　　　　　　　　[5] *D&M* 1424.
[6] Article 4(5).　　　[7] *D&M* 1327.　　　[8] Article 4(3).　　　[9] Giuliano–Lagarde Report, 23.
[10] Article 9(1).　　　[11] Article 9(2).

subject matter of the security is immovable property, the formal requirements of the law of the country where the property is situated must
be satisfied if those are imposed irrespective of the law governing the
contract.[12]

Capacity

The capacity of companies is excluded from the scope of the Rome
Convention.[13] The capacity of a company is limited by its constitution
which is interpreted according to the law of the place of its incorporation.[14]
According to *Dicey and Morris*,[15] this means that any contract entered into
by a company which is *ultra vires* will not be an act of the company and
will consequently be void. It may be doubted whether this is completely
correct. It is not correct where an English company acts *ultra vires*: the
validity of its acts cannot be called into question against a person dealing
with the company on the ground of lack of capacity.[16] The laws applicable to European Union companies have been, to an extent, harmonized in
this respect.[17] However, in dealing with a company from outside the
European Union a person runs the risk of being prejudiced by a restriction on the company's capacity of which he is unaware, something which
has not been true for anyone dealing with an English company for nearly
thirty years. In addition, a company's capacity may be further restricted,
but not increased, by the law governing the contract.[18]

Power of officers to bind the company[19]

The Rome Convention excludes from its scope 'the question whether an
agent is able to bind a principal, or an organ to bind a company or body
corporate . . . to a third party'.[20] In accordance with the general law applicable to agents,[21] whether a company's officer has *actual* authority should
be determined by the law governing the relationship between the
company and the officer. Whether a director has been validly appointed[22]

---

[12] Article 9(6).   [13] Article 1(2)(f); Giuliano–Lagarde Report, 13.

[14] *The Saudi Prince* [1982] 2 Lloyd's Rep 255; *Sierra Leone Telecommunication Co Ltd v Barclays Bank plc* [1998] 2 All ER 821.   [15] *D&M* 1110.

[16] Companies Act 1985, s 35.

[17] First Company Law Directive 68/151 [1968] OJ 41 Article 9.

[18] *First Russian Insurance Co v London & Lancashire Insurance Co* [1928] Ch 922, 935; *Rae v Lazard Investment Co Ltd* [1963] 1 WLR 555, 573.

[19] *Bowstead & Reynolds on Agency* (16th edn) ch 12; Verhagen, *Agency in Private International Law* (Martinus Nijhoff, 1995).   [20] Article 1(2)(f).

[21] *D&M* 1464.

[22] *Sierra Leone Telecommunications Co Ltd v Barclays Bank plc* [1998] 2 All ER 821.

and who are the corporation's officers authorized to deal on its behalf[23] should be and is determined by the law of the place of incorporation.

The protection accorded to third parties dealing with a company acting without capacity may be contrasted with that given to those dealing with agents of the company who lack authority. According to *Dicey and Morris* whether an agent has *ostensible* authority to bind his principal should be determined by the law applicable to the contract concluded between the agent and the third party.[24] On its face this is a strange rule as, where an agent purports to contract with a third party on behalf of his principal, the agent may not be a party to any contract with the third party.[25] What is presumably meant is that the law applicable to the putative contract that the agent has concluded on behalf of his principal is to govern the obligations of the principal.

The rule suggested by *Dicey and Morris* has much to commend it. That a principal may be bound by contracts entered into by someone who lacks actual authority but possesses ostensible authority is most easily justifiable by the general rule that a party may be bound according to the objective appearance of agreement that he has created.[26] This being so, in principle the law which should be applied to determine whether there is a contract between the principal and the third party is that which would generally be applied to determine the existence and validity of a contract. Under the Rome Convention this is determined by the putative governing law. This is the law which would govern the contract if the contract were valid.[27]

This rule makes sense from the perspective of the third party: he expects his rights to be determined by the law governing the contract he has entered into. From the principal's perspective it may be less satisfactory. The principal may be bound because of a choice of law to which it is not a party or, perhaps more accurately, is only a party to as a result of a choice made by the third party and the ostensible agent. To avoid this unfortunate result *Dicey and Morris* recommend that the law which should be applied to govern the contract between the agent and the third party is that with the 'closest and most real connection' to the contract, ignoring any choice made.[28] Whilst sensible, it is submitted that it is meaningless to describe this as the law applicable to the contract concluded between the agent and the third party as this is not, following the enactment of the Rome Convention, the method for determining the law applicable to any contract for any other purpose.

---

[23] *Carl-Zeiss Stiftung v Rayner & Keeler Ltd (No 2)* [1967] 1 AC 853.

[24] *D&M* 1474–1475; *Presentaciones Musicales SA v Secunda* [1994] Ch 271; *Merrill Lynch Capital Services Inc v Municipality of Piraeus* [1997] CLC 1214.

[25] In England he will have given a warranty of authority.

[26] Reynolds (1994) 110 LQR 21.   [27] Article 8(1).   [28] *D&M* 1478.

Another approach would be to apply the protection afforded by Article 8(2) of the Rome Convention, which allows a party to rely upon the law of the country in which he has his habitual residence to establish that he did not consent, if it appears from the circumstances that it would not be reasonable to apply the putative governing law. It may be wondered, however, where the habitual residence of a body corporate is, indeed whether it can have one at all.[29] Indirectly applying the Rome Convention leads to conformity of result with the approach generally taken in relation to the objective appearance of agreement but would render the exclusion of the ability of an agent to bind his principal from the scope of the Convention otiose, which is presumably not what was intended.

III. PROPRIETARY CONSEQUENCES

Immovable property

Proprietary validity

The general rule in English law, as in other systems, is that the *lex situs* is the governing law for proprietary issues relating to immovable property. It is generally thought that the *lex situs* in this context does not mean the domestic law of the *situs* but the law which would be applied by the courts of the *situs*. The distinction between movable and immovable property which, in common with other systems, the English conflicts of laws adopts, is not the same as the distinction which English domestic law adopts between personalty and realty. For example, a mortgage over English land is an interest in an immovable despite the fact that it is classified as personalty by English domestic law.[30] It is for the law of the *situs* of the thing to determine whether that thing is to be characterized as movable or immovable. The *lex situs* rule applies to capacity, formal validity, and essential validity.

The justification usually given for the application of the *lex situs* as the applicable law for interests in immovable property is that '[a]ny other rule would be ineffective, because in the last resort land can only be dealt with in a manner which the *lex situs* allows'.[31] This incorrectly assumes, however, that the courts of the place where the property is situated will recognize and enforce an English judgment only where the conclusion reached is the same as that it would have reached. Further, it cannot be assumed that, even if the courts of the *situs* would not recognize and

---

[29] Article 4(2) makes specific provision for corporate bodies whilst Article 8(2) fails to do so.
[30] *Re Hoyles* [1911] 1 Ch 179.   [31] *D&M* 958.

enforce the English judgment, that this would necessarily mean that the English judgment would be a dead letter. If, for example, the land has been sold and the proceeds are now situated within the English court's jurisdiction, the determination of the interests in the proceeds in a manner inconsistent with that of the *lex situs* of the original land would not prevent enforcement. The *lex situs* rule is, however, certain, accords with the parties' probable expectations, and deters forum shopping.

One potential difficulty is that it may be necessary to ascertain the scope of application of a relevant foreign law. For example, an English company gives a charge over Ruritanian land to an English bank. In a wholly domestic context in Ruritania unregistered charges given over land would be void. The question then becomes the potentially difficult one of ascertaining whether the Ruritanian law was one which applied to charges over Ruritanian land or charges created by Ruritanian companies. If the latter, it may be that a Ruritanian court would not have applied the registration requirements, in which case the English courts should do likewise.[32] The scope of application of registration requirements is probably most easily discoverable by the mode of registration, whether in a land registry or a companies' register.

Priorities

Where there is more than one security interest created over foreign land, should the *lex situs* or the *lex fori* govern the order of priorities? *Dicey and Morris* suggest that it is 'possible' that the priority of claims is governed by the *lex situs*.[33] It is submitted that it would be convenient to apply the same system of law to determine both the validity and priority of a security interest over land. The justification for applying the *lex situs* is equally strong in both cases. The *lex situs* is a single unchanging system of law. The application of the *lex fori* has the advantage that it may give a uniform result when applied to charges granted over assets in disparate jurisdictions. Its application may, however, encourage forum shopping.

Tangible movable property

Proprietary validity

The validity of a transfer of proprietary rights in tangible movables is governed by the law of the country where they are situated at the time of

---

[32] cf *Bank of Africa v Cohen* [1909] 2 Ch 129.
[33] D&M 170; *Norton v Florence Land and Public Works* (1877) 7 Ch D 332; *Macmillan Inc v Bishopsgate Investment Trust plc (No 3)* [1996] 1 WLR 387, 399.

assignment.[34] Where the goods remain in one jurisdiction, this rule has great merit. The rule is certain and probably corresponds with reasonable expectations. In *Winkworth v Christie*[35] artwork was stolen from the plaintiff in England. The goods were taken to Italy and sold to the defendant who purchased them in good faith. The goods were later sent to England where they were claimed by the plaintiff. English law determined that the thief did not have good title. It was held that, if by Italian law the defendant acquired good title from the thief, this would be recognized by the English court.

Where, however, a charge is granted over movables in different jurisdictions, the *situs* of which change over time, the justification for applying the *lex situs* of each asset at the time that the charge is granted to determine validity is far from overwhelming. It would make little sense, however, to have one rule for the transfer of interests in individual movables and another for general voluntary transfers.

Priorities

It is often stated that priorities in movables are an issue for the *lex fori*.[36] However, it was suggested in *Macmillan Inc v Bishopsgate Investment Trust plc (No 3)* by Staughton LJ that the *lex situs* should and does determine the priority in tangible movables.[37] Which is correct?

It would follow from *Winkworth v Christie* that, if A Ltd gives a fixed charge to B bank over goods situated in country X which A Ltd then sells to C Ltd, the question of whether C Ltd takes free of B bank's charge will be determined by the law of X.

One difficulty, however, is that the *lex situs* of tangible movables may change, unlike the *lex situs* of immovables or the law governing an intangible movable. The following example, drawn from by *Dicey and Morris*, is instructive. D Ltd grants a fixed charge over goods situated in country X to E bank. The goods are then taken to country Y. D Ltd there sells the goods to F Ltd representing that it has an unencumbered title. F Ltd takes in good faith. The validity of E bank's charge will be determined by the law of X. The law of Y should determine the consequences of the second transaction. If by the law of Y a bona fide purchaser acquired good title then F Ltd's title would prevail against E bank.[38]

Again, the difficulty of ascertaining the scope of a foreign law may arise. If by the law of Y a non-possessory security is void as against a bona fide purchaser unless registered, the question arises as to whether

---

[34] *Cammell v Sewell* (1858) 5 H&N 728.　　[35] [1980] Ch 496.　　[36] D&M 169.
[37] [1996] 3 WLR 387, 399.　　[38] D&M 972.

the registration requirements apply to foreign mortgages. Again, this may be capable of being answered by the mode of registration.

If the second transaction is not a sale but the creation of a second charge in favour of G bank, which charge should have priority? One answer would be to apply exactly the same approach. After all, why should mortgagees be treated differently from purchasers? If both charges have been validly created, the law of Y would determine the consequences of the second transaction. If by the law of Y the first charge created prevailed, E bank's charge should have priority.

Unlike the situation where the issue is whether a security right is lost to a bona fide purchaser, questions of priority can lead to grave difficulties where more than two jurisdictions are involved. If the goods are transferred to a third state, Z, where a further security interest is created in favour of H bank, which law or laws are to determine priority? Again, assuming that all three charges have been validly created, one solution would be to determine whether E bank has priority over G bank according to the law of Y, and for the law of Z to determine the consequences of the third transaction. If by the law of Z, unregistered charges (including foreign charges)[39] over movables are void as against other creditors, H bank's charge should have priority. However, difficulty may arise as a result of inconsistent solutions adopted by the different jurisdictions leading to circularity problems (H bank having priority over G bank which has priority over E bank which in turn has priority over H bank). The complexities increase where a company grants successive charges over movables situated in a number of different jurisdictions.

The difficulties of determining priorities by the consequences of each successive transaction by the law of the *situs* of each asset at the relevant time, whilst not insuperable, are obvious. The application of the *lex fori* may be justifiable as it provides a single system of law by which to rank the various claims, each of which may be governed by different laws over assets which may be situated in a number of jurisdictions which change over time. This approach has been adopted with ships—movables with the unhappy habit of changing the jurisdiction in which they are situated. The leading authority is the decision of the Privy Council in *The Halcyon Isle*.[40] An English bank had a mortgage on a ship which was repaired in New York by American ship repairers. The repair bill was unpaid and the ship was arrested in Singapore. The ship was sold but the proceeds were insufficient to meet both the claims of the mortgagee and the repairers. Who had priority? If the repairs had taken place in Singapore the ship repairers would not have had a maritime lien over the ship and the mortgagees would have had priority. Under the law of New York the repairers

---

[39] Whether foreign or domestic. See *D&M* 972.   [40] [1981] AC 221.

would have a maritime lien giving them priority. It was held by the majority that the *lex fori* (Singapore) should be applied to the dispute and that the mortgagees were entitled to priority.

This result has justifiably been criticized for failing to distinguish between the proprietary validity of the repairers' claim and the issue of priority.[41] The validity of the maritime lien should have been determined by the law of New York as the *lex situs* at the relevant time. Under Singaporean domestic law, in these cases where a maritime lien does exist it would have had priority.

Applying the *lex fori* to issues of priority, however, may encourage forum shopping, something which the English rules on jurisdiction will not necessarily prevent. Alternatives, which are, however, without authority, include the *lex situs* of each asset at the time of the last transaction and the *lex situs* of each asset at the time of the hearing.

Intangible movables

Debts

Article 12 of the Rome Convention on the Law Applicable to Contractual Obligations[42] provides:

1. The mutual obligations of assignor and assignee under a voluntary assignment of a right against another person ('the debtor') shall be governed by the law which under this Convention applies to the contract between the assignor and the assignee.
2. The law governing the right to which the assignment relates shall determine its assignability, the relationship between the assignee and the debtor, the conditions under which the assignment can be invoked against the debtor and any question whether the debtor's obligations have been discharged.

If a company sells receivables to a factor, the law governing the contractual rights between assignor and assignee is uncontroversial. A sale of receivables, just like any other contract, is governed by the applicable law under the Rome Convention. If the sale is ineffective, the applicable law will determine any remedy the assignee may have against the assignor (for example, damages). Article 12(1) appears to be included for the purposes of clarity.

More controversial, however, is the extent to which Article 12 is determinative of the proprietary consequences of assignment. Some commentators have taken the view that the proprietary consequences of assignment

---

[41] P North and JJ Fawcett (eds), *Cheshire and North's Private International Law* (Butterworths, 13th edn, 1999), (hereafter 'C & N') 83–84. [42] Contracts (Applicable Law) Act 1990, Sch 1.

are outside the scope of the Convention.[43] Some support for this may be derived from the Giuliano–Lagarde Report on the Convention which states that, 'since the Convention is concerned only with the law applicable to contractual obligations, property rights . . . are not governed by these provisions'.[44]

It is submitted, however, that both *Dicey and Morris* and *Cheshire and North* are correct in the view that Article 12(2) is determinative of the ownership of rights assigned.[45] A proprietary interest in a chose in action cannot be vindicated in any way except through bringing a claim.[46] The person who is *owed* a debt must, definitionally, *own* the debt. Article 12(2) clearly envisages that the obligations of the debtor are determined by the law governing the right assigned. Whether the right is capable of assignment ('assignability'), whether notice by an assignee is required ('conditions under which the assignment can be invoked'), and the relationship (if any) between debtor and assignee are all clearly governed by the law applicable to the right assigned. To whom the obligation is owed, and consequently who owns the right, is determined by the law governing the right assigned.

Further, the same principles would appear to apply regardless of whether the assignment is absolute or by way of security. It also follows that, as the law governing the obligation determines to whom the obligation is owed, where there is more than one assignment the law governing the right assigned determines to which of the assignees the right has been transferred. Priority should therefore be determined by the law governing the right assigned.[47]

Even if the language of the Convention could be ignored, it is submitted that this result is justifiable in principle. There will only be one law governing the right in question and, where there are multiple assignments, in different places, governed by different laws, it provides a single system which will determine the order of priority. Further, the debtor and original creditor may have expressly or impliedly chosen a system of law to govern the obligation. Where this has been done, the debtor will legitimately expect the obligations he is under, including to whom they are owed, to be determined by the law governing the right chosen. If, for example, by the law chosen to govern, a right may not be assigned until notice is given to the debtor, it would be unsatisfactory to allow rights to be acquired against the debtor by applying a system of law which imposed no such requirement.

---

[43] Goode, *Commercial Law* (Penguin, 2nd edn 1995) 1127–1129; Moshinsky (1992) 108 LQR 591; Struycken [1998] LMCLQ 345, 346. [44] Giuliano–Lagarde Report, 10.
[45] *D&M* 982; *C&N* 962. [46] Unless there is a right of set-off. [47] *D&M* 982.

One potential disadvantage of the approach suggested is that, if a creditor makes a global assignment of present and future debts, different laws may apply to the different debts. An assignee could not, therefore, look to a single law to determine which debts are assignable and what is necessary to perfect the assignments and obtain priority (for example, whether notice to debtors is required). Whilst real, this disadvantage should not be exaggerated. A supplier who wishes to assign the debts owed by purchasers may, if the contracts of sale were on a standard form, have stipulated that the same law was to apply to each sale. Even where no law has been expressly stipulated for, the law of the place of the central administration of the supplier, the party rendering the characteristic performance, would be presumed to apply to all the debts.[48]

It is submitted that confusion in understanding the principles applicable to the transfer of title to intangible property is caused by the search for a *lex situs*. Application of the *lex situs* initially appears attractive as it conforms with the approach taken in relation to tangible property. Any *situs* that intangible property may have, however, is a metaphysical one that it is deemed by the courts to have: 'something with no physical existence can hardly have a location in space'.[49] The application of any particular law cannot be justified by appeals to the analogy of the application of the *lex situs* to tangible property.[50] If it were thought helpful, the law governing the obligation could be deemed to be the *lex situs* without any more artificiality than any other system of law.

However, some important commentators disagree with the interpretation of Article 12 of the Rome Convention suggested here and favour the application of the *lex situs* of the debt to determine proprietary issues.[51] In the context of taxation, the *lex situs* of a debt is deemed to be the place where the debtor resides.[52] Since this will generally[53] be the place where the debt will be enforced and is a single law which will rarely change, the application of this system of law would make considerable sense when applied to the proprietary effect of a single debt.

It makes little sense, however, in the context of global assignments of existing and future debts as the places of residence of the various debtors may be unascertainable and multifarious. Those who have supported the application of the *lex situs* have suggested that an exception should be made for global assignments and the law of the assignor's place of residence

---

[48] Article 4(2).   [49] *D&M* 924.

[50] cf Goode, *Commercial Law* (Penguin, 2nd edn, 1995) 1128; Moshinsky (1992) 108 LQR 591, 607.

[51] Goode, *Commercial Law* (Penguin, 2nd edn, 1995) 1128; Moshinsky (1992) 108 LQR 591; Struycken [1998] LMCLQ 345.

[52] *Kwok Chi Leung Karl v Commissioner of Estate Duty* [1988] 1 WLR 1035.

[53] Not always: *Re Helbert Wagg & Co Ltd* [1956] Ch 323.

applied.[54] We might ask, however, what is to be deemed to be a global assignment for these purposes? The assignment of two debts or more where the residence of the debtors is different?

Assuming that the interpretation of Article 12(2) adopted here is correct, the scope of the type of rights covered by Article 12(2) remains unclear. The determinative law under Article 12(2) is that 'governing the right to which the assignment relates'. On its face the reference to the 'right' assigned is capable of encompassing all forms of intangible movables and not simply contractual obligations. It may be presumed, however, that the scope of the rights covered by Article 12(2) is the same as that for the Rome Convention generally. Obligations under trusts,[55] shares,[56] and contracts of insurance (but not reinsurance) which cover risks situated in the territories of the member states of the European Community would not, for example, be covered.[57] The common law would therefore apply. It is submitted, however, that *Dicey and Morris* are correct that the common law was and is essentially the same as Article 12.[58] This cannot be said with certainty, however, as the common law rules were not and are not entirely clear.

Negotiable instruments

If, according to the law governing the right, the right is vested in the owner of a piece of paper representing the right an incidental question arises: who is the owner of the instrument? Negotiable instruments are tangible movables. In accordance with the general approach to tangible movables,[59] validity of a transfer of proprietary rights in an instrument is governed by the *lex situs cartae* at the time of the assignment.[60] It is, therefore, misleading to ask which is the law (singular) which determines negotiablity as reference must be made both to the law governing the obligation and to the *lex situs cartae*. If the *lex situs cartae* is English law, the ownership of the certificates will not pass to a bona fide purchaser free of any defects in the title of the transferor unless there is an English custom or statute to the effect that the instrument is negotiable.[61]

---

[54] Goode, *Commercial Law* (Penguin, 2nd edn, 1995) 1128; Moshinsky (1992) 108 LQR 591, 609.
[55] Article 1(2)(g).
[56] Article 2(e); *Macmillan Inc v Bishopsgate Investment Trust plc (No 3)* [1996] 1 WLR 387.
[57] Article 1(3).
[58] *D&M* 984; *Lee v Abdy* (1886) 17 QBD 309; *Republica de Guatemala v Nunez* [1927] 1 KB 699; *D&M* 957–960.
[59] Should the law determining the ownership of the share certificates be determined by English conflicts rules or by the conflicts rules of the place of incorporation? See further *D&M* ch 3.
[60] *Alcock v Smith* [1892] 1 Ch 238, 255, 267–268; *Embiricos v Anglo-Austrian Bank* [1904] 2 KB 870, 874, [1905] 1 KB 677, 683.
[61] *Picker v London and County Banking Co* (1887) 18 QBD 515.

Shares

The leading modern authority on the law applicable to the validity and priority of proprietary rights in shares is the Court of Appeal's decision in *Macmillan Inc v Bishopsgate Investment Trust plc (No 3)*.[62] Unfortunately, the members of the Court of Appeal did not speak with one voice. They were agreed that the *lex situs* of the shares should apply but there was no unanimity as to where the *lex situs* of shares actually is. Aldous LJ's view was that shares are situated at the place of incorporation. Staughton LJ agreed, unless the shares are negotiable instruments by English law when, presumably, the *lex situs* of the shares would be the *lex situs cartae*. Staughton LJ also considered it arguable that the *lex situs* may, in certain cases, be the law of the place where the share register is kept. Auld LJ's opinion was that the *lex situs* will be the country where the share register is kept, normally but not always the place of incorporation, unless the shares are negotiable when the *lex situs* will be the *lex situs cartae*. The Court of Appeal's decision was considered by Neuberger J in *Re Harvard Securities Ltd (in liq)*,[63] but this decision does little to clarify the position.[64]

Again, it is submitted that attempting to discern a *lex situs* tends to confuse more than it helps. Whilst it is sometimes said that a shareholder has rights *in* the company this is purely metaphorical. All an owner of shares in a company has are rights against the company and other shareholders.[65] The system of law governing these rights is the law of the place of incorporation. Applying the same principles set out above, who is owed an obligation should be and is determined by the law governing the obligation. The ownership of shares should, therefore, be determined by the law of the place of incorporation. This is a convenient result as there will only be one place of incorporation.

If, according to the law of the place of incorporation, the shares are negotiable, the rights against the company and other shareholders are vested in the owner of the share certificates. The approach set out above in relation to negotiable instruments should therefore be adopted.

What if the shares are not negotiable and the share register is in a different country from the place of incorporation? If the law of the place of incorporation provides that valid inscription on the register determines title to the shares, the law of the place of the share register should determine who has been validly registered.

---

[62] [1996] 1 WLR 387; see Johnson 'The Law Applicable to Shares' in van Houtte, *The Law of Cross Border Securities Transactions* (Sweet & Maxwell, 1998).   [63] [1997] 2 BCLC 369.
[64] Stevens [1999] CFILR 139.
[65] *Colonial Bank v Whinney* (1886) 1 App Cas 426; *Re VGM Holdings* [1942] Ch 235, 241; *Borland's Trustee v Steel Bros* [1901] Ch 279, 288.

It is submitted that this approach was that taken by the Court of Appeal in *Colonial Bank v Cady*[66] and is consistent with the rather vaguer speeches given in the House of Lords in the same case.[67] American[68] and Canadian[69] authority also supports it.

Securites held through intermediaries

This topic has been the subject of an earlier colloquium and it would be inappropriate for me to set out my views at length.[70] Where securities are held by an intermediary for the benefit of a client which the client then uses for security, which law or laws is or are to determine the validity of any security right created and any question of priorities?

The starting point, it is submitted, is to determine what sort of interest the client has. It may be that the client has a proprietary interest, possibly by way of a trust, in the securities themselves. This will be determined according to the normal rules for determining interests in securities. If the client does have a proprietary interest in the securities themselves the validity and priority of the security interest in them will be determined as above. This appears to have been assumed to be the case in both *Macmillan Inc v Bishopsgate Investment Trust (No 3)*[71] and *Re Harvard Securities (In liquidation)*.[72]

Sometimes, however, by the applicable law the client does not have an interest in the securities themselves. In Europe, when securities are deposited with a central securities depository (Euroclear or Clearstream), the depositor does not have any interest in the securities but merely a right against the depository dealt with. The validity and priority of any security right taken over this interest should be determined by the law governing the right against the depository.

Both the complexity and the obscurity of the current law have led to legislative intervention. Regulation 23 of the Financial Markets and Insolvency (Settlement Finality) Regulations 1999[73] provides that for certain

---

[66] (1888) 38 Ch D 388, 399 (Cotton LJ) , 403 (Lindley LJ), 408 (Bowen LJ).

[67] 15 App Cas 267, 272 (Lord Halsbury LC), 276–277 (Lord Watson), 281 (Lord Bramwell), 283 (Lord Herschell).

[68] *Jellenik v Huron Copper Mining Co* (1899) 177 US 1, 13; *Direction der Disconto-Gesellsschaft v United States Steel Corporation* (1924) 267 US 22, 28; *United Cigarette Machine Co Inc v Canadian Pacific Railway Co* (1926) 12 F 2d 634, 636; *Pennsylvania Co for Insurance on Lives and Granting Annuities v United Railways of Havana & Regla Warehouses Ltd* (1939) 26 F Supp 379, 380; American Law Institute, *Second Restatement of the Conflict of Laws*, text to s 303.

[69] *Braun v The Custodian* [1944] 3 DLR 412,428, [1944] 4 DLR 209, 214; *Hunt v The Queen* (1968) 67 DLR (2d) 373, 378.

[70] *Oxford Colloquium on Collateral and Conflict of Laws* (1998) 12 JIBFL Supplement. See also Benjamin (1998) 47 ICLQ 923; Benjamin, *The Law of Global Custody* (Sweet & Maxwell, 1997) chs 3, 6, and 7.   [71] [1996] 1 WLR 387.

[72] [1997] 2 BCLC 369.

[73] Enacting Art 9(2) of the Directive on Settlement Finality and Payment Security Systems 98/26/EC.

transactions the law of the place where the register, account, or central-ized deposit system is located is to apply. This provision is not, however, free from difficulty. Where, for example, the register and central deposi-tory are in different jurisdictions it is unclear which law is to apply.

Preferred and deferred claims

The priorities as between claimants to a limited fund administered by a court is said to be a procedural matter that is determinable by the law of the forum.[74] The scope of this proposition is uncertain. Whether a partic-ular unsecured creditor (for example, employees or the Revenue) should be granted preferential status in an English winding-up of a company is clearly determined by English insolvency law and not by any other sys-tem of law.[75] An interesting example is *Ex p Melbourn*. A husband and wife married in Batavia. The husband settled 75,000 guilders upon his wife. The husband went into bankruptcy in England. By Batavian law a marriage settlement which was not registered was to be postponed to other claims in a husband's bankruptcy. It was held that so long as the claim was valid, the order of priorities was to be determined by the *lex fori* which allowed her to prove *pari passu* with the other creditors. It might be objected that such a rule encourages forum shopping as it is one thing for a foreign creditor who wishes to prove in England to be denied an advantage conferred by a foreign law but quite another to be placed in a better position by the application of English law.[76]

IV. ENGLISH REGISTRATION RULES

Under Part XII of the English Companies Act 1985 certain charges if unregistered are void against the liquidator, administrator or any credi-tor of the company. The requirement of registration applies to any com-pany registered in England and Wales, regardless of the *situs* of the property.[77] The requirement of registration is extended to charges created or acquired by companies outside Great Britain[78] which have an estab-lished place of business in England and Wales and the property charged is in England and Wales.[79] Even where the liquidation is a foreign one the

---

[74] *D&M* 169–170; *C&N* 82–84.
[75] *Ex p Melbourn* (1870) LR 6 Ch App 64, 67–70; *Harrison v Sterry* (1809) 5 Cranch 289, 298; *The Colorado* [1923] P 102; cf *Cook v Gregson* (1854) 2 Drew 286.
[76] Smart, *Cross Border Insolvency* (Butterworths, 2nd edn 1998) 313.
[77] Companies Act 1985, s 395.
[78] Charges created by Scottish companies do not therefore need to be registered.
[79] The Companies Act 1989, s 703D contains provisions intended to replace this regime. It is very doubtful whether this will ever be brought into force.

charge will be void against the liquidator unless registered.[80] Where an English company creates a charge over tangible movables situated abroad, any applicable registration requirements of both English law and the *lex situs* will need to be complied with to be certain that the charge will be valid upon the company's winding-up.

V. SET-OFF

Set-off outside insolvency

The procedural question as to whether any claim that the defendant has against the claimant should be tried in the same hearing is a matter for the *lex fori*.[81] Set-off may, however, not merely be a procedural issue but a substantive one operating so as wholly or partially to extinguish the claimant's cause of action. Here the proper approach should be to apply the law governing the claim that the defendant asserts has been extinguished to establish the effect of any set-off.[82] Similarly the issue of mutuality (for example, whether one claim is proprietary) should be determined by ordinary conflicts principles.

One potential disadvantage of this approach is that it is possible that the two claims may be governed by different laws, one of which permits set-off whilst the other does not. This could lead to the potentially lopsided result that one claim would be subject to a defence of set-off whilst the other would not. This might be resolved by only allowing set-off where the *lex causae* of both claims permit it.

Set-off within insolvency

In England, where a company goes into liquidation where there are mutual debts between a creditor and the company set-off is mandatory[83] and automatic.[84] The effect of this in an international context was determined in *Re Bank of Credit and Commerce International SA (No 10)*.[85] The English winding up was ancillary to the main proceedings in Luxembourg, where BCCI SA was incorporated. A judicially sanctioned agreement had authorized the transmission of funds collected elsewhere for distribution according

---

[80] *NV Slavenburg's Bank v Intercontinental Natural Resources Ltd* [1980] 1 WLR 1076.

[81] *Meyer v Dresser* (1864) 16 CB(NS) 646; Case C–341/93, *Danavern Productions A/S v Schuhfabriken Otterbeck GmbH & Co* [1995] ECR I–2053.

[82] *D&M* 169 n 12; Wood, *English and International Set Off* (Sweet & Maxwell, 1989) ch 23.

[83] Insolvency Rules 1986, 4.90; *National Westminster Bank Ltd v Halesowen Presswork and Assemblies Ltd* [1972] AC 785.   [84] *Stein v Blake* [1996] AC 243.

[85] [1997] Ch 213.

to the law of Luxembourg. The rules of set-off which would be applied in Luxembourg would be far more restrictive than those applied in England. Scott V-C held that, even in an ancillary winding-up, the English insolvency set-off provisions were mandatory and could not be disapplied, regardless of the law governing the claims or the place of residence of the creditors who had entered proofs in the English winding-up. Before any assets were transferred to Luxembourg the English liquidators were required to retain sufficient funds to compensate those creditors who would be prejudiced by the application of the Luxembourg rules of set-off.

The result is unfortunate but the blame probably does not lie with Scott V-C. Clearly identical claims will be treated differently in the principal and ancillary liquidations. Some claimants with no connection with England, whose debts and claims are not governed by English law and who may have no expectation that English law will apply, will be able to prove in an English winding-up and take the benefit of English law's extremely generous insolvency set-off provisions. However, as the set-off legislation is, on its face, subject to no territorial restriction and gives no guidance as to what criteria might be applied to confine it, it is difficult to see what alternative Scott V-C had.[86]

Where there is no English winding-up, the insolvency set-off provisions will not apply. The English courts have, however, a very wide jurisdiction to wind up companies. Any company registered in England may be wound up and any company incorporated outside the United Kingdom may be wound up if there is a 'sufficient connection' between the company and England, and there are persons who would benefit from the making of the order.[87]

VI. CLAWBACK

As has been seen in the context of set-off, in English insolvency proceedings the courts have consistently applied English insolvency law and ignored any foreign insolvency law. Where, for example, it is sought to recover a payment as having been a preference, the claim as it arises from English insolvency proceedings will be governed by English law.[88]

Whether avoidance of dispositions of a company's property after the commencement of winding-up under section 127 of the Insolvency Act 1986 applies to assets situated abroad is unclear. Property is defined for the purposes of the Act as including 'every description of property wherever

---

[86] Smart, *Cross Border Insolvency* (Butterworths, 2nd edn 1998) 320.
[87] *D&M* Rule 155.   [88] *Rousou v Rousou* [1955] 3 All ER 486.

situated'[89] which indicates that section 127 should be given extraterritorial effect. However, section 128 which avoids attachments put into force or effect after the commencement of the winding-up, does not apply to attachments in foreign jurisdictions.[90] This might indicate that a similar approach will be taken under section 127.

The approach which will be taken in relation to the law applicable to claims to set aside transactions defrauding creditors which do not arise from the commencement of insolvency proceedings is unclear. The correct characterization of such claims is uncertain. If such claims are characterized as based upon unjust enrichment[91] the general rules applicable to such claims may be applied.

VII. CONCLUSION

Much has been omitted. Whether choice of law rules are appropriate cannot be definitively assessed unless considered in conjunction with the rules concerning jurisdiction.[92] The recognition and effect of foreign insolvency proceedings has not been discussed. In order to keep the chapter within reasonable limits the applicability of the doctrine of renvoi has been largely ignored. However, it is hoped that the complexity of this area of law has been demonstrated.

[89] Insolvency Act 1986, s 346.   [90] *Mitchell v Carter* [1997] 1 BCLC 673.
[91] cf *Bowling v Cox* [1926] AC 751; *Rousou v Rousou* [1955] 3 All ER 486; *Re Jogia* [1988] 1 WLR 484 where the claim was characterized as 'quasi-contractual'.
[92] Briggs (1998) 47 ICLQ 877.

PART 4

Uniform Law

12

The UNIDROIT Mobile Equipment Convention

PROFESSOR SIR ROY GOODE

(*St John's College, Oxford*)

I. DEVELOPMENTS IN THE HARMONIZATION OF THE LAW
GOVERNING SECURITY IN MOVABLES

The sharp movement from planned to market economies has made the role of security for payment even more important than formerly; and with the globalization of markets has come a pressing need to ensure as far as possible that a security interest created under the law of one juris-diction will be recognized in others. Hence over the past decade there have been renewed attempts to secure a measure of harmonization of national laws affecting cross-border security interests. There are many kinds of instrument that can be used for the harmonization of different aspects of commercial law. They include instruments which have, or are intended to be given, the force of law, such as model laws, multilateral con-ventions, and instruments produced by supranational organizations such as the European Union; contract-based uniform rules of the kind published by the International Chamber of Commerce, such as the Uniform Customs and Practice for Documentary Credits; and 'soft law', exemplified by international restatements by scholars such as the UNIDROIT Principles of International Commercial Contracts and the Principles of European Contract Law prepared by the Commission on European Contract Law. However, contract-based instruments are inapposite to regulate transac-tions involving third party rights, while international restatements can at most be of persuasive influence.[1] For the regulation of such rights it is necessary to resort to legally binding instruments, in particular model laws, multilateral conventions, and EC Directives. All three types of instrument have been employed in the field of security interests. Of par-ticular importance are the following.

---

[1] Particularly as a guide to legislators and to arbitral tribunals who decide not to apply any national law to the dispute. The project for the preparation of a European Civil Code, under the direction of Professor Christian von Bar, is expected to include a treatment of security interests, and already a preliminary position paper has been prepared for the project by Professor Ulrich Drobnig.

The EU Directive on settlement finality in payment and securities systems

This Directive[2] is designed to ensure the reduction of systemic risk in cross-border payment and settlement systems, in particular by ensuring that national insolvency laws do not result in the unwinding of a netting. Article 9(2) of the Directive lays down a conflict of laws rule governing uncertificated securities held as collateral by system participants and/or central banks, and provides that the rights of such participants shall be governed by the law of the member state in which the register is maintained. This very useful rule is nevertheless restricted in scope, and intense negotiations are under way to broaden it so as to cover all rights held by way of collateral through an account with a securities intermediary. The intention is to secure a uniform rule to cover indirect holdings in securities through a fungible account with a custodian or other securities intermediary and to ensure that the rights of the holder of the collateral are determined by the location of the record maintained by the intermediary in question, without reference to the (artificially determined) *situs* of the underlying securities.[3]

The EBRD Model Personal Property Security Law

The 1994 Model Law on Personal Property Security is designed to provide developing countries with the framework of a modern legal regime governing security interests in personal property. The Model Law rightly concentrates on principles of attachment, perfection, and priority of security interests and does not seek to emulate the sophistication of codifications such as Article 9 of the American Uniform Commercial Code. The Model Law has attracted a great deal of interest and comment, much of it favourable.

The UNCITRAL Draft Convention on assignment in receivables financing

The Working Group set up by the United Nations Commission on International Trade Law to produce a text for a Convention on assignment in receivables financing has now completed its work and submitted

---

[2] 98/26/EC, OJ L166/45, 11 June 1998, adopted on 19 May 1998.

[3] For a detailed discussion, see *The Oxford Colloquium on Collateral and the Conflict of Laws*, published as a Special Supplement to Butterworths' *Journal of International Banking and Financial Law*, September 1998. For the follow-up seminar in London, see Richard Potok (1999) 14 JIBFL 279. More recently the European Commission has prepared a broader Directive (c4/PN D (2000) 16.6.2000).

a text for consideration by the Commission at its meeting in June/July 2000. A number of matters, including the title of the Convention, remain to be settled. A brief description of the key features of this important Convention, which builds on the 1988 UNIDROIT Convention on International Factoring, is given below.

The Draft UNIDROIT Convention on International Interests in Mobile Equipment

This ambitious draft Convention, prepared by the International Institute for the Unification of Private Law (UNIDROIT), has four major objectives:

- to give international protection to security and title-retention interests in high value mobile equipment, in particular airframes, air engines, helicopters, railway rolling stock, and space property;
- to provide holders of such interests with effective rights and remedies against debtors;
- to offer an international registration system by which such holders can protect the priority of their interests worldwide, both outside and within the debtor's insolvency, while third parties can discover the existence of those interests;
- by these means to give intending creditors and credit rating agencies greater confidence in the effectiveness of such interests, particularly in countries whose laws have traditionally been hostile to non-possessory security, and thereby facilitate the extension of credit for the acquisition of capital mobile equipment on reasonable terms, especially to developing countries, enhance the rating of receivables, and reduce borrowing costs.

A brief description is given of the UNCITRAL Draft Convention on receivables financing. The remainder of this chapter is devoted to the UNIDROIT mobile equipment Convention.

II. THE UNCITRAL DRAFT RECEIVABLES FINANCING CONVENTION

This Convention is concerned with assignments effected in cross-border receivables financing transactions, whether they are outright assignments (as in factoring transactions) or assignments by way of security (for example, for bank loans). The Convention covers both the assignment of international receivables and the international assignment of receivables, including assignments of existing and future receivables by way of security. The elements of internationality differ as between these two categories. An assignment of international receivables is one in which the assignor and the debtor are located in different states, even if the assignor and the assignee are in the same state, so that the assignment is local. An international assignment of receivables is one in which the assignor and the assignee are located in different states, even if the assignor and the debtor are in the same state, so that the transaction under which the assigned receivable arises is local. This breadth of the internationality concept is matched by the range of transactions covered, namely, trade receivables (such as those purchased under factoring and invoice discounting agreements or assigned as security for loans), financial receivables (including those arising from securitizations, swaps and other derivatives, repos, charge-backs, and clearing-house transactions), and consumer receivables.

A number of the provisions broadly track the 1988 UNIDROIT Convention on International Factoring. Like the UNIDROIT Convention, the UNCITRAL draft Convention attaches high importance to party autonomy. On the other hand, contractual provisions which interfere with modern receivables financing will not necessarily affect assignees. So, as under the UNIDROIT Convention, a contractual prohibition against assignment will not affect the rights of the assignee.

The Convention lays down substantive rules governing the creation and notification of assignments but merely prescribes a uniform conflicts rule on other issues, such as the relationship between assignor and assignee and between assignee and debtor and the determination of priorities. Relations between assignor and assignee are governed by the law chosen by the parties or, if none, by the law of the state with which the contract of assignment has the closest connection. Relations between assignee and debtor are determined by the law governing the receivable. Priorities are determined by the law of the state in which the assignor is located, a much more sensible rule than the traditional *lex situs*. An optional annex prescribes alternative substantive priority rules, the first set based on registration and the second on the order of the competing assignments.

III. THE UNIDROIT MOBILE EQUIPMENT CONVENTION: AN OUTLINE

Progress towards a Diplomatic Conference

UNIDROIT, which is responsible for this Convention, has worked in close collaboration with the International Civil Aviation Organization (ICAO), the International Air Transport Association (IATA), the private Aviation Working Group and the Aircraft Protocol Group as regards the application of the Convention to aircraft objects. This public-private partnership, involving two international intergovernmental organizations, a non-governmental international association with UN observer status, and a private industry grouping, is one of the most striking features of this ambitious project. The text of the draft Convention and draft Aircraft Protocol have been reviewed by Joint Sessions of the UNIDROIT Committee of governmental experts and the ICAO Legal Sub-Committee at meetings in Rome and Montreal in 1999 and 2000. The work of the Joint Sessions was completed at the third and final meeting in Rome, 20–30 March 2000. The texts of the two instruments, as amended by the ICAC Legal Committee at its 31st session in August/September 2000, were approved by the Governing Council of UNIDROIT and the Council of ICAC for submission to a Diplomatic Conference in 2001. As stated above, the Convention provides a regime for the creation, registration, enforcement, and priority of international interests in mobile equipment, that is, interests in aircraft, railway rolling stock, and space property arising in favour of a chargee under a security agreement or held by a person who is the conditional seller under a conditional sale agreement or the lessor under a leasing agreement.

Apart from listing the categories of equipment to be covered, the provisions of the Convention itself are not equipment-specific and will be controlled, as regards each of the three categories of object, by equipment-specific Protocols. While texts have been prepared for all three categories, only the aircraft equipment Protocol is ready for submission to the forthcoming Diplomatic Conference. The railway equipment Protocol has been reviewed by a Steering and Revisions Committee convened by UNIDROIT and involving the participation of key players, including OTIF,[4] and the next stage is for this to be examined by a Committee of Governmental Experts. The space objects Protocol has been reviewed by a restricted informal group of experts. It is hoped, however, that the Diplomatic Conference will approve provisions in the draft Convention for a fast-track procedure that will allow these Protocols to be adopted without the need for further Diplomatic Conferences.

Key elements

The UNIDROIT Convention promises to be one of the most important conventions ever to be made in the sphere of transactional commercial law. Copies of the two texts as finalized are set out in Appendices 4 and 5. The key elements of the Convention are as follows:

- If the formalities required for the creation of an international interest are complied with, then the international interest will be recognized in

---

[4] L'Organisation intergouvernmentale pour les transports internationaux ferroviaires.

every Contracting State, even if that state's national law does not ordinarily recognize non-possessory security rights or other rights of a kind
created by the Convention.

- The Convention supports a broad principle of party autonomy in contractual relationships, but with certain safeguards dictated by fundamental policy considerations.
- It contains an underlying attachment to the concept of predictability.
This is manifested in different ways. For example, the Article on interpretation, while generally following Article 7 of the Vienna Convention
on Contracts for the International Sale of Goods, substitutes predictability for good faith as an interpretative guide. Similarly, the priority rules give priority according to the date of registration in the
International Registry, irrespective of whether the first to register had
actual knowledge of a prior unregistered interest, in order to provide a
bright line rule and avoid factual disputes as to whether a person did
or did not have knowledge.
- There is a set of basic default remedies which the parties can exclude
or, for the most part, add to or vary.
- There are provisions for speedy judicial relief pending final determination of the claim and covering preservation of the object and its
value, possession, control, or custody of the object, immobilization of
the object, and/or lease or management of the object and the income
from it.
- There is an international registration system. In practice, there would
be different systems for different types of equipment. The Register
would be electronically operated and asset-based, so that registrations
and searches would be against identified equipment. The system
would be operated by a Registrar as an independent operator under
the overall supervision of a Supervisory Authority. Again, the designation of Registrar and Supervisory Authority will vary with the category of equipment.
- A set of simple priority rules governs priority disputes between the
holder of a registered international interest and other interests, and the
recognition of registered international interests in the insolvency of
the debtor. They do not, however, affect special rules of insolvency law
governing the avoidance of preferences and fraudulent transfers or
special rules of insolvency procedure relating to the enforcement of
rights to property under the control or supervision of the insolvency
administrator. The international security interest would not displace
security interests created under national law, but a registered international interest would have priority over national interests.
- There are provisions relating to the assignment of and subrogation to
secured claims and international interests.

- The registration facilities are extended to allow for the registration of categories of non-consensual right or interest declared by Contracting States and also notice of national interests, that is, interests in an object created by an internal transaction, where the centre of the main interests of all parties is situated, and the relevant object is located, in the same Contracting State.

A novel feature of the Convention is that, in relation to any category of equipment covered by the Convention, it will be triggered only by the coming into force of a Protocol relating to that category of equipment and will take effect subject to the provisions of the Protocol. This is necessary in order to ensure that the Convention provisions can be adapted to the specific needs of particular sectors. This two-instrument approach was the subject of some debate. At one time certain interests favoured a series of stand-alone equipment-specific Conventions rather than the two-instrument approach represented by a non-equipment-specific Convention and a set of equipment-specific Protocols. But the latter has many advantages, including the lightening of the Convention text, the avoidance of the discord that might result between Conventions drafted by different hands, the availability of a menu of Protocols from which states could choose and the facility of a fast-track procedure for new Protocols that would obviate the need for further Diplomatic Conferences. The two-instrument approach was endorsed by the third Joint Session and subsequently by the ICAO Legal Committee.

IV. A CLOSER LOOK AT THE CONVENTION

It is not possible in a chapter of this length to cover the Convention and Protocol in any great detail. But it may be of interest to identify some of the key problems which had to be addressed and which demonstrate the complexities inherent in international law-making.

Sphere of application

One of the hardest tasks in the preparation of a commercial law convention is to define its sphere of application. This is a task involving both policy and technical considerations. There are several elements in the process. First, it is necessary to describe and define the types of transaction to which the Convention is to apply. Secondly, where the Convention is to be limited to cross-border transactions, thought needs to be given to the concept of internationality. Thirdly, the connecting factor which provides the link to a Contracting State has to be identified. As will be seen, in the context of international interests in mobile equipment some of these elements proved particularly difficult to capture.

Types of equipment

The identification of the various classes of equipment to be covered went through a fairly protracted process, partly because of the difficulty of defining the three essential ingredients, namely that the equipment is mobile, is of high value, and is uniquely identifiable (this last requirement stems from the fact that registration in the International Registry will be against assets, not against debtors). At one stage there was a list covering not only aircraft, railway rolling stock, and space property but also oil rigs, containers, and a residual category embracing any other categories of uniquely identifiable object. Then the list disappeared, to be replaced by a more general formulation applying the Convention to interests in a uniquely identifiable object of a category of such objects specified in a Protocol. Finally, the list was restored but is restricted to three categories: airframes, aircraft engines, and helicopters; railway rolling stock; and space property. The remaining two categories, together with the residual category, have disappeared, though the Convention contains provisions empowering UNIDROIT to create working groups to assess the feasibility of extending the Convention to other categories of high-value, uniquely identifiable equipment.

Value

The Convention does not seek to define airframes etc, nor does it specifically mention high value except in the Preamble; these matters are left to be worked out in the relevant Protocol, and this has entailed the input of a considerable amount of technical expertise into each of the three Protocols so far drafted. The ingredient of high value in the Aircraft Protocol is not addressed directly in value terms but rather in terms of horsepower, thrust, or carrying capacity.

Mobility

The element of mobility proved more troublesome. In a sense every tangible object is mobile, including the fountain pen that accompanies its owner from one country to another. The underlying idea is to cover objects of a kind regularly used in two or more countries in the course of business. However, the particular equipment used may never in fact move to another country at all. The example given, and one which caused some perplexity, was that of the railway train running round a circuit in the city of Kansas. Could that be the subject of an international interest? The answer is yes, and for the very practical reason that the creditor could never be sure that the train would not be moved elsewhere. In the case of an aircraft the problem would be still more acute. So the decision was taken to treat the mobility element, and hence the internationality of the interest, as satisfied by the nature of the object itself. The problem is rarely likely to arise in relation to aircraft or space property, but it is quite possible that in relation to railway rolling stock the Convention would apply to a purely internal transaction. For such a transaction, defined as one where the centre of the main interests of all the parties is situated, and the object is located, in the same Contracting State at the time of the conclusion of the transaction,[5] Article S allows the relevant Contracting State to exclude the application of the Convention except in relation to its priority rules. This exception reflects the fact that it is open to the holder of an interest created by an internal transaction (referred to as a 'national interest') to protect its priority by registration of notice of the interest in the International Registry.[6]

Types of transaction

Article 2 of the Convention defines an international interest in mobile equipment as an interest, constituted under Article 6, in a uniquely identifiable object of a category of such objects listed in Article 3 and designated in the Protocol:

(a) granted by the chargor under a security agreement;
(b) vested in a person who is the conditional seller under a title reservation agreement; or
(c) vested in a person who is the lessor under a leasing agreement.[7]

The Convention does not determine into which of these three categories an international interest falls; that is a characterization issue to be determined in accordance with the rules of the *lex fori*. However, in North America conditional sale agreements and certain types of lease are treated as security agreements. It was therefore necessary to provide that an interest falling within (a) does not also fall within (b) or (c). An international interest in an object extends to proceeds, but these are confined by definition to proceeds arising from the total or partial loss or physical destruction of the object or its total or partial confiscation, condemnation, or requisition.[8]

---

[5] Article 1(1)(n).   [6] Articles 15(1)(e), 19(6).   [7] With or without an option to purchase.
[8] Article 1(1)(w).

Since the Convention is primarily concerned with consensual security and quasi-security interests it does not apply to outright sales. However, it allows for a Protocol to extend the scope of the Convention to encompass outright sales, and the Aircraft Protocol does precisely this in order to secure for such sales the benefits of the registration system and the priority rules. There are also provisions enabling a Contracting State to make a declaration rendering given classes of non-consensual interest registrable as if they were international interests and separate provisions enabling declarations that other classes of non-consensual interest are to have priority without registration, even over a registered international interest.

Connecting factor

In order for the Convention to apply the debtor must be situated in a Contracting State at the time of conclusion of the agreement.[9]

Relationship of the international interest to equivalent interests under national law

The international interest is a creature of the Convention and in principle does not owe its existence or effect to national law. An interest falling within Article 2 and constituted in accordance with the formal requirements of Article 6 is an international interest whether or not it has any counterpart in national law or fulfils the requirements for an interest created under national law.[10] In most cases a domestic security interest or title retention will simultaneously constitute an international interest, so that the two will coexist. However, the creditor will usually find it advantageous to rely on the interest in its capacity of international interest, which will in most cases give it stronger rights than under national law.

While the international interest is not the product of national law, it is the applicable national law which determines whether the object is one of which the chargor, conditional seller, or lessor has power to dispose, an essential prerequisite of an international interest.[11]

---

[9] Article 3(1). A wide meaning is given to 'situated' by Art 4.

[10] The phrase 'interest created under national law' covers both national interests as defined (ie, those arising in an internal transaction) and interests created under national law in connection with cross-border transactions. For brevity, interests created under national law are referred to hereafter as domestic interests.   [11] Article 6.

Default remedies

Chapter III of the Convention provides a series of basic default remedies: possession, control, sale or lease of the object, collection or receipt of income or profits arising from its management or use, or application for a court order authorizing any of these remedies. Foreclosure is also available but only with the consent of the debtor and other interested persons or with leave of the court. The parties are free to exclude or modify these remedies, and to agree on additional remedies permitted by the applicable law to the extent that they are not inconsistent with the mandatory provisions of Chapter III as set out in Article 14. Unless otherwise agreed, 'default' means a substantial default,[12] but it is open to the parties to agree in writing as to the events constituting default and as to any other events triggering the default remedies.[13] Of particular importance in the context of high-value asset financing are the provisions of Article 12 empowering the court to grant various forms of relief, on evidence of default being adduced, pending final determination of the claim. These consist of preservation of the object and its value, possession, control, or custody of the object, immobilization of the object and lease or management of the object and its income.[14] At one time sale was included, but for some delegates this was considered incompatible with the interim nature of the relief and was dropped. The Aircraft Protocol adds two additional remedies, namely de-registration of the aircraft (ie, removal from its nationality registration) and exportation of the aircraft. This remedy enables the creditor to have the aircraft re-registered in a different state.

Registration

The registration system lies at the heart of the Convention. Registration fulfils the twin objectives of giving public notice of the international interest and securing the creditor's priority, including priority against general creditors in the debtor's insolvency. Though conceptually there is a single system, it is envisaged that there will be separate registration systems for different categories of object. Registration is against the object, not the debtor. It is for this reason that the Convention is confined to objects that are uniquely identifiable, typically by manufacturer's serial number, and

---

[12] Article 10(2). Alternatives to the word 'substantial' were suggested, such as 'fundamental', 'material' and 'major', but since these terms are not synonymous and different terms are used in different legal systems the Drafting Group concluded that it was best to retain 'substantial' as a neutral term, and that it was an advantage if this was not a term in current use in the context of default remedies.

[13] Article 10(1). Typical 'events of default' which are not technically breaches because there is no promise not to allow them to occur are liquidation, reorganization, receivership, and the like.   [14] The court may impose terms for relief under Art 12(2).

does not cover other types of asset, future property, or proceeds apart from insurance and other loss-related proceeds. The provisions of the Convention are predicated on the assumption that the system will be electronic and available on-line, so that registration and responses to searches will be effected automatically and without human intervention. The role of the Registrar will therefore be to administer the system, not to examine documents or data transmitted to the Registry. Each registration will be dated and timed so as to establish a precise priority point. Contracting States may require registration to be effected through national access points, taking advantage of existing national electronic registration systems, while searches could be effected direct from any point anywhere in the world having an electronic link with the Registry.

The rules have been devised for maximum flexibility. So long as the equipment has been identified, the creditor can register not only a fully-fledged international interest but also a prospective international interest, that is, an interest in an identified object which lacks only some element, such as signature of the agreement or acquisition by the debtor, to make it a complete international interest. When the missing element is later supplied, the international interest then coming into being has priority from the time of registration of the prospective interest. The register will also record assignments and prospective assignments of international interests, acquisitions of international interests by legal or contractual subrogation, subordinations, registrable non-consensual rights and interests, notices of (unregistered) national interests, and, for cases where the Convention is extended to cover outright sales, then sales or prospective sales. The registration provisions also cover amendment, extension, or discharge of a registration. The primary role of the Registrar is to ensure the efficient operation of the Registry.

The Registrar, conceived as an independent operator rather than an employee, will be answerable to a Supervisory Authority, though the latter cannot give directions affecting entries on the register, which are the sole prerogative of the courts of the state in which the Registrar has its centre of administration.[15] National courts of other states will have no power to make orders binding the Registrar.[16] So if there is a complaint that a security interest is improperly registered, the remedy of the person named as debtor is to obtain an *in personam* order from a court of competent jurisdiction requiring the creditor to procure removal of the entry from the register. That should usually suffice. But if the *in personam* order is not complied with, the courts of the state where the Registrar has its main centre of administration may (but are not bound to) direct the Registrar to take such steps as will give effect to the order.[17] Liability for

---

[15] Article 43.　　[16] Article 43(4).　　[17] Article 43(3).

errors, omissions, and system malfunctions is imposed on the Registrar.[18] In principle, liability is strict and therefore includes system failures not resulting from negligence by the Registrar. There is a bracketed provision for exceptions, as yet to be defined. Liability is limited to compensatory damages. The Registrar is required to provide insurance or a financial guarantee.

Priorities

The priority rules are remarkably simple. A registered interest has priority over a subsequently registered interest and over an unregistered interest.[19] For the sake of simplicity, refinements of the kind found in national laws are omitted. So the fact that the holder of the registered international interest had actual knowledge of an earlier unregistered interest does not affect the holder's priority. Similarly, where the security agreement covers future advances, the creditor has priority as to those advances even if they were made with knowledge of a subsequent interest. Thus the limitation on tacking imposed by English law does not apply to a Convention interest. The proper course for the intending junior incumbrancer is to obtain a subordination agreement from the holder of the registered interest. An international interest is effective in insolvency proceedings against the debtor provided that the interest was registered prior to the commencement of the insolvency proceedings.[20] This is without prejudice to any other ground of validity available under the applicable law.[21] However, the Convention provisions do not affect any rules of insolvency law relating to the avoidance of a transaction as a preference or as a transfer in fraud of creditors, or any rules of insolvency procedure relating to the enforcement of rights in respect of property under the control or supervision of the insolvency administrator.[22] This last provision is designed to preserve local insolvency law rules designed to restrict enforcement of security pending a reorganization.

Assignments

An international interest can be assigned and the assignment entered on the register. An assignment carries with it associated rights to payment or

[18] Article 28(1).
[19] The definition of 'unregistered interest' in Article 1(1)(mm) covers both registrable and unregistrable interests. Accordingly even interests of a kind outside the scope of the Convention altogether are overridden by a registered international interest, subject to the transitional provisions of Article 55 (of which there are alternative versions) and to the rule that a pre-existing right or interest arising under the law of a state which has not become a Contracting State remains unaffected (Art 55(3)). [20] Article 29(1).
[21] Article 29(2). [22] Article 29(3).

other performance.[23] The default provisions in Chapter III apply *mutatis mutandis* to assignments by way of security where the assignor defaults. One variant of paragraph 1(c) of Article 32, concerning the debtor's duty to make payment or give other performance in favour of the assignee, makes this dependent on the debtor's written consent to the assignment. This provision, inserted on the proposal of the Aviation Working Group, runs counter to the usual rule in legal systems by which an assignment may be made without the debtor's consent, and is intended to avoid the problems confronting an assignee who wishes to collect from a debtor who has been given notice of a conflicting assignment. The final decision awaits the Diplomatic Conference.

Non-consensual rights or interests

These are the subject of Articles 38 and 39 and have been referred to earlier.

Jurisdictional issues

In a Convention of this kind it was inevitable that the treatment of juris-diction would prove complex. Considerable attention was devoted to it, and the outcome is a Chapter devoted exclusively to jurisdiction.[24] The primary rule is one of party autonomy. The parties are free to choose the court or courts of any Contracting State to have jurisdiction in respect of any claim brought under the Convention, and the choice of forum is not invalid by reason of the fact that the chosen state has no connection with the parties or the transaction.[25] They cannot, however, confer jurisdiction to make orders against the Registrar.[26] As regards claims for interim relief under Article 12, in the absence of party choice a distinction is drawn between orders under paragraphs 1(a), (b), and (c) of Article 12 and orders under paragraph (d). The former require access to the object, and accordingly only the courts of a Contracting State on the territory of which the object is situated have jurisdiction. By contrast, the courts of the Contracting State on the territory of which the debtor is situated are given non-exclusive jurisdiction under paragraph (d), relating to lease or management of the object and the income from it. As stated earlier, juris-diction to make orders against the Registrar is confined to the courts of the state where the Registrar has its centre of administration. This is a sensible rule, since it limits jurisdiction to the court which is in a position to exercise control and avoids the possibility of conflicting orders from

---

[23] Article 31 (a Working Group will consider proposals for revision of this Article).
[24] Chapter XII.   [25] Article 41.   [26] Article 43(4).

national courts of different states. Finally, general jurisdiction is determined by the *lex fori.*[27]

V. THE PROTOCOLS

The Aircraft Protocol

The Aircraft Protocol reflects the spirit of the Convention/Protocol approach, which is to make such adjustments to the Convention as are necessary to meet the needs of the particular sector concerned while not disturbing the Convention's basic structure. The Aircraft Protocol shows how it is possible to make quite significant changes while working within the basic framework. Article X(2) requires Contracting States to ensure that speedy relief is given under Article 12 within such number of calendar days from the date of filing of the application for relief as is specified in a declaration made by the Contracting State in which the application is made. It remains to be seen whether this provision will survive. Undoubtedly some states will feel concerns as to the constitutional propriety of legislating a timetable for judicial decisions, while others may feel that it is not practicable to do so, since even the court's ability to control its own docket is dependent on outside factors, such as the efficiency with which the parties themselves conduct the proceedings. Equally interesting are the alternative sets of provisions designed to ensure that in the event of insolvency the insolvency administrator will, within a designated waiting period, either cure all defaults and agree to perform future obligations or surrender the aircraft. The stronger version of these provisions, which obviously have implications for the general body of creditors, is modelled on section 1110 of the American Federal Bankruptcy Code and a comparable statutory provision for railway rolling stock. There are various other, more minor, additions and amendments designed to meet the specific needs of the aviation industry.

The Rail and Space Protocols

These are not yet ready to go forward to the Diplomatic Conference, though they are likely to receive examination from committees of governmental experts during 2001. They are both patterned on the Aircraft Protocol, albeit with significant modifications. For example, the Rail Protocol dispenses with any need for the debtor's consent to an assignment, and has a number of other provisions particular to rail, such as a

[27] Article 44.

system in North America for allocation of identification numbers to railway rolling stock by a designated regional authority rather than by the manufacturer.

VI. CONCLUSION

The UNIDROIT Convention, with its associated Protocols, represents one of the most innovative international instruments in the history of international commercial law, not only in its substantive provisions but also in the processes leading to the present texts. What the project has amply demonstrated is the enormous impetus that can be given to work on an international instrument if governments are kept in regular touch as the work proceeds and if the private sector is actively involved in the work in its formative stages, not merely in a consultative capacity but as a major player. Also important, and hitherto rather neglected, is the raising of awareness of the project, through articles, seminars, and conferences, as it proceeds through its various stages, rather than waiting until the instrument has been concluded at a Diplomatic Conference. This approach has at least two significant advantages. Obtaining an early input of views from outsiders helps to identify and eradicate weaknesses and make the text more responsive to commercial needs; and the process of education and involvement also helps to mobilize the industry support which is so vital if governments are to be persuaded to ratify the instrument. Next year UNIDROIT celebrates its 75th anniversary. Conclusion of the UNIDROIT Convention on International Interests in Mobile Equipment would make the birthday party a particularly joyous occasion.[28]

[28] The texts of the draft Convention and Protocol in the form sent out to Member States of UNIDROIT and ICAO are reproduced in Appendix IV at the end of this volume.

PART 5

Cross-Border Insolvency

13

An Insolvency Practitioner's Perspective

MARK HOMAN

(*PricewaterhouseCoopers*)

I. WHAT IS CROSS-BORDER INSOLVENCY?

The term cross-border insolvency is used somewhat loosely by insolvency practitioners, sometimes simply to indicate the existence of some international aspect such as the presence of assets or subsidiaries in a foreign jurisdiction. True cross-border insolvency refers to the situation where a single debtor company has entered formal insolvency proceedings in more than one jurisdiction and there is, at least potentially, a conflict of laws affecting the conduct of the debtor's affairs.

II. THE PROBLEM

As this book has been in gestation it has perhaps developed more towards considering the security issues. My brief, however, is to present the problem posed by cross-border insolvency as seen from the perspective of the insolvency practitioner. This chapter will touch on some security realization issues, but this is only incidental because security is normally realized in the context of an insolvency. It attempts only to deal with the insolvency practitioner's main conflict of laws problems among the many issues he has to deal with. Thankfully, my brief does not presume that I will have the answers, although I shall offer a few suggestions.

Well, what *is* the problem?

The background is that, as business becomes more international, companies entering insolvency proceedings increasingly find themselves subject to the jurisdiction of more than one country.

The problem is that there is a business to run. Trying to run a business in insolvency proceedings (which inevitably means in crisis) at the same time as sorting out an international conflict of laws dispute is almost impossible. The business problems occur and have to be resolved more quickly than the international process for the resolution of such conflicts will normally accommodate. Even if running the business consists of no more than liquidating its assets, that in itself can be quite a business in a large international corporation.

Whether it involves a trading concern or realization of the assets, insolvency is a commercial problem not a legal one. But it is a commercial problem that has to be resolved in a legal framework. That legal framework needs to be responsive to the commercial difficulties if it is to achieve the objective of maximizing the estate for creditors.

Substitute a foreign legal framework for the one with which the insolvency practitioner is familiar and he is in some difficulty. If it is a framework which is not responsive to the commercial problems, he is in considerable difficulty. If instead you substitute not just a foreign law but a clash between foreign law and his familiar national framework so that he has a conflict of laws dispute on his hands, he is in deep trouble. Administering an insolvency under two laws at once is rather like playing chess without breaking the rules of draughts; the rooks and knights cannot move and the queen and king can only move diagonally one square at a time; pawns can only move diagonally to capture, but you are not sure whether they have to leap over the captured piece or not!

I shall, incidentally, refer to two conflicting proceedings since, although there is in theory scope for any number of conflicting proceedings, it is rare to have more than two in respect of any one company. Despite the European flavour of this book, I shall also deal more with UK/US matters. This is because the universal (not to say imperialist) approach of UK and US courts leads to some interesting transatlantic problems that are not so frequently encountered between the UK and, say, France, or Germany both of which adopt a more territorial approach.

The diversity of insolvency systems around the world is such that the scope for differences is enormous, but by way of example they may differ as to:

- who has authority over the debtor's affairs; debtor management in possession or an office holder;
- the extent of that authority;
- the extent of court involvement in the process;
- the role of the creditors' committee;
- the ranking of creditors' claims, including the treatment of security and quasi-security interests, priority claims, interest on claims, late claims, tax claims, claims in foreign currency, and the date to which claims are calculated (unless, exceptionally, these are synchronized);
- undoing antecedent, pre-bankruptcy transactions;
- whether the thrust of any rescue effort is toward trying to rescue the legal entity through its reconstruction or rescue the business through a going concern sale;
- the extent of extraterritorial reach—some countries adopt the approach that proceedings are purely local (for example, France, Germany, Japan);

others take a universal approach assuming worldwide jurisdiction over companies susceptible to local insolvency proceedings and their worldwide assets;
- the attitude of the jurisdiction to rival proceedings in other jurisdictions;
- reporting requirements.

The inevitable result of such clashes of jurisdiction is at best huge uncertainty, cost, and delay and, at worst, strife and paralysis. The costs increase dramatically whether there is a jurisdictional battle or a negotiated reconciliation of conflicting proceedings. Even in the latter event many problems require legal advice under both laws as well as in relation to the conflict between them and costs can easily treble.

The first and most crucial problem is who speaks for the company. If post-filing credit is required ('debtor in possession finance' to some or 'administrator's borrowing' to others or just 'trade credit'), and it may be required immediately, for example to pay wages, the insolvency office holder or debtor in possession needs to know that he has authority to borrow in the eyes of both jurisdictions and is recognized as the corporate governance of the company by both courts rather than being seen by one of them as acting illegally.

Equally, the providers of credit need to know that the borrowing is *intra vires* in the eyes of both courts and that the super-priority or security which they require is effective under both laws.

III. PRIMARY AND ANCILLARY PROCEEDINGS

The most serious problems arise where there are conflicting 'main' or 'primary' proceedings with international effect. This occurs as a result of courts assuming worldwide jurisdiction over companies having some connection with their territory by reference to criteria other than incorporation, such as place of business, employment, or presence of assets in the jurisdiction. This leads them into conflict with the courts in the territory of incorporation. In its worst form, both courts may appoint someone with (in the eyes of that court) worldwide authority over the company's affairs, each appointee being a trespasser in the eyes of the other court.

The difficulties are lessened somewhat where there is a primary proceeding, usually under the laws of the company's 'home' territory based on incorporation, and secondary or ancillary proceedings, in other jurisdictions. Since ancillary proceedings are normally of local effect only, being restricted to assets of the debtor situated in the second jurisdiction, they cause far less difficulty with jurisdictional clashes. Nevertheless, there is initial uncertainty while the territorial scope of each proceeding is clarified and the location of assets and status of assets in any third jurisdiction is worked out.

IV. THE COMMERCIAL CONTEXT

The introduction of a stay on creditor action at the commencement of an insolvency process is a watershed in the life of the business. It can provide a company or a business with a breathing space from creditor pressures, which enables it to reorganize. It can provide the opportunity to shed unprofitable activities, onerous contracts, etc, so that a new and successful business can emerge from the wreckage either in the original corporate entity or in the hands of a new owner following a going concern sale.

At the same time, the company's public declaration of insolvency, which the stay necessarily entails, puts on notice all those who do business with the company that the future is uncertain. This can cause a crisis of confidence, which can be damaging or even fatal, in some businesses extremely quickly. Suppliers may be uncertain whether they will be paid for goods ordered, employees may be tempted away to jobs offering a more secure future, and customers will be uncertain about receiving their supplies and the availability of after sales support.

Whether the underlying business is, on balance, assisted or damaged by the introduction of the stay will depend very much on the nature of that business. Banks close more or less instantly, computer service companies may last a week, shipbuilders many months but only until the work in progress is complete. Manufacturers of goods that do not represent a high-risk decision for customers can survive for long periods if viability can be restored. That sets a time frame for any reconstruction or sale.

What is clear is that if a rescue is to be achieved:

- Pre-insolvency rescues are to be preferred where possible, particularly where the publicity that goes with a stay would be seriously damaging to rescue prospects. Formal insolvency represents only a last chance when all else has failed.
- The process is assisted if third parties can be given confidence by a professional office holder (or a debtor in possession) who can present a vision of a solution and credible assurances of payment for goods and services.
- Because a sale of the business is usually more quickly achieved than an arrangement with creditors, there will often be cases when a recon-

struction of the company cannot be implemented in time to avoid the collapse of the underlying business, and sale of the business to new owners is the only possible way in which a going concern outcome can be achieved.
• Speed and confidence are often crucial.

There are many insolvency systems that are not conducive to getting the best commercial result, essentially because they are too slow and uncertain. For example, systems that require a demonstration of balance sheet insolvency as one of the entry criteria can involve damaging delays.

Unitary or 'single gateway' insolvency proceedings with an initial 'observation phase' can lose vital days compared with the UK system where experts are available who can rapidly identify which of a variety of procedures the company is going to be most suited by.

Debtor in possession proceedings involve rather slower business decision making than office holder proceedings and, in management's attempts to rescue the company, opportunities to rescue the *business* through a going concern sale may be lost.

But all of these problems pale into insignificance in comparison to the situation where a company is subject to two simultaneous primary proceedings. The delay and uncertainty that this entails inevitably means that the company suffers a process slower and more expensive than the worst of both worlds.

Unfortunately the delay and uncertainty is most prevalent at the very start of the case, in the crucial early days when, in order to hold the business together, the debtor in possession or insolvency office holder needs to present a vision of a solution around which wavering customers, suppliers, and employees can coalesce. In its simplest form this may amount to no more than 'please carry on working/supplying against my orders while I attempt to sell the business as a going concern and I will see that you get paid'. However, even this simple statement can only be made from a platform of some confidence in the legal regime, in his authority, and in what assets fall under his control.

The problem is the insolvency practitioner (or debtor in possession) needs certainty and he needs it now, on appointment, not later in some international court of appeal.

V. SECURED CREDITORS

The type of insolvency regime that a company ends up in is also of considerable importance to the secured creditor, not only from the point of view of whether the regime overall is conducive to producing a constructive commercial outcome, but also the treatment it affords to his security.

Is the asset, which forms the security, to become a part of the insolvent estate, or is it free to be dealt with by the secured creditor or his receiver outside it? If it does form part of the estate, is there compensation for depreciation and delay in realizing it? Does anything rank ahead of it? For example, in Russia, security forms part of the estate with secured creditors having a second tier claim, against the estate as a whole, for the amount of their security, ranking after the costs and expenses of the bankruptcy and the first tier claims of employees and tort claimants. It is therefore impossible for a creditor advancing money on security to have any real notion of its worth in an insolvency. This rather defeats the object of having secured interests in the first place, which is to lower the cost of loan finance.

There is a separate bundle of commercial issues which affects secured lenders and which, essentially, amounts to: 'In what context am I going to be able to realize my security if at all, and what will it be worth in that context?' That is not the subject of this chapter save only to mention the case of Lancer Boss, a construction plant manufacturing business the key activities of which spanned a UK company and a German company, each placed in local insolvency proceedings with different officials and different groups of creditors with different interests. The German insolvency office holder disposed of the German half of the business rapidly, for enough money to obtain a useful return for German creditors, but in the process rendered the UK half of the business worth very substantially less. This produced howls of anguish and cries for reform of cross-border insolvency laws. Those cries were misplaced. They missed the essential point that the UK lenders had secured themselves on the assets of half a business. The problem lay in the organizational structure of the group and the fact that the UK lenders had loaned to an entity that did not have a complete business, but was dependent on a sister company with a different office holder and different creditors with a different agenda. The problem could have arisen just as much had both companies been English.

VI. AVOIDING CROSS-BORDER INSOLVENCY PROBLEMS

The first and most obvious point to be made about avoiding problems of a clash of jurisdictions is that the worse the insolvency regime the greater the advantage to all concerned in finding a pre-insolvency work-out solution. So to avoid a company being torn apart in a clash of formal insolvency proceedings it may be worth going an extra mile in the search for a solution that avoids formal proceedings. However, this in itself can have extra complications because of legal differences. Beware, for example, wrongful trading in the UK, the French law on abusive support of an insolvent company, and the threat of equitable subordination under US law.

Furthermore, differences in culture and perception as to how parties will fare in formal proceedings can affect behaviour in the work-out phase. For example, there is a tendency for US management (of, say, an English parented multinational group with US interests) to file in Chapter 11 rather than suffer creditor imposed sanctions during a work-out.

The second way of avoiding the clash of jurisdictions is to win the battle of the jurisdictions before it even starts. Take the same example of an English parented multinational group with US interests; it may be possible for a floating charge holder to appoint an administrative receiver of the parent in England and for the receiver then to take control of the boards of group companies with such alacrity that the directors do not have the opportunity to file in the US. This requires meticulous planning, but the effort may be preferable to having the whole group placed in Chapter 11.

While the pre-emptive strike may work to prevent a US filing, it may not work the same way in reverse. If the directors (of an English company) make a pre-emptive strike (as did the Maxwell Communications Corporation) by filing for Chapter 11, that does not protect their company against UK creditors who are not respectful of the US stay, nor does it protect them from English proceedings for wrongful trading.

They therefore need to file in England as well. It is an interesting question as to whether they need leave of the US Court to do so! It is also interesting to note that one consequence of a pre-emptive Chapter 11 filing may be that the English floating charge holder is denied the opportunity of appointing an administrative receiver (to do so would amount to a breach of the US stay), with the result that there may be a UK administration proceeding instead.

'The battle of the jurisdictions' is therefore an extra dimension in pre-insolvency strategy in multinational cases.

The third way of avoiding a clash of jurisdictions is to exit from one of the proceedings as quickly as possible, for example by an application under section 304 of the US Bankruptcy Code to allow a company's insolvency to be dealt with purely under English proceedings. A Chapter 11 case can be dismissed if a foreign proceeding is pending and various factors are satisfied; in particular if the foreign (ie non-US) proceeding includes just treatment of all holders of claims against the estate, protection of US claim holders against prejudice and inconvenience, prevention of preferential or fraudulent dispositions of the estate's property, and a regime which respects comity. It is only necessary for the foreign distribution scheme to be substantially in accordance with US Bankruptcy Law. Deference to a foreign proceeding is not precluded merely because a US creditor is accorded a lower priority under the foreign proceeding. Unfortunately, the wide discretion of US Bankruptcy Judges as to whether to defer to foreign proceedings in this way results in unpredictability in the treatment of such applications and does little to alleviate the problems of uncertainty referred to earlier.

It is worth noting that the English Court is prepared to defer to foreign proceedings in the same way, even in respect of English incorporated companies, if it is in the interests of creditors globally. This has, for example, been done where a provisional liquidation was originally embarked upon to secure control over the company's affairs with an English court stay, but it was later found that the assets were all capable of being dealt with under the rival foreign proceeding and simplification appeared to benefit creditors without any English creditor being significantly disadvantaged. It may also have been a factor that the stay in the foreign (US) proceeding appeared strong enough to prevent the immediate resuscitation of the English liquidation on a creditor's petition.

VII. THE MYTH OF MAXWELL

The Maxwell Communications Corporation (MCC) case has been claimed by some commentators as providing the solution to a clash of primary proceedings. There are in fact two myths involved in such claims.

MCC was the English incorporated parent of a group of 400 companies. The parent alone had some US$3 billion of liabilities and US$ 2 billion of assets. The directors caused it to file for Chapter 11 proceedings on 16 December 1991. It was placed in administration by the High Court in London on 20 December 1991.

From an English perspective MCC had very little connection with the US. Arguably it had no US place of business. It had one US resident director (the Chief Executive of its US subsidiaries). It had virtually no US creditors (other than the London branches of US banks participating in a syndicated loan put together through a European bank). US debt traders bought in subsequently, but they were not a relevant factor at the time. It had no directly held US assets apart from one inter-company receivable.

However, from a US perspective, 80 per cent of its assets were situated in the US (albeit held through two layers of English intermediate holding companies) and this was sufficient to persuade the US court not only to accept the company's filing, but to insist on retaining the company under its jurisdiction subject to the full panoply of US bankruptcy laws and to appoint an Examiner to 'ensure the integrity of the US Bankruptcy process'.

The first myth is the 'American myth' that the filing of MCC in Chapter 11 'saved the day for American creditors in the face of the threat from English liquidators'.

There were in fact virtually no US creditors for whom the day needed to be saved, nor was there in reality anything to be saved at all. MCC was a holding company with no synergy between its subsidiaries, which were worth more sold separately than held together. And even if they had been held together, the lingering smell of fraud would have caused the company's securities to trade at a discount. It was by any reckoning a de facto liquidation. The US Examiner agreed totally with this analysis (arrived at with the assistance of JP Morgan hired jointly by the Examiner and the English administrators). He also endorsed the English administrators' approach to the realization of the assets through sale of subsidiaries as separate going concerns, in one case through an independent public offering.

The second myth is that the MCC case provides the role model for dealing with cross-border cases where there is a clash between contemporaneous primary proceedings.

Filing an application under sections 304 and 305 of the US Bankruptcy Code to dismiss MCC's US bankruptcy proceedings was contemplated, but rejected as too risky given the attitude of the US Bankruptcy Court, the timescale for any appeal, and the extent of the emergencies facing MCC group companies to which the parent had previously acted as 'banker'. A consensual solution was therefore sought.

The first essential mechanism in the Maxwell solution was a protocol (an agreement between the Examiner and the administrator approved by both courts) under which the US court recognized the English administrators as the corporate governance of the debtor in possession for the purposes of the Chapter 11 proceeding. This avoided the nightmare scenario of the company having two worldwide heads both acting as trespassers. However, the US court subjected certain of the administrators' actions to the approval of the Examiner or the US court. The administrators protected themselves from criticism by obtaining English court approval for this fettering of their powers.

The protocol introduced a number of tensions into the case. First, this was because the fettering of the administrators' powers extended to fettering their ability to dismiss management of US subsidiaries without the Examiner's approval. This created a new dynamic in the case in that US management's agenda took on a significance which it would not have had in an English proceeding. Secondly, the creditors' committee, at least in the early stages, adopted the adversarial style of a US creditors' committee which seeks to exert control over a debtor in possession. It sought to do so in a way which was potentially incompatible with the exercise of fiduciary duties by a UK office holder who cannot allow his decisions to be *directed* by a creditors' committee, not least because he has fiduciary responsibility to the court and to all of the creditors and exposure to negligence suits as a result of his actions.

The second stage of the Maxwell solution was a combined US Chapter 11 plan and English Scheme of Arrangement, providing a single distribution mechanism approved by the creditors. This was crucial. It would not have been possible to have a legal US liquidation proceeding under Chapter 7 and an English liquidation because the distribution plans in those two proceedings are rigid and they differ from each other.

The greater flexibility of Chapter 11 and a UK Scheme of Arrangement allowed the administrators to devise a distribution plan which was lawful in both countries. Differences in priority claims, the treatment of interest, foreign currency claims, and late claims were all finessed, essentially by being generous to the minorities to prevent there being any disadvantage to groups of creditors who could form a class with a blocking vote. It was fortunate that the facts of the case made this possible at a price that was acceptable to the general body of creditors and did not inflict such damage on either country's approach as to cause the courts to reject it. Whether this solution does provide a model for other cases depends entirely on the fact patterns being suitable.

The existence of a UK debenture containing a floating charge, for example, would have caused an entirely different set of problems. A receiver appointed by a floating charge holder might be able to file a motion to dismiss the Chapter 11 proceedings if he were appointed before the Chapter 11 was filed (on the grounds that the directors had no authority to file). But with a Chapter 11 predating the receivership, it is not clear that the receiver would even have standing to apply to the US Court under sections 304 and 305. He is not a 'foreign representative' of the debtor for this purpose. With a Chapter 11 on foot he would also have had considerable difficulty in seeking to become the 'designated person' under the US Bankruptcy Rules to act for the debtor in possession. His prime duty to the debenture holder would have been inconsistent with the debtor in possession's duty as a fiduciary to the general body of creditors. With a receivership instead of an administration there is thus a far greater risk of the US court appointing a trustee and treating the receiver as a trespasser, with the English court taking the reciprocal approach to the trustee. Even with an administrator instead of a receiver, the existence of a valid floating charge would have made it impossible to reconcile the two distribution schemes.

It was also fortuitous that MCC was only a holding company and there was no need to run a business while subject to the legal uncertainty which prevailed. It would probably have been too demanding to be simultaneously on two continents operating under two conflicting laws while managing trading relationships with hundreds of third parties.

In the event, even the approval in both courts of the combined US Chapter 11 plan and UK Scheme of Arrangement did not resolve everything. It was only subsequently that the creditors learned which set of avoidance laws applied to antecedent transactions. The avoidance laws differ in that English law looks at the directors' intentions and US law looks instead at whether creditors have been preferred as a result of non-ordinary course transactions. It was the administrators' duty as debtor in possession under a confirmed plan in a full US Chapter 11 proceeding to pursue avoidance claims under US law. Ultimately, the matter was decided in the Second Circuit Court of Appeal.[1] The court ruled that it had discretion to apply comity even after confirmation of a Chapter 11 plan, and that the fact that the predominance of the contacts of the challenged transactions were with England required that comity be exercised in favour of English law. This has left comity as something of a wild card to be played at any time in US Chapter 11 proceedings.

The *Maxwell* case would have been much simpler if comity had been exercised at the outset to allow the whole insolvency process to be dealt with under English law alone.

The discussion of comity in the Second Circuit's judgment in *Re Maxwell Communications Corp plc* when read with sections 304 and 305 may give some encouragement to the US Bankruptcy Court to apply comity at the outset in future. In two other cases, *Atlantic Computers* and *Re Gercke*,[2] orders were made on grounds of comity under section 304, blocking the commencement of US bankruptcy proceedings to allow those cases to be dealt with in England. In the case of *Ionica plc*,[3] the company's Chapter 11 petition was dismissed to enable the case to be dealt with in England. These cases set a much more realistic, commercially sensible precedent than the *Maxwell* case.

VIII. CONVENTIONS AND MODEL LAWS—DO THEY HELP?

The EC Convention on Insolvency Proceedings stalled (according to choice) either on British non-co-operation with Europe during the BSE

---

[1] *Re Maxwell Communications Corp plc* 593 F 3d 1036 (2nd Cir 1996).
[2] *Atlantic Computers* is unreported; *Re Gercke* 122 BR 621 (Bankr D Dist Col 1991).
[3] 241 BR 829 (Bankr SDNY 1999).

crisis or on issues to do with sovereignty over Gibraltar. The current situation is that there is a move to resurrect the Convention as a Council Regulation of the European Union.[4] This does not require unanimity of member states.

If adopted:

- The Regulation will not apply to insurance companies and credit institutions.
- The court of the state in which the centre of a debtor's main interests is situated (provided that is within the European Community) will have jurisdiction to open universal insolvency proceedings. This is critical because the law applicable to the proceedings is the law of the state opening the proceedings.
- The Regulation should in theory normally avoid there being two main proceedings.
- It will provide a Europe-wide stay.
- It provides Europe-wide recognition of the office holder.
- The opening of secondary proceedings will be limited to territories where there are establishments where the debtor carries out activities. Mere presence of assets will not be sufficient.
- Secondary proceedings will be territorial, limited to assets in the territory. Where there is no establishment, but just assets, the assets will therefore be able to be recovered for the main proceeding free from rival proceedings or creditor attachment.
- There is provision for some co-operation between territorial and main proceedings.
- The office holder has power to open secondary proceedings which will help to deal with problems with local management or local creditors.

However, the Regulation is a compromise and as a result too much open to interpretation.

The Regulation provides a rebuttable presumption that the place of the registered office will determine the centre of main interests, but the recitals expand on this to say that 'centre of main interests' should correspond to the place where the debtor conducts the administration of his interests on a regular basis and is therefore ascertainable by third parties. This is helpful, but still leaves an element of uncertainty, not least because of the circularity involved in the court having jurisdiction by reference to its own decision on where the centre of main interest lies, thus opening the question of jurisdiction up to challenge. In addition any state will be

---

[4] Since this chapter was drafted the Regulation has been adopted. It comes into force in May 2002.

able to refuse on public policy grounds to recognize insolvency proceedings opened in any other state.

Whether this provides quite the certainty which the insolvency office holder needs is somewhat doubtful. In MCC, for example, the registered office was in England, the head office was arguably in England, but it could equally well have been argued that the administration of its interests was conducted wherever Robert Maxwell was at the time, since, by a board resolution, he had been constituted a committee of one with all the powers of the board. At times the group's interests were administered from the communication centre of his yacht which sailed from jurisdiction to jurisdiction. From a US perspective (not that the US is intended to be party to the EU Regulation) it might have been contended that MCC's main interests (looked at on a group basis) were administered from New York. There also appears to be a certain amount of scope for forum shopping, particularly as the only evidence before the court will often be that presented by the debtor.

Secondary proceedings may be opened in another contracting state where the debtor possesses an establishment. An establishment is a place of operations through which the debtor carries on a non-transitory economic activity with human means and goods. Various states agreed to abandon the presence of assets as a basis for proceedings, provided the concept of establishment can be interpreted 'in a broad manner'. This compromise too hints at uncertainty and scope for forum shopping.

That said, the Regulation would still be a step in the right direction.

The second main development in the area of international co-operation is the UNCITRAL model law, implemented so far only in Eritrea.[5] The Model Law has many similarities with the draft EU Regulation and its definitions of main proceedings, non-main proceedings, establishment, etc, but with subtle differences. A main proceeding takes place where 'the debtor has the centre of its main interests', but without further elaboration. The effect of recognizing a foreign main proceeding under the Model Law stays local actions against the debtor's assets but does not of course provide a community-wide stay in the sense of the EU Regulation.

Unlike the EU Regulation, there does not appear to be an express presumption against two main proceedings. Article 28 provides that after recognition of a foreign main proceeding, local proceedings may only be commenced if the debtor has assets in the state and, with certain exceptions, those proceedings should be restricted to the assets of the debtor within the state. However, prior to recognition of a foreign main proceeding it would seem that a state may commence a rival main proceeding.

---

[5] At the time this chapter was drafted.

For a foreign non-main proceeding to be recognized the debtor has to have an establishment in the foreign state but, in contrast to the EU approach, local non-main proceedings can be commenced on an assets only test.

All in all the EU and UNCITRAL approaches may, if adopted, reduce the scope for a clash of proceedings, but they fall some way short of eliminating it and will not therefore remove all the uncertainties that afflict the administration of cross-border cases.

IX. SOME OUTSTANDING QUESTIONS

Fortunately, I have been invited to write about a problem, not about a solution. International conventions may eventually ease the problem a little, but for as long as nations wish to apply local laws to foreign entities based on a presence in their territories of a place of business or establishment, assets, jobs, or some lesser connection, clashes will occur.

Forgoing everything except the incorporation test would have the benefit of clarity, but regrettably this is probably politically unrealistic.

Perhaps the best hope is for judges to recognize the damage to creditor interests that can be caused by a clash of proceedings and to weigh this heavily in the exercise of their discretion to dismiss proceedings at the outset in the interests of comity. Where there is a reluctance to dismiss at the outset, it may be a practical proposition to delay the decision rather than impose a conflict of jurisdictions at the outset. This may be achieved by protecting the estate with a stay coupled with provisional liquidation or some other temporary proceeding pending fact finding to allow an informed decision to be made, but this too creates uncertainty and may not be a sensible commercial approach in a going concern situation.

14

The Insolvency Issues

PROFESSOR IAN F FLETCHER

*(Herbert Smith Professor of International Commercial Law,
University College London)*

and

HAMISH ANDERSON

(Partner, Norton Rose, London)

This chapter is concerned with the effect of the insolvency of the debtor upon the rights of a secured creditor. In particular, it is concerned with the assessment of 'bankruptcy risk' which should be conducted at the inception of a security transaction.

For the purposes of examining the issues which arise, the chapter takes as its premise a security transaction in respect of tangible movable property of high value which will, in the ordinary course of usage, move from one jurisdiction to another. An aircraft provides an excellent example of the sort of asset in question although there will be no attempt to examine the special features of aviation financing practice or the registration and regulatory considerations which arise in respect of security over aircraft. For present purposes, the important point is to identify the possibility of security being taken in one jurisdiction and the subject matter of the security being located in another jurisdiction when questions of enforcement arise. The assumed facts are that a bank is willing to advance credit to a borrower against security of a type in respect of which that possibility arises. It will also be assumed that both parties are corporate although it should be noted that the ability of individuals to assume a domicile of choice adds an additional layer of complication if, for example, the borrower is unincorporated. In this chapter the creditor is called 'B' and the debtor is called 'D'.

According to conventional principles of private international law, the capacity of the parties will be determined by reference to the laws of the country in which they are incorporated and the governing law of the transaction will usually, but not invariably, be determined by the express choice of the parties. So far as proprietary rights are concerned, the general rule in respect of tangible movable property is that the validity of a transfer and its effects on proprietary rights are governed by the laws of the country in which the property is located at the time of the transfer. However, it should be noted that the application of this approach to security interests, particularly non-possessory security interests, can raise difficult problems where there are competing claims. (This topic falls outside the scope of this chapter.)

The focus of this chapter is on making such a transaction 'bankruptcy proof'. It will be assumed that there is a genuine extension of credit in reliance on the security.[1] It will also be assumed that it has not been possible to reduce or eliminate bankruptcy risk through the use of special purpose companies or other similar techniques. In such circumstances, it is necessary to consider the impact of D's insolvency upon the rights of B. 'Insolvency' for these purposes means the commencement of formal insolvency proceedings rather than merely default. The chapter begins by examining, in very general comparative terms, the issues which arise and the range of possible legal rules which may be encountered. It then moves on to a more detailed account of the approach of English law to some fundamental cross-border insolvency problems and to a commentary on current international initiatives.

I. INTERACTION OF LEGAL SYSTEMS

Analysis of the hypothetical scenario with which this chapter is concerned has identified the interaction of four different legal jurisdictions although, on the facts of any given case, two or more of those jurisdictions could be the same. The four jurisdictions are the law of the location of B, the law of the location of D, the law of the place of the transaction, and the jurisdiction within which the subject matter of the security is located. The traditional Latin terminology, which has the merit of some degree of international recognition, is *lex domicilii*, *lex loci contractus*, and *lex situs*. At first sight, only the jurisdiction within which the movable subject matter of the security is situated is capable of changing from time to time. However, this presupposes an English common law concept of corporate domicile, which is neither as absolute as might be supposed nor shared by civil law jurisdictions. Corporate domicile in English law, is usually regarded as immutably determined by the place of incorporation but a number of English companies have effected redomicile by private legislation. Another possibility in some jurisdictions, but not in England,[2] is for a corporation to be incorporated in more than one jurisdiction. In civil law jurisdictions the concept of domicile is more flexible. It relates to the company's principal establish-

---

[1] Tax-driven financing may involve defeasances to ensure the performance of obligations.
[2] In the absence of special legislation such as the National Bank of New Zealand Limited Act 1985.

ment or 'seat' thereby admitting the possibility of transfer from one jurisdiction to another by the movement of the centre of administration.[3] The starting position for a creditor wishing to take security is, therefore, a basic set of up to four relevant legal systems with some potential for change in the identity of those systems during the lifetime of the security transaction.

The insolvency of D introduces the possibility of a fifth legal jurisdiction, namely that in which the insolvency proceedings occur (*lex concursus*).[4] As before, this jurisdiction may prove to be the same as one of the other legal systems, which already has to be taken into account. Of those other legal systems, the jurisdiction of D's domicile is, in practice, most likely to be the jurisdiction within which insolvency proceedings are commenced. The jurisdiction where the subject matter of the security is located is another (but less likely) possibility. However, it is of the very essence of cross-border security and insolvency issues that the range of possibilities is much wider.[5] From the point of view of insolvency practitioners undertaking an appointment, the relevant legal jurisdictions are usually readily identifiable at the time of appointment or shortly thereafter. However, from the point of view of a bank seeking to obtain security, the problems of risk assessment are altogether more profound because the logical first step in making a transaction 'bankruptcy proof' is to identify the jurisdictions in which insolvency proceedings might occur in order to assess the effects of the insolvency laws of those jurisdictions upon the transaction in question. The necessary acknowledgement that the jurisdiction within which the insolvency proceedings are commenced need not be any of the four legal systems which are directly relevant to the inception of the transaction makes this an extremely open question.

II. SIGNIFICANCE OF INSOLVENCY PROCEEDINGS

The effects of insolvency proceedings on B's security rights can be profound. Most systems of insolvency law include provisions enabling

---

[3] See generally: David Lewis, 'Corporate Redomicile' (1995) 16 Co Law 295

[4] The insolvency of B could introduce yet another system of law. However, the effects of insolvency proceedings in respect of B are likely to be much less profound because of the general principle that the insolvency representative will have no greater rights against D or its property taken in security than those which could have been exercised by B itself in the absence of insolvency proceedings. That said, the insolvency of B is not necessarily without significance. See, for example, *Re Bank of Credit and Commerce International SA (No 11)* [1997] 1 BCLC 80 dealing with rights of set-off against a creditor company in liquidation.

[5] By contrast, in a 'domestic' insolvency all five (or six) legal systems are, of course, one and the same.

transactions occurring within a specified period prior to the formal commencement of the insolvency proceedings to be set aside. A particularly relevant example for any creditor taking security is the avoidance of 'preferences'. Even though the existence of rules directed to this mischief is commonplace, the approach of different jurisdictions varies considerably. Thus in England the rules apply only to transactions which are influenced by a subjective desire to confer a benefit on the recipient.[6] However, in the United States, the rules are effects-based enabling a much wider class of transaction to be attacked, albeit limited to transactions in a much shorter period prior to the commencement of the proceedings and excluding transactions in the ordinary course of business.[7]

In some jurisdictions, the commencement of insolvency proceedings can lead to the recharacterization of transactions. For example, a finance lease might be treated as a disguised security and invalidated for non-compliance with formalities. Other possibilities are the subordination of security rights to special priorities such as tax and employment claims or super-priority for finance obtained within the insolvency procedure. The insolvency representative may have exceptional powers to terminate onerous obligations.

It is increasingly common to find both terminal and reorganizational procedures in a developed system of insolvency law. Under the latter in particular, the remedies of a secured creditor are likely to be temporarily suspended and the insolvency representative may be able to compel dealings with the subject matter of the security which are contrary to the wishes of the secured creditor. A considerable quantity of academic work now exists providing comparative guides to different insolvency laws. Generally speaking, procedures in different countries have broadly similar purposes. Thus, the function of a terminal procedure is to reduce the available assets to cash and to distribute that cash amongst the claimants in accordance with some predetermined order of priority. A reorganizational procedure is directed primarily to rescue and may not, of itself, have any lasting effects on creditors' rights. Since insolvency procedures in different jurisdictions serve similar purposes, it is hardly surprising that they tend to contain rules which address common problems. An insolvency procedure almost inevitably incorporates a defined commencement date, regulation of subsequent creditor activity, clawback of antecedent activity, rules on set-off, and powers of collection, realization, and distribution. For present purposes, it is the range of solutions to these common problems which is of interest to the secured creditor.

---

[6] Section 239 Insolvency Act 1986.
[7] Section 547 US Bankruptcy Code. Generally, 'effects' based rules are more likely to be encountered internationally than 'intention'-based rules which follow the English model.

Although the concept of security is more or less universally recognized, different jurisdictions exhibit varying degrees of sympathy to upholding secured creditors' rights. The underlying policy tensions in this area reflect an intention to accord priority either to the importance of ensuring the availability of finance for enterprise within the economy (pro-creditor) or the importance of preserving existing enterprises and employment (pro-debtor). Whether such abstract distinctions can reasonably be maintained for much longer is questionable since it is fairly obvious that both objectives are important. Indeed, faced with the collapse of the 'Tiger economies' in the Far East, the introduction of new insolvency laws reflecting both these objectives was the price of international financial support.

In assessing insolvency risk and attempting to make a transaction 'bankruptcy proof', B needs to take an informed view of the potential effects of the systems most likely to be encountered. Alongside the detailed rules, one very important consideration is whether the jurisdiction in question permits 'debtor in possession' insolvency proceedings or whether it requires the appointment of an insolvency representative to administer the process. An insolvency representative will usually be found to be required to have regard to the interests of the creditors or, as a minimum, to balance the competing interests of the debtor and the creditors. By contrast, in debtor in possession proceedings, management is concerned with survival and provisions which enable management to invoke compulsory disclosure and clawback powers against its own counterparties can come as an unwelcome surprise to creditors whose own jurisdictions have no equivalent procedure. It also has to be recognized that these considerations can give rise to 'forum shopping'. This leads directly to the issue of jurisdiction.

III. JURISDICTION

By way of preliminary comment, it should be observed that not all legal systems include insolvency laws. Insolvency is a risk inherent in a market economy which admits the possibility of profit and loss. In a planned economy it is possible to manage without an insolvency code. Thus, the emergence of new market economies from the former communist bloc was accompanied by the enactment of new insolvency codes or the resurrection of old codes which had fallen into disuse. In the Far East, a different situation was encountered with insolvency laws on the statute book which were unused in practice, sometimes for cultural reasons and sometimes because the courts were an ineffective means of enforcement. The absence of insolvency law and creditor remedies can pose as great a problem for the secured lender as can the existence of insolvency laws with unwelcome effects (although the nature of the problem is entirely different). Globally, the 1990s witnessed considerable legislative activity in the enactment of new insolvency laws. A surviving example of a jurisdiction without insolvency laws is Liberia although it is possible to obtain recognition in Liberia of the foreign liquidation of a Liberian company.

There are currently two major initiatives to harmonize the international approach to jurisdiction in insolvency proceedings. These are the Council Regulation of the European Union and the UNCITRAL Model Law, which are discussed later under the heading 'Forthcoming developments relating to recognition of foreign insolvency proceedings'. Apart from these pending initiatives, the only treaties currently in force apply in Latin America and Scandinavia. Although these measures are long established,[8] the exercise in harmonization which they embody is limited in nature because of the similarities of the constituent legal systems.[9] The task of harmonizing disparate insolvency laws, such as that being undertaken by the European Union, is of a quite different order.

Pending the more or less universal adoption of a harmonized approach to insolvency jurisdiction, if B wishes to make a security transaction 'bankruptcy proof' it will have to continue to consider the basis on which different countries assert jurisdiction. It is not unduly difficult to summarize the range of different approaches which may be encountered in this context even though the detail of the rules in any given jurisdiction can be a subject of considerable complexity. It can be assumed with reasonable safety that D can be wound up in the jurisdiction of its own incorporation. So far as taking jurisdiction to wind up D is concerned, substantially the same is true where a company has its 'seat', ie its domicile as understood in civil law. However, whilst winding-up in the jurisdiction of incorporation will usually (but not invariably) be recognized in other jurisdictions, a winding-up jurisdiction founded on the civil law concept of domicile may not automatically be recognized in common law jurisdictions which equate domicile with the place of incorporation. With that qualification, jurisdiction founded on domicile is relatively predictable. Long-arm jurisdiction is much less so.

The more conventional bases of long-arm jurisdiction are the presence of some of D's assets or business activity within the jurisdiction. However, some countries, for example Denmark and Norway, adopt a comparatively restrained approach to jurisdiction on such grounds. England provides a contrasting example. The jurisdiction is at all times discretionary

---

[8] The Latin American treaties date back to 1889 and the Nordic Convention was signed in 1933.

[9] Similarly, the Insolvency Act 1986 harmonizes insolvency law within the United Kingdom.

but is founded on concepts of 'sufficient connection' and prospective benefit to creditors coupled with the existence of jurisdiction over one or more persons interested in the distribution of D company's assets. It has even been held that the existence of claims of a type which can only be pursued by a liquidator after winding-up has commenced is capable of satisfying the requirement for prospective benefit.[10] Arguably, long-arm jurisdiction to conduct 'main' (as opposed to 'ancillary' or 'secondary' winding-up proceedings) is no longer consonant with contemporary notions of comity. In any event, if the proposed European Union regulation becomes law, England's long-arm jurisdiction will be curtailed.[11]

It is also possible to encounter winding-up jurisdiction based on the local nationality or residence of the petitioning creditor. France provides an example.

In the United States, there is a common jurisdictional base for terminal and reorganizational proceedings under the US Bankruptcy Code. A foreign company with a place of business or assets within the jurisdiction can file. However, this degree of consistency cannot be assumed elsewhere: the jurisdictional base can vary depending on the nature of the proceedings. As noted, in England there is a long-arm jurisdiction to wind up foreign unregistered companies but the principal reorganizational procedure, administration, is confined to companies incorporated within the jurisdiction. This divergence is sufficient to illustrate the point that B, in assessing 'bankruptcy risk', must have regard to the fact that the courts of a country may assert insolvency jurisdiction for different purposes in different circumstances. Some degree of control can be exerted through covenants but it is hardly likely that the courts of any country would decline to accept jurisdiction, where it would otherwise exist, solely on the ground that the circumstances bringing D within its jurisdiction had involved a breach of banking covenants.

IV. UNITY AND UNIVERSALITY

These principles of international insolvency (or their rejection) are second only to jurisdiction in terms of practical importance for B. Unity contrasts with plurality in that, in the event of insolvency, the affairs, business and property of the insolvent company should be subjected to a single procedure. Universality contrasts with territoriality. Where the principle of universality is applied, the insolvency procedure will deal with D's assets

---

[10] *Stocznia Gdanska SA v Latreefers Inc* [2000] CPLR 65 [1999] 1 BCLC 271.
[11] See further: House of Lords, Session 1995–96 7th Report, Select Committee on the European Communities: *Convention on Insolvency Proceedings* (HL paper 59).

and undertaking worldwide but, where territoriality applies, the procedure will be limited to assets within the jurisdiction. However, it does not follow that, because a given legal system embraces the principles of unity and universality, that proceedings instituted within that jurisdiction will be respected or even recognized in other jurisdictions. Thus, from the point of view of B, determination of which of these principles applies serves to inform as to the likely consequences of the proceedings in question within the jurisdiction of inception, the *lex concursus*, but does not necessarily have any impact on the assessment of 'bankruptcy risk' elsewhere.

In practice, insolvency proceedings commenced within the country of D's domicile will generally be found to deal with (or purport to deal with) all of D's assets and liabilities worldwide. Japan is an exception. Japanese insolvency proceedings currently do not relate to assets outside the jurisdiction (the corollary being that Japan does not recognize the effect of foreign proceedings over local assets) although foreign creditors' claims are admissible in Japanese proceedings. Security rights in respect of foreign assets will be recognized in Japanese proceedings but may be subordinated to tax claims even if the security rights take priority in the jurisdiction where the subject matter of the security is located.

Although the international trend is towards universality, the same is not true of unity (except as regards other proceedings within the jurisdiction in which the insolvency proceedings have been commenced). The failure of harmonization initiatives to keep pace with an increasingly international trading environment appears to have led to more rather than less plurality of proceedings. In the absence of an international framework, judicial ingenuity has produced *ad hoc* solutions. Pioneering work was done in this respect by the High Court in London and the United States Bankruptcy Court for the Southern District of New York in the case of *Maxwell Communications Corp plc*. The company was subject to an administration order in England and Chapter 11 proceedings in the United States. The insolvency representatives appointed in both proceedings entered into an agreement for co-operation which was approved by orders of the courts to which they were answerable.[12] The result of the agreement was parallel proceedings neither of which were ancillary to the other. The example has subsequently been followed elsewhere and has been actively encouraged by Committee J of the International Bar Association which developed and promulgated its own Cross-Border Insolvency Concordat.

---

[12] Of the numerous reported proceedings which resulted from this case, see especially the judgment of Hoffmann J reported at [1992] BCC 757, aff'd CA at 767 (*Re Maxwell Communications Corporation plc, Barclays Bank v Homan*), and the corresponding judgment of Judge Brozman during the American stage of the same episode: 170 BR 800, 801–807 (Bankr SDNY 1994).

Where insolvency proceedings are instituted outside the jurisdiction of domicile, they will frequently be found to espouse the principle of universality provided that the debtor company is not already subject to insolvency proceedings in another jurisdiction. However, where such proceedings are instituted and D is already (or, possibly, becomes) subject to separate insolvency proceedings in its jurisdiction of domicile, then it is likely that the 'non-domicillary' proceedings will be regarded as ancillary or secondary. This approach is born of pragmatism. In England, despite some five centuries of statutory insolvency law, the law on ancillary liquidations is almost entirely judge made and remains ill-defined.[13]

In summary, the attitude of any given jurisdiction to the principles of unity and universality is a matter to be taken into account by B in assessing 'bankruptcy risk' in relation to security but those principles do not, of themselves, reduce the possibility of other proceedings in other jurisdictions. Their real significance lies in assessment of the prospective consequences of proceedings commenced in the subject jurisdiction.

V. CHOICE OF LAW

A seemingly universal principle of private international law is that procedure is governed by the domestic law of the country in which proceedings are instituted, namely, the *lex fori*. Indeed, it is difficult to see how it could be otherwise. The corollary is that matters of substance are governed by the law to which the domestic court is directed by its own rules of private international law, namely, the *lex causae*. The distinction is not necessarily easily drawn and the classification of an issue as procedural can neatly circumvent the need to refer to foreign law. For present purposes, the question is whether insolvency law is procedural or substantive and, in general terms, the answer is that it contains elements of both. From the point of view of B, the important point is that issues as to the validity and priority of security are substantive issues in respect of which the court having the conduct of the insolvency proceedings will, where appropriate under its own rules of private international law, refer to foreign law. Purely procedural impediments to the assertion or enforcement of security rights under the relevant foreign legal system will be disregarded because they will yield to the corresponding procedural requirements (if any) applied by the domestic court.

'Choice of law' in this context does not mean choice by the parties in the manner which is familiar, for example, in the rules of private international law applicable to contracts. When insolvency proceedings are

---

[13] See further *Re Bank of Credit and Commerce International SA (No 11)*, n 4 above.

opened in a jurisdiction, the courts of that jurisdiction can be expected to apply domestic, not foreign, insolvency law. There are, however, exceptions where the courts in one jurisdiction act in aid of the courts in another jurisdiction. In England, the relevant statutory provision[14] expressly confers a discretion to apply either domestic insolvency law or the equivalent provisions of the law of the requesting court. By this circuitous route, insolvency proceedings in jurisdiction 1 can expose counterparties to a 'bankruptcy risk' in jurisdiction 2 in circumstances where the risk did not exist in jurisdiction 1 and no insolvency proceedings have been commenced in jurisdiction 2. The example is not unique. It would appear that a similar result could be obtained in the United States[15] and Australia.[16]

It follows that establishing the validity of security under applicable foreign legal systems is merely the starting point for determining the effect of the insolvency proceedings upon the rights of the secured creditor. In this respect, various issues arise which will depend in part on the nature of the proceedings. An overarching consideration is public policy. No court can be expected to enforce rights which offend local concepts of public policy. This issue is much more likely to arise in respect of the remedies purportedly conferred by the security transaction but could, conceivably, arise in respect of the subject matter of a security. In this connection, the European Convention on Human Rights may have increasing significance by developing the concept of public policy in those jurisdictions which have adopted it.

VI. EXTRA-TERRITORIALITY

The insolvency of D company is likely to have maximum impact on B where the subject matter of the security is located within the jurisdiction in which the insolvency proceedings have been commenced. This is, however, merely an observation on practicalities. Insolvency laws can and do purport to have extra-territorial effect. This is not simply a function of adherence to the principle of universality since a domestic theory of universality does not presuppose the assumption of jurisdiction to regulate conduct in other countries. There are two reasons why an insolvency proceeding which sets out to address the assets and liabilities of D company worldwide may nonetheless refrain from interference in the internal affairs of another jurisdiction. First, there is the purely practical

---

[14] Section 426(5) Insolvency Act 1986. See further below, under the heading 'Effects of recognition in England'.   [15] Section 304 US Bankruptcy Code.
[16] Section 581 Corporations Law.

consideration that orders may well prove to be unenforceable and unenforceable orders bring a legal system into disrepute. Secondly, there are considerations of comity. Comity and universality are not contradictory approaches. Rather, proper respect for considerations of comity is more likely to promote the principles of unity and universality by not precluding local proceedings and local remedies for local issues.

The issues which arise from the extra-territorial application of insolvency laws include the effect on other proceedings in foreign jurisdictions, the scope of a stay or moratorium in reorganizational proceedings, and the ability of the office holder in insolvency proceedings which are commenced in jurisdiction 1 to use clawback provisions to attack transactions which occurred in jurisdiction 2.

One of the purposes of terminal insolvency proceedings is to put an end to the multiplicity of individual proceedings for the recovery of debt and to replace them with an orderly administration of claims. A consequence of the commencement of insolvency proceedings is likely to be found to be a stay on further proceedings in the same jurisdiction where the insolvency proceedings have been opened. Such a rule exists in English law but is not treated by the English courts as being applicable to proceedings in a court outside the United Kingdom.[17] Where this is possible in a cross-border insolvency case, individual creditors can use proceedings in foreign jurisdictions to circumvent the insolvency process and to achieve a priority. There are various ways, short of attempting to control the conduct of litigation in foreign courts, by which a legal system can respond to this problem. A personal order could be made to restrain a creditor located within the jurisdiction in which insolvency proceedings have commenced from having recourse to foreign courts. A variation on this theme is to treat a creditor who resorts to such proceedings as being in contempt of the insolvency proceedings. The distinction between treating the rule of local insolvency law as having extra-territorial effect and these measures is somewhat artificial and difficult to reconcile with considerations of comity. A more acceptable approach is for a creditor making foreign recoveries to be required to bring those recoveries into account before being allowed to participate in the insolvency process. This solution has been adopted in a number of civil and common law jurisdictions.

The extra-territorial effect of a stay on foreign proceedings and remedies raises more difficult policy issues when the stay in question forms a part of a reorganizational procedure. Whereas a terminal insolvency procedure which respects the proprietary rights of secured creditors is unlikely

---

[17] Section 130 Insolvency Act 1986; *Re Oriental Inland Steam Co, ex parte Scinde Railway Co* (1874) LR 9 Ch App 557.

to seek to impose any impediments on the enforcement on security abroad, a moratorium for the purposes of reorganization raises entirely different considerations. The stay on the enforcement of security is a cornerstone of Chapter 11 proceedings in the United States, of administration in the United Kingdom, and of the multiplicity of other reorganizational procedures derived from those models. Here, considerations of comity may more readily yield to the overriding imperative of achieving a stay if the procedure is to enjoy any prospect of success. The first question is always whether the stay purports to be extra-territorial. The automatic stay in Chapter 11 proceedings[18] has worldwide effect and it has been assumed, but not yet decided, that the English courts would take a similar view of the effect of an administration order.[19] Rules requiring a creditor to bring receipts into account have little relevance where the receipts in question represent security realizations and the underlying purpose of the stay is to prevent realizations rather than to make distributions to creditors.

From a practical point of view a worldwide stay becomes an issue of recognition when B is attempting to enforce security in a foreign jurisdiction. B must always consider not only the steps which may be taken to give the stay local effect, for example orders in aid of secondary proceedings, but also the possible consequences for B within the jurisdiction in which the insolvency proceedings have been commenced. If, as is frequently the case with international lending institutions, there is a local presence or local assets within that jurisdiction, then proceeding to enforce security elsewhere may nonetheless attract adverse consequences. In some cases, creditors can and will conclude that insolvency proceedings occurring in a jurisdiction other than that where their security is located and with which they have no other dealings, can be disregarded. However, a decision deliberately to flout the insolvency laws of any jurisdiction should take into account not merely present connections but also the possibility of future connections or involvement in other proceedings in the courts of that country. In the case of a major financial institution, it is not a course which will be lightly undertaken.

Extra-territorial clawback provisions raise similar issues. However, in this instance, B can be the subject of a targeted attack by the insolvency representative in the 'foreign' proceedings rather than simply being put in the position of considering whether it can safely exercise local remedies which are available to it. For the reasons explained under the heading of 'Choice of law' above, circumstances can arise where the targeted

---

[18] Section 362 US Bankruptcy Code.
[19] *Banque Indosuez v Ferromet Resources Inc* [1993] BCLC 112.

attack is made in accordance with the provisions of local insolvency law even though there are no local insolvency proceedings.

The extra-territorial application of transactional avoidance rules is not necessarily as controversial as an extra-territorial stay. For example, the transaction in question may have been entered into between a debtor company and a creditor both of whom are domiciled in the jurisdiction within which the insolvency proceedings have commenced. The only foreign element might be the choice of a foreign governing law or the fact that the transaction was concluded in a foreign jurisdiction. In such circumstances, there would seem to be no obvious policy objections to the domestic clawback rules having the same effects that they would have had on a purely domestic transaction. The position is less clear when the counterparty is domiciled outside the jurisdiction or the subject matter of the transaction is an asset located outside the jurisdiction. English law approaches these issues through the exercise of discretion. The issue arose in the context of rules concerning 'transactions at an undervalue' which enable certain office holders in English insolvency proceedings to attack gratuitous transactions and transactions where the inflow of benefit to D company is not commensurate with the outflow to the counterparty.[20] The drafting of the relevant legislation does not incorporate any territorial limitation. The court nonetheless approached the matter on the basis that it had a discretion which it would only exercise so as to permit proceedings against a foreign counterparty if satisfied that there was a sufficient connection with England. Factors to be taken into account included the location of the counterparty, the connection with the insolvent, the nature and purpose of the transaction under attack, and the location of any property involved. Critically the court added that these considerations would also include: 'whether under any relevant foreign law the defendant acquired an unimpeachable title free from any claims even if the insolvent had been adjudged bankrupt or wound-up locally'.[21]

A further protection is that, under English law, the court's leave to serve process abroad may also be required, thereby introducing an additional discretion. The result is unpredictable and therefore unsatisfactory from the point of view of B. However, it is a pragmatic approach and it is difficult to see how clear predetermined rules could avoid the risk of injustice in individual cases, through either facilitating claims which amounted to an exorbitant exercise of jurisdiction, or, alternatively, by preventing claims being pursued with resultant injustice to the general body of creditors.

---

[20] *Re Paramount Airways Ltd* [1993] Ch 223.   [21] ibid, 240.

VII. LENDER LIABILITY

'Lender liability' is a compendious term used to describe a variety of potential liabilities which lenders can incur to debtors and third parties. Some such liabilities are of a general nature, for example breach of contract, and only qualify as lender liability because the breach in question is the breach of a lending contract. Other heads of liability are much more specific. Two which are of particular concern to secured creditors are environmental liability and liability arising from control of D.

Environmental liability is much more likely to arise in the jurisdiction within which the subject matter of the security is located than as a feature of the insolvency proceedings as such. However, liability for control of D may take a form which can only arise in the context of insolvency proceedings. An example under English law is 'wrongful trading'.[22] This is a liability incurred by the directors of an insolvent company who fail to take all available steps to minimize loss to creditors after the inevitability of an insolvent liquidation becomes apparent (or ought to have become apparent if they had kept themselves properly informed). It is not a liability which attaches to lenders as such but a lender could, at least in theory, constitute a 'shadow director'.[23] Hitherto the English courts have resisted the imposition of liability under this heading on creditors[24] but the possibility of liability in a future case cannot be entirely discounted. Similarly, in extreme circumstances, a creditor could be liable as a party to 'fraudulent trading' if it accepts money which it knows to have been procured by a fraud perpetrated for the very purpose of making the payment.[25] The existence of provisions providing sanctions against fraud will not occasion surprise in any jurisdiction although they may be found in criminal law rather than in the insolvency code. A much wider variety of approaches to trading whilst insolvent may be encountered with differences arising both from the standard of culpability demanded and the range of persons capable of being held responsible. Arguably, this remains one of the genuine areas of difference by which the 'debtor friendliness' of a jurisdiction can be assessed because of the effect of such sanctions on the risk undertaken by entrepreneurs.

There is also a risk, which appears to be most pronounced in France, of a lender incurring liability by continuing to extend credit to an insolvent debtor and thereby giving other creditors a false impression of its creditworthiness.

---

[22] Section 214 Insolvency Act 1986.

[23] ie a person who is not a member of the board of directors but nonetheless exercises some controlling influence over the activities of the company (*Secretary of State for Trade and Industry v Deverell* [2000] 2 All ER 365 (CA).   [24] *Re PTFTZM Ltd* [1995] BCC 280.

[25] *Re Gerald Cooper Chemicals Ltd* [1978] Ch 262.

VIII. HOW INSOLVENCY LAW APPROACHES CROSS-BORDER ISSUES

The next sections of this chapter assume that insolvency proceedings involving D have been opened in at least one country (*forum concursus*). To avoid an over-elaborate discussion, the issues will be approached mainly from the standpoint of English law. As already explained, the rules of jurisdiction to be found in the insolvency laws of many countries are drawn in such a way as to make them potentially applicable to debtors having various kinds and levels of contact with the country in question, apart from the more obvious case where D is a 'subject' of that system of law by virtue of having undergone incorporation there.

Given that the asset to which the security relates is movable, its location at any particular moment may be a material question for the purpose of determining whether the insolvency law of the *forum concursus* will be interposed between B and its attempted exercise of its anticipated rights as a secured creditor. If the asset happens to be located in the *forum concursus* at the time when B seeks to assert its rights, the application of the insolvency law of that forum would appear to be nigh inescapable except perhaps under rare circumstances where the private international law of the *forum concursus* has the effect of regarding the asset in question as excluded from the scope of the insolvency proceedings taking place in that jurisdiction. If the asset in question was not so situate at the opening of proceedings, but was brought there subsequently, it is possible that the courts of that country could uphold the claims of B to exercise its rights over the asset. To do so, however, would involve B in the exacting task of satisfying the *forum concursus* as to the validity and extent of its claim to the asset in question, which would entail B showing that the original transaction is recognized according to the private international law of that forum. Because of the lack of standardized private international laws there is a considerable diversity between different countries' laws in terms of the rules for recognition of foreign legal proceedings, or transactions intended to have legal effects, and the final outcome will obviously be dependent on the precise nature of the relevant rule as applied to the circumstances of the instant case.[26]

---

[26] eg in some systems, the issue of validity of a security interest arising from contractual agreement may be referred to the governing law of the contract (as established by means of the choice of law rule of *that* system); in other systems, more emphasis may be placed upon the *situs* of the asset at one or more relevant times (with the possibility that a *cumulative* test has to be satisfied, involving reference to the laws of two or possibly more systems). Additional complications can arise from the requirement of registration as an inescapable precondition to the perfection of security, which may apply irrespective of the *situs* of the asset or of the governing law of the contract: cf *Re Weldtech Equipment Ltd* [1991] BCLC 393.

The more commonly encountered situation, for the purposes of the present discussion, involves the process of recognition of foreign insolvency proceedings by a court before which a claim has arisen in connection with the asset over which B asserts security. If it is also the case that the asset itself is currently located within the jurisdiction in question, the court's ultimate findings can be readily given effect without more ado. Matters are more complex, however, where the asset is located elsewhere, because its final destiny will be further dependent on the attitude of the court of the *situs* towards the respective claims by the 'rival' courts, namely the court presently seized, as against the *forum concursus*, to decide questions of title to the asset in question.

If it is alleged that the foreign insolvency proceedings have the consequence of suspending B's powers of enforcement of security—or of rendering the security wholly or partially voidable in accordance with further processes under the *lex concursus*—then the first and most obvious questions to be resolved are whether such foreign proceedings are recognized according to the law of the country before whose court the issue has arisen, and, if so, what effects are to be accorded in consequence of such recognition. Where there is only one set of foreign insolvency proceedings, the challenge to B's security will typically be mounted by the office-holder appointed under those proceedings. However, other parties may have an interest in attacking B's status as a secured creditor, including any holders of subordinate or competing interests in the same asset, whose own position would be enhanced by the elimination of B's entitlement. A less common situation arises when there are concurrent insolvency proceedings in different jurisdictions, thereby presenting the courts of third states (within whose jurisdiction some asset of D is presently situated) with the task of determining which office-holder has the proper standing to request turnover of the asset in question. Logically, the court must first determine which of the office-holders has the pre-eminent claim, according to the rule of recognition found within its own system of private international law. Thereafter, any question concerning the impact of the foreign insolvency proceedings upon the status of B's security can be resolved by application of the relevant rules belonging to the foreign law in question, as already identified by the private international law rules of the forum before which the matter is currently being decided.

IX. ENGLISH PRINCIPLES OF RECOGNITION

In keeping with the disparate character of private international laws, it can be noted that the principles on which recognition is accorded to foreign insolvency proceedings under the laws of different countries exhibit considerable variation. Even within a single country—notably in the case of England and Wales—there can be significant differences between the principles applied in recognition of bankruptcies of individuals, and those applicable to corporate insolvencies.[27] Although this chapter is concerned with the latter, it is also to be observed that in the course of development of the English law rules of recognition (which have hitherto been almost entirely based upon case decisions) some principles have been applied interchangeably between individual and corporate cases.

The following principles of recognition are derived from the cases:

1. English law strongly favours the law of a company's country of incorporation as having the strongest claim to control questions concerning the formation, regulation, and ultimately the demise of the company as a legal entity endowed with personality and capacity. Similarly, the courts of the state of incorporation are considered to have enduring competence to serve as the forum for insolvency proceedings whose ultimate effect will be to bring about the winding-up and dissolution of the company. Therefore, winding-up proceedings which have commenced in that jurisdiction will be recognized in England, even in situations where the company's central management and control are shown to be located in some other jurisdiction. As a further consequence of such recognition, English law recognizes the standing of the office-holder appointed in proceedings opened in the company's country of incorporation, and will assist him in any efforts to claim, protect, and also to administer and dispose of the company's English assets, subject to it being shown that the capacity to do so is conferred under the law of his original appointment.[28] This involves an inquiry into the provisions of the *lex concursus*, to confirm that its intended scope of application extends to D's assets 'wherever situate'.[29]

2. Where insolvency proceedings have commenced in a country other than that in which the company underwent incorporation, the position is less certain in view of the lack of reported English authority directly

---

[27] For a more detailed account of the divergent approaches of English law (and of the laws of countries that have been influenced by English law and doctrine) towards recognition of individual and company insolvency respectively, see IF Fletcher, *Insolvency in Private International Law* (1999), 92–104, 165–172, and 178–185.

[28] See eg *Sea Insurance Co v Rossia Insurance Co of Petrograd* (1924) 20 Ll L Rep 308 (CA); *Bank of Ethiopia v National Bank of Egypt* [1937] 1 Ch 513; *Banco de Bilbao v Sancha* [1938] 2 KB 176 (CA).

[29] *Macaulay v Guaranty Trust of New York* (1927) 44 TLR 99; *Onassis v Drewry* (1949) 83 Ll L R 308 (CA). In the United Kingdom itself, insolvency proceedings are designed to have extraterritorial effect upon D's property 'wherever situated': see Insolvency Act 1986, s 436 (definition of 'property').

in point. However, there is a line of cases in which English courts have applied the notion of 'secondary' or 'ancillary' proceedings in relation to concurrent liquidations taking place in England and in a foreign country. The approach has been to regard the proceedings which are based in the company's state of incorporation as the 'primary' proceedings, while those which are commenced in a state in which the company has maintained a branch of its business are, logically, to be treated as of an ancillary character for the purpose of co-ordination.[30] This implies a readiness on the part of English law to recognize proceedings opened in a country in which the company has had a place of business, while reserving the right to accord primacy of effect to any proceedings that are opened in the state of incorporation. As might be expected, such cases have tended to present themselves before the English courts in relation to companies which were either formed in England, or which had a branch there.

The position is more uncertain for cases in which the company has not had sufficiently close links with England as to give rise to the possibility of insolvency proceedings (whether primary or ancillary) being commenced here. In such a situation, where the English court is essentially 'neutral', it might be reasonable to suppose that the approach to recognition of foreign insolvency proceedings (in the absence of any treaty- or statute-based obligation to accord such recognition) would be closely modelled on that which has been developed towards foreign proceedings in general, namely to have regard to the actual circumstances under which the foreign court's exercise of jurisdiction took place. If satisfied that the foreign court enjoyed 'jurisdiction in the international sense' (as determined, for this purpose, by the criteria accepted by English private international law), English courts have been prepared to recognize foreign judgments in civil or commercial proceedings. Notably, however, such recognition has not been accorded in cases where the exercise of jurisdiction was based on an 'extended' or 'exorbitant' ground such as the presence of assets, or temporary personal presence alone. This restrictive approach has been maintained even where it is the case that English law itself embodies a rule of extended jurisdiction similar to that utilized in the foreign proceedings.[31] In the absence of a thorough revision and restatement of the English law concerning recognition of foreign insol-

---

[30] *Re Matheson Brothers Ltd* (1884) 27 Ch D 225; *Re Commercial Bank of South Australia* (1886) 33 Ch D 174; *Re English, Scottish and Australian Chartered Bank* [1893] 3 Ch 385; *Re Bank of Credit and Commerce International SA (No 3)* [1993] BCLC 106, 111 *(the same) (No 10)* [1996] 4 All ER 796.

[31] cf *Re Trepca Mines Ltd* [1960] 1 WLR 1273, 1281; *Société Co-opérative Sidmetal v Titan International Ltd* [1966] 1 QB 828, 838–841.

vency proceedings, it is suggested that (unless there are strong reasons to the contrary in a given case) English courts should be prepared to recognize foreign insolvency proceedings commenced in a country in which the company has had a place of business, or has carried on business for a measurable period, or in which the company's central management and control is or has been based.[32]

X. EFFECTS OF RECOGNITION IN ENGLAND

The primary consequence of recognition being accorded to a foreign insolvency proceeding, so far as English law is concerned, is that the office-holder has standing to invoke the assistance of the courts of this country, on the basis that he represents the collective interests of all parties with claims against the insolvent debtor and its property. Since the nineteenth century, English courts have followed a liberal policy in terms of the giving of such assistance, and in the facilitation of cross-border cooperation in cases of concurrent proceedings relating to the same debtor. This tradition was originally based upon case precedents alone, since there were no statutory provisions relating to such matters in the case of corporate (as opposed to individual) insolvency prior to 1986.[33] The enactment of section 426 of the Insolvency Act 1986 supplied a new, statutory basis for obtaining assistance from United Kingdom courts in matters of corporate (as well as individual) insolvency. However, since access to the section 426 procedure is limited to cases in which the foreign proceedings are commenced in a country which has been expressly designated as a 'relevant' country for the purposes of section 426, it is important to bear in mind that the case-based system of assistance remains intact, and is available for use in cases originating from other foreign jurisdictions apart from the twenty foreign countries and territories that have thus far been designated.[34] Where applicable, however, the terms of assistance available under section 426 have a number of special features that can

---

[32] So argued in Fletcher, n 27 above, 93–96 and at 167–169. See also P Smart, *Cross-Border Insolvency* (2nd edn, 1998) 164–182.

[33] Under the Bankruptcy Act 1914, s 122 (and previously, under 118 Bankruptcy Act 1883, and 74 of the Act of 1869) a requirement to provide mutual aid and auxiliary assistance in bankruptcy was imposed upon the courts of the United Kingdom and on 'every British court elsewhere having jurisdiction in bankruptcy or insolvency'. From the mid-20th century onward, the practice based upon this series of Empire-wide enactments was transformed into a network of arrangements maintained among independent members of the Commonwealth, with the original provisions' effects being confined to the dwindling number of colonial or dependent territories.

[34] See s 426(11) Insolvency Act 1986, together with SI 1986 s 2123; SI 1996 s 253 and SI 1998 s 2766.

provide practical advantages by comparison to the assistance available at common law. The two forms of assistance will be briefly described:

1. At common law, an office-holder in foreign corporate insolvency proceedings can apply directly for orders and remedies that will enable him to perform the duties and functions which he is mandated to perform under the law governing his appointment. Although (in contrast to the position which has obtained since the mid-eighteenth century in the case of individual bankruptcy) English law does not regard foreign corporate insolvency proceedings as producing any direct or automatic change of ownership of the company's assets situate outside the state in which the proceedings have commenced,[35] the courts are prepared to entertain an application for a vesting order in favour of the foreign liquidator, so as to confer title to the company's property (movable or immovable) that is situate here. An alternative—and equally effective—remedy that is available is for the court to appoint the foreign liquidator to be a receiver of the company's English property. The order of appointment can embody such further powers as the court considers appropriate, such as the power of sale, and the power to deal with the proceeds in accordance with the provisions of the law of his appointment, or to do so subject to some proviso taking account of any special factors such as locally prevalent claims or charges.[36] In the case of foreign proceedings whose nature is analogous to the court-appointed receivership known to English law, recognition and assistance is available on terms which are, if anything, more liberal than those applicable to foreign liquidations. The competence of the foreign court can for this purpose be derived from the fact of the company's incorporation under the law of that country, or alternatively from the company's submission to the jurisdiction of the foreign court through participation in the proceedings from which the receivership has arisen.[37]

Where the foreign proceedings are non-liquidation proceedings whose aim is to bring about the restructuring of a financially troubled company, such as the Chapter 11 proceeding under the US Bankruptcy

---

[35] Contrast the cases following *Solomons v Ross* (1764) 1 Hy Bl 131n, holding that a foreign bankruptcy effects the immediate divesting of the bankrupt's English property that is of a *movable* character, in favour of the foreign trustee (or equivalent). This doctrine was not applicable to *immovable* property in England: *Waite v Bingley* (1882) 21 Ch D 674.

[36] cf the bankruptcy cases, *Re Kooperman* [1928] WN 101, *Re Levy's Trusts* (1885) 30 Ch D 119; *Re Osborne* (1931–32) 15 B & C R 189.

[37] *Macaulay v Guaranty Trust of New York* (1927) 44 TLR 99; *Schemmer v Property Resources Ltd* [1975] Ch 273 (see especially at 287–288, per Goulding J, for suggestions of further grounds on which English law might recognize the validity of the foreign court's exercise of jurisdiction to appoint a receiver).

Code, it may be stated that English law has gradually come to terms with the special challenges posed by such operations in a cross-border context. In the controversial, and much misunderstood, case of *Felixstowe Dock and Railway Co v US Lines Inc*,[38] Hirst J indicated his readiness, in principle, to accord the usual assistance under the doctrine of comity towards a Delaware-registered company, as debtor in possession, which was undergoing Chapter 11 proceedings in the US Bankruptcy Court for the Southern District of New York. In the light of the evidence before him, however, the learned judge declined to set aside a *Mareva* injunction preventing the removal of the company's English assets to the United States, on the ground that the substance and effect of the plan of reorganization proposed by the company did not offer the same advantages to the European creditors as were in prospect for creditors in the United States. In the general chorus of negative sentiment that this decision provoked from across the Atlantic, it was perhaps too easy to overlook the indications of more positive judicial intentions towards Chapter 11 that were planted within the judgment of Hirst J. The potential for inter-jurisdictional co-operation in the attempted rescue or restructuring of a company was demonstrated to considerable effect in the subsequent proceedings in the case of *Maxwell Communications Corp plc* described under the heading of 'Unity and universality' (part IV above). The vital premises on which that judicial co-operation was founded were the recognition by each system of the validity of the proceedings opened under the law of the other—an administration order made by the English High Court, and Chapter 11 proceedings conducted from New York—combined with the acceptance of the necessary consequences of such recognition in terms of the standing of the office holders appointed by each court. This, it is submitted, offers a valuable basis for future co-operation in cross-border cases falling outside the scope of section 426, as explored below.

2. In cases where a United Kingdom court's assistance is sought under the provisions of section 426, the problem of restricted access to this procedure has already been noted. Only if the request comes from a *court* in a *relevant country or territory* (as defined in section 426(11)) does it fall within the ambit of the section. Thus, the office-holder cannot apply directly to the court here, but must first induce the court in the country of appointment to address a request pursuant to section 426 to a competent court in some part of the United Kingdom. If those conditions are met, there are at least two substantial advantages of access to the section 426 procedure, by comparison to that available at common law.

---

[38] [1989] QB 360.

First, section 426(4) and (5) are so drafted as to make it obligatory for the United Kingdom court to assist the foreign court.[39] Secondly, in subsection (5) the nature of the assistance the United Kingdom court is empowered to provide to the requesting court is expressed as including 'the insolvency law which is applicable by *either court* in relation to comparable matters falling within its jurisdiction' (emphasis added). A proviso to subsection (5), whose precise effect is not wholly clear, states that: 'In exercising its discretion under this subsection, a court shall have regard in particular to the rules of private international law'. The full implications of these statutory provisions are being progressively explored in litigation, but a number of propositions have already been the subject of reported decisions up to the level of the Court of Appeal: (a) although the United Kingdom court is under an obligation to give assistance, it retains a discretion as to the precise nature of the assistance which ought to be provided in a given case, and will be necessarily mindful of its wider responsibilities to uphold the principles of law and justice; (b) nevertheless, the essential spirit in which the court should respond is that if the assistance requested can properly be granted, then it should be given unless there is some good reason for not doing so;[40] (c) in formulating its response to the request, the United Kingdom court has available to it its own general jurisdiction and powers vested in it under the laws of this country, in addition to the provisions of domestic 'insolvency law' (as defined by section 426(10)(a)) and so much of the law of the country from which the request is received as corresponds to the contents of domestic insolvency law;[41] (d) by means of the 'ambidextrous' powers of assistance conferred by section 426(5), a court in the United Kingdom can provide assistance using provisions within the United Kingdom insolvency law (which is of particular relevance where the law of the requesting country contains no comparable provision);[42] (e) alterna-

---

[39] Section 426(4) states: 'The courts having jurisdiction in relation to insolvency law in any part of the United Kingdom *shall assist* the courts having the corresponding jurisdiction in any other part of the United Kingdom or in any relevant country or territory' (emphasis added).

[40] *Hughes v Hannover* [1997] 1 BCLC 497, 513–514, per Morritt LJ, quoting with approval the judgment of Rattee J in *Re Bank of Credit and Commerce International SA (No 9)* [1994] 3 All ER 764, 785. See also *Re Southern Equities Corpn Ltd, England v Smith* [2000] BCC 123 (CA).   [41] *Hughes v Hannover*, n 40 above, at 517.

[42] As in *Re Bank of Credit and Commerce International SA* (No 9), n 40 above, a case in which the English court dealt with a letter of request from the Grand Court of the Cayman Islands in respect of a Cayman Islands company. It was held that, in such circumstances, the English court had jurisdiction to apply English clawback rules even though there were no equivalent provisions under Cayman Islands law and the English court would have had no jurisdiction to entertain the applications if the applicants had applied direct to the English court. See also *Re Dallhold Estates (UK) Pty Ltd* [1992] BCLC 621.

tively, it may be the case that the law of the country from which the request is received is more apt to deliver the assistance that is desired, but that the United Kingdom happens to be the preferred or necessary venue for carrying out the relevant procedures. In such cases, the Court of Appeal have held that a request which satisfies the formal requirements of section 426 remains subject to the general principle that the United Kingdom court is required to give the assistance in the manner requested, and should not withhold it by reason of a divergence of practices between the two systems when concerned with domestic insolvency cases. The fact that the Secretary of State has seen fit to designate the foreign country in question for the purposes of section 426 should be taken as indicative that the legal process in that other country is of an acceptable standard, viewed from the standpoint of public policy in the United Kingdom. Courts should therefore refrain from adopting a view of the foreign law that would effectively stigmatize it as oppressive.[43]

XI. SECTION 426 AND CHOICE OF LAW

From the above summary of the results thus far of cases brought under section 426 it will be noted that there is an absence of clarification of the meaning and scope of the proviso to subsection (5), which requires the United Kingdom court to 'have regard in particular to the rules of private international law'. This question is of direct relevance for the purposes of this chapter, because of the potential need to examine the validity of B's security if this should be challenged or impeached under the insolvency law of a country which qualifies as a relevant country within the meaning of section 426, or under the insolvency law of this country itself.

The subject of 'choice of avoidance law' is still underdeveloped in the private international law of this country, and awaits a suitable case in which to receive direct judicial attention. The issue was addressed by courts in the United States in the course of deciding whether to allow the administrators of Maxwell Communications Corp plc to bring action in that jurisdiction with a view to avoiding a transaction (allegedly amounting to a voidable preference) entered into by the directors of MCC shortly before insolvency proceedings commenced.[44] The avoidance rule

---

[43] *Re Southern Equities Corpn Ltd, England v Smith*, n 40 above. For a note of reservation regarding the wider implications of the judgment of the Court of Appeal, see (2000) 13 *Insolvency Intelligence*, p 38. (Leave to appeal to the House of Lords was refused.)

[44] *Re Maxwell Communications Corp plc*, 170 BR 800, 801–807 (Bankr SDNY 1994) (Judge Brozman); affd 186 BR 807, 812–815 (SDNY 1995) (Scheindlin, USDJ); affd 593 F 3d 1036 (2nd Cir 1996) (Cardamone, Circuit Judge). For further comment see Fletcher [1997] JBL at 476–480.

of section 547 of the United States Bankruptcy Code is considerably more favourable from the office holder's point of view, by comparison to section 239 of the Insolvency Act 1986. Although the United States proceedings were confined to establishing whether the United States courts could exercise jurisdiction over the matter, and if so whether they should do so, this question was treated as depending on whether the transaction in question was properly governed by the law of one of the states of the United States, or by English law. Judge Brozman (with whose analysis and approach neither of the appellate judges expressed any disagreement) opted for a 'classical' assessment of the relative strengths of the various contacts linking the parties to the transaction with a particular country and its law. These contacts included D's 'home country' (regarded as its state of incorporation—here England), D's operational 'nerve centre', and the locations of the assets and creditors with which D's business is primarily conducted, as well as the particular circumstances surrounding the transaction under attack. Having concluded that the balance of factors indicated the transaction's validity should be tested according to the English avoidance law, the learned judge dismissed the suit. It may be noted that she had declined to adopt the solution proposed by the court-appointed *amicus curiae* (Professor Jay L Westbrook) who advocated a more direct and predictable test for selecting the system of law whose avoidance rule would be applied, utilizing D's 'home country' as the single connecting factor for this purpose.[45] Although, on the facts in *Maxwell Communications Corp plc* itself, this would also have led to the application of the English avoidance rule, the judge was apparently concerned that too mechanistic a rule might give rise to intellectually unsatisfactory results in subsequent cases.

By way of a historic footnote to the above comments, it may be observed that the questions of choice of avoidance law, and of the appropriate jurisdiction in which to bring proceedings for transactional avoidance, were apparently at the forefront of ministerial considerations underlying the introduction of section 426 in its current form. During the course of proceedings on what was then the Insolvency Bill 1984, a new clause was introduced which was destined to become section 426 of the Act of 1986. The following justification was offered for the terms proposed:

The new clause will give courts sufficient flexibility in all types of insolvency proceedings to solve complicated matters involving one or more of the insolvency jurisdictions in the United Kingdom in the manner best suited to the facts before them in any particular case. For example, if a company registered in England and

---

[45] For further elaboration see Westbrook, 'Choice of Avoidance Law in Global Insolvencies', (1991) 17 Brook J Int'l L 499–538.

Wales enters into an under-value transaction with a person in Scotland and then subsequently goes into liquidation and the liquidator wishes to bring the matter before the court, it is not clear at present whether he should go to the English or Scottish court and whether it should apply to [*sic*] the law of England or that of Scotland in determining whether the transaction should be set aside. Under the new clause, a liquidator could go in the first instance to the English court. If that court felt that the matter would more appropriately be dealt with under the law of Scotland, the English court would issue a request to the Scottish court to assist the liquidator. *The Scottish court could then deal with the matter by applying its rules of private international law to determine the law applicable to the transaction in question'.*[46] (emphasis added)

While it appears from the above statement that the clause was intended to provide a vehicle for the application of rules of private international law in cases of transactional avoidance, it is equally clear that no precise intentions were present in the mind of Parliament as to the laying down of any particular choice of law rule for that purpose. Either it was assumed that such rules already formed a settled part of the respective bodies of private international law in the various parts of the United Kingdom, or it was anticipated that the courts would proceed to develop such rules for the future, drawing on existing principles. Whatever may be the truth of the matter, the development of such rules for modern purposes has still to take place. It is submitted that it would not be satisfactory—and would appear to fly in the face of the Parliamentary expectations voiced above—for a court simply to conclude that, provided it is in a position to exercise jurisdiction in an application for avoidance, it should proceed to apply its own avoidance rule irrespective of the connecting factors that can be shown to have some material relationship to the transaction and the parties. Such a response would amount to an abnegation of the very purpose for which private international law exists.

XII. ENGLISH RECOGNITION OF DISCHARGE OF OBLIGATIONS UNDER
FOREIGN PROCEEDINGS

Although English law has followed a relatively liberal policy towards the according of recognition of foreign insolvency proceedings, and in assisting the foreign office holder on the basis of such recognition, there is at least one respect in which the state of the authorities produces a less than satisfactory position. This arises in the case of a debtor which, despite having undergone insolvency proceedings in the foreign country whose

---

[46] Hansard, HC Standing Committee E, 18 June 1985, col 423 (Mr Trippier). Consider: *Reid v Ramlort* [1999] BPIR 133.

jurisdiction is recognized according to English private international law, happens to be subject to a liability whose governing law is English. Although it is the case that English law regards its own insolvency proceedings as giving rise to universal effects—and thus resulting in the discharge of all D's liabilities that are comprised in those proceedings, irrespective of their governing law—this line of reasoning is abandoned in relation to foreign proceedings and their effects. The primary rule is that a foreign discharge will be recognized as valid and effective if it can be shown that the substantive obligation has been released according to the law by which it is governed.[47] Where, however, the consequence of applying the English choice of law rules on contractual obligations (which, since 1991, are mainly supplied by the provisions of the Rome Convention of 19 June 1980[48]) is that the applicable law is that of England itself, recognition of the foreign discharge is precluded by the dogmatic (and, it is submitted, illogical and indefensible) rule laid down in a decision of the Court of Appeal in 1890, to the effect that a contract made and to be performed in England can only be discharged through some legal process occurring under, or subject to, English law.[49] What is required, surely, is a properly formulated, supplementary rule of recognition as part of English contract law itself, to allow foreign legal proceedings which otherwise meet the criteria for jurisdictional competence and due process (in particular, fair opportunity for B to participate in the foreign insolvency proceedings) to be capable of bringing about the discharge of an obligation governed by English law. The existing state of the law is particularly unsatisfactory in the context of any attempt, by means of proceedings taking place in its home country, to restructure an ailing company with multi-jurisdictional connections. Under the *Gibbs* rule, a creditor whose claim is governed by English law, and who may even have been party to the foreign proceedings under which debts were to be discharged under the terms of a scheme or composition, could subsequently seek to recover the balance of the debt by action in the English court, followed by enforcement against any assets of the company which happen to be found in this country. Such an outcome is difficult to justify, and is conspicuously at odds with the professed purposes of modern

---

[47] See eg, *Potter v Brown* (1804) 5 East 124; *Ellis v M'Henry* (1871) LR 6 CP 228, 234 *et seq.*

[48] This EU Convention was given legal effect, as from 1 April 1991, by the Contracts (Applicable Law) Act 1990.

[49] *Gibbs & Sons v La Société Industrielle et Commerciale des Métaux* (1890) 25 QBD 399. The decision was commended as correct by the House of Lords in *National Bank of Greece and Athens SA v Metliss* [1958] AC 509, 523; *Adams v National Bank of Greece SA* [1961] AC 255, 287. For criticism of the *Gibbs* case and its consequences, see F Piggott, *Foreign Judgments and Jurisdiction* (3rd edn, 1910) Part III, Book VI, 127–137; IF Fletcher, n 27 above, at 104–109.

English insolvency law, with its emphasis upon the promotion of a 'rescue' culture.

XIII. FORTHCOMING DEVELOPMENTS RELATING TO RECOGNITION OF FOREIGN PROCEEDINGS

Two major developments at international level have given rise to the prospect of changes to the English law of international insolvency in the near future. The implications for recognition of foreign proceedings and of their effects are noted here.

First, as the culmination of some four decades of work towards the conclusion of a uniform regime for the member states of the European Union, pertaining to questions of insolvency, a Council Regulation on Insolvency Proceedings was adopted in May 2000 (with entry into force postponed until 31 May 2002). The regulation will not harmonize the substantive laws and insolvency procedures of the member states, but will instead control the circumstances under which proceedings can be opened in any of those states, in relation to a debtor whose centre of main interests is located within the territory of one of them (Article 3). The regulation further provides for recognition to be accorded as of right to proceedings opened in any European Union state in circumstances falling within its ambit, and goes on to specify the extraterritorial effects which shall accompany such recognition. Additionally, there are a series of provisions (Articles 4–15) which supply uniform choice of law rules to indicate the law applicable to numerous issues arising in the context of an international insolvency. Of particular relevance are the choice of law provisions, commencing with Article 4 which specifies that unless otherwise provided the law applicable to insolvency proceedings and their effects shall be that of the member state within whose territory the proceedings are opened. This rule is expressly stated to include the determination of the conditions under which set-offs may be invoked, and also questions relating to the voidness, voidability or unenforceability of legal acts detrimental to all the creditors.[50] In relation to the issues considered in this chapter, the impact of the basic rule would be that, assuming D to have become the subject of insolvency proceedings in a European Union member state in which D's centre of main interests is located, the avoidance rule of the state of opening would be applicable to determine the validity of any transaction impeached by the office holder, and the consequence of its

---

[50] EU Regulation, Art 4(2)(d), (m). In the case of set-off, the further provisions of Art 6 should be noted, whereby if the law of the state of opening proceedings happens to deny set-off, it can nevertheless be demanded where such a right is allowed according to the law applicable to the insolvent debtor's claim.

application would be respected and enforced in all other member states with regard to assets within their jurisdiction. In relation to B's assertion that it enjoys a security interest over an asset of D, Article 5 supplies a choice of law rule in favour of the law of the *situs* of the asset at the time of opening of proceedings, provided the location is within the territory of another member state. To the extent that the law of the *situs* recognizes B's rights, and allows them to be exercised notwithstanding the opening of insolvency proceedings elsewhere against D, this may be done. However, Article 5(4) expressly preserves the role of the *lex concursus* in relation to actions aimed at bringing about the avoidance of the security. Consequently, it is the law of the state of opening of proceedings that will determine the issue of the validity of B's security.

A further aspect of the European Union regulation that may be noted is that the connecting factor chosen to provide the basis for EU-wide jurisdiction (and hence as the test for recognition purposes also) is essentially a *functional* one, involving the determination of the place which, at the time of opening, constitutes the 'centre' of D's 'main interests'. Although no definition of the expression is provided, Article 3(1) supplies a rebuttable presumption that, in the case of a company or legal person, the place of the registered office shall be presumed to be the centre of its main interests in the absence of proof to the contrary. Hence, the traditional English law approach, based on the 'state of incorporation' test, will be modified in such a way that, where it can be shown that the company conducts the administration of its interests on a regular basis at an ascertainable location in some other state than that in which its registered office is situated,[51] it is in the state from which the administration is conducted that proceedings must be opened. All member states, including the state of incorporation, are required to recognize the validity and effects of those proceedings. The regulation also allows the opening of insolvency proceedings to take place in a member state in which D has an establishment (as defined in Article 2(h)), but such proceedings are expressly restricted in their effects to the assets of D situated in the territory of the state in which the establishment is located.[52]

The second notable development will occur as a consequence of the prospective implementation of the UNCITRAL Model Law on Cross-Border Insolvency.[53] This instrument, which was adopted by the United

---

[51] See the observations regarding the nature and purpose of the 'centre of main interests' concept in the paragraph numbered as (13) in the Preambles to the EU Regulation.

[52] EU Regulation, Art 3(2). On the definition of 'establishment', see n 55 below, and related text.

[53] The Model Law has been well received. It has already been adopted by New Zealand (although not implemented), Mexico and Eritrea. Proposals for its adoption in the United States has reached an advanced stage and legislation in South Africa is also pending. The current position in the UK is explained below at p 286.

Nations Commission on International Trade Law on 30 May 1997, differs from an international convention in that it is not dependent on attracting a minimum number of adherents in order to take effect, nor does it require reciprocal international undertakings between states in order to do so. Instead, any state which is persuaded of the merits of the principle of international co-operation is eligible to take unilateral action, using the form and means appropriate to its internal legal system, to enact provisions within its own law that will enable the courts and officials of that state to interact with courts and office-holders abroad in cross-border insolvency matters. The Model Law does not embody any rules of choice of law, not does it impose any mandatory regime for the exercise of jurisdiction. However, its provisions for recognition of a foreign proceeding, and for the giving of assistance to the foreign representative appointed under that proceeding, are predicated upon the requirement that a foreign proceeding can only receive recognition if it has opened either in the state in which D has its centre of main interests (defined in Article 2(b) as a 'foreign main proceeding'), or in a state in which D has an establishment (defined in Article 2(c) as a 'foreign non-main proceeding'). The identity of terminology between the Model Law and the European Union Regulation with respect to the two fundamental bases for exercise of jurisdiction is by no means coincidental, and this conceptual symmetry is reinforced by the use of a rebuttable presumption (imported by Article 16(3)) to the effect that D's registered office (or habitual residence in the case of an individual) is presumed to be the centre of D's main interests.[54] The correlation is further reinforced through the definition of the term 'establishment', as supplied by Article 2(f), which is in substance identical to that offered by Article 2(h) of the European Union Regulation.[55] Therefore, while the two instruments are otherwise very different in nature, and are designed to operate in different ways and to relate to separate (albeit overlapping) constituencies of states, there is a welcome compatibility, and complementarity, between their conceptual foundations. Between them, these two instruments establish a powerful demonstration of the worldwide trend towards international recognition and co-operation, based upon commonly agreed standards of jurisdictional propriety.

---

[54] This is, in practice, a compromise between the common law and civil law concepts of corporate domicile.

[55] The definition of 'establishment' in Art 2(f) of the Model Law differs from its counterpart in Art 2(h) of the EU Regulation in one respect only, namely by the addition of the concluding words 'or services'. The definition in the Model Law states: 'establishment means any place of operations where D carries out a non-transitory economic activity with human means and goods or services'.

The Insolvency Act 2000 includes an enabling section (section 14) to authorize the Secretary of State, by means of a statutory instrument, to give effect to the UNCITRAL Model Law (with or without modifications) and, for that purpose, to modify the application of insolvency law and to amend any provision of section 426 Insolvency Act 1986. When in due course acted upon, this provision will give rise to a situation whereby English courts will be required to recognize, and to give assistance to, a foreign representative obtaining appointment under a foreign main proceeding (with a number of significant effects following automatically upon such recognition)[56], and will be required to recognize, and at their discretion provide assistance including various forms of remedial relief, in the case of a foreign non-main proceeding.[57] While these principles for according recognition and assistance do not represent a radical divergence from the traditional approach of English law, there are some significant modifications that are worthy of note. First, the introduction of the functionally designed test based on D's centre of main interests represents a transition from the 'state of incorporation' to the 'real seat' theory of jurisdiction (and also of recognition) in insolvency matters. Secondly, the acceptance of the more circumscribed authority and scope of proceedings opened on the basis of the existence of an establishment of D (which essentially equates to the maintenance of a place of business in the jurisdiction in question) is particularly useful, as it allows such proceedings to fulfil their primary purpose of protecting the expectations of local creditors whose dealings with D have been conducted through that place of business, while at the same time a firm proposition is established that such proceedings are to be co-ordinated with the primary administration of D's estate that is based upon the centre of main interests.

XIV. DESTABILIZING EFFECTS OF INSOLVENCY

As described, there are developments nearing completion which will introduce important changes to the international insolvency process, both within the enclosed membership of the European Union and— potentially—between an unlimited number of states worldwide which may in due course decide to enact the UNCITRAL Model Law. However, for the immediate future it must be acknowledged that these changes have not yet come into effect. Even when they do so, the European Union Regulation will only operate in relation to 14 of the 15 states which are

---

[56] Model Law, Arts 17, 20–24.　　　　[57] Model Law, Arts 17, 21–24.

currently European Union members,[58] and then only with regard to cases where D's centre of main interests is located in the territory of one of them. The Model Law, for its part, should certainly have a positive impact on international recognition and co-operation in cross-border cases, but again it must be noted that the benefits of this will be obtainable only from the courts of those states which enact it. For the foreseeable future, therefore, the global picture both in terms of the exercise of jurisdiction in insolvency matters, and in the areas of international recognition and enforcement and choice of law, will be not be standardized. Hence it will be subject to significant variations which will have the potential to destabilize debtor-creditor relationships which are accompanied by the taking of security. Even more significantly, none of the international initiatives to date have contemplated the harmonization of the substantive insolvency laws, and related procedures, of the individual states. These aspects of national laws carry still more destabilizing capabilities.

It can therefore be seen that those who are engaging in secured lending in relation to movable assets will need to take into account the fact that the secured party's expectations of recourse to the object of the security may be partly or even totally defeated (or at the very least, delayed in its capability to be exercised) as a consequence of D becoming subject to insolvency proceedings in a number of different countries in addition to the one whose law governed the transaction by which the security was originally created. This may also occur where, by the time insolvency commences, the object of the security happens to be in a different jurisdiction to that in which it was originally. This is an unwelcome paradox, since it is a primary objective of the taking of security that it shall prevail—and thus protect B—in the event of D's insolvency.

The moral of the above reflections is that it is essential when embarking on an international transaction involving the taking of security over movable property to calculate the various jurisdictions in which insolvency proceedings could foreseeably take place, and to project the impact of such proceedings on the secured party's position, having regard also to the factor of mobility of the security itself. This is a complex assessment, involving as it may the investigation of the insolvency laws, and the private international law rules, of a number of different countries.

---

[58] Denmark is omitted from the operation of the Regulation, because its enactment is based upon Arts 61(c) and 67(1) of the Treaty establishing the European Community. These provisions were implanted by the Treaty on European Union (the Amsterdam Treaty), which entered into force in 1999, and from which Denmark negotiated a permanent exemption. The Amsterdam Treaty further allows the United Kingdom and the Republic of Ireland the facility to opt in or out of any measures enacted pursuant to these provisions, and on this occasion both states elected to participate.

Given the number of variables, it would be imprudent to assume that the risks of destabilization can be eliminated entirely. Nevertheless, in structuring security transactions, and designing the terms and conditions to which D is to be subject, every effort should be made to ensure that such risks are anticipated and, where possible, minimized by means of suitably worded provisions in the documentation employed.

Appendix 1
The Colloquium Case Study

The following case study defined the scope of the chapters in this volume and served as a focus for discussion at the Colloquium, held at St John's College Oxford in April 2000.

Note 1: The case study is in skeletal form. Further factual assumptions will be made as necessary.

Note 2: It is intended to concentrate on the proprietary effects of the security, whilst not ignoring the contractual and other personal issues.

I. BACKGROUND

1. The company creating the security is incorporated in jurisdiction A, the security is created whilst the asset is in jurisdiction B and the asset ends up in jurisdiction C. The company is managed and controlled in jurisdiction D.

2. The asset concerned is a large item of valuable movable equipment (such as rolling stock or an aircraft). The asset is funded by a bank, which either provides the finance for the company to acquire the asset (and is granted a security interest in it by the company) or acquires the asset itself and leases it to the company under a finance lease. (In this case study, the expression 'security' includes such a lease.)

3. The company leases (or sub-leases) the asset to an operator and the bank has a security interest in the income stream payable by the operator to the company. The operator is in jurisdiction E.

4. All security is created in accordance with the laws of jurisdiction B.

5. The company goes into insolvency proceedings in jurisdiction A at a time when the asset is in jurisdiction C.

6. The following issues then arise. The main question to be considered in each case is how each of the jurisdictions concerned (England, the United States, France, and Germany) will decide which law will govern each issue. As a subsidiary matter, the substantive differences of the approach of the four jurisdictions can be used to highlight the problems which can arise in practice.

II. THE ISSUES

7. The company's liquidator claims that the security is ineffective because the company did not have the capacity to grant it, its directors did not have the authority to execute it or were acting in breach of duty in doing so (to the

knowledge of the bank), or the company was insolvent at the time it was created.

8. The liquidator of the company claims that the security was not created in accordance with the requirments of one of the jurisdictions.

9. Another financial institution claims an interest in the asset or in the income stream as a result of a security interest created over it in one of the jurisdictions.

10. A purchaser of the asset or an outright assignee of the income stream in one of the jurisdictions claims title free from the bank's rights.

11. A repairer of the asset in jurisdiction C claims a lien over the asset in respect of work done on it.

12. The company has accounts with the bank in one of the jurisdictions, all of which are in credit. The liquidator of the company denies the bank a right of set-off.

13. The operator claims that it is entitled to retain possession of the asset as against the company and the bank.

14. The company's liquidator, or a third party creditor, tries to put the company into insolvency proceedings in jurisdiction C.

Appendix 2
Article 9 of the Uniform Commercial Code (selected provisions)

1994 ARTICLE 9:

§ 9–103. Perfection of Security Interest in Multiple State Transactions.

(1) Documents, instruments and ordinary goods.

    (a) This subsection applies to documents and instruments and to goods other than those covered by a certificate of title described in subsection (2), mobile goods described in subsection (3), and minerals described in subsection (5).

    (b) Except as otherwise provided in this subsection, perfection and the effect of perfection or non-perfection of a security interest in collateral are governed by the law of the jurisdiction where the collateral is when the last event occurs on which is based the assertion that the security interest is perfected or unperfected.

    (c) If the parties to a transaction creating a purchase money security interest in goods in one jurisdiction understand at the time that the security interest attaches that the goods will be kept in another jurisdiction, then the law of the other jurisdiction governs the perfection and the effect of perfection or non-perfection of the security interest from the time it attaches until thirty days after the debtor receives possession of the goods and thereafter if the goods are taken to the other jurisdiction before the end of the thirty-day period.

    (d) When collateral is brought into and kept in this state while subject to a security interest perfected under the law of the jurisdiction from which the collateral was removed, the security interest remains perfected, but if action is required by Part 3 of this Article to perfect the security interest,

        (i) if the action is not taken before the expiration of the period of perfection in the other jurisdiction or the end of four months after the collateral is brought into this state, whichever period first expires, the security interest becomes unperfected at the end of that period and is thereafter deemed to have been unperfected as against a person who became a purchaser after removal;

        (ii) if the action is taken before the expiration of the period specified in subparagraph (i), the security interest continues perfected thereafter;

        (iii) for the purpose of priority over a buyer of consumer goods (subsection (2) of Section 9–307), the period of the effectiveness of a filing in the jurisdiction from which the collateral is removed is governed by the rules with respect to perfection in subparagraphs (i) and (ii).

(2) Certificate of title.
- (a) This subsection applies to goods covered by a certificate of title issued under a statute of this state or of another jurisdiction under the law of which indication of a security interest on the certificate is required as a condition of perfection.
- (b) Except as otherwise provided in this subsection, perfection and the effect of perfection or non-perfection of the security interest are governed by the law (including the conflict of laws rules) of the jurisdiction issuing the certificate until four months after the goods are removed from that jurisdication and thereafter until the goods are registered in another jurisdiction, but in any event not beyond surrender of the certificate. After the expiration of that period, the goods are not covered by the certificate of title within the meaning of this section.
- (c) Except with respect to the rights of a buyer described in the next paragraph, a security interest, perfected in another jurisdiction otherwise than by notation on a certificate of title, in goods brought into this state and thereafter covered by a certificate of title issued by this state is subject to the rules stated in paragraph (d) of subsection (1).
- (d) If goods are brought into this state while a security interest therein is perfected in any manner under the law of the jurisdiction from which the goods are removed and a certificate of title is issued by this state and the certificate does not show that the goods are subject to the security interest or that they may be subject to security interests not shown on the certificate, the security interest is subordinate to the rights of a buyer of the goods who is not in the business of selling goods of that kind to the extent that he gives value and receives delivery of the goods after issuance of the certificate and without knowledge of the security interest.

(3) Accounts, general intangibles and mobile goods.
- (a) This subsection applies to accounts (other than an account described in subsection (5) on minerals) and general intangibles (other than uncertificated securities) and to goods which are mobile and which are of a type normally used in more than one jurisdiction, such as motor vehicles, trailers, rolling stock, airplanes, shipping containers, road building and construction machinery and commercial harvesting machinery and the like, if the goods are equipment or are inventory leased or held for lease by the debtor to others, and are not covered by a certificate of title described in subsection (2).
- (b) The law (including the conflict of laws rules) of the jurisdiction in which the debtor is located governs the perfection and the effect of perfection or non-perfection of the security interest.
- (c) If, however, the debtor is located in a jurisdiction which is not a part of the United States, and which does not provide for perfection of the security interest by filing or recording in that jurisdiction, the law of the jurisdiction in the United States in which the debtor has its major executive office in the United States governs the perfection and the

effect of perfection or non-perfection of the security interest through filing. In the alternative, if the debtor is located in a jurisdiction which is not a part of the United States or Canada and the collateral is accounts or general intangibles for money due or to become due, the security interest may be perfected by notification to the account debtor. As used in this paragraph, 'United States' includes its territories and possessions and the Commonwealth of Puerto Rico.

(d) A debtor shall be deemed located at his place of business if he has one, at his chief executive office if he has more than one place of business, otherwise at his residence. If, however, the debtor is a foreign air carrier under the Federal Aviation Act of 1958, as amended, it shall be deemed located at the designated office of the agent upon whom service of process may be made on behalf of the foreign air carrier.

(e) A security interest perfected under the law of the jurisdiction of the location of the debtor is perfected until the expiration of four months after a change of the debtor's location to another jurisdiction, or until perfection would have ceased by the law of the first jurisdiction, whichever period first expires. Unless perfected in the new jurisdiction before the end of that period, it becomes unperfected thereafter and is deemed to have been unperfected as against a person who became a purchaser after the change.

(4) Chattel paper.

The rules stated for goods in subsection (1) apply to a possessory security interest in chattel paper. The rules stated for accounts in subsection (3) apply to a non-possessory security interest in chattel paper, but the security interest may not be perfected by notification to the account debtor.

(5) Minerals.

Perfection and the effect of perfection or non-perfection of a security interest which is created by a debtor who has an interest in minerals or the like (including oil and gas) before extraction and which attaches thereto as extracted, or which attaches to an account resulting from the sale thereof at the wellhead or minehead are governed by the law (including the conflict of laws rules) of the jurisdiction wherein the wellhead or minehead is located.

(6) Investment property.

(a) This subsection applies to investment property.

(b) Except as otherwise provided in paragraph (f), during the time that a security certificate is located in a jurisdiction, perfection of a security interest, the effect of perfection or non-perfection, and the priority of a security interest in the certificated security represented thereby are governed by the local law of that jurisdiction.

(c) Except as otherwise provided in paragraph (f), perfection of a security interest, the effect of perfection or non-perfection, and the priority of a security interest in an uncertificated security are governed by the local law of the issuer's jurisdiction as specified in Section 8–110(d).

(d) Except as otherwise provided in paragraph (f), perfection of a security interest, the effect of perfection or non-perfection, and the priority of a security interest in a security entitlement or securities account are governed by the local law of the securities intermediary's jurisdiction as specified in Section 8–110(e).

(e) Except as otherwise provided in paragraph (f), perfection of a security interest, the effect of perfection or non-perfection, and the priority of a security interest in a commodity contract or commodity account are governed by the local law of the commodity intermediary's jurisdiction. The following rules determine a 'commodity intermediary's jurisdiction' for purposes of this paragraph:

(i) If an agreement between the commodity intermediary and commodity customer specifies that it is governed by the law of a particular jurisdiction, that jurisdiction is the commodity intermediary's jurisdiction.

(ii) If an agreement between the commodity intermediary and commodity customer does not specify the governing law as provided in subparagraph (i), but expressly specifies that the commodity account is maintained at an office in a particular jurisdiction, that jurisdiction is the commodity intermediary's jurisdiction.

(iii) If an agreement between the commodity intermediary and commodity customer does not specify a jurisdiction as provided in subparagraphs (i) or (ii), the commodity intermediary's jurisdiction is the jurisdiction in which is located the office identified in an account statement as the office serving the commodity customer's account.

(iv) If an agreement between the commodity intermediary and commodity customer does not specify a jurisdiction as provided in subparagraphs (i) or (ii) and an account statement does not identify an office serving the commodity customer's account as provided in subparagraph (iii), the commodity intermediary's jurisdiction is the jurisdiction in which is located the chief executive office of the commodity intermediary.

(f) Perfection of a security interest by filing, automatic perfection of a security interest in investment property granted by a broker or securities intermediary, and automatic perfection of a security interest in a commodity contract or commodity account granted by a commodity intermediary are governed by the local law of the jurisdiction in which the debtor is located.

REVISED ARTICLE 9:

§ 9–301. Law Governing Perfection and Priority of Security Interests.

Except as otherwise provided in Sections 9–303 through 9–306, the following rules determine the law governing perfection, the effect of perfection or non-perfection, and the priority of a security interest in collateral:

(1) Except as otherwise provided in this section, while a debtor is located in a jurisdiction, the local law of that jurisdiction governs perfection, the effect of perfection or nonperfection, and the priority of a security interest in collateral.

(2) While collateral is located in a jurisdiction, the local law of that jurisdiction governs perfection, the effect of perfection or nonperfection, and the priority of a possessory security interest in that collateral.

(3) Except as otherwise provided in paragraph (4), while negotiable documents, goods, instruments, money, or tangible chattel paper is located in a jurisdiction, the local law of that jurisdiction governs:

    (A) perfection of a security interest in the goods by filing a fixture filing;

    (B) perfection of a security interest in timber to be cut; and

    (C) the effect of perfection or nonperfection and the priority of a nonpossessory security interest in the collateral.

(4) The local law of the jurisdiction in which the wellhead or minehead is located governs perfection, the effect of perfection or nonperfection, and the priority of a security interest in as-extracted collateral.

§ 9–307. Location of Debtor.

    (a) **['Place of business.']** In this section, 'place of business' means a place where a debtor conducts its affairs.

    (b) **[Debtor's location: general rules.]** Except as otherwise provided in this section, the following rules determine a debtor's location:

        (1) A debtor who is an individual is located at the individual's principal residence.

        (2) A debtor that is an organization and has only one place of business is located at its place of business.

        (3) A debtor that is an organization and has more than one place of business is located at its chief executive office.

    (c) **[Limitation of applicability of subsection (b).]** Subsection (b) applies only if a debtor's residence, place of business, or chief executive office, as applicable, is located in a jurisdiction whose law generally requires information concerning the existence of a nonpossessory security interest to be made generally available in a filing, recording, or registration system as a condition or result of the security interest's obtaining priority over the rights of a lien creditor with respect to the collateral. If subsection (b) does not apply, the debtor is located in the District of Columbia.

    (d) **[Continuation of location: cessation of existence, etc.]** A person that ceases to exist, have a residence, or have a place of business continues to be located in the jurisdiction specified by subsections (b) and (c).

    (e) **[Location of registered organization organized under State law.]** A registered organization that is organized under the law of a State is located in that State.

    (f) **[Location of registered organization organized under federal law; bank branches and agencies.]** Except as otherwise provided in subsection (i), a registered organization that is organized under the law of the United States and a branch or agency of a bank that is not organized under the law of the United States or a State are located:

     (1) in the State that the law of the United States designates, if the law designates a State of location;

     (2) in the State that the registered organization, branch, or agency designates, if the law of the United States authorizes the registered organization, branch, or agency to designate its State of location; or

     (3) in the District of Columbia, if neither paragraph (1) nor paragraph (2) applies.

(g) **[Continuation of location: change in status of registered organization.]** A registered organization continues to be located in the jurisdiction specified by subsection (e) or (f) notwithstanding:

     (1) the suspension, revocation, forfeiture, or lapse of the registered organization's status as such in its jurisdiction or organization; or

     (2) the dissolution, winding up, or cancellation of the existence of the registered organization.

(h) **[Location of United States.]** The United States is located in the District of Columbia.

(i) **[Location of foreign bank branch or agency if licensed in only one State.]** A branch or agency of a bank that is not organized under the law of the United States or a State is located in the State in which the branch or agency is licensed, if all branches and agencies of the bank are licensed in only one State.

(j) **[Location of foreign air carrier.]** A foreign air carrier under the Federal Aviation Act of 1958, as amended, is located at the designated office of the agent upon which service of process may be made on behalf of the carrier.

(k) **[Section applies only to this part.]** This section applies only for purposes of this part.

Appendix 3

Council Regulation (EC) No 1346/2000
of 29 May 2000
on insolvency proceedings

THE COUNCIL OF THE EUROPEAN UNION

Having regard to the Treaty establishing the European Community, and in particular Articles 61(c) and 67(1) thereof,

Having regard to the initiative of the Federal Republic of Germany and the Republic of Finland,

Having regard to the opinion of the European Parliament,[1]

Having regard to the opinion of the Economic and Social Committee,[2]

Whereas:

(1) The European Union has set out the aim of establishing an area of freedom, security and justice.

(2) The proper functioning of the internal market requires that cross-border insolvency proceedings should operate efficiently and effectively and this Regulation needs to be adopted in order to achieve this objective which comes within the scope of judicial cooperation in civil matters within the meaning of Article 65 of the Treaty.

(3) The activities of undertakings have more and more cross-border effects and are therefore increasingly being regulated by Community law. While the insolvency of such undertakings also affects the proper functioning of the internal market, there is a need for a Community act requiring coordination of the measures to be taken regarding an insolvent debtor's assets.

(4) It is necessary for the proper functioning of the internal market to avoid incentives for the parties to transfer assets or judicial proceedings from one Member State to another, seeking to obtain a more favourable legal position (forum shopping).

(5) These objectives cannot be achieved to a sufficient degree at national level and action at Community level is therefore justified.

(6) In accordance with the principle of proportionality this Regulation should be confined to provisions governing jurisdiction for opening insolvency proceedings and judgments which are delivered directly on the basis of the insolvency proceedings and are closely connected with such proceedings. In addition, this Regulation should contain provisions regarding the recognition of those judgments and the applicable law which also satisfy that principle.

---

[1] Opinion delivered on 2 March 2000 (not yet published in the Official Journal).
[2] Opinion delivered on 26 January 2000 (not yet published in the Official Journal).

(7) Insolvency proceedings relating to the winding-up of insolvent companies or other legal persons, judicial arrangements, compositions and analogous proceedings are excluded from the scope of the 1968 Brussels Convention on Jurisdiction and the Enforcement of Judgments in Civil and Commercial Matters,[3] as amended by the Conventions on Accession to this Convention.[4]

(8) In order to achieve the aim of improving the efficiency and effectiveness of insolvency proceedings having cross-border effects, it is necessary, and appropriate, that the provisions on jurisdiction, recognition and applicable law in this area should be contained in a Community law measure which is binding and directly applicable in Member States.

(9) This Regulation should apply to insolvency proceedings, whether the debtor is a natural person or a legal person, a trader or an individual. The insolvency proceedings to which this Regulation applies are listed in the Annexes. Insolvency proceedings concerning insurance undertakings, credit institutions, investment undertakings holding funds or securities for third parties and collective investment undertakings should be excluded from the scope of this Regulation. Such undertakings should not be covered by this Regulation since they are subject to special arrangements and, to some extent, the national supervisory authorities have extremely wide-ranging powers of intervention.

(10) Insolvency proceedings do not necessarily involve the intervention of a judicial authority; the expression 'court' in this Regulation should be given a broad meaning and include a person or body empowered by national law to open insolvency proceedings. In order for this Regulation to apply, proceedings (comprising acts and formalities set down in law) should not only have to comply with the provisions of this Regulation, but they should also be officially recognised and legally effective in the Member State in which the insolvency proceedings are opened and should be collective insolvency proceedings which entail the partial or total divestment of the debtor and the appointment of a liquidator.

(11) This Regulation acknowledges the fact that as a result of widely differing substantive laws it is not practical to introduce insolvency proceedings with universal scope in the entire Community. The application without exception of the law of the State of opening of proceedings would, against this background, frequently lead to difficulties. This applies, for example, to the widely differing laws on security interests to be found in the Community. Furthermore, the preferential rights enjoyed by some creditors in the insolvency proceedings are, in some cases, completely different. This Regulation should take account of this in two different ways. On the one hand, provision should be made for special rules on applicable law in the case of particularly significant rights and legal relationships (eg rights in rem and contracts of employment). On the other hand, national proceedings covering only assets situated in the State of opening should also be allowed alongside main insolvency proceedings with universal scope.

---

[3] OJ L299, 31.12.1972, p 32.
[4] OJ L204, 2.8.1975, p 28; OJ L304, 30.10.1978, p 1; OJ L388, 31.12.1982, p 1; OJ L285, 3.10.1989, p 1; OJ C15, 15.1.1997, p 1.

(12) This Regulation enables the main insolvency proceedings to be opened in the Member State where the debtor has the centre of his main interests. These proceedings have universal scope and aim at encompassing all the debtor's assets. To protect the diversity of interests, this Regulation permits secondary proceedings to be opened to run in parallel with the main proceedings. Secondary proceedings may be opened in the Member State where the debtor has an establishment. The effects of secondary proceedings are limited to the assets located in that State. Mandatory rules of coordination with the main proceedings satisfy the need for unity in the Community.

(13) The 'centre of main interests' should correspond to the place where the debtor conducts the adminstration of his interests on a regular basis and is therefore ascertainable by third parties.

(14) This Regulation applies only to proceedings where the centre of the debtor's main interests is located in the Community.

(15) The rules of jurisdiction set out in this Regulation establish only international jurisdiction, that is to say, they designate the Member State the courts of which may open insolvency proceedings. Territorial jurisdiction within that Member State must be established by the national law of the Member State concerned.

(16) The court having jurisdiction to open the main insolvency proceedings should be enabled to order provisional and protective measures from the time of the request to open proceedings. Preservation measures both prior to and after the commencement of the insolvency proceedings are very important to guarantee the effectiveness of the involvency proceedings. In that connection this Regulation should afford different possibilities. On the one hand, the court competent for the main insolvency proceedings should be able also to order provisional protective measures covering assets situated in the territory of other Member States. On the other hand, a liquidator temporarily appointed prior to the opening of the main insolvency proceedings should be able, in the Member States in which an establishment belonging to the debtor is to be found, to apply for the preservation measures which are possible under the law of those States.

(17) Prior to the opening of the main insolvency proceedings, the right to request the opening of insolvency proceedings in the Member State where the debtor has an establishment should be limited to local creditors and creditors of the local establishment or to cases where main proceedings cannot be opened under the law of the Member State where the debtor has the centre of his main interest. The reason for this restriction is that cases where territorial insolvency proceedings are requested before the main insolvency proceedings are intended to be limited to what is absolutely necessary. If the main insolvency proceedings are opened, the territorial proceedings become secondary.

(18) Following the opening of the main insolvency proceedings, the right to requrest the opcning of insolvency proceedings in a Member State where the debtor has an establishment is not restricted by this Regulation. The liquidator in the main proceedings or any other person empowered under the national law of that Member State may request the opening of secondary insolvency proceedings.

(19) Secondary insolvency proceedings may serve different purposes, besides the protection of local interests. Cases may arise where the estate of the debtor is too complex to administer as a unit or where differences in the legal systems concerned are so great that difficulties may arise from the extension of effects deriving from the law of the State of the opening to the other States where the assets are located. For this reason the liquidator in the main proceedings may request the opening of secondary proceedings when the efficient administration of the estate so requires.

(20) Main insolvency proceedings and secondary proceedings can, however, contribute to the effective realisation of the total assets only if all the concurrent proceedings pending are coordinated. The main condition here is that the various liquidators must cooperate closely, in particular by exchanging a sufficient amount of information. In order to ensure the dominant role of the main insolvency proceedings, the liquidator in such proceedings should be given several possibilities for intervening in secondary insolvency proceedings which are pending at the same time. For example, he should be able to propose a restructuring plan or composition or apply for realisation of the assets in the secondary insolvency proceedings to be suspended.

(21) Every creditor, who has his habitual residence, domicile or registered office in the Community, should have the right to lodge his claims in each of the insolvency proceedings pending in the Community relating to the debtor's assets. This should also apply to tax authorities and social insurance institutions. However, in order to ensure equal treatment of creditors, the distribution of proceeds must be coordinated. Every creditor should be able to keep what he has received in the course of insolvency proceedings but should be entitled only to participate in the distribution of total assets in other proceedings if creditors with the same standing have obtained the same proportion of their claims.

(22) This Regulation should provide for immediate recognition of judgments concerning the opening, conduct and closure of insolvency proceedings which come within its scope and of judgments handed down in direct connection with such insolvency proceedings. Automatic recognition should therefore mean that the effects attributed to the proceedings by the law of the State in which the proceedings were opened extend to all other Member States. Recognition of judgments delivered by the courts of the Member States should be based on the principle of mutual trust. To that end, grounds for non-recognition should be reduced to the minimum necessary. This is also the basis on which any dispute should be resolved where the courts of two Member States both claim competence to open the main insolvency proceedings. The decision of the first court to open proceedings should be recognised in the other Member States without those Member States having the power to scrutinise the court's decision.

(23) This Regulation should set out, for the matters covered by it, uniform rules on conflict of laws which replace, within their scope of application, national rules of private international law. Unless otherwise stated, the law of the Member State of the opening of the proceedings should be applicable (*lex concursus*). This rule on conflict of laws should be valid both for the main proceedings and for local

proceedings; the *lex concursus* determines all the effects of the insolvency proceedings, both procedural and substantive, on the persons and legal relations concerned. It governs all the conditions for the opening, conduct and closure of the insolvency proceedings.

(24) Automatic recognition of insolvency proceedings to which the law of the opening State normally applies may interfere with the rules under which transactions are carried out in other Member States. To protect legitimate expectations and the certainty of transactions in Member States other than that in which proceedings are opened, provisions should be made for a number of exceptions to the general rule.

(25) There is a particular need for a special reference diverging from the law of the opening State in the case of rights in rem, since these are of considerable importance for the granting of credit. The basis, validity and extent of such a right in rem should therefore normally be determined according to the *lex situs* and not be affected by the opening of insolvency proceedings. The proprietor of the right in rem should therefore be able to continue to assert his right to segregation or separate settlement of the collateral security. Where assets are subject to rights in rem under the *lex situs* in one Member State but the main proceedings are being carried out in another Member State, the liquidator in the main proceedings should be able to request the opening of secondary proceedings in the jurisdiction where the rights in rem arise if the debtor has an establishment there. If a secondary proceeding is not opened, the surplus on sale of the asset covered by rights in rem must be paid to the liquidator in the main proceedings.

(26) If a set-off is not permitted under the law of the opening State, a creditor should nevertheless be entitled to the set-off if it is possible under the law applicable to the claim of the insolvent debtor. In this way, set-off will acquire a kind of guarantee function based on legal provisions on which the creditor concerned can rely at the time when the claim arises.

(27) There is also a need for special protection in the case of payment systems and financial markets. This applies for example to the position-closing agreements and netting agreements to be found in such systems as well as to the sale of securities and to the guarantees provided for such transactions as governed in particular by Directive 98/26/EC of the European Parliament and of the Council of 19 May 1998 on settlement finality in payment and securities settlement systems.[5] For such transactions, the only law which is material should thus be that applicable to the system or market concerned. This provision is intended to prevent the possibility of mechanisms for the payment and settlement of transactions provided for in the payment and set-off systems or on the regulated financial markets of the Member States being altered in the case of insolvency of a business partner. Directive 98/26/EC contains special provisions which should take precedence over the general rules in this Regulation.

(28) In order to protect employees and jobs, the effects of insolvency proceedings on the continuation or termination of employment and on the rights and

---

[5] OJ L166, 11.6.1998, p 45.

obligations of all parties to such employment must be determined by the law applicable to the agreement in accordance with the general rules on conflict of law. Any other insolvency-law questions, such as whether the employees' claims are protected by preferential rights and what status such preferential rights may have, should be determined by the law of the opening State.

(29) For business considerations, the main content of the decision opening the proceedings should be published in the other Member States at the request of the liquidator. If there is an establishment in the Member State concerned, there may be a requirement that publication is compulsory. In neither case, however, should publication be a prior condition for recognition of the foreign proceedings.

(30) It may be the case that some of the persons concerned are not in fact aware that proceedings have been opened and act in good faith in a way that conflicts with the new situation. In order to protect such persons who make a payment to the debtor because they are unaware that foreign proceedings have been opened when they should in fact have made the payment to the foreign liquidator, it should be provided that such a payment is to have a debt-discharging effect.

(31) This Regulation should include Annexes relating to the organisation of insolvency proceedings. As these Annexes relate exclusively to the legislation of Member States, there are specific and substantiated reasons for the Council to reserve the right to amend these Annexes in order to take account of any amendments to the domestic law of the Member States.

(32) The United Kingdom and Ireland, in accordance with Article 3 of the Protocol on the position of the United Kingdom and Ireland annexed to the Treaty on European Union and the Treaty establishing the European Community, have given notice of their wish to take part in the adoption and application of this Regulation.

(33) Denmark, in accordance with Articles 1 and 2 of the Protocol on the position of Denmark annexed to the Treaty on European Union and the Treaty establishing the European Community, is not participating in the adoption of this Regulation, and is therefore not bound by it nor subject to its application.

HAS ADOPTED THIS REGULATION:

CHAPTER 1
GENERAL PROVISIONS

Article 1
Scope

1. This Regulation shall apply to collective insolvency proceedings which entail the partial or total divestment of a debtor and the appointment of a liquidator.

2. This Regulation shall not apply to insolvency proceedings concerning insurance undertakings, credit institutions, investment undertakings which provide services involving the holding of funds or securities for third parties, or to collective investment undertakings.

Article 2

Definitions

For the purposes of this Regulation:

(a) 'insolvency proceedings' shall mean the collective proceedings referred to in Article 1(1). These proceedings are listed in Annex A;

(b) 'liquidator' shall mean any person or body whose function is to administer or liquidate assets of which the debtor has been divested or to supervise the administration of his affairs. Those persons and bodies are listed in Annex C;

(c) 'winding-up proceedings' shall mean insolvency proceedings within the meaning of point (a) involving realising the assets of the debtor, including where the proceedings have been closed by a composition or other measure terminating the insolvency, or closed by reason of the insufficiency of the assets. Those proceedings are listed in Annex B;

(d) 'court' shall mean the judicial body or any other competent body of a Member State empowered to open insolvency proceedings or to take decisions in the course of such proceedings;

(e) 'judgment' in relation to the opening of insolvency proceedings or the appointment of a liquidator shall include the decision of any court empowered to open such proceedings or to appoint a liquidator;

(f) 'the time of the opening of proceedings' shall mean the time at which the judgment opening proceedings becomes effective, whether it is a final judgment or not;

(g) 'the Member State in which assets are situated' shall mean, in the case of:

— tangible property, the Member State within the territory of which the property is situated,

— property and rights ownership of or entitlement to which must be entered in a public register, the Member State under the authority of which the register is kept,

— claims, the Member State within the territory of which the third party required to meet them has the centre of his main interests, as determined in Article 3(1);

(h) 'establishment' shall mean any place of operations where the debtor carries out a non-transitory economic activity with human means and goods.

Article 3

International jurisdiction

1. The courts of the Member State within the territory of which the centre of a debtor's main interests is situated shall have jurisdiction to open insolvency proceedings. In the case of a company or legal person, the place of the registered office shall be presumed to be the centre of its main interests in the absence of proof to the contrary.

2. Where the centre of a debtor's main interests is situated within the territory of a Member State, the courts of another Member State shall have jurisdiction to open insolvency proceedings against that debtor only if he possesses an establishment within the territory of that other Member State. The effects of those proceedings shall be restricted to the assets of the debtor situated in the territory of the latter Member State.

3. Where insolvency proceedings have been opened under paragraph 1, any proceedings opened subsequently under paragraph 2 shall be secondary proceedings. These latter proceedings must be winding-up proceedings.

4. Territorial insolvency proceedings referred to in paragraph 2 may be opened prior to the opening of main insolvency proceedings in accordance with paragraph 1 only:

    (a) where insolvency proceedings under paragraph 1 cannot be opened because of the conditions laid down by the law of the Member State within the territory of which the centre of the debtor's main interests is situated; or

    (b) where the opening of territorial insolvency proceedings is requested by a creditor who has his domicile, habitual residence or registered office in the Member State within the territory of which the establishment is situated, or whose claim arises from the operation of that establishment.

Article 4

Law applicable

1. Save as otherwise provided in this Regulation, the law applicable to insolvency proceedings and their effects shall be that of the Member State within the territory of which such proceedings are opened, hereafter referred to as the 'State of the opening of proceedings'.

2. The law of the State of the opening of proceedings shall determine the conditions for the opening of those proceedings, their conduct and their closure. It shall determine in particular:

    (a) against which debtors insolvency proceedings may be brought on account of their capacity;

    (b) the assets which form part of the estate and the treatment of assets acquired by or devolving on the debtor after the opening of the insolvency proceedings;

    (c) the respective powers of the debtor and the liquidator;

    (d) the conditions under which set-offs may be invoked;

    (e) the effects of insolvency proceedings on current contracts to which the debtor is party;

    (f) the effects of the insolvency proceedings on proceedings brought by individual creditors, with the exception of lawsuits pending;

    (g) the claims which are to be lodged against the debtor's estate and the treatment of claims arising after the opening of insolvency proceedings;

(h) the rules governing the lodging, verification and admission of claims;
(i) the rules governing the distribution of proceeds from the realisation of assets, the ranking of claims and the rights of creditors who have obtained partial satisfaction after the opening of insolvency proceedings by virtue of a right in rem or through a set-off;
(j) the conditions for and the effects of closure of insolvency proceedings, in particular by composition;
(k) creditors' rights after the closure of insolvency proceedings;
(l) who is to bear the costs and expenses incurred in the insolvency proceedings;
(m) the rules relating to the voidness, voidability or unenforceability of legal acts detrimental to all the creditors.

Article 5

Third parties' rights in rem

1. The opening of insolvency proceedings shall not affect the rights in rem of creditors or third parties in respect of tangible or intangible, moveable or immoveable assets—both specific assets and collections of indefinite assets as a whole which change from time to time—belonging to the debtor which are situated within the territory of another Member State at the time of the opening of proceedings.

2. The rights referred to in paragraph 1 shall in particular mean:
(a) the right to dispose of assets or have them disposed of and to obtain satisfaction from the proceeds of or income from those assets, in particular by virtue of a lien or a mortgage;
(b) the exclusive right to have a claim met, in particular a right guaranteed by a lien in respect of the claim or by assignment of the claim by way of a guarantee;
(c) the right to demand the assets from, and/or to require restitution by, anyone having possession or use of them contrary to the wishes of the party so entitled;
(d) a right in rem to the beneficial use of assets.

3. The right, recorded in a public register and enforceable against thrid parties, under which a right in rem within the meaning of paragraph 1 may be obtained, shall be considered a right in rem.

4. Paragraph 1 shall not preclude actions for voidness, voidability or unenforceability as referred to in Article 4(2)(m).

Article 6

Set-off

1. The opening of insolvency proceedings shall not affect the right of creditors to demand the set-off of their claims against the claims of the debtor, where such a set-off is permitted by the law applicable to the insolvent debtor's claim.

2. Paragraph 1 shall not preclude actions for voidness, voidability or unenforceability as referred to in Article 4(2)(m).

Article 7

Reservation of title

1. The opening of insolvency proceedings against the purchaser of an asset shall not affect the seller's rights based on a reservation of title where at the time of the opening of proceedings the asset is situated within the territory of a Member State other than the State of opening of proceedings.

2. The opening of insolvency proceedings against the seller of an asset, after delivery of the asset, shall not constitute grounds for rescinding or terminating the sale and shall not prevent the purchaser from acquiring title where at the time of the opening of proceedings the asset sold is situated within the territory of a Member State other than the State of the opening of proceedings.

3. Paragraphs 1 and 2 shall not preclude actions for voidness, voidability or unenforceability as referred to in Article 4(2)(m).

Article 8

Contracts relating to immoveable property

The effects of insolvency proceedings on a contract conferring the right to acquire or make use of immoveable property shall be governed solely by the law of the Member State within the territory of which the immoveable property is situated.

Article 9

Payment systems and financial markets

1. Without prejudice to Article 5, the effects of insolvency proceedings on the rights and obligations of the parties to a payment or settlement system or to a financial market shall be governed solely by the law of the Member State applicable to that system or market.

2. Paragraph 1 shall not preclude any action for voidness, voidability or unenforceability which may be taken to set aside payments or transactions under the law applicable to the relevant payment system or financial market.

Article 10

Contracts of employment

The effects of insolvency proceedings on employment contracts and relationships shall be governed solely by the law of the Member State applicable to the contract of employment.

Article 11

Effects on rights subject to registration

The effects of insolvency proceedings on the rights of the debtor in immoveable property, a ship or an aircraft subject to registration in a public register shall be determined by the law of the Member State under the authority of which the register is kept.

Article 12

Community patents and trade marks

For the purposes of this Regulation, a Community patent, a Community trade mark or any other similar right established by Community law may be included only in the proceedings referred to in Article 3(1).

Article 13

Detrimental acts

Article 4(2)(m) shall not apply where the person who benefited from an act detrimental to all the creditors provides proof that:

— the said act is subject to the law of a Member State other than that of the State of the opening of proceedings, and
— that law does not allow any means of challenging that act in the relevant case.

Article 14

Protection of third-party purchasers

Where, by an act concluded after the opening of insolvency proceedings, the debtor disposes, for consideration, of:

— an immoveable asset, or
— a ship or an aircraft subject to registration in a public register, or
— securities whose existence presupposes registration in a register laid down by law,

the validity of that act shall be governed by the law of the State within the territory of which the immoveable asset is situated or under the authority of which the register is kept.

Article 15

Effects of insolvency proceedings on lawsuits pending

The effects of insolvency proceedings on a lawsuit pending concerning an asset or a right of which the debtor has been divested shall be governed solely by the law of the Member State in which that lawsuit is pending.

CHAPTER II

RECOGNITION OF INSOLVENCY PROCEEDINGS

Article 16

Principle

1. Any judgment opening insolvency proceedings handed down by a court of a Member State which has jurisdiction pursuant to Article 3 shall be recognised in all the other Member States from the time that it becomes effective in the State of the opening of proceedings.

This rule shall also apply where, on account of his capacity, insolvency proceedings cannot be brought againts the debtor in other Member States.

2. Recognition of the proceedings referred to in Article 3(1) shall not preclude the opening of the proceedings referred to in Article 3(2) by a court in another Member State. The latter proceedings shall be secondary insolvency proceedings within the meaning of Chapter III.

Article 17
Effects of recognition

1. The judgment opening the proceedings referred to in Article 3(1) shall, with no further formalities, produce the same effects in any other Member State as under this law of the State of the opening of proceedings, unless this Regulation provides otherwise and as long as no proceedings referred to in Article 3(2) are opened in that other Member State.

2. The effects of the proceedings referred to in Article 3(2) may not be challenged in other Member States. Any restriction of the creditors' rights, in particular a stay or discharge, shall produce effects vis-à-vis assets situated within the territory of another Member State only in the case of those creditors who have given their consent.

Article 18
Powers of the liquidator

1. The liquidator appointed by a court which has jurisdiction pursuant to Article 3(1) may exercise all the powers conferred on him by the law of the State of the opening of proceedings in another Member State, as long as no other insolvency proceedings have been opened there nor any preservation measure to the contrary has been taken there further to a request for the opening of insolvency proceedings in that State. He may in particular remove the debtor's assets from the territory of the Member State in which they are situated, subject to Articles 5 and 7.

2. The liquidator appointed by a court which has jurisdiction pursuant to Article 3(2) may in any other Member State claim through the courts or out of court that moveable property was removed from the territory of the State of the opening of proceedings to the territory of that other Member State after the opening of the insolvency proceedings. He may also bring any action to set aside which is in the interests of the creditors.

3. In exercising his powers, the liquidator shall comply with the law of the Member State within the territory of which he intends to take action, in particular with regard to procedures for the realisation of assets. Those powers may not include coercive measures or the right to rule on legal proceedings or disputes.

Article 19
Proof of the liquidator's appointment

The liquidator's appointment shall be evidenced by a certified copy of the original decision appointing him or by any other certificate issued by the court which has jurisdiction.

A translation into the official language or one of the official languages of the Member State within the territory of which he intends to act may be required. No legalisation or other similar formality shall be required.

Article 20

Return and imputation

1. A creditor who, after the opening of the proceedings referred to in Article 3(1) obtains by any means, in particular through enforcement, total or partial satisfaction of his claim on the assets belonging to the debtor situated within the territory of another Member State, shall return what he has obtained to the liquidator, subject to Articles 5 and 7.

2. In order to ensure equal treatment of creditors a creditor who has, in the course of insolvency proceedings, obtained a dividend on his claim shall share in distributions made in other proceedings only where creditors of the same ranking or category have, in those other proceedings, obtained an equivalent dividend.

Article 21

Publication

1. The liquidator may request that notice of the judgment opening insolvency proceedings and, where appropriate, the decision appointing him, be published in any other Member State in accordance with the publication procedures provided for in that State. Such publication shall also specify the liquidator appointed and whether the jurisdiction rule applied is that pursuant to Article 3(1) or Article 3(2).

2. However, any Member State within the territory of which the debtor has an establishment may require mandatory publication. In such cases, the liquidator or any authority empowered to that effect in the Member State where the proceedings referred to in Article 3(1) are opened shall take all necessary measures to ensure such publication.

Article 22

Registration in a public register

1. The liquidator may request that the judgment opening the proceedings referred to in Article 3(1) be registered in the land register, the trade register and any other public register kept in the other Member States.

2. However, any Member State may require mandatory registration. In such cases, the liquidator or any authority empowered to that effect in the Member State where the proceedings referred to in Article 3(1) have been opened shall take all necessary measures to ensure such registration.

Article 23

Costs

The costs of the publication and registration provided for in Articles 21 and 22 shall be regarded as costs and expenses incurred in the proceedings.

Article 24

Honouring of an obligation to a debtor

1. Where an obligation has been honoured in a Member State for the benefit of a debtor who is subject to insolvency proceedings opened in another Member State, when it should have been honoured for the benefit of the liquidator in those proceedings, the person honouring the obligation shall be deemed to have discharged it if he was unaware of the opening of proceedings.

2. Where such an obligation is honoured before the publication provided for in Article 21 has been effected, the person honouring the obligation shall be presumed, in the absence of proof to the contrary, to have been unaware of the opening of insolvency proceedings; where the obligation is honoured after such publication has been effected, the person honouring the obligation shall be presumed, in the absence of proof to the contrary, to have been aware of the opening of proceedings.

Article 25

Recognition and enforceability of other judgments

1. Judgments handed down by a court whose judgment concerning the opening of proceedings is recognised in accordance with Article 16 and which concern the course and closure of insolvency proceedings, and compositions approved by that court shall also be recognised with no further formalities. Such judgments shall be enforced in accordance with Articles 31 to 51, with the exception of Article 34(2), of the Brussels Convention on Jurisdiction and the Enforcement of Judgments in Civil and Commercial Matters, as amended by the Conventions of Accession to this Convention.

The first subparagraph shall also apply to judgments deriving directly from the insolvency proceedings and which are closely linked with them, even if they were handed down by another court.

The first subparagraph shall also apply to judgments relating to preservation measures taken after the request for the opening of insolvency proceedings.

2. The recognition and enforcement of judgments other than those referred to in paragraph 1 shall be governed by the Convention referred to in paragraph 1, provided that that Convention is applicable.

3. The Member States shall not be obliged to recognise or enforce a judgment referred to in paragraph 1 which might result in a limitation of personal freedom or postal secrecy.

Article 26[6]

Public policy

Any Member State may refuse to recognise insolvency proceedings opened in another Member State or to enforce a judgment handed down in the context of such proceedings where the effects of such recognition or enforcement would be

---

[6] Note the Declaration by Portugal concerning the application of Articles 26 and 37 (OJ C183, 30.6.2000, p 1).

manifestly contrary to that State's public policy, in particular its fundamental principles or the constitutional rights and liberties of the individual.

CHAPTER III
SECONDARY INSOLVENCY PROCEEDINGS

Article 27
Opening of proceedings

The opening of the proceedings referred to in Article 3(1) by a court of a Member State and which is recognised in another Member State (main proceedings) shall permit the opening in that other Member State, a court of which has jurisdiction pursuant to Article 3(2), of secondary insolvency proceedings without the debtor's insolvency being examined in that other State. These latter proceedings must be among the proceedings listed in Annex B. Their effects shall be restricted to the assets of the debtor situated within the territory of that other Member State.

Article 28
Applicable law

Save as otherwise provided in this Regulation, the law applicable to secondary proceedings shall be that of the Member State within the territory of which the secondary proceedings are opened.

Article 29
Right to request the opening of proceedings

The opening of secondary proceedings may be requested by:

- (a) the liquidator in the main proceedings;
- (b) any other person or authority empowered to request the opening of insolvency proceedings under the law of the Member State within the territory of which the opening of secondary proceedings is requested.

Article 30
Advance payment of costs and expenses

Where the law of the Member State in which the opening of secondary proceedings is requested requires that the debtor's assets be sufficient to cover in whole or in part the costs and expenses of the proceedings, the court may, when it receives such a request, require the applicant to make an advance payment of costs or to provide appropriate security.

Article 31
Duty to cooperate and communicate information

1. Subject to the rules restricting the communication of information, the liquidator in the main proceedings and the liquidators in the secondary proceedings shall be duty bound to communicate information to each other. They shall immediately communicate any information which may be relevant to the other proceedings, in

particular the progress made in lodging and verifying claims and all measures aimed at terminating the proceedings.

2. Subject to the rules applicable to each of the proceedings, the liquidator in the main proceedings and the liquidators in the secondary proceedings shall be duty bound to cooperate with each other.

3. The liquidator in the secondary proceedings shall give the liquidator in the main proceedings an early opportunity of submitting proposals on the liquidation or use of the assets in the secondary proceedings.

Article 32

Exercise of creditors' rights

1. Any creditor may lodge his claim in the main proceedings and in any secondary proceedings.

2. The liquidators in the main and any secondary proceedings shall lodge in other proceedings claims which have already been lodged in the proceedings for which they were appointed, provided that the interests of creditors in the latter proceedings are served thereby, subject to the right of creditors to oppose that or to withdraw the lodgement of their claims where the law applicable so provides.

3. The liquidator in the main or secondary proceedings shall be empowered to participate in other proceedings on the same basis as a creditor, in particular by attending creditors' meetings.

Article 33

Stay of liquidation

1. The court, which opened the secondary proceedings, shall stay the process of liquidation in whole or in part on receipt of a request from the liquidator in the main proceedings, provided that in that event it may require the liquidator in the main proceedings to take any suitable measure to guarantee the interest of the creditors in the secondary proceedings and of individual classes of creditors. Such a request from the liquidator may be rejected only if it is manifestly of no interest to the creditors in the main proceedings. Such a stay of the process of liquidation may be ordered for up to three months. It may be continued or renewed for similar periods.

2. The court referred to in paragraph 1 shall terminate the stay of the process of liquidation:

— at the request of the liquidator in the main proceedings,
— of its own motion, at the request of a creditor or at the request of the liquidator in the secondary proceedings if that measure no longer appears justified, in particular, by the interests of creditors in the main proceedings or in the secondary proceedings.

Article 34

Measures ending secondary insolvency proceedings

1. Where the law applicable to secondary proceedings allows for such proceedings to be closed without liquidation by a rescue plan, a composition or a comparable measure, the liquidator in the main proceedings shall be empowered to propose such a measure himself.

Closure of the secondary proceedings by a measure referred to in the first subparagraph shall not become final without the consent of the liquidator in the main proceedings; failing his agreement, however, it may become final if the financial interests of the creditors in the main proceedings are not affected by the measure proposed.

2. Any restriction of creditors' rights arising from a measure referred to in paragraph 1 which is proposed in secondary proceedings, such as a stay of payment or discharge of debt, may not have effect in respect of the debtor's assets not covered by those proceedings without the consent of all the creditors having an interest.

3. During a stay of the process of liquidation ordered pursuant to Article 33, only the liquidator in the main proceedings or the debtor, with the former's consent, may propose measures laid down in paragraph 1 of this Article in the secondary proceedings; no other proposal for such a measure shall be put to the vote or approved.

Article 35

Assets remaining in the secondary proceedings

If by the liquidation of assets in the secondary proceedings it is possible to meet all claims allowed under those proceedings, the liquidator appointed in those proceedings shall immediately transfer any assets remaining to the liquidator in the main proceedings.

Article 36

Subsequent opening of the main proceedings

Where the proceedings referred to in Article 3(1) are opened following the opening of the proceedings referred to in Article 3(2) in another Member State, Articles 31 to 35 shall apply to those opened first, in so far as the progress of those proceedings so permits.

Article 37[7]

Conversion of earlier proceedings

The liquidator in the main proceedings may request that proceedings listed in Annex A previously opened in another Member State be converted into winding-up proceedings if this proves to be in the interests of the creditors in the main proceedings.

The court with jurisdiction under Article 3(2) shall order conversion into one of the proceedings listed in Annex B.

---

[7] Note the Declaration by Portugal concerning the application of Articles 26 and 37 (OJ C183, 30.6.2000, p 1).

Article 38

Preservation measures

Where the court of a Member State which has jurisdiction pursuant to Article 3(1) appoints a temporary administrator in order to ensure the preservation of the debtor's assets, that temporary administrator shall be empowered to request any measures to secure and preserve any of the debtor's assets situated in another Member State, provided for under the law of that State, for the period between the request for the opening of insolvency proceedings and the judgment opening the proceedings.

CHAPTER IV

PROVISION OF INFORMATION FOR CREDITORS AND LODGEMENT OF THEIR CLAIMS

Article 39

Right to lodge claims

Any creditor who has his habitual residence, domicile or registered office in a Member State other than the State of the opening of proceedings, including the tax authorities and social security authorities of Member States, shall have the right to lodge claims in the insolvency proceedings in writing.

Article 40

Duty to inform creditors

1. As soon as insolvency proceedings are opened in a Member State, the court of that State having jurisdiction or the liquidator appointed by it shall immediately inform known creditors who have their habitual residences, domiciles or registered offices in the other Member States.

2. That information, provided by an individual notice, shall in particular include time limits, the penalties laid down in regard to those time limits, the body or authority empowered to accept the lodgement of claims and the other measures laid down. Such notice shall also indicate whether creditors whose claims are preferential or secured in rem need lodge their claims.

Article 41

Content of the lodgement of a claim

A creditor shall send copies of supporting documents, if any, and shall indicate the nature of the claim, the date on which it arose and its amount, as well as whether he alleges preference, security in rem or a reservation of title in respect of the claim and what assets are covered by the guarantee he is invoking.

Article 42

Languages

1. The information provided for in Article 40 shall be provided in the official language or one of the official languages of the State of the opening of proceedings. For that purpose a form shall be used bearing the heading 'Invitation to lodge a claim. Time limits to be observed' in all the official languages of the institutions of the European Union.

2. Any creditor who has his habitual residence, domicile or registered office in a Member State other than the State of the opening of proceedings may lodge his claim in the official language or one of the official languages of that other State. In that event, however, the lodgement of his claim shall bear the heading 'Lodgement of claim' in the official language or one of the official languages of the State of the opening of proceedings. In addition, he may be required to provide a translation into the official language or one of the official languages of the State of the opening of proceedings.

CHAPTER V
TRANSITIONAL AND FINAL PROVISIONS

Article 43
Applicability in time

The provisions of this Regulation shall apply only to insolvency proceedings opened after its entry into force. Acts done by a debtor before the entry into force of this Regulation shall continue to be governed by the law which was applicable to them at the time they were done.

Article 44
Relationship to Conventions

1. After its entry into force, this Regulation replaces, in respect of the matters referred to therein, in the relations between Member States, the Conventions concluded between two or more Member States, in particular:

(a) the Convention between Belgium and France on Jurisdiction and the Validity and Enforcement of Judgments, Arbitration Awards and Authentic Instruments, signed at Paris on 8 July 1899;

(b) the Convention between Belgium and Austria on Bankruptcy, Winding-up, Arrangements, Compositions and Suspension of Payments (with Additional Protocol of 13 June 1973), signed at Brussels on 16 July 1969;

(c) the Convention between Belgium and the Netherlands on Territorial Jurisdiction, Bankruptcy and the Validity and Enforcement of Judgments, Arbitration Awards and Authentic Instruments, signed at Brussels on 28 March 1925;

(d) the Treaty between Germany and Austria on Bankruptcy, Winding-up, Arrangements and Compositions, signed at Vienna on 25 May 1979;

(e) the Convention between France and Austria on Jurisdiction, Recognition and Enforcement of Judgments on Bankruptcy, signed at Vienna on 27 February 1979;

(f) the Convention between France and Italy on the Enforcement of Judgments in Civil and Commercial Matters, signed at Rome on 3 June 1930;

(g) the Convention between Italy and Austria on Bankruptcy, Winding-up, Arrangements and Compositions, signed at Rome on 12 July 1977;

(h) the Convention between the Kingdom of the Netherlands and the Federal Republic of Germany on the Mutual Recognition and Enforcement of Judgments and other Enforceable Instruments in Civil and Commercial Matters, signed at The Hague on 30 August 1962;

(i) the Convention between the United Kingdom and the Kingdom of Belgium providing for the Reciprocal Enforcement of Judgments in Civil and Commercial Matters, with Protocol, signed at Brussels on 2 May 1934;

(j) the Convention between Denmark, Finland, Norway, Sweden and Iceland on Bankruptcy, signed at Copenhagen on 7 November 1933;

(k) the European Convention on Certain International Aspects of Bankruptcy, signed at Istanbul on 5 June 1990.

2. The Conventions referred to in paragraph 1 shall continue to have effect with regard to proceedings opened before the entry into force of this Regulation.

3. This Regulation shall not apply:

(a) in any Member State, to the extent that it is irreconcilable with the obligations arising in relation to bankruptcy from a convention concluded by that State with one or more third countries before the entry into force of this Regulation;

(b) in the United Kingdom of Great Britain and Northern Ireland, to the extent that is irreconcilable with the obligations arising in relation to bankruptcy and the winding-up of insolvent companies from any arrangements with the Commonwealth existing at the time this Regulation enters into force.

Article 45

Amendment of the Annexes

The Council, acting by qualified majority on the initiative of one of its members or on a proposal from the Commission, may amend the Annexes.

Article 46

Reports

No later than 1 June 2012, and every five years thereafter, the Commission shall present to the European Parliament, the Council and the Economic and Social Committee a report on the application of this Regulation. The report shall be accompanied if need be by a proposal for adaptation of this Regulation.

Article 47

Entry into force

This Regulation shall enter into force on 31 May 2002.

Council Regulation (EC) No 1346/2000   317

This Regulation shall be binding in its entirety and directly applicable in the Member States in accordance with the Treaty establishing the European Community.

Done at Brussels, 29 May 2000.

For the Council
The President
A. COSTA

ANNEX A
Insolvency proceedings referred to in Article 2(a)

BELGIË—BELGIQUE
— Het faillissement/La faillite
— Het gerechtelijk akkoord/Le concordat judiciaire
— De collectieve schuldenregeling/Le règlement collectif de dettes

DEUTSCHLAND
— Das Konkursverfahren
— Das gerichtliche Vergleichsverfahren
— Das Gesamtvollstreckungsverfahren
— Das Insolvenzverfahren

ΕΛΛΑΣ
— Πτώχευση
— Η ειδική εκκαθάριση
— Η προσωρινή διαχείριση εταιρίας. Η διοίκηση και η διαχείριση των πιστωτών
— Η υπαγωγή επιχείρησης υπό επίτροπο με σκοπό τη σύναψη συμβιβασμού με τους πιστωτές

ESPAÑA
— Concurso de acreedores
— Quiebra
— Suspensión de pagos

FRANCE
— Liquidation judiciaire
— Redressement judiciaire avec nomination d'un administrateur

IRELAND
— Compulsory winding-up by the court
— Bankruptcy

— The administration in bankruptcy of the estate of persons dying insolvent
— Winding-up in bankruptcy of partnerships
— Creditors' voluntary winding-up (with confirmation of a Court)
— Arrangements under the control of the court which involve the vesting of all or part of the property of the debtor in the Official Assignee for realisation and distribution
— Company examinership

ITALIA
— Fallimento
— Concordato preventivo
— Liquidazione coatta amministrativa
— Amministrazione straordinaria
— Amministrazione controllata

LUXEMBOURG
— Faillite
— Gestion contrôlée
— Concordat préventif de faillite (par abandon d'actif)
— Régime spécial de liquidation du notariat

NEDERLAND
— Het faillissement
— De surséance van betaling
— De schuldsaneringsregeling natuurlijke personen

ÖSTERREICH
— Das Konkursverfahren
— Das Ausgleichsverfahren

PORTUGAL

— O processo de falência
— Os processos especiais de recuperação de empresa, ou seja:
    — A concordata
    — A reconstituição empresarial
    — Areestruturação financeira
    — A gestão controlada

SUOMI—FINLAND

— Konkurssi/konkurs
— Yrityssaneeraus/företagssanering

SVERIGE

— Konkurs
— Företagsrekonstruktion

UNITED KINGDOM

— Winding up by or subject to the supervision of the court
— Creditors' voluntary winding up (with confirmation by the court)
— Administration
— Voluntary arrangements under insolvency legislation
— Bankruptcy or sequestration

ANNEX B

Winding-up proceedings referred to in Article 2(c)

BELGIË—BELGIQUE

— Het faillissement/La faillite

DEUTSCHLAND

— Das Konkursverfahren
— Das Gesamtvollstreckungsverfahren
— Das Insolvenzverfahren

ΕΛΛΑΣ

— Πτώχευση
— Η ειδική εκκαδάριση

ESPAÑA

— Concurso de acreedores
— Quiebra
— Suspensión de pagos basada en la insolvencia definitiva

FRANCE

— Liquidation judiciaire

IRELAND

— Compulsory winding up
— Bankruptcy
— The administration in bankruptcy of the estate of persons dying insolvent
— Winding-up in bankruptcy of partnerships
— Creditors' voluntary winding up (with confirmation of a court)

— Arrangments under the control of the court which involve the vesting of all or part of the property of the debtor in the Official Assignee for realisation and distribution

ITALIA

— Fallimento
— Liquidazione coatta amministrativa

LUXEMBOURG

— Faillite
— Régime spécial de liquidation du notariat

NEDERLAND

— Het faillissement
— De schuldsaneringsregeling natuurlijke personen

ÖSTERREICH

— Das Konkursverfahren

PORTUGAL

— O processo de falência

SUOMI—FINLAND

— Konkurssi/konkurs

SVERIGE

— Konkurs

UNITED KINGDOM

— Winding up by or subject to the supervision of the court

— Creditors' voluntary winding up (with
  confirmation by the court)
— Bankruptcy or sequestration

ANNEX C

Liquidators referred to in Article 2(b)

BELGIË—BELGIQUE

— De curator/Le curateur
— De commissaris inzake opschorting/Le
  commissaire au sursis
— De schuldbemiddelaar/Le médiateur
  de dettes

DEUTSCHLAND

— Konkursverwalter
— Vergleichsverwalter
— Sachwalter (nach der
  Vergleichsordnung)
— Verwalter
— Insolvenzverwalter
— Sachwalter (nach der
  Insolvenzordnung)
— Treuhänder
— Vorläufiger Insolvenzverwalter

ΕΛΛΑΣ

— Ο σύνδικο
— Ο προσωρινός διαχειριστής. Η
  διοικούσα επιτροπή των πιοτωτών
— Ο ειδικός εκκαδαριστής
— Ο επίτροπος

ESPAÑA

— Depositario-administrador
— Interventor o Interventores
— Síndicos
— Comisario

FRANCE

— Représentant des créanciers
— Mandataire liquidateur
— Administrateur judiciaire
— Commissaire à l'exécution de plan

IRELAND

— Liquidator
— Official Assignee
— Trustee in bankruptcy
— Provisional Liquidator
— Examiner

ITALIA

— Curatore
— Commissario

LUXEMBOURG

— Le curateur
— Le commissaire
— Le liquidateur
— Le conseil de gérance de la section
  d'assainissement du notariat

NEDERLAND

— De curator in het faillissement
— De bewindvoerder in de surséance van
  betaling
— De bewindvoerder in de
  schuldsaneringsregeling natuurlijke
  personen

ÖSTERREICH

— Masseverwalter
— Ausgleichsverwalter
— Sachwalter
— Treuhänder
— Besondere Verwalter
— Vorläufiger Verwalter
— Konkursgericht

PORTUGAL

— Gestor judicial

— Liquidatário judicial
— Commissão de credores

SUOMI—FINLAND

— Pesänhoitaja/boförvaltare
— Selvittäjä/utredare

SVERIGE

— Förvaltare

— God man
— Rekonstruktör

UNITED KINGDOM

— Liquidator
— Supervisor of a voluntary arrangement
— Administrator
— Official Receiver
— Trustee
— Judicial factor

Appendix 4

Draft Convention on International Interests in Mobile Equipment

The States Parties to this Convention,

Aware of the need to acquire and use mobile equipment of high value or particular economic significance and to facilitate the financing of the acquisition and use of such equipment in an efficient manner,

Recognising the advantages of asset-based financing and leasing for this purpose and desiring to facilitate these types of transaction by establishing clear rules to govern them,

Mindful of the need to ensure that interests in such equipment are recognised and protected universally,

Desiring to provide broad economic benefits for all interested parties,

Believing that such rules must reflect the principles underlying asset-based financing and leasing and promote the autonomy of the parties necessary in these transactions,

Conscious of the need to establish a legal framework for international interests in such equipment and for that purpose to create an international registration system for their protection,

Have agreed upon the following provisions:

CHAPTER I

SPHERE OF APPLICATION AND GENERAL PROVISIONS

Article 1

Definitions

In this Convention, except where the context otherwise requires, the following terms are employed with the meanings set out below:

(a) 'agreement' means a security agreement, a title reservation agreement or a leasing agreement;

(b) 'assignment' means a contract which, whether by way of security or otherwise, confers on the assignee rights in the international interest;

(c) 'associated rights' means all rights to payment or other performance by a debtor under an agreement which are secured by or associated with the object;

(d) 'commencement of the insolvency proceedings' means the time at which the insolvency proceedings are deemed to commence under the applicable insolvency law;

(e) 'conditional buyer' means a buyer under a title reservation agreement;

(f) 'conditional seller' means a seller under a title reservation agreement;

(g) 'contract of sale' means a contract for the sale of an object by a seller to a buyer which is not an agreement as defined in (a) above;

(h) 'court' means a court of law or an administrative or arbitral tribunal established by a Contracting State;

(i) 'creditor' means a chargee under a security agreement, a conditional seller under a title reservation agreement or a lessor under a leasing agreement;

(j) 'debtor' means a chargor under a security agreement, a conditional buyer under a title reservation agreement, a lessee under a leasing agreement or a person whose interest in an object is burdened by a registrable non-consensual right or interest;

(k) 'insolvency administrator' means a person authorised to administer the reorganisation or liquidation, including one authorised on an interim basis, and includes a debtor in possession if permitted by the applicable insolvency law;

(l) 'insolvency proceedings' means collective judicial or administrative proceedings, including interim proceedings, in which the assets and affairs of the debtor are subject to control or supervision by a court for the purposes of reorganisation or liquidation;

(m) 'interested persons' means:
   (i) the debtor;
   (ii) any person who, for the purpose of assuring performance of any of the obligations in favour of the creditor, gives or issues a suretyship or demand guarantee or a standby letter of credit or any other form of credit insurance;
   (iii) any other person having rights in or over the object;

(n) 'internal transaction' means a transaction of a type listed in Article 2(2)(a) to (c) where the centre of the main interests of all parties to such transaction is situated, and the relevant object is located (as specified in the Protocol), in the same Contracting State at the time of the conclusion of the transaction;

(o) 'international interest' means an interest to which Article 2 applies;

(p) 'International Registry' means the international registration facilities established for the purposes of this Convention or the Protocol;

(q) 'leasing agreement' means an agreement by which a lessor grants a right to possession or control of an object (with or without an option to purchase) to a lessee in return for a rental or other payment;

(r) 'national interest' means an interest in an object created by an internal transaction;

(s) 'non-consensual right or interest' means a right or interest conferred by law to secure the performance of an obligation, including an obligation to a State or State entity;

(t) 'notice of a national interest' means a notice that a national interest has been registered in a public registry in the Contracting State making a declaration to the Protocol pursuant to Article 48(1);

(u) 'object' means an object of a category to which Article 2 applies;

(v) 'pre-existing right or interest' means a right or interest of any kind in an object created or arising under the law of a Contracting State before the entry into force of this Convention in respect of that State, including a right or interest of a category covered by a declaration pursuant to Article 39 and to the extent of that declaration;

(w) 'proceeds' means money or non-money proceeds of an object arising from the total or partial loss or physical destruction of the object or its total or partial confiscation, condemnation or requisition;

(x) 'prospective assignment' means an assignment that is intended to be made in the future, upon the occurrence of a stated event, whether or not the occurrence of the event is certain;

(y) 'prospective international interest' means an interest that is intended to be created or provided for in an object as an international interest in the future, upon the occurrence of a stated event (which may include the debtor's acquisition of an interest in the object), whether or not the occurrence of the event is certain;

(z) 'prospective sale' means a sale which is intended to be made in the future, upon the occurrence of a stated event, whether or not the occurrence of the event is certain;

(aa) 'Protocol' means, in respect of any category of object and associated rights to which this Convention applies, the Protocol in respect of that category of object and associated rights;

(bb) 'registered' means registered in the International Registry pursuant to Chapter V;

(cc) 'registered interest' means an international interest, a registrable non-consensual right or interest or a national interest specified in a notice of a national interest registered pursuant to Chapter V;

(dd) 'registrable non-consensual right or interest' means a non-consensual right or interest registrable pursuant to a declaration deposited under Article 38;

(ee) 'Registrar' means, in respect of the Protocol, the person or body designated by that Protocol or appointed under Article 16(2)(b);

(ff) 'regulations' means regulations made or approved by the Supervisory Authority pursuant to the Protocol;

(gg) 'sale' means a transfer of ownership of an object pursuant to a contract of sale;

(hh) 'secured obligation' means an obligation secured by a security interest;

(ii) 'security agreement' means an agreement by which a chargor grants or agrees to grant to a chargee an interest (including an ownership interest) in or over an object to secure the performance of any existing or future obligation of the chargor or a third person;

(jj) 'security interest' means an interest created by a security agreement;

(kk) 'Supervisory Authority' means, in respect of the Protocol, the Supervisory Authority referred to in Article 16(1);

(ll) 'title reservation agreement' means an agreement for the sale of an object on terms that ownership does not pass until fulfilment of the condition or conditions stated in the agreement;

(mm) 'unregistered interest' means a consensual interest or non-consensual right or interest (other than an interest to which Article 39 applies) which has not been registered, whether or not it is registrable under this Convention; and

(nn) 'writing' means a record of information (including information communicated by teletransmission) which is in tangible or other form and is capable of being reproduced in tangible form on a subsequent occasion and which indicates by reasonable means a person's approval of the record.[1]

Article 2
The international interest

1.—This Convention provides for the constitution and effects of an international interest in certain categories of mobile equipment and associated rights.

2.—For the purposes of this Convention, an international interest in mobile equipment is an interest, constituted under Article 6, in a uniquely identifiable object of a category of such objects listed in paragraph 3 and designated in the Protocol:

(a) granted by the chargor under a security agreement;
(b) vested in a person who is the conditional seller under a title reservation agreement; or
(c) vested in a person who is the lessor under a leasing agreement.

An interest falling within sub-paragraph (a) does not also fall within sub-paragraph (b) or (c).

3.—The categories referred to in the preceding paragraphs are:

(a) airframes, aircraft engines and helicopters;
(b) railway rolling stock; and
(c) space property.

4.—This Convention does not determine whether an interest to which paragraph 2 applies falls within sub-paragraph (a), (b) or (c) of that paragraph.

5.—An international interest in an object extends to proceeds of that object.

Article 3
Sphere of application

1.—This Convention applies when, at the time of the conclusion of the agreement creating or providing for the international interest, the debtor is situated in a Contracting State.

2.—The fact that the creditor is situated in a non-Contracting State does not affect the applicability of this Convention.

---

[1] It was noted that this definition should be further reviewed.

Article 4
Where debtor is situated

1.—For the purposes of this Convention, the debtor is situated in any Contracting State:

    (a) under the law of which it is incorporated or formed;

    (b) where it has its registered office or statutory seat;

    (c) where it has its centre of administration; or

    (d) where it has its place of business.

2.—A reference in this Convention to the debtor's place of business shall, if it has more than one place of business, mean its principal place of business or, if it has no place of business, its habitual residence.

Article 5
Interpretation and applicable law

1.—In the interpretation of this Convention, regard is to be had to its purposes as set forth in the preamble, to its international character and to the need to promote uniformity and predictability in its application.

2.—Questions concerning matters governed by this Convention which are not expressly settled in it are to be settled in conformity with the general principles on which it is based or, in the absence of such principles, in conformity with the applicable law.

3.—References to the applicable law are to the domestic rules of the law applicable by virtue of the rules of private international law of the forum State.

4.—Where a State comprises several territorial units, each of which has its own rules of law in respect of the matter to be decided, and where there is no indication of the relevant territorial unit, the law of that State decides which is the territorial unit whose rules shall govern. In the absence of any such rule, the law of the territorial unit with which the case is most closely connected shall apply.

CHAPTER II

CONSTITUTION OF AN INTERNATIONAL INTEREST

Article 6
Formal requirements

An interest is constituted as an international interest under this Convention where the agreement creating or providing for the interest:

    (a) is in writing;

    (b) relates to an object of which the chargor, conditional seller or lessor has power to dispose;

    (c) enables the object to be identified in conformity with the Protocol; and

    (d) in the case of a security agreement, enables the secured obligations to be determined, but without the need to state a sum or maximum sum secured.

CHAPTER III
DEFAULT REMEDIES

Article 7
Remedies of chargee

1.—In the event of default as provided in Article 10, the chargee may, to the extent that the chargor has at any time so agreed, exercise any one or more of the following remedies:

(a)   take possession or control of any object charged to it;
(b)   sell or grant a lease of any such object;
(c)   collect or receive any income or profits arising from the management or use of any such object, or apply for a court order authorising or directing any of the above acts.

2.—Any remedy given by sub-paragraph (a), (b) or (c) of the preceding paragraph or by Article 12 shall be exercised in a commercially reasonable manner. A remedy shall be deemed to be exercised in a commercially reasonable manner where it is exercised in conformity with a provision of the security agreement except where such a provision is manifestly unreasonable.

3.—A chargee proposing to sell or grant a lease of an object under paragraph 1 otherwise than pursuant to a court order shall give reasonable prior notice in writing of the proposed sale or lease to:

(a)   interested persons specified in Article 1(m)(i) and (ii); and
(b)   interested persons specified in Article 1(m)(iii) who have given notice of their rights to the chargee within a reasonable time prior to the sale or lease.

4.—Any sum collected or received by the chargee as a result of exercise of any of the remedies set out under paragraph 1 shall be applied towards discharge of the amount of the secured obligations.

5.—Where the sums collected or received by the chargee as a result of the exercise of any remedy given in paragraph 1 exceed the amount secured by the security interest and any reasonable costs incurred in the exercise of any such remedy, then unless otherwise ordered by the court the chargee shall pay the excess to the holder of the registered interest ranking immediately after its own or, if there is none, to the chargor.

Article 8
Vesting of object in satisfaction; redemption

1.—At any time after default as provided in Article 10, the chargee and all the interested persons may agree that ownership of (or any other interest of the chargor in) any object covered by the security interest shall vest in the chargee in or towards satisfaction of the secured obligations.

2.—The court may on the application of the chargee order that ownership of (or any other interest of the chargor in) any object covered by the security interest shall vest in the chargee in or towards satisfaction of the secured obligations.

3.—The court shall grant an application under the preceding paragraph only if the amount of the secured obligations to be satisfied by such vesting is reasonably commensurate with the value of the object after taking account of any payment to be made by the chargee to any of the interested persons.

4.—At any time after default as provided in Article 10 and before sale of the charged object or the making of an order under paragraph 2, the chargor or any interested person may discharge the security interest by paying in full the amount secured, subject to any lease granted by the chargee under Article 7(1)(b). Where, after such default, the payment of the amount secured is made in full by an interested person other than the debtor, that person is subrogated to the rights of the chargee.

5.—Ownership or any other interest of the chargor passing on a sale under Article 7(1)(b) or passing under paragraph 1 or 2 of this Article is free from any other interest over which the chargee's security interest has priority under the provisions of Article 28.

Article 9
Remedies of conditional seller or lessor

In the event of default under a title reservation agreement or under a leasing agreement as provided in Article 10, the conditional seller or the lessor, as the case may be, may:

    (a) terminate the agreement and take possession or control of any object to which the agreement relates; or

    (b) apply for a court order authorising or directing either of these acts.

Article 10
Meaning of default

1.—The debtor and the creditor may at any time agree in writing as to the events that constitute a default or otherwise give rise to the rights and remedies specified in Articles 7 to 9 and 12.

2.—In the absence of such an agreement, 'default' for the purposes of Articles 7 to 9 and 12 means a substantial default.

Article 11
Additional remedies

Any additional remedies permitted by the applicable law, including any remedies agreed upon by the parties, may be exercised to the extent that they are not inconsistent with the mandatory provisions of this Chapter as set out in Article 14.

Article 12
Relief pending final determination

1.—A Contracting State shall ensure that a creditor who adduces evidence of default by the debtor may, pending final determination of its claim and to the extent that the debtor has at any time so agreed, obtain from a court speedy relief in the form of such one or more of the following orders as the creditor requests:

  (a) preservation of the object and its value;
  (b) possession, control or custody of the object;
  (c) immobilisation of the object; and/or
  (d) lease or management of the object and the income therefrom.

2.—In making any order under the preceding paragraph, the court may impose such terms as it considers necessary to protect the interested persons in the event that the creditor:

  (a) in implementing any order granting such relief, fails to perform any of its obligations to the debtor under this Convention or the Protocol; or
  (b) fails to establish its claim, wholly or in part, on the final determination of that claim.

3.—Before making any order under paragraph 1, the court may require notice of the request to be given to any of the interested persons.

4.—Nothing in this Article affects the application of Article 7(2) or limits the availability of forms of interim relief other than those set out in paragraph 1.

Article 13
Procedural requirements

Subject to Article 52(2), any remedy provided by this Chapter shall be exercised in conformity with the procedure prescribed by the law of the place where the remedy is to be exercised.

Article 14
Derogation

In their relations with each other, the parties may, by agreement in writing, derogate from or vary the effect of any of the preceding provisions of this Chapter, except as stated in Articles 7(2) to (5), 8(3) and (4), 12(2) and 13.

CHAPTER IV

THE INTERNATIONAL REGISTRATION SYSTEM

Article 15
The International Registry

1.—An International Registry shall be established for registrations of:

  (a) international interests, prospective international interests and registrable non-consensual rights and interests;

    (b) assignments and prospective assignments of international interests;

    (c) acquisitions of international interests by legal or contractual subrogation;

    (d) subordinations of interests referred to in sub-paragraph (a) of this paragraph; and

    (e) notices of national interests.

2.—Different international registries may be established for different categories of object and associated rights.

3.—For the purposes of this Chapter and Chapter V, the term 'registration' includes, where appropriate, an amendment, extension or discharge of a registration.

Article 16
The Supervisory Authority and the Registrar

1.—There shall be a Supervisory Authority as provided by the Protocol.

2.—The Supervisory Authority shall:

    (a) establish or provide for the establishment of the International Registry;

    (b) except as otherwise provided by the Protocol, appoint and dismiss the Registrar;

    (c) ensure that any rights required for the continued effective operation of the International Registry are such as may be assigned in the event of a change of Registrar;

    (d) after consultation with the Contracting States, make or approve and ensure the publication of regulations pursuant to the Protocol dealing with the operation of the International Registry;

    (e) establish administrative procedures through which complaints concerning the operation of the International Registry can be made to the Supervisory Authority;

    (f) supervise the Registrar and the operation of the International Registry;

    (g) at the request of the Registrar, provide such guidance to the Registrar as the Supervisory Authority thinks fit;

    (h) set and periodically review the structure of fees to be charged for the services and facilities of the International Registry;

    (i) do all things necessary to ensure that an efficient notice-based electronic registration system exists to implement the objectives of this Convention and the Protocol; and

    (j) report periodically to Contracting States concerning the discharge of its obligations under this Convention and the Protocol.

3.—The Supervisory Authority may enter into any agreement requisite for the performance of its functions, including any agreement referred to in Article 26(3).

4.—The Supervisory Authority shall own all proprietary rights in the data and archives of the International Registry.

5.—The Registrar shall ensure the efficient operation of the International Registry and perform the functions assigned to it by this Convention, the Protocol and the regulations.

CHAPTER V
MODALITIES OF REGISTRATION

Article 17
Registration requirements

1.—The Protocol and regulations shall specify the requirements, including the criteria for the identification of the object:

(a) for effecting a registration;

(b) for making searches and issuing search certificates, and, subject thereto,

(c) for ensuring the confidentiality of information and documents of the International Registry.

2.—Such requirements shall not include any evidence that a consent to registration required by Article 19(1), (2) or (3) has been given.

3.—Registration shall be effected in chronological order of receipt at the International Registry data base, and the file shall record the date and time of receipt.

4.—The Protocol may provide that a Contracting State may designate an entity in its territory as the entity through which the information required for registration shall or may be transmitted to the International Registry.

Article 18
When registration takes effect

1.—A registration shall be valid only if made in conformity with Article 19 and shall take effect upon entry of the required information into the International Registry data base so as to be searchable.

2.—A registration shall be searchable for the purposes of the preceding paragraph at the time when:

(a) the International Registry has assigned to it a sequentially ordered file number; and

(b) the registration information, including the file number, is stored in durable form and may be accessed at the International Registry.

3.—If an interest first registered as a prospective international interest becomes an international interest, that international interest shall be treated as registered from the time of registration of the prospective international interest.

4.—The preceding paragraph applies with necessary modifications to the registration of a prospective assignment of an international interest.

5.—A registration shall be searchable in the International Registry data base according to the criteria prescribed by the Protocol.

Article 19
Who may register

1.—An international interest, a prospective international interest or an assignment or prospective assignment of an international interest may be registered, and any such registration amended or extended prior to its expiry, by either party with the consent in writing of the other.

2.—The subordination of an international interest to another international interest may be registered by or with the consent in writing at any time of the person whose intrest has been subordinated.

3.—A registration may be discharged by or with the consent in writing of the party in whose favour it was made.

4.—The acquisition of an international interest by legal or contractual subrogation may be registered by the subrogee.

5.—A registrable non-consensual right or interest may be registered by the holder thereof.

6.—A notice of a national interest may be registered by the holder thereof.

Article 20
Duration of registration

Registration of an international interest remains effective until discharged or until expiry of the period specified in the registration.

Article 21
Searches

1.—Any person may, in the manner prescribed by the Protocol or regulations, make or request a search of the International Registry concerning interests registered therein.

2.—Upon receipt of a request therefor, the Registrar, in the manner prescribed by the Protocol or regulations, shall issue a registry search certificate with respect to any object:

  (a) stating all registered information relating thereto, together with a statement indicating the date and time of registration of such information; or
  (b) stating that there is no information in the International Registry relating thereto.

Article 22
List of declared non-consensual rights or interests

The Registrar shall maintain a list of declarations, withdrawals of declaration and of the categories of non-consensual right or interest communicated to the Registrar by the depositary State as having been declared by Contracting States in conformity with Article 39 and the date of each such declaration. Such list shall be recorded and searchable in the name of the declaring State and shall be made available as provided in the Protocol or regulations to any person requesting it.

Article 23
Evidentiary value of certificates

A document in the form prescribed by the regulations which purports to be a certificate issued by the International Registry is *prima facie* proof:

(a) that it has been so issued; and

(b) of the facts recited in it, including the date and time of a registration.

Article 24
Discharge of registration

1.—Where the obligations secured by a registered security interest or the obligations giving rise to a registered non-consensual right or interest have been discharged, or where the conditions of transfer of title under a registered title reservation agreement have been fulfilled, the holder of such interest shall procure the discharge of the registration upon written demand by the debtor delivered to or received at its address stated in the registration.

2.—Where a prospective international interest or a prospective assignment of an international interest has been registered, the intending creditor of intending assignee shall procure the discharge of the registration upon written demand by the intending debtor or assignor which is delivered to or received at its address stated in the registration before the intending creditor or assignee has given value or incurred a commitment to give value.

3.—Where the obligations secured by a national interest specified in a registered notice of a national interest have been discharged, the holder of such interest shall procure the discharge of the registration upon written demand by the debtor delivered to or received at its address stated in the registration.

Article 25
Access to the international registration facilities

No person shall be denied access to the registration and search facilities of the International Registry on any ground other than its failure to comply with the procedures prescribed by this Chapter.

CHAPTER VI
PRIVILEGES AND IMMUNITIES OF THE SUPERVISORY AUTHORITY AND THE REGISTRAR

Article 26
Legal personality; immunity

1.—The Supervisory Authority shall have international legal personality where not already possessing such personality.

2.—The Supervisory Authority and its officers and employees shall enjoy [functional] immunity from legal or administrative process.

3.— (a) The Supervisory Authority shall enjoy exemption from taxes and such other privileges as may be provided by agreement with the host State.

(b) For the purposes of this paragraph, 'host State' means the State in which the Supervisory Authority is situated.

4.—Except for the purposes of Article 27(1) and in relation to any claim made under that paragraph and for the purposes of Article 43:

(a) the Registrar and its officers and employees shall enjoy functional immunity from legal or administrative process;

(b) the assets, documents, databases and archives of the International Registry shall be inviolable and immune from seizure or other legal or administrative process.

5.—The Supervisory Authority may waive the immunity conferred by paragraph 4.

CHAPTER VII
LIABILITY OF THE REGISTRAR

Article 27
Liability and insurance

1.—The Registrar shall be liable for compensatory damages for loss suffered by a person directly resulting from an error or omission of the Registrar and its officers and employees or from a malfunction of the international registration system [except . . .]

2.—The Registrar shall provide insurance or a financial guarantee covering the liability referred to in the preceding paragraph to the extent provided by the Protocol.

CHAPTER VIII
EFFECTS OF AN INTERNATIONAL INTEREST AS AGAINST THIRD PARTIES

Article 28
Priority of competing interests

1.—A registered interest has priority over any other interest subsequently registered and over an unregistered interest.

2.—The priority of the first-mentioned interest under the preceding paragraph applies:

(a) even if the first-mentioned interest was acquired or registered with actual knowledge of the other interest; and

(b) even as regards value given by the holder of the first-mentioned interest with such knowledge.

3.—The buyer of an object acquires its interest in it:

(a) subject to an interest registered at the time of its acquisition of that interest; and

(b) free from an unregistered interest even if it has actual knowledge of such an interest.

4.—The priority of competing interests under this Article may be varied by agreement between the holders of those interests, but an assignee of a subordinated interest is not bound by an agreement to subordinate that interest unless at the time of the assignment a subordination had been registered relating to that agreement.

5.—Any priority given by this Article to an interest in an object extends to proceeds.

6.—This Convention does not determine priority as between the holder of an interest in an item held prior to its installation on an object and the holder of an international interest in that object.

Article 29
Effects of insolvency

1.—In insolvency proceedings against the debtor an international interest is effective if prior to the commencement of the insolvency proceedings that interest was registered in conformity with this Convention.

2.—Nothing in this Article impairs the effectiveness of an international interest in the insolvency proceedings where that interest is effective under the applicable law.

3.—Nothing in this Article affects any rules of insolvency law relating to the avoidance of a transaction as a preference or a transfer in fraud of creditors or any rules of insolvency procedure relating to the enforcement of rights to property which is under the control or supervision of the insolvency administrator.

CHAPTER IX[2]
ASSIGNMENTS OF INTERNATIONAL INTERESTS AND RIGHTS OF SUBROGATION

Article 30
Formal requirements of assignment

1.—The holder of an international interest ('the assignor') may make an assignment of it to another person ('the assignee') wholly or in part.

2.—An assignment of an international interest shall be valid only if it:

[2] At the third Joint Session the Chairman invited three delegations to develop proposals designed to bring Chapter IX more into line with those national legal systems under which an assignment of associated rights would carry with it the interest securing those rights. A proposal containing two alternatives was discussed but there was insufficient time to give the alternatives full consideration. Substantial support for the approach taken in the proposal was expressed. However, it was agreed that the alternatives required further careful study by experts and a number of delegations expressed their wish to proceed with further informal consultations. This matter was not further discussed at the 31st Session of the ICAO Legal Committee.

(a) is in writing;
(b) enables the international interest and the object to which it relates to be identified;
(c) in the case of an assignment by way of security, enables the obligations secured by the assignment to be determined in accordance with the Protocol but without the need to state a sum or maximum sum secured.

Article 31
Effects of assignment

1.—An assignment of an international interest in an object made in conformity with the preceding Article transfers to the assignee, to the extent agreed by the parties to the assignment:

(a) all the interests and priorities of the assignor under this Convention; and
(b) all associated rights.

2.—Subject to paragraph 3, the applicable law shall determine the defences and rights of set-off available to the debtor against the assignee.

3.—The debtor may at any time by agreement in writing waive all or any of the defences and rights of set-off referred to in the preceding paragraph, but the debtor may not waive defences arising from fraudulent acts on the part of the assignee.

4.—In the case of an assignment by way of security, the assigned rights revest in the assignor, to the extent that they are still subsisting, when the obligations secured by the assignment have been discharged.

Article 32
Debtor's duty to assignee

1.—To the extent that an international interest has been assigned in accordance with the provisions of this Chapter, the debtor in relation to that interest is bound by the assignment, and, in the case of an assignment within Article 31(1)(b), has a duty to make payment or give other performance to the assignee, if but only if:

(a) the debtor has been given notice of the assignment in writing by or with the authority of the assignor;
(b) the notice identifies the international interest [; and
(c) the debtor [consents in writing to the assignment, whether or not the consent is given in advance of the assignment or identifies the assignee] [has not been given prior notice in writing of an assignment in favour of another person]].

2.—Irrespective of any other ground on which payment or performance by the debtor discharges the latter from liability, payment or performance shall be effective for this purpose if made in accordance with the preceding paragraph.

3.—Nothing in the preceding paragraph shall affect the priority of competing assignments.

Article 33
Default remedies in respect of assignment by way of security

In the event of default by the assignor under the assignment of an international interest made by way of security, Articles 7, 8 and 10 to 13 apply in the relations between the assignor and the assignee (and, in relation to associated rights, apply in so far as they are capable of application to intangible property) as if references:

(a) to the secured obligation and the security interest were references to the obligation secured by the assignment of the international interest and the security interest created by that assignment;

(b) to the chargee and chargor were references to the assignee and assignor of the international interest;

(c) to the holder of the international interest were references to the holder of the assignment; and

(d) to the object were references to the assigned rights relating to the object.[3]

Article 34
Priority of competing assignments

Where there are competing assignments of international interests and at least one of the assignments is registered, the provisions of Article 28 apply as if the references to an international interest were references to an assignment of an international interest.

Article 35
Assignee's priority with respect to associated rights

Where the assignment of an international interest has been registered, the assignee shall, in relation to the associated rights transferred by virtue of or in connection with the assignment, have priority under Article 28 only to the extent that such associated rights relate to:

(a) a sum advanced and utilised for the purchase of the object;

(b) the price payable for the object; or

(c) the rentals payable in respect of the object, and the reasonable costs referred to in Article 7(5).

Article 36
Effects of assignor's insolvency

The provisions of Article 29 apply to insolvency proceedings against the assignor as if references to the debtor were references to the assignor.

---

[3] The Drafting Committee of the third Joint Session noted that this provision would require further technical consideration. However, this matter was not discussed by the third Joint Session Plenary, nor by the 31st Session of the ICAO Legal Committee.

Article 37
Subrogation

1.—Subject to paragraph 2, nothing in this Convention affects the acquisition of an international interest by legal or contractual subrogation under the applicable law.

2.—The priority between any interest within the preceding paragraph and a competing interest may be varied by agreement in writing between the holders of the respective interests.

CHAPTER X

NON-CONSENSUAL RIGHTS OR INTERESTS

Article 38
Registrable non-consensual rights or interests

A Contracting State may at any time in a declaration deposited with the depositary of the Protocol list the categories of non-consensual right or interest which shall be registrable under this Convention as regards any category of object as if the right or interest were an international interest and be regulated accordingly. Such a declaration may be modified from time to time.

Article 39
Priority of non-registrable non-consensual rights or interests

1.—A Contracting State may at any time in a declaration deposited with the depositary of the Protocol declare, generally or specifically, those categories of non-consensual right or interest (other than a right or interest to which Article 38 applies) which under that State's law would have priority over an interest in the object equivalent to that of the holder of the international interest and shall have priority over a registered international interest, whether in or outside the insolvency of the debtor. Such a declaration may be modified from time to time.

2.—A declaration made under the preceding paragraph may be expressed to cover categories that are created after the deposit of that declaration.

3.—An international interest has priority over a non-consensual right or interest of a category not covered by a declaration deposited prior to the registration of the international interest.

CHAPTER XI

APPLICATION OF THE CONVENTION TO SALES

Article 40
Sale and prospective sale

This Convention shall apply to the sale or prospective sale of an object as provided for in the Protocol with any modifications therein.

CHAPTER XII

JURISDICTION

Article 41
Choice of forum

Subject to Articles 42 and 43, the courts of a Contracting State chosen by the parties to a transaction have exclusive jurisdiction in respect of any claim brought under this Convention, unless otherwise agreed between the parties, whether or not the chosen forum has a connection with the parties or the transaction.

Article 42
Jurisdiction under Article 12(1)

1.—The courts of a Contracting State chosen by the parties and the courts on the territory of which the object is situated may exercise jurisdiction to grant relief under Article 12(1)(a), (b), (c) and Article 12(4) in respect of that object.

2.—The courts of a Contracting State chosen by the parties and the courts on the territory of which the debtor is situated may exercise jurisdiction to grant relief under Article 12(1)(d) and Article 12(4) if the enforcement of such relief is limited to the territory of the forum.

3.—A court may exercise jurisdiction under the preceding paragraphs even if the final determination of the claim referred to in Article 12(1) will or may take place in a court of another Contracting State or in an arbitral tribunal.

Article 43
Jurisdiction to make orders against the Registrar

1.—The courts of the place in which the Registrar has its centre of administration shall have exclusive jurisdiction to award damages against the Registrar under Article 27.

2.—Where a person fails to respond to a demand made under Article 24(1) or (2) and that person has ceased to exist or cannot be found for the purpose of enabling an order to be made against it requiring it to procure discharge of the registration, the courts referred to in paragraph 1 shall have exclusive jurisdiction, on the application of the debtor or intending debtor, to make an order directed to the Registrar requiring the Registrar to discharge the registration.

3.—Where a person fails to comply with an order of a court having jurisdiction under this Convention or, in the case of a national interest, an order of a court of competent jurisdiction requiring that person to procure the amendment or discharge of a registration, the courts referred to in paragraph 1 may direct the Registrar to take such steps as will give effect to that order.

4.—Except as otherwise provided by the preceding paragraphs, no court may make orders or give judgments or rulings against or purporting to bind the Registrar.

Article 44
General jurisdiction

Except as provided by Articles 41, 42 and 43, the courts of a Contracting State having jurisdiction under the law of that State may exercise jurisdiction in respect of any claim brought under this Convention.

CHAPTER XIII
RELATIONSHIP WITH OTHER CONVENTIONS

Article 45
Relationship with the UNIDROIT Convention on International Financial Leasing

The Protocol may determine the relationship between this Convention and the *UNIDROIT Convention on International Financial Leasing*, opened for signature in Ottawa on 28 May 1988.

Article 46
Relationship with the [draft] UNCITRAL Convention on Assignment
[in Receivables Financing] [of Receivables in International Trade]

[This Convention shall supersede the [draft] UNCITRAL Convention on Assignment [in Receivables Financing] [of Receivables in International Trade] as it relates to the assignment of receivables which are associated rights related to international interests in objects of the categories referred to in Article 2(3).][4]

CHAPTER XIV
FINAL PROVISIONS

Article 47
Entry into force

1.—This Convention enters into force on the first day of the month following the expiration of six months after the date of deposit of the [third/fifth] instrument of ratification, acceptance, approval or accession but only as regards a category of objects to which a Protocol applies:

    (a) as from the time of entry into force of that Protocol;

    (b) subject to the terms of that Protocol; and

    (c) as between Contracting States Parties to that Protocol.

2.—This Convention and the Protocol shall be read and interpreted together as a single instrument.

Article 48
Internal transactions

1.—A Contracting State may declare at the time of ratification, acceptance, approval of, or accession to the Protocol that this Convention shall not apply to a transaction which is an internal transaction in relation to that State.

---

[4] This provision may be modified or deleted depending on the final form of the future UNCITRAL Convention.

2.—Notwithstanding the preceding paragraph, the provisions of Articles 7(3) and 8(1), Chapter V, Article 28, and any provisions of this Convention relating to registered interests shall apply to an internal transaction.

Article 49
Protocols on Railway Rolling Stock and Space Property

1.—The International Institute for the Unification of Private Law (UNIDROIT) shall communicate the text of any preliminary draft Protocol relating to a category of objects falling within Article 2(3)(b) or (c) prepared by a working group convened by UNIDROIT to all Contracting States Parties to the Convention through their adherence to any existing Protocol, all Member States of UNIDROIT and all Member States of any intergovernmental Organisation represented in the working group. Such States shall be invited to participate in intergovernmental negotiations for the completion of a draft Protocol on the basis of such a preliminary draft Protocol.

2.—UNIDROIT shall also communicate the text of any preliminary draft Protocol prepared by a working group to relevant non-governmental Organisations as UNIDROIT considers appropriate. Such non-governmental Organisations shall be invited to submit comments on the text of the preliminary draft Protocol to UNIDROIT or, as appropriate, to participate as observers in the preparation of a draft Protocol.

3.—Upon completion of a draft Protocol, as provided by the preceding paragraphs, the draft Protocol shall be submitted to the Governing Council of UNIDROIT for approval with a view to adoption by the General Assembly of UNIDROIT and such other intergovernmental Organisations as may be determined by UNIDROIT.

4.—The procedure for the adoption of Protocols covered by this Article shall be determined by the States participating in their preparation.]

Article 50
Other future Protocols

1.—UNIDROIT may create working groups to assess the feasibility of extending the application of this Convention, through one or more Protocols, to objects of any category of high-value mobile equipment, other than a category referred to in Article 2(3), each member of which is uniquely identifiable, and associated rights relating to such objects.

2.—The Protocols referred to in the preceding paragraph shall be prepared and adopted in accordance with the procedures provided for under Article 49.

Article 51
Determination of courts

A Contracting State may declare at the time of ratification, acceptance, approval of, or accession to the Protocol the relevant 'court ' or 'courts' for the purposes of Article 1 and Chapter XII of this Convention.

Article 52
Declarations regarding remedies

1.—A Contracting State may declare at the time of signature, ratification, acceptance, approval of, or accession to the Protocol that while the charged object is situated within, or controlled from its territory the chargee shall not grant a lease of the object in that territory.

2.—A Contracting State at the time of signature, ratification, acceptance, approval of, or accession to the Protocol shall declare whether or not any remedy available to the creditor under any provision of this Convention which is not there expressed to require application to the court may be exercised only with leave of the court.

Article 53
Declarations regarding relief pending final determination

A Contracting State may declare at the time of signature, ratification, acceptance, approval of, or accession to the Protocol that it will not apply the provisions of Article 12, wholly or in part.

Article 54
Reservations, declarations and non-application of reciprocity principle

1.—No reservations are permitted except those expressly authorised in this Convention and the Protocol.

2.—No declarations are permitted except those expressly authorised in this Convention and the Protocol.

3.—The provisions of this Convention subject to any reservation or declaration shall be binding on the Contracting States that do not make such reservations or declarations in their relations vis-à-vis the reserving or declaring Contracting State.

Article 55
Transitional provisions

Alternative A

[This Convention does not apply to a pre-existing right or interest, which shall retain the priority it enjoyed before this Convention entered into force.]

Alternative B[5]

1.—Except as provided by paragraph 2, this Convention does not apply to a pre-existing right or interest.

2.—Any pre-existing right or interest of a kind referred to in Article 2(2) shall retain the priority it enjoyed before this Convention entered into force if it is registered in the International Registry before the expiry of a transitional period of

---

[5] The ICAO Legal Committee, while maintaining both alternatives A and B, expressed the view that in case alternative B was selected, the fees charged with respect to these transactions should be nominal.

[10 years] after the entering into force of this Convention in the Contracting State under the law of which it was created or arose. Where such a pre-existing right or interest is not so registered, its priority shall be determined in accordance with Article 28.

3.—The preceding paragraph does not apply to any right or interest in an object created or arising under the law of a State which has not become a Contracting State.]

[Remaining Final Provisions to be prepared by the Diplomatic Conference]

Appendix 5

Draft Protocol to the Convention on International Interests in Mobile Equipment on Matters Specific to Aircraft Equipment

The states parties to this protocol,

Considering it necessary to implement the Convention on International Interests in Mobile Equipment as it relates to aircraft equipment, in the light of the purposes set out in the preamble to the Convention,

Mindful of the need to adapt the Convention to meet the particular requirements of aircraft finance and to extend the sphere of application of the Convention to include contracts of sale of aircraft equipment,

Have agreed upon the following provisions relating to aircraft equipment:

CHAPTER I

SPHERE OF APPLICATION AND GENERAL PROVISIONS

Article I
Defined terms

1.—In this Protocol, except where the context otherwise requires, terms used in it have the meanings set out in the Convention.

2.—In this Protocol the following terms are employed with the meanings set out below:

(a) 'aircraft' means aircraft as defined for the purposes of the Chicago Convention which are either airframes with aircraft engines installed thereon or helicopters;

(b) 'aircraft engines' means aircraft engines (other than those used in military, customs or police services) powered by jet propulsion or turbine or piston technology and:

    (i) in the case of jet propulsion aircraft engines, have at least 1750 lbs of thrust or its equivalent; and

    (ii) in the case of turbine-powered or piston-powered aircraft engines, have at least 550 rated take-off shaft horsepower or its equivalent, together with all modules and other installed, incorporated or attached accessories, parts and equipment and all data, manuals and records relating thereto;

(c) 'aircraft objects' means airframes, aircraft engines and helicopters;

(d) 'aircraft register' means a register maintained by a State or a common mark registering authority for the purposes of the Chicago Convention;

(e) 'airframes' means airframes (other than those used in military, customs or police services) that, when appropriate aircraft engines are installed thereon, are type certified by the competent aviation authority to transport:

  (i) at least eight (8) persons including crew; or

  (ii) goods in excess of 2750 kilograms,

together with all installed, incorporated or attached accessories, parts and equipment (other than aircraft engines), and all data, manuals and records relating thereto;

(f) 'authorised party' means the party referred to in Article XIII(2);

(g) 'Chicago Convention' means the *Convention on International Civil Aviation*, opened for signature in Chicago on 7 December 1944, as amended, and its annexes;

(h) 'common mark registering authority' means the authority maintaining a register in accordance with Article 77 of the Chicago Convention as implemented by the Resolution adopted on 14 December 1967 by the Council of the International Civil Aviation Organization on nationality and registration of aircraft operated by international operating agencies;

(i) 'de-registration of the aircraft' means deletion or removal of the registration of the aircraft from its aircraft register in accordance with the Chicago Convention;

(j) 'guarantee contract' means a contract entered into by a person as guarantor;

(k) 'guarantor' means a person who, for the purpose of assuring performance of any obligations in favour of a creditor secured by a security agreement or under an agreement, gives or issues a suretyship or demand guarantee or a standby letter of credit or any other form of credit insurance;

(l) 'helicopters' means heavier-than-air machines (other than those used in military, customs or police services) supported in flight chiefly by the reactions of the air on one or more power-driven rotors on substantially vertical axes and which are type certified by the competent aviation authority to transport:

  (i) at least five (5) persons including crew; or

  (ii) goods in excess of 450 kilograms,

together with all installed, incorporated or attached accessories, parts and equipment (including rotors), and all data, manuals and records relating thereto;

(m) 'insolvency-related event' means:

  (i) the commencement of the insolvency proceedings; or

  (ii) the declared intention to suspend or actual suspension of payments by the debtor where the creditor's right to institute insolvency proceedings against the debtor or to exercise remedies under the Convention is prevented or suspended by law or State action;

(n) 'primary insolvency jurisdiction' means the Contracting State in which the centre of the debtor's main interests is situated, which for this purpose shall be deemed to be the place of the debtor's statutory seat or, if there is none, the place where the debtor is incorporated or formed, unless proved otherwise;

(o) 'registry authority' means the national authority or the common mark registering authority, maintaining an aircraft register in a Contracting State and responsible for the registration and de-registration of an aircraft in accordance with the Chicago Convention; and

(p) 'State of registry' means, in respect of an aircraft, the State on the national register of which an aircraft is entered or the State of location of the common mark registering authority maintaining the aircraft register.

Article II

Application of Convention as regards aircraft objects

1.—The Convention shall apply in relation to aircraft objects as provided by the terms of this Protocol.

2.—The Convention and this Protocol shall be known as the Convention on International Interests in Mobile Equipment as applied to aircraft objects.

Article III

Application of Convention to sales

The following provisions of the Convention apply in relation to a sale and shall do so as if references to an international interest, a prospective international interest, the debtor and the creditor were references to a contract of sale, a prospective sale, the seller and the buyer respectively:

Articles 3 and 4;
Article 15(1)(a);
Article 17;
Article 18(3);
Article 19(1) (as regards registration of a contract of sale or a prospective sale);
Article 24(2) (as regards a prospective sale); and
Article 29.

In addition, the general provisions of Article 1, Article 5, Chapters IV to VII, Article 28 (other than Article 28(3) which is replaced by Article XIV(1)), Chapter X, Chapter XII (other than Article 42), Chapter XIII and Chapter XIV (other than Article 55) shall apply to contracts of sale and prospective sales.

Article IV

Sphere of application

1.—Without prejudice to Article 3(1) of the Convention, the Convention shall also apply if an aircraft is registered in an aircraft register of a Contracting State. And in such circumstances the application of the Convention shall be from the earlier of:

(a) the date the aircraft is so registered; and

(b) the date of an agreement providing that the aircraft shall be so registered.

2.—For the purposes of the definition of 'internal transaction' in Article 1 of the Convention:

(a) an airframe is located in the State of registry of the aircraft of which it is a part;

(b) an aircraft engine is located in the State of registry of the aircraft on which it is installed or, if it is not installed on an aircraft, where it is physically located; and

(c) a helicopter is located in its State of registry, at the time of the conclusion of the agreement creating or providing for the interest.

3.—The parties may, by agreement in writing, exclude the application of Article XI and, in their relations with each other, derogate from or vary the effect of any of the provisions of this Protocol except Article IX (2)-(4).

Article V
Formalities, effects and registration of contract of sale

1.—For the purposes of this Protocol, a contract of sale is one which:

(a) is in writing;

(b) relates to an aircraft object of which the seller has power to dispose; and

(c) enables the aircraft object to be identified in conformity with this Protocol.

2.—A contract of sale transfers the interest of the seller in the aircraft object to the buyer according to its terms.

3.—Registration of a contract of sale remains effective indefinitely. Registration of a prospective sale remains effective unless discharged or until expiry of the period, if any, specified in the registration.

Article VI
Representative capacities

A person may enter into an agreement or a sale, and register an international interest in, or a sale of, an aircraft object, in an agency, trust or other representative capacity. In such case, that person is entitled to assert rights and interests under the Convention.

Article VII
Description of aircraft objects

A description of an aircraft object that contains its manufacturer's serial number, the name of the manufacturer and its model designation is necessary and sufficient to identify the object for the purposes of Articles 6(c) and 30(2)(b) of the Convention and Article V(1)(c) of this Protocol.

Article VIII
Choice of law

1.—The parties to an agreement, or a contract of sale, or a related guarantee contract or subordination agreement may agree on the law which is to govern their contractual rights and obligations under the Convention, wholly or in part.

2.—Unless otherwise agreed, the reference in the preceding paragraph to the law chosen by the parties is to the domestic rules of law of the designated State or, where that State comprises several territorial units, to the domestic law of the designated territorial unit.

CHAPTER II

DEFAULT REMEDIES, PRIORITIES AND ASSIGNMENTS

Article IX
Modification of default remedies provisions

1.—In addition to the remedies specified in Chapter III of the Convention, the creditor may, to the extent that the debtor has at any time so agreed and in the circumstances specified in that Chapter:

    (a) procure the de-registration of the aircraft; and

    (b) procure the export and physical transfer of the aircraft object from the territory in which it is situated.

2.—The creditor shall not exercise the remedies specified in the preceding paragraph without the prior consent in writing of the holder of any registered interest ranking in priority to that of the creditor.

3.—   (a) Article 7(2) of the Convention shall not apply to aircraft objects.

    (b) In relation to aircraft objects the following provisions shall apply:

        (i) any remedy given by the Convention shall be exercised in a commercially reasonable manner;

        (ii) an agreement between the debtor and the creditor as to what is a commercially reasonable manner shall be conclusive.

4.—A chargee giving ten or more calendar days' prior written notice of a proposed sale or lease to interested persons shall be deemed to satisfy the requirement of providing 'reasonable prior notice' specified in Article 7(3) of the Convention. The foregoing shall not prevent a chargee and a chargor or a guarantor from agreeing to a longer period of prior notice.

Article X
Modification of provisions regarding relief pending final determination

1.—This Article applies only where a Contracting State has made a declaration to that effect under Article XXVIII(2) and to the extent stated in such declaration.

2.—For the purposes of Article 12(1) of the Convention, 'speedy' in the context of obtaining relief means within such number of calendar days from the date of filing of the application for relief as is specified in a declaration made by the Contracting State in which the application is made.

3.—Article 12(1) of the Convention applies with the following being added immediately after sub-paragraph (d):

> '(e) sale and application of proceeds therefrom',
>   and Article 42(2) applies with the insertion after the words 'Article 12(1)(d)' of the words 'and (e)'.

4.—Ownership or any other interest of the debtor passing on a sale under the preceding paragraph is free from any other interest over which the creditor's international interest has priority under the provisions of Article 28 of the Convention.

5.—The creditor and the debtor or any other interested person may agree in writing to exclude the application of Article 12(2) of the Convention.

6.—With regard to the remedies in Article IX(1):

> (a) they shall be made available by the registry authority and other administrative authorities, as applicable, in a Contracting State no later than [five] working days after the creditor notifies such authorities that the relief specified in Article IX(1) is granted or, in the case of relief granted by a foreign court, recognised by a court of that Contracting State, and that the creditor is entitled to procure those remedies in accordance with this Convention; and
> (b) the applicable authorities shall expeditiously cooperate with and assist the creditor in the exercise of such remedies in conformity with the applicable aviation safety laws and regulations.

Article XI

Remedies on insolvency

1.—This Article applies only where a Contracting State that is the primary insolvency jurisdiction has made a declaration pursuant to Article XXVIII(3).

[Alternative A]

2.—Upon the occurrence of an insolvency-related event, the insolvency administrator or the debtor, as applicable, shall, subject to paragraph 7, give possession of the aircraft object to the creditor no later than the earlier of:

> (a) the end of the waiting period; and
> (b) the date on which the creditor would be entitled to possession of the aircraft object if this Article did not apply.

3.—For the purposes of this Article, the 'waiting period' shall be the period specified in a declaration of the Contracting State which is the primary insolvency jurisdiction.

4.—References in this Article to the 'insolvency administrator' shall be to that person in its official, not in its personal, capacity.

5.—Unless and until the creditor is given the opportunity to take possession under paragraph 2:

> (a) the insolvency administrator or the debtor, as applicable, shall preserve the aircraft object and maintain it and its value in accordance with the agreement; and

> (b) the creditor shall be entitled to apply for any other forms of interim relief available under the applicable law.

6.—Sub-paragraph (a) of the preceding paragraph shall not preclude the use of the aircraft object under arrangements designed to preserve the aircraft object and maintain it and its value.

7.—The insolvency administrator or the debtor, as applicable, may retain possession of the aircraft object where, by the time specified in paragraph 2, it has cured all defaults and has agreed to perform all future obligations under the agreement. A second waiting period shall not apply in respect of a default in the performance of such future obligations.

8.—With regard to the remedies in Article IX(1) :

> (a) they shall be made available by the registry authority and the administrative authorities in a Contracting State, as applicable, no later than five working days after the date on which the creditor notifies such authorities that it is entitled to procure those remedies in accordance with this Convention; and
>
> (b) the applicable authorities shall expeditiously cooperate with and assist the creditor in the exercise of such remedies in conformity with the applicable aviation safety laws and regulations.

9.—No exercise of remedies permitted by the Convention or this Protocol may be prevented or delayed after the date specified in paragraph 2.

10.—No obligations of the debtor under the agreement may be modified without the consent of the creditor.

11.—Nothing in the preceding paragraph shall be construed to affect the authority, if any, of the insolvency administrator under the applicable law to terminate the agreement.

12.—No rights or interests, except for preferred non-consensual rights or interests of a category covered by a declaration pursuant to Article 39(1), shall have priority in the insolvency over registered interests.

13.—The Convention as modified by Article IX of this Protocol shall apply to the exercise of any remedies under this Article.

[Alternative B]

2.—Upon the occurrence of an insolvency-related event, the insolvency administrator or the debtor, as applicable, upon the request of the creditor, shall give notice to the creditor within the time specified in a declaration of a Contracting State pursuant to Article XXVIII(3) whether it will:

> (a) cure all defaults and agree to perform all future obligations, under the agreement and related transaction documents; or
>
> (b) give the creditor the opportunity to take possession of the aircraft object, in accordance with the applicable law.

3.—The applicable law referred to in sub-paragraph (b) of the preceding paragraph may permit the court to require the taking of any additional step or the provision of any additional guarantee.

4.—The creditor shall provide evidence of its claims and proof that its international interest has been registered.

5.—If the insolvency administrator or the debtor, as applicable, does not give notice in conformity with paragraph 2, or when he has declared that he will give possession of the aircraft object but fails to do so, the court may permit the creditor to take possession of the aircraft object upon such terms as the court may order and may require the taking of any additional step or the provision of any additional guarantee.

6.—The aircraft object shall not be sold pending a decision by a court regarding the claim and the international interest.

Article XII
Insolvency assistance

The courts of a Contracting State in which an aircraft object is situated shall, in accordance with the law of the Contracting State, co-operate to the maximum extent possible with foreign courts and foreign insolvency administrators in carrying out the provisions of Article XI.

Article XIII
De-registration and export authorisation

1.—Where the debtor has issued an irrevocable de-registration and export request authorisation substantially in the form annexed to this Protocol and has submitted such authorisation for recordation to the registry authority, that authorisation shall be so recorded.

2.—The person in whose favour the authorisation has been issued (the 'authorised party') or its certified designee shall be the sole person entitled to exercise the remedies specified in Article IX(1) and may do so only in accordance with the authorisation and applicable aviation safety laws and regulations. Such authorisation may not be revoked by the debtor without the consent in writing of the authorised party. The registry authority shall remove an authorisation from the registry at the request of the authorised party.

3.—The registry authority and other administrative authorities in Contracting States shall expeditiously co-operate with and assist the authorised party in the exercise of the remedies specified in Article IX.

Article XIV
Modification of priority provisions

1.—A buyer under a registered contract of sale takes its interest free from an interest subsequently registered and from an unregistered interest, even if the buyer has actual knowledge of the unregistered interest, but subject to a previously registered interest.

2.—The provisions of Article 28(1)–(4) of the Convention shall determine the priority of the holders of interests in an aircraft engine and Article 28(6) shall not apply.

3.—Ownership of an aircraft engine shall not pass by virtue of its installation on, or removal from, an airframe or an aircraft.

Article XV
Modification of assignment provisions

1.—Article 30(2) of the Convention applies with the following being added immediately after sub-paragraph (c):

'(d) is consented to in writing by the debtor, whether or not the consent is given in advance of the assignment or identifies the assignee.'[1]

[**2.**—Article 35 of the Convention applies as if the words following the phrase 'under Article 28' were omitted].

CHAPTER III

REGISTRY PROVISIONS RELATING TO INTERNATIONAL INTERESTS IN AIRCRAFT OBJECTS

Article XVI
The Supervisory Authority and the Registrar

1.—The Supervisory Authority shall be Y.

2.—The first Registrar shall operate the International Registry for a period of five years from the date of entry into force of this Protocol. Thereafter, the Registrar shall be appointed or re-appointed at regular five-yearly intervals by the Supervisory Authority.

Article XVII
First regulations

The first regulations shall be made by the Supervisory Authority so as to take effect on the entry into force of this Protocol.

Article XVIII
Designated entry points

1.—At the time of ratification, acceptance, approval of, or accession to this Protocol, a Contracting State may, subject to paragraph 2, designate an entity in its territory as the entity through which the information required for registration shall or may be transmitted to the International Registry.

2.—A Contracting State may make a designation under the preceding paragraph only in relation to:

(a) international interests in, or sales of, helicopters or airframes pertaining to aircraft for which it is the State of registry;

(b) registrable non-consensual rights or interests created under its domestic law; and

(c) notices of national interests.

---

[1] The removal of square brackets in Article 32(1)(c) Convention may have implications for this provision.

Article XIX
Additional modifications to Registry provisions

1.—For the purposes of Article 18(5) of the Convention, the search criterion for an aircraft object shall be its manufacturer's serial number, supplemented as necessary to ensure uniqueness. Such supplementary information shall be specified in the regulations.

2.—For the purposes of Article 24(2) of the Convention and in the circumstances there described, the holder of a registered prospective international interest or a registered prospective assignment of an international interest shall take such steps as are within its power to procure the discharge of the registration no later than five calendar days after the receipt of the demand described in such paragraph.

3.—The fees referred to in Article 16(2)(h) of the Convention shall be determined so as to recover the reasonable costs of establishing, operating and regulating the International Registry and the reasonable costs of the Supervisory Authority associated with the performance of the functions, exercise of the powers, and discharge of the duties contemplated by Article 16(2) of the Convention.

4.—The centralised functions of the International Registry shall be operated and administered by the Registrar on a twenty-four hour basis. The various entry points shall be operated during working hours in their respective territories.

5.—The insurance or financial guarantee referred to in Article 27(2) shall cover all liability of the Registrar under the Convention.

CHAPTER IV
JURISDICTION

Article XX
Modification of jurisdiction provisions

For the purposes of Articles 42 and 44 of the Convention and subject to Article 41 of the Convention, a court of a Contracting State also has jurisdiction where that State is the State of registry.

Article XXI
Waivers of sovereign immunity

1.—Subject to paragraph 2, a waiver of sovereign immunity from jurisdiction of the courts specified in Articles 41, 42 or 44 of the Convention or relating to enforcement of rights and interests relating to an aircraft object under the Convention shall be binding and, if the other conditions to such jurisdiction or enforcement have been satisfied, shall be effective to confer jurisdiction and permit enforcement, as the case may be.

2.—A waiver under the preceding paragraph must be in a writing that contains a description of the aircraft object.

CHAPTER V
RELATIONSHIP WITH OTHER CONVENTIONS

Article XXII
Relationship with the Convention on the International Recognition of Rights in Aircraft

The Convention shall, for a Contracting State that is a party to the *Convention on the International Recognition of Rights in Aircraft*, opened for signature in Geneva on 19 June 1948, supersede that Convention as it relates to aircraft, as defined in this Protocol, and to aircraft objects. However, with respect to rights or interests not covered or affected by the present Convention, the Geneva Convention shall not be superseded.

Article XXIII
Relationship with the Convention for the Unification of Certain Rules Relating to the Precautionary Attachment of Aircraft

1.—The Convention shall, for a Contracting State that is a Party to the *Convention for the Unification of Certain Rules Relating to the Precautionary Attachment of Aircraft*, opened for signature in Rome on 29 May 1933, supersede that Convention as it relates to aircraft, as defined in this Protocol.

2.—A Contracting State Party to the above Convention may declare, at the time of ratification, acceptance, approval of, or accession to this Protocol, that it will not apply this Article.

Article XXIV
Relationship with the UNIDROIT Convention on International Financial Leasing

The Convention shall supersede the *UNIDROIT Convention on International Financial Leasing* as it relates to aircraft objects.

CHAPTER VI
FINAL PROVISIONS

Article XXV
Adoption of Protocol

1.—This Protocol is open for signature at the concluding meeting of the Diplomatic Conference for the adoption of the Protocol to the Convention on International Interests in Mobile Equipment on Matters specific to Aircraft Equipment and will remain open for signature by all Contracting States at [. . . .] until [. . . .].

2.—This Protocol is subject to ratification, acceptance or approval of Contracting States which have signed it.

3. This Protocol is open for accession by all States which are not signatory States as from the date it is open for signature.

4.—Ratification, acceptance, approval or accession is effected by the deposit of a formal instrument to that effect with the depositary.

Article XXVI
Entry into force

1.—This Protocol enters into force on the first day of the month following the expiration of three months after the date of deposit of the [third/fifth] instrument of ratification, acceptance, approval or accession.

2.—For each Contracting State that ratifies, accepts, approves or accedes to this Protocol after the deposit of the [third/fifth] instrument of ratification, acceptance, approval or accession, this Protocol enters into force in respect of that Contracting State on the first day of the month following the expiration of three months after the date of the deposit of its instrument of ratification, acceptance, approval or accession.

Article XXVII
Territorial units

1.—If a Contracting State has two or more territorial units in which different systems of law are applicable in relation to the matters dealt with in this Protocol, it may, at the time of ratification, acceptance, approval or accession, declare that this Protocol is to extend to all its territorial units or only to one or more of them and may substitute its declaration by another declaration at any time.

2.—These declarations are to be notified to the depositary and are to state expressly the territorial units to which this Protocol extends.

3.—If a Contracting State makes no declaration under paragraph 1, this Protocol is to extend to all territorial units of that Contracting State.

Article XXVIII
Declarations relating to certain provisions

1.—A Contracting State may declare, at the time of ratification, acceptance, approval of, or accession to this Protocol, that it will apply any one or more of Articles VIII, XII and XIII of this Protocol.

2.—A Contracting State may declare, at the time of ratification, acceptance, approval of, or accession to this Protocol, that it will apply Article X of this Protocol wholly or in part. If it so declares with respect to Article X(2), it shall specify the time-period required thereby.

3.—A Contracting State may declare, at the time of ratification, acceptance, approval of, or accession to this Protocol, that it will apply the entirety of Alternative A, or the entirety of Alternative B of Article XI and, if so, shall specify the types of insolvency proceeding, if any, to which it will apply Alternative A and the types of insolvency proceeding, if any, to which it will apply Alternative B. A Contracting State making a declaration pursuant to this paragraph shall specify the time-period required by Article XI.

4.—The courts of Contracting States shall apply Article XI in conformity with the declaration made by the Contracting State which is the primary insolvency jurisdiction.

Article XXIX
Subsequent declarations

1.—A Contracting State may make a subsequent declaration at any time after the date on which the Protocol enters into force for that Contracting State, by the deposit of an instrument to that effect with the depositary.

2.—Any such subsequent declaration shall take effect on the first day of the month following the expiration of six months after the date of deposit of the instrument in which such declaration is made with the depositary. Where a longer period for that declaration to take effect is specified in the instrument in which such declaration is made, it shall take effect upon the expiration of such longer period after its deposit with the depositary.

3.—Notwithstanding the previous paragraphs, this Protocol shall continue to apply, as if no such subsequent declaration had been made, in respect of all rights and interests arising prior to the effective date of that subsequent declaration.

Article XXX
Withdrawal of declarations and reservations

Any Contracting State which makes a declaration under, or a reservation to this Protocol may withdraw it at any time by a formal notification in writing addressed to the depositary. Such withdrawal is to take effect on the first day of the month following the expiration of six months after the date of the receipt of the notification by the depositary.

Article XXXI
Denunciations

1.—This Protocol may be denounced by any Contracting State at any time after the date on which it enters into force for that Contracting State, by the deposit of an instrument to that effect with the depositary.

2.—Any such denunciation shall take effect on the first day of the month following the expiration of [six/twelve] months after the date of deposit of the instrument of denunciation with the depositary. Where a longer period for that denunciation to take effect is specified in the instrument of denunciation, it shall take effect upon the expiration of such longer period after its deposit with the depositary.

3.—Notwithstanding the previous paragraphs, this Protocol shall continue to apply, as if no such denunciation had been made, in respect of all rights and interests arising prior to the effective date of that denunciation.

Article XXXII
Establishment and responsibilities of Review Board

1.—A five-member Review Board shall promptly be appointed to prepare yearly reports for the Contracting States addressing the matters specified in sub-paragraphs (a)-(d) of paragraph 2.

2.—At the request of not less than twenty-five per cent of the Contracting States, conferences of the Contracting States shall be convened from time to time to consider:

(a) the practical operation of this Protocol and its effectiveness in facili-tating the asset-based financing and leasing of aircraft objects;
(b) the judicial interpretation given to the terms of the Convention, this Protocol and the regulations;
(c) the functioning of the international registration system and the performance of the Registrar and its oversight by the Supervisory Authority; and
(d) whether any modifications to this Protocol or the arrangements relating to the International Registry are desirable.

Article XXXIII
Depositary arrangements

1.—This Protocol shall be deposited with the [. . . .].

2.—The [depositary] shall:

(a) inform all Contracting States of this Protocol and [. . . .] of:
   (i) each new signature or deposit of an instrument of ratification, acceptance, approval or accession, together with the date thereof;
   (ii) each declaration made in accordance with this Protocol;
   (iii) the withdrawal of any declaration;
   (iv) the date of entry into force of this Protocol; and
   (v) the deposit of an instrument of denunciation of this Protocol together with the date of its deposit and the date on which it takes effect;
(b) transmit certified true copies of this Protocol to all signatory States, to all States acceding to the Protocol and to [. . . .];
(c) provide the Registrar with the contents of each instrument of ratifi-cation, acceptance, approval, accession, declaration or withdrawal of a declaration, so that the information contained therein may be made publicly accessible; and
(d) perform such other functions customary for depositaries.

FORM OF IRREVOCABLE DE-REGISTRATION AND EXPORT REQUEST AUTHORISATION

[Insert Date]

To: [Insert Name of Registry Authority]

Re: Irrevocable De-Registration and Export Request Authorisation

The undersigned is the registered [operator] [owner]* of the [insert the airframe/helicopter manufacturer name and model number] bearing manufacturer's serial number [insert manufacturer's serial number] and registration [number] [mark] [insert registration number/mark] (together

---

* Select the term that reflects the relevant nationality registration criterion

with all installed, incorporated or attached accessories, parts and equipment, the '**aircraft**').

This instrument is an irrevocable de-registration and export request authorisation issued by the undersigned in favour of [insert name of creditor] ('the **authorised party**') under the authority of Article XIII of the Protocol to the [UNIDROIT] Convention on Interntional Interests in Mobile Equipment on Matters specific to Aircraft Equipment. In accordance with that Article, the undersigned hereby requests:

(i)   recognition that the authorised party or the person it certifies as its designee is the sole person entitled to:

    (a)   procure the de-registration of the aircraft from the [insert name of aircraft register] maintained by the [insert name of registry authority] for the purposes of Chapter III of the Chicago Convention of 1944 on International Civil Aviation; and

    (b)   procure the export and physical transfer of the aircraft from [insert name of country]; and

(ii)   confirmation that the authorised party or the person it certifies as its designee may take the action specified in clause (i) above on written demand without the consent of the undersigned and that, upon such demand, the authorities in [insert name of country] shall co-operate with the authorised party with a view to the speedy completion of such action.

The rights in favour of the authorised party established by this instrument may not be revoked by the undersigned without the written consent of the authorised party.

Please acknowledge your agreement to this request and its terms by appropriate notation in the space provided below and lodging this instrument in [insert name of registry authority].

    [insert name of operator/owner]

_____

Agreed to and lodged this   By: [insert name of signatory]
[insert date]   Its: [insert title of signatory]

_____

[insert relevant notational details]

Index